O-LEVEL MATHEMATICS
A CONSOLIDATION COURSE

O-LEVEL MATHEMATICS

A CONSOLIDATION COURSE

J.S. Fairhurst, B.Sc.
Assistant Head of Mathematics,
George Abbot Comprehensive School, Guildford

Stanley Thornes (Publishers) Ltd

First published 1984 by
Stanley Thornes (Publishers) Ltd
Educa House
Old Station Drive
Leckhampton
CHELTENHAM GL53 0DN

British Library Cataloguing in Publication Data

Fairhurst, J.S.
    O Level mathematics.
    1. Mathematics — 1961 —
    I. Title
    510   QA39.2

    ISBN 0-85950-110-8

Typeset by Tech-Set, Gateshead, Tyne & Wear.
Printed and bound in Great Britain at The Pitman Press, Bath.

CONTENTS

PREFACE

After a period of radical change, the content of school mathematics has settled to a blend in which old and new topics are largely integrated. Examination Boards have recognised this and are replacing 'traditional' and 'modern' syllabuses with new courses, such as London Syllabus 'B' and Cambridge Syllabus 'D', which combine the best of both. This book is written in full support of this unification. 'Modern' and 'traditional' topics are developed side by side and interrelated wherever possible.

Equally, the book is written in support of students preparing for their first public examinations. Each topic is broken down into manageable sections, key definitions and techniques are explained simply, and illustrated by a large number of worked examples and exercises which have been developed, over a long period, in the light of the author's experience using the material with his own O-level groups.

However, this is not only a classroom exercise book. It is also offered as a revision text, containing the necessary notes and explanations from which the individual student, working at home in the run up to the examination, may consolidate what he or she has previously learned.

I would like to thank Mrs J. Barstow and Mr S.A. Lugg for their helpful comments and suggestions on the initial drafts of this book, Mr M. Berezicki for working through the exercises, and Mr R.C. Day for proof-reading the final text.

I would like also to acknowledge the following Examination Boards for their kind permission to reproduce questions selected from past examination papers:

Associated Examining Board   (AEB)
University of Cambridge Local Examinations Syndicate   (C)
Joint Matriculation Board   (JMB)
University of London University Entrance and School Examinations Council   (LU)
Oxford Delegacy of Local Examinations   (Ox)
Oxford and Cambridge Schools Examination Board   (O & C)
Southern Universities' Joint Board   (SUJB)
Welsh Joint Education Committee   (WJEC)

Responsibility for the answers to these questions is the author's alone.

J.S. Fairhurst

1 NUMBERS

TYPES OF NUMBERS

Numbers that are used in the normal, simple process of counting, i.e. $1, 2, 3, 4, 5, 6, 7$, etc., are called *natural numbers*. Natural numbers are necessarily whole numbers, or *integers*. However, the set of integers includes zero and negative whole numbers as well. Thus, of the set of numbers $\{-4, -3, -2, -1, 0, +1, +2\}$ only $+1$ and $+2$ are natural numbers although *all* are examples of integers.

Numbers that are not integers may be *fractions* (e.g. $\frac{3}{4}$ or $-2\frac{1}{4}$) or *decimal fractions* (e.g. 0.38 or -1.1).

Any integer or fraction is a *rational number*. So, too, are decimal numbers that terminate (such as 0.38 or 1.1) and decimal numbers that recur (e.g. $0.333\,333\ldots$ or $2.182\,182\,182\ldots$). Decimals that go on for ever, with *no* recurring pattern, are called *irrational numbers*. Two examples of irrational numbers are π and $\sqrt{2}$.

All these types of numbers — natural numbers, integers, fractions, decimals, rational numbers, irrational numbers — are *real numbers* that may be shown as points on a *number line* (see Fig. 1.1).

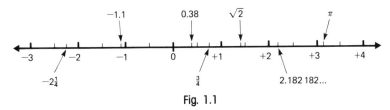

Fig. 1.1

Remember that 0 is an integer and is therefore both a real and a rational number.

RELATING NUMBERS

The *sum* of two numbers is found by *adding* them together. Thus the sum of 3 and 2 is $3 + 2 = 5$.

The *difference* between two numbers is found by *subtracting* the smaller number from the larger one. Thus the difference between 3 and 2 is $3 - 2 = 1$.

1

The *product* of two numbers is found by *multiplying* them. The product of 3 and 2 is $3 \times 2 = 6$.

Take great care when combining negative numbers. Remember in particular the following points:

(*i*) Adding a negative number is like subtracting a positive one:

$$6 + (-2) = 6 - (+2) = +4$$

(*ii*) Subtracting a negative number is like adding a positive one:

$$6 - (-2) = 6 + (+2) = +8$$

(*iii*) Multiplying a negative number by a positive number gives a negative number:

$$6 \times (-2) = -12$$

(*iv*) But multiplying two negative numbers together gives a positive result:

$$-6 \times (-2) = +12$$

(*v*) Division behaves exactly like multiplication:

$$6 \div (-2) = -3$$
$$-6 \div (-2) = +3$$

EXERCISE 1a

1. Which of the following numbers are integers: $7, 7.7, -2, \frac{2}{7}$, $0.18, \sqrt{2}$?

2. Which if the following numbers are real: $3, 5.23, 0.555\,555\ldots,$ $\frac{5}{9}, -3, 0.000\,01$?

3. Is zero
    (a) a natural number   (b) an integer
    (c) a real number   (d) a rational number?

4. Which if these are irrational: $0.151\,151\ldots, 0, -1\frac{1}{2}, \frac{3}{4}, \sqrt{2}$, $\pi, \sqrt{4}$?

5. Find the sum of 15 and 5. What is their product? What is their difference?

6. Work out
    (a) $12 + (-3)$ (b) $2 - 5$ (c) $6 - (-8)$
    (d) $9 + (-3)$ (e) $9 - (-3)$ (f) $-12 + (-4)$
    (g) $-11 - (-2)$ (h) $8 \times (-6)$ (i) $10 \div (-5)$
    (j) $-3 \times (-7)$ (k) $-16 \div (-8)$ (l) $36 \div (-6)$.

FACTORS

One number is a *factor* of another number if the first number divides the second number exactly. For example, 5 is a factor of 40 since $40 \div 5 = 8$. Similarly, 2 is a factor of 40 since $40 \div 2 = 20$. On the other hand, 7 is *not* a factor of 40 since $40 \div 7$ does *not* give a whole number. The complete set of factors of 40 is $\{1, 2, 4, 5, 8, 10, 20, 40\}$.

Any number is divisible by itself and also by 1. So it follows that *any* number must have itself and 1 as factors. A *prime* number is one that has no other factors (except itself and one). For example, 13 is a prime number since it has only two factors: 13 and 1; 2 is also prime — the only even prime number, since all other even numbers have 2 as a factor. (1 is a special case and is not regarded as a prime number.)

The *highest common factor*, or HCF, of two numbers is the highest number that is a factor of both. For example, the factors of 40 are

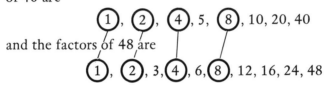

and the factors of 48 are

The factors common to both 40 and 48 are 1, 2, 4 and 8. The *highest* common factor is 8.

MULTIPLES

One number is a *multiple* of another number if the first number is exactly divisible by the second number. For example, 4 is a multiple of 2; 6 is another multiple of 2 and is also a multiple of 3. Do not confuse multiples and factors — they are opposites. Thus 40 is a multiple of 1, 2, 4, 5, 8, 10, 20 and 40, and these numbers are factors of 40.

The *lowest common multiple*, or LCM, of two numbers is the lowest number that is a multiple of *both*. For example, multiples of 6 are

$$6, 12, 18, (24), 30, 36, 42, (48), 54, 60, 66, (72), 78, \ldots$$

and multiples of 8 are

$$8, 16, (24), 32, 40, (48), 56, 64, (72), 80, 88, 96, 104, \ldots$$

The multiples common to both 6 and 8 are 24, 48, 72, ... The *lowest* common multiple is 24.

1. Complete this list of factors of 36: 1, 2, 3, –, –, –, –, –, 36.

2. Complete this list of factors of 108: 1, –, –, –, –, –, 12, –, 27, –, –, 108.

3. What is the HCF of 36 and 108?

4. List all the factors of
   (a) 16   (b) 24.

5. What is the HCF of 16 and 24?

6. List the factors of
   (a) 13   (b) 17.
   What sort of numbers are these?

7. Which of the following are prime numbers: 1, 2, 3, 4, 5, 7, 9, 11, 15, 27?

8. Can an even number be prime?

9. Complete this list of multiples of 5: 5, 10, –, –, –, –, 35, –, –, 50.

10. List six multiples of
    (a) 6   (b) 15.

11. What is the LCM of
    (a) 5 and 6   (b) 6 and 15.

12. Find the LCM of
    (a) 3 and 4   (b) 6 and 8   (c) 6 and 12.

13. Find the LCM and the HCF of 3, 5 and 15.

14. Find the LCM and the HCF of 10, 25 and 60.

15. T = {multiples of 3 up to 39} and F = {multiples of 4 up to 40}.
    (a) List the elements of T.
    (b) List the elements of F.

    Copy the Venn diagram from Fig. 1.2 and mark on it the members of T and F. (The first few have been done for you.)
    (c) Write down three multiples common to 3 and 4.
    (d) What is the LCM of 3 and 4?

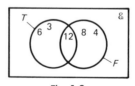

Fig. 1.2

16. Copy the Venn diagram in Fig. 1.3 which shows two sets:
    $S = \{$factors of 72$\}$ and $F = \{$factors of 54$\}$.

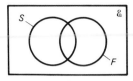

Fig. 1.3

(a) List the members of sets S and F and mark them on your diagram.

(b) What factors are common to 72 and 54?

(c) What is the HCF of 72 and 54?

NUMBERS IN BASE 10

The number 7 6 7 3 means 'seven thousand six hundred and seventy-three'. Each digit in the number has a *place value*, i.e. it is recognised to mean thousands or hundreds or tens or units according to its place in the number. Thus, in the number 7673 the digit '7' means seven thousands in the first position and seven tens in the other.

Notice especially how the number 7 6 7 3 0 differs from 7 6 7 3; the value of every digit is changed by the extra zero at the end of the number.

Place value	Ten thousands 10 000	Thousands 1000	Hundreds 100	Tens 10	Units 1
Digit	—	7	6	7	3
	7	6	7	3	0

If a zero is placed at the right of 7 6 7 3, each digit moves one place to the left and takes a new place value of ten times the previous value. Thus 7 6 7 3 0 is ten times larger than 7 6 7 3.

A decimal point is used to locate the units column (immediately to its left). The place values of the digits to the right of the decimal point are then fractions: tenths, hundredths, thousandths, ... So 7 6 . 7 3 means seven tens, six units, seven tenths and three hundredths.

5

Place value	Hundreds 100	Tens 10	Units 1	•	Tenths $\frac{1}{10}$	Hundredths $\frac{1}{100}$
Digit		7	6	•	7	3
	7	6	7	•	3	

Again, notice that shifting the digits to the left, so that the number reads 767.3, increases the place value of each digit ten times. Thus

$$76.73 \times 10 = 767.3$$

Conversely, moving the digits to the right is equivalent to *division* by ten, since the place value of every digit is decreased:

$$76.73 \div 10 = 7.673$$

Moving the digits *two* places left or right effectively multiplies or divides the number by 100 (i.e. 10×10); moving *three* places effectively multiplies or divides the number by 1000 ($10 \times 10 \times 10$), and so on.

$$7673 \div 100 = 76.73$$

$$123 \div 1000 = 0.123$$

STANDARD FORM

Any number, no matter how large or small, may be written in *standard form* or *scientific notation*; that is, as a number between 1 and 10 multipled by an appropriate power of 10. For example

$$253.7 = 2.537 \times 100 = 2.537 \times 10^2$$

Since the first part of standard form must be written as a value between 1 and 10, the digits of the original number (253.7) have to be moved two places to the right. This effectively divides the number by 100, so to compensate we multiply by 100 (written as 10^2 in standard form). Similarly

$$1234.5 = 1.2345 \times 10^3$$

$$67890 = 6.7890 \times 10^4$$

The digits of small numbers, such as 0.000543, have to be moved to the *left* if they are to be written as a value between 1 and 10. This effectively multiplies the number so we must *divide* to compensate. This is shown by *multiplying* by a *negative* power of 10.

Examples
$$0.000543 = 5.43 \div 10\,000 = 5.43 \times 10^{-4}$$
$$0.068 = 6.8 \div 100 = 6.8 \times 10^{-2}$$
$$0.00789 = 7.89 \div 1000 = 7.89 \times 10^{-3}$$

EXERCISE 1c Work out:

1. (a) 23×10 (b) 23×100 (c) $23 \times 10\,000$
   (d) 2.3×100

2. (a) $2300 \div 10$ (b) $2300 \div 100$ (c) $2300 \div 1000$
   (d) $2300 \div 10^6$

3. (a) 3.45×10 (b) 3.45×100 (c) $3.45 \times 10\,000$
   (d) 3.45×10^6

4. (a) $345 \div 10$ (b) $345 \div 100$ (c) $345 \div 10\,000$
   (d) $345 \div 10^6$.

Write the following in standard form:

5. (a) 78.9 (b) 542.1 (c) $32\,000$
   (d) $32\,000\,000$

6. (a) 0.0134 (b) $0.000\,51$ (c) 0.01
   (d) $0.000\,011$

7. (a) 3456 (b) 0.3456 (c) $0.000\,345\,6$
   (d) $0.000\,000\,034\,56$

8. (a) 52×10^2 (b) 0.5×10^3 (c) 278.1×10^6
   (d) 3054.7×10^7.

WORKING WITH DECIMALS

Addition and Subtraction

Decimal points must be placed underneath each other.

Example $3.56 - 0.0503$.

Rewrite 3.56 as 3.5600 then:

$$
\begin{array}{r}
^{5\,9\,1}\\
3.5\cancel{6}\cancel{0}\cancel{0}\\
-\,0.0503\\
\hline
3.5097
\end{array}
$$

Multiplication

To multiply two decimals:

(*i*)   multiply the numbers, disregarding the decimal points;

(*ii*)   count the total number of decimal places;

(*iii*)   place the decimal point in your answer to (*i*) so that it has the same number of decimal places that you counted in (*ii*).

Example 0.0003 × 0.02.

(*i*)   3 × 2 = 6

(*ii*)   0.0003 has 4 decimal places
0.02   has 2 decimal places
Total: 6 decimal places

(*iii*)   Placing a decimal point in (*i*) so that there are 6 decimal places gives 0.000 006, i.e.

$$0.0003 \times 0.02 = 0.000\,006$$

Division

To divide two decimals:

(*i*)   move the digits of the dividing number to the left, to make it a whole number;

(*ii*)   compensate for (*i*) by moving the digits of the other (divided) number in *exactly* the same way;

(*iii*)   divide.

Example 5.49 ÷ 0.9.

(*i*)   0.9 → 9   by moving the digits one place to the left

(*ii*)   5.49 → 54.9   by moving the digits one place to the left, as in (*i*)

(*iii*)   54.9 ÷ 9   = 6.1, i.e.

$$5.49 \div 0.9 = 6.1$$

EXERCISE 1d   *Without* using a calculator, work out:

1. (a) 5.41 + 0.39   (b) 4.51 − 3.78
   (c) 2.1 + 0.009   (d) 2.1 − 0.009

2. (a) 2.3×0.02 (b) 0.023×0.02
   (c) $5.4 \div 0.002$ (d) $0.054 \div 0.002$

3. (a) $7.11 - 6.031$ (b) $102.1 + 0.0002$
   (c) 121×0.0011 (d) $121 \div 0.0011$

4. (a) $0.001\,44 \div 1.2$ (b) $2 \div 0.0005$
   (c) $10.8 \div 0.009$ (d) $1080 \div 0.036$

5. (a) $(0.003)^2$ (b) $(0.01)^2$
   (c) 0.013×90 (d) 1001×10.01

6. (a) $\dfrac{0.04 \times 0.12}{0.24}$ (b) $\dfrac{3.0 \times 6.3}{0.009}$

   (c) $\dfrac{5.6 \times 0.2}{0.08}$

7. (a) $\dfrac{0.03 - 0.003}{0.3}$ (b) $\dfrac{1.12 + 0.09}{1.1}$

   (c) $\dfrac{2.02 + 0.18}{0.0022}$

8. (a) $\dfrac{(0.04)^2}{0.016}$ (b) $\dfrac{0.288}{(1.2)^2}$

   (c) $\dfrac{(0.05)^2}{0.125}$

9. (a) $\dfrac{0.003 \times 0.4}{0.2 \times 1.2}$ (b) $\dfrac{0.6(1.1 - 0.02)}{0.9 \times (0.4)^2}$

   (c) $\dfrac{0.08 \times 0.09}{0.006 \times 1.2}$

10. (a) $\dfrac{0.08 \times 0.006}{0.0096 \times 0.02}$ (b) $\dfrac{3.9 \times 0.028}{0.026 \times 2.1}$

    (c) $\dfrac{1.44 \times 1.08}{3.6 \times 4.8}$.

APPROXIMATING DECIMALS

Sometimes, a number is given to more decimal places (d.p.) than is desirable, in which case it may be *rounded off* provided that some indication of the rounding off process is given. (If there is no indication of rounding off then a number is assumed to be exact.)

How a number rounds off in the *second* decimal place depends upon the digit in the *third*; rounding off in the *third* place depends upon the digit in the *fourth*; and so on. The digits 0, 1, 2, 4 round off leaving the digit in the preceding place unaltered. The digits 5, 6, 7, 8, 9 round *up* increasing the digit in the preceding place by 1.

Examples
$$0.1465 \approx 0.147 \quad (3 \text{ d.p.})$$
$$0.1465 \approx 0.15 \quad (2 \text{ d.p.})$$
$$0.1465 \approx 0.1 \quad (1 \text{ d.p.})$$

Notice that the rounding off depends *only* upon the digit in the next place. For example, to round off 0.1465 to one decimal place it is sufficient to know that the second decimal place contains the digit 4; subsequent digits are irrelevant and must *not* affect the rounding off.

Alternatively, we may wish to round off to a given number of *significant figures* (s.f.). The digits 1, 2, 3, 4, 5, 6, 7, 8, 9 are *always* significant. Zero is significant when it is part of the number, i.e. when it follows other significant digits; it is *not* significant when it is a 'spacer', locating the decimal point.

Examples

234.7   has *four* significant figures

203.85   has *five* significant figures

0.000 234   has *three* significant figures (the zeros are 'spacers' only)

0.0560   also has *three* significant figures since the last digit, 0, is part of the number, indicating that it is neither 0.0561 nor 0.0559.

Notice that figures may be significant on either side of the decimal point. Thus 345, 34.5, 3.45, 0.003 45 are all examples of numbers with three significant figures.

In numbers that do not contain a decimal point, deciding whether a zero is significant or not is impossible unless the context is known. For example, in the sequence 98, 99, 100, 101, ... the number 100 is exact; both zeros *are* significant. However, suppose you were lucky enough to win £98.86½ in some competition; almost certainly, you would say to people 'I've won £100' — that is, you would be rounding off to *one* significant figure, and the two zeros of the value £100 would be *non*-significant. This ambiguity underlines the importance of declaring an approximation when one is made.

Example
$$2342 \approx 2340 \quad (3 \text{ s.f.})$$
$$\approx 2300 \quad (2 \text{ s.f.})$$
$$\approx 2000 \quad (1 \text{ s.f.})$$

ESTIMATION

Rounding off numbers to one significant figure is useful when a rough estimate of some calculation is required.

Example Without using a calculator, estimate, to one significant figure, the answer to 219.3×587.14.

Very roughly

$$219.3 \approx 200$$
and
$$587.14 \approx 600$$
So
$$219 \times 587.14 \approx 200 \times 600 = 120\,000$$

So to *one* significant figure. the answer to 219.3×587.14 is $100\,000$.

CALCULATORS

It is good practice to make this sort of estimate whenever you use a calculator — after all, it is very easy to push a wrong button! For example, the decimal point may not register when I enter 219.3 (or so I think) into my calculator. It gives as the answer to the above multiplication

$$219.3 \times 587.14 = 1\,287\,598$$

But, because we made an estimate and are expecting an answer of around $100\,000$, we know that this answer of around $1\,000\,000$ is ten times too large and the error in the use of the calculator is apparent. Double checking, we find

$$219.3 \times 587.14 = 128\,759.8$$

which *is* about what we expected.

Most calculators display numbers to eight or ten figures. This is too many for O-level or CSE work, so your calculations will usually need to be rounded off. A good rule is work to *five* significant figures throughout a problem and give *answers* to *three* significant figures.

Example An eight-digit calculator shows $\sqrt{3}$ to be 1.732 050 8. So write down in your working $\sqrt{3} = 1.7321$ (rounding up the fifth digit because of the 5 in the next place).

Give as your answer

$$\sqrt{3} = 1.73 \quad \text{(3 s.f.)}$$

EXERCISE 1e

1. Round off to 2 d.p.:
   (a) 7.767   (b) 9.785   (c) 10.005   (d) 10.004
   (e) 6.666.

2. Round off to 3 s.f.:
   (a) 5.0467   (b) 12.123   (c) 121.5   (d) 10.06
   (e) 10.03.

3. Round off the following, (a) to 3 d.p. and (b) to 3 s.f.:
   (i) 0.1234   (ii) 0.001 234   (iii) 123.4567.

4. How many significant figures are there in the numbers
   (a) 123   (b) 1203   (c) 1230   (d) 123.0
   (e) 0.001 002 3 (f) 0.001 00   (g) 3.00   (h) 3
   (i) 10.00   (j) 6×10^6.

5. Estimate to *one* significant figure only the results of the following calculations:
   (a) 231×170 (b) 0.9157×6017 (c) 975.7×1109
   (d) 53.97×62.98 (e) 0.198×0.054 (f) $0.869 \div 0.032$
   (g) $0.0098 \div 0.119$.

6. Place the decimal point in the following calculations:
   (a) $237.1 \times 56.2 = 1\,332\,502$
   (b) $23.54 \times 11.45 = 269\,533$
   (c) $36\,543 \div 243.1 = 150\,321$
   (d) $41.67 \div 0.003 = 138\,900$.

7. An eight-digit calculator shows $\sqrt{7}$ to be 2.645 751 3; how would you record this in your working, and what would your answer be to $\sqrt{7} = \ldots$?

8. An eight-digit calculator shows the following:
   $$\cos 45° = 0.707\,106\,7 \qquad \tan 30° = 0.577\,350\,2.$$
   Copy these down rounding off to 5 s.f. (as you would from the calculator). Find to 3 s.f.
   (a) $2\cos 45° - \tan 30°$ (b) $\cos 45° - 2\tan 30°$.

9. State the largest and the smallest four-digit number that would round off to

   (a) 1.11   (b) 1.24   (c) 1.42   (d) 1.54

   (e) 1.55   (f) 1.00.

10. (a) A number is given as 1.24 (3 s.f.). What is the smallest number that could round up to this value? What is the largest value that would round down?

   (b) Elsewhere, a number is given as 1.240 (4 s.f.). What is the smallest number that would round up to this and what is the largest that would round down?

METRIC MEASUREMENT

The metric system of measurement is based upon ten, just like the number system. The common prefixes and their meanings are as follows:

kilo-	1000 times	e.g. 1 kilometre (km)	$= 1000$ metres (m)
		1 kilogram (kg)	$= 1000$ grams (g)
milli-	$\frac{1}{1000}$	e.g. 1 milligram (mg)	$= \frac{1}{1000}$ g
		1 millimetre (mm)	$= \frac{1}{1000}$ m
centi-	$\frac{1}{100}$	e.g. 1 centimetre (cm)	$= \frac{1}{100}$ m

Note that   1 metric tonne (t) $= 1000$ kg

1 cubic metre (m^3) $= 1000$ litres

1 cubic centimetre (cm^3) $= 1$ millilitre (ml)

1 litre of water has a mass of 1 kg

Be careful when dealing with areas and volumes. For although 100 centimetres make a metre, 10 000 (i.e. 100×100) *square* centimetres make a *square* metre and 1 000 000 (i.e. $100 \times 100 \times 100$) *cubic* centimetres make a *cubic* metre.

EXERCISE 1f 1. How many watts are there in a kilowatt? How many amps in a milliamp?

2. There are 10 mm in 1 cm. How many square millimetres are there in 1 cm^2?. How many cubic millimetres are there in 3 cm^3?

3. How many grams are there in 2.534 tonnes?

4. Find the volume of the tank illustrated in Fig. 1.4
   (a) in cubic metres   (b) in cubic centimetres
   (c) in litres.

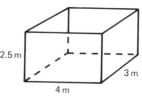

2.5 m

3 m

4 m

Fig. 1.4

5. A bath is 2 m long and 80 cm wide; it holds 960 litres of water when full. How high is it?

6. Find the length, in metres, of a roll of wallpaper 11 yards long, given that 1 yard is 1.1 m. Now give your answer to the nearest centimetre.

   The same roll of wallpaper is 21 inches wide. Given that 1 inch = 2.54 cm, how wide is the wallpaper, to the nearest millimetre?

7. The density of copper is $8.8 \, g/cm^3$. Find, in kilograms, the mass of 2 m^3 of copper.

8. At a particular pressure, 11.4 litres of hydrogen have a mass of 1 g. What is the density of hydrogen in g/cm^3? What is the mass of 39.9 litres of hydrogen?

9. One pint is equivalent to 583 ml. If I order 2 pints of milk per day from the milkman, how many litres is this? Correct your answer to one decimal place.

   Later the same day, I buy 1 gallon (8 pints) of motor oil, only to find later that the can actually contains 5 litres. Is this more or less than I intended to buy, and by how much?

10. Convert 54 km/h to m/s. How long would it take to travel 67.5 cm at this speed (give your answer in milliseconds)?

11. A particle travels 32 mm in 4 milliseconds. How far would it travel in 3 h at this speed?

NUMBERS IN BASES OTHER THAN TEN

Human-beings naturally work in base ten — or *denary* — as we have ten fingers. But other bases do exist. For example, computers work in base two, or *binary*.

Numbers written in other bases have different place values from those written in base ten. However, it must be possible to count one unit whatever base is used, and the digit on the extreme right *always* represents units. For example, the number 1 1 0 0 1 written in base two represents a value considerably less than eleven thousand and one. It is denoted $1 1 0 0 1_2$ and means:

Place value (base 2)	Sixteens 16	Eights 8	Fours 4	Twos 2	Units 1
Digit	1	1	0	0	1

The denary (base ten) value of the number is

$$(1 \times 16) + (1 \times 8) + (0 \times 4) + (0 \times 2) + (1 \times 1) = 25$$

Notice that the place value of the digits doubles (since this is base two) as we move left.

If the digits in this number were all forced to the left by an extra 0 placed on the right of the number, then the place value of each digit — and hence the value of the whole number — would double. Thus, as $1 1 0 0 1_2$ represents the denary value 25 so $1 1 0 0 1 0_2$ represents the denary value $2 \times 25 = 50$.

Similarly, in base three, the place value of the digits starts with units on the extreme right and *trebles* as we move left. Thus the base three number $2 2 1 2_3$ means:

Place value (base 3)	Twenty-sevens 27	Nines 9	Threes 3	Units 1
Digit	2	2	1	2

The base ten value of the number is

$$(2 \times 27) + (2 \times 9) + (1 \times 3) + (2 \times 1)$$
$$= \quad 54 \; + \; 18 \; + \; 3 \; + \; 2 \; = \; 77$$

In base three, an extra 0 on the end *trebles* the number. Thus, as $2 2 1 2_3$ represents the denary value 77 so $2 2 1 2 0_3$ represents the denary value $3 \times 77 = 231$.

In base four, the place value *quadruples* as we move left from *units* on the extreme right, then *fours, sixteens, sixty-fours*. Base five goes *units, fives, twenty-fives* and so on.

In base two, the number 10_2 means two (i.e. one lot of twos and no units); it follows that we shall never need the digit 2 while working in binary. Nor shall we need 3 (represented by 11_2) nor anything other than 0 and 1. Similarly, in base three, we need only three digits: 0, 1, and 2; in base four we need four digits: 0, 1, 2 and 3; and so on.

Note also that a number in a base other than ten should be 'spelled out'. Thus 10_2 is read as 'one zero, base two'.

CONVERTING BASES TO DENARY

The simplest way to convert a number from its base to base ten is to consider the place value of each digit, as above.

Example Convert 21221_3 to base ten.

Place value	81	27	9	3	1
Digit	2	1	2	2	1

The number is

$$(2 \times 81) + (1 \times 27) + (2 \times 9) + (2 \times 3) + (1 \times 1)$$
$$= \quad 162 \quad + \quad 27 \quad + \quad 18 \quad + \quad 6 \quad + \quad 1$$
$$= \quad 214$$

CONVERTING FROM DENARY

To convert a base ten number into a different base, base n, the base ten number must repeatedly be divided by n, recording the remainders at each stage. These remainders — in reverse order — make the number in the new base.

Example (*i*) Convert 87 to base two,

$87 \rightarrow$ base 2	Remainders
$87 \div 2 = 43$	1
$43 \div 2 = 21$	1
$21 \div 2 = 10$	1
$10 \div 2 = 5$	0
$5 \div 2 = 2$	1
$2 \div 2 = 1$	0
$1 \div 2 = 0$	1

Reading the remainders *in reverse order* gives

$$87 = 1010111_2$$

Example (*ii*) Convert 87 to base five.

87 → base 5	Remainders
$87 \div 5 = 17$	2
$17 \div 5 = 3$	2
$3 \div 5 = 0$	3

Reading the remainders *in reverse order* gives

$$87 = 322_5$$

ADDITION AND SUBTRACTION IN BINARY

Addition and subtraction may be completed in binary provided that particular attention is paid to the carrying and borrowing processes which arise frequently.

Example $10011 + 101$.

$$\begin{array}{r} 10011 \\ +101 \\ \hline 11000 \\ \hline 111 \end{array}$$
Since $1 + 1 = 10$ in base 2, the 0 is placed in the units column and the 1 carried over into the twos column. Here the carrying process arises three times.

Remember, when subtracting in base 2 a *two* (not ten) is borrowed from the next column.

Example $1011 - 101$.

$$\begin{array}{r} \overset{2}{1}011 \\ -101 \\ \hline 110 \end{array}$$
In the fours column, 1 cannot be subtracted from 0. Therefore an eight is borrowed from the eights column, which appears as 2 in the fours column (1 eight = 2 fours).

ADDITION AND SUBTRACTION IN OTHER BASES

Addition and subtraction works in the same way in *any* base.

Examples (*i*) Find $123_5 + 334_5$.

$$\begin{array}{r} 1\,2\,3 \\ +\,3\,3\,4 \\ \hline 1\,0\,1\,2 \\ \hline 1\,1 \end{array}$$

$3 + 4 = 7$, which is 12_5, so 1 must be carried to the next (fives) column. Similarly in the next column, it is necessary to carry again.

(*ii*) Find $32_4 - 23_4$.

$$\begin{array}{r} 2\,4+ \\ 3\,2 \\ 2\,3 \\ \hline 0\,3 \end{array}$$

In base 4 we borrow from the next column. So $4 + 2 - 3 = 3$ in the units column; and $2 - 2 = 0$ in the fours column.

1. Complete the table and so work out the denary (base 10) value of (a) 2112_4 (b) 1221_4.

Place value (base 4)		...	...	Fours 4	Units 1
Digit	(a)	2	1	1	2
	(b)	1	2	2	1

2. Work out the base ten value of these base 4 numbers:
   (a) 22_4 (b) 33_4 (c) 220_4 (d) 330_4.

3. What is the base 10 value of the following:
   (a) 13_4 (b) 13_7 (c) 13_9 (d) 13_{12}.

4. Convert these binary numbers to denary:
   (a) 110_2 (b) 1100_2 (c) 10010_2
   (d) 1001001_2.

5. Find the equivalent to 15 in
   (a) base 4   (b) base 7   (c) base 3.

6. Find the equivalent to 42 in
   (a) base 5   (b) base 7   (c) base 2.

7. Add the following in binary:
   (a) $\begin{array}{r} 1011 \\ +101 \\ \hline \end{array}$
   (b) $\begin{array}{r} 100101 \\ +1011 \\ \hline \end{array}$

8. Subtract the following binary numbers:
   (a) $\begin{array}{r} 11011 \\ -1101 \\ \hline \end{array}$
   (b) $\begin{array}{r} 110110 \\ -11101 \\ \hline \end{array}$

9. The binary number representing 11 is 1011_2. Without any further working, *write down* the binary number that represents
   (a) 22   (b) 44   (c) 88.

10. Find the base 3 number equivalent to
    (a) 12   (b) 36   (c) 108.

11. Write these binary numbers as base 10 numbers:
    (a) 101_2 (b) 1101_2 (c) 100100_2 (d) 1111_2.

12. Write as binary numbers
    (a) 7   (b) 12   (c) 25   (d) 37.

13. Convert 65
    (a) to base 3   (b) to base 5.

14. Convert to base 10
    (a) 332_5 (b) 332_6.

15. Work out the following in binary arithmetic:
    (a) $\begin{array}{r} 1101 \\ +111 \\ \hline \end{array}$
    (b) $\begin{array}{r} 10111 \\ +1011 \\ \hline \end{array}$
    (c) $\begin{array}{r} 1101 \\ -110 \\ \hline \end{array}$

16. Convert to binary
    (a) 27   (b) 64.

    Use your answers to *write down* the binary values of 27×64 without further working.

17. Convert 41
    (a) to binary   (b) to octal (base 8)
    (c) to hexadecimal (base 16).

18. Complete the following table:

	Base 10	Base 8	Base 6	Base 4	Base 3	Base 2
(a)	111					
(b)		111				
(c)			111			
(d)				111		
(e)					111	
(f)						111

19. Work out in base 4

(a) $123_4 + 11_4$ (b) $321_4 - 123_4$ (c) $123_4 \times 11_4$.

20. Find the base of the following calculations:

(a) $\begin{array}{r} 2\,0\,3 \\ +\,2\,2 \\ \hline 2\,3\,1 \end{array}$ (b) $\begin{array}{r} 3\,1\,2 \\ -\,3\,5 \\ \hline 2\,4\,4 \end{array}$ (c) $\begin{array}{r} 1\,0\,5 \\ -\,4\,3 \\ \hline 7\,2 \end{array}$

MISCELLANEOUS EXERCISE 1

1. Which of the following are (a) real numbers   (b) natural number   (c) integers   (d) rational numbers?

$$-101, -96.1, 0, \tfrac{1}{2}, 1, \sqrt{11}, 11, 12.7, 101$$

2.

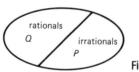

Fig. 1.5

The Venn diagram (Fig. 1.5) shows the set of all real numbers, which are either rational or irrational.

(a) Copy the diagram and put into it both the set of integers, I, and the set of natural numbers, N.

(b) For each of the following numbers, state *all* of the sets, using the letters I, N, P, Q, to which each belongs:

(i) π,   (ii) $3\tfrac{1}{7}$,   (iii) 4,   (iv) -4.   (LU)

3. (a) Evaluate 0.03×0.06.

(b) Estimate, to one significant figure, $\dfrac{23.96 \times 29.7}{(60.2)^2}$

(c) Express 0.0072 in the standard form $A \times 10^n$ where n is an integer and $1 \leqslant A < 10$.   (AEB '81)

4. Given that $26.389 \times 97.23 = 2565.8025$, *write down* the values of

   (a) $26\,389 \times 9723$ (b) $0.002\,638\,9 \times 0.097\,23$.

5. Given that $23.31 \div 3.15 = 7.4$, *write down* the answers to the following:

   (a) $23.31 \div 7.4$ (b) 3.15×74 (c) $2.331 \div 315$.

6. A boy's calculator lets him down: the decimal point fails to show. He uses it for the following calculations. Place the decimal point for him.

   (a) $45.6 \times 97.82 = 4\,460\,592$ (b) $12\,310.2 \div 42 = 2931$

   (c) $134.342 \div (2.02 \times 10^{-2}) = 6\,650\,594$.

7. Express 539.8×10^{-2} as an ordinary number correct (a) to two significant figures (b) to two decimal places (c) to the nearest integer.   (SUJB)

8. Write down the number $0.050\,506$ correct to

   (a) $4\,\text{d.p.}$ (b) $4\,\text{s.f.}$ (c) $1\,\text{d.p.}$ (d) $1\,\text{s.f.}$

9. Pluto, the furthest planet, is $7\,300\,000\,000$ miles from the Sun. The nearest star, Alpha Centauri, is $23\,520\,000\,000\,000$ miles from the Sun. A light year is $5\,880\,000\,000\,000$ miles.

   (a) Write these astronomical distances in scientific notation.

   (b) Estimate to 1 s.f. the number of light years between the Sun and Alpha Centauri.

   (c) Estimate to 1 s.f. the number of miles in a light day.

10. The mass of an atom of hydrogen is approximately 1.66×10^{-24} g, and that of an atom of oxygen is approximately 2.66×10^{-23} g.

    (a) Find, giving the answer in standard form to three significant figures, the mass of a molecule of water, which consists of two atoms of hydrogen and one of oxygen.

    (b) The given masses are correct to three significant figures. Find the maximum possible error in your answer to (a), and show that this answer is not necessarily *correct* to three significant figures.

    For parts (c) and (d), use your answer to (a), approximating it to *two* significant figures.

    (c) Find, giving your answer in standard form, the approximate number of molecules in 1 g of water.

    (d) Find, to the nearest whole number, the percentage by mass of oxygen in water.   (LU)

11. (a) Write down as a single number
$$7 \times 10^4 + 1 \times 10^2 + 4 \times 10 + 7.$$

   (b) If $x = 1 \times 2^5 + 1 \times 2^3 + 1 \times 2^1$, write x as a single binary number.

   Without further working, write down the binary values of

   (i) $\frac{1}{2}x$ (ii) $2x$.

12. Complete the following calculations:

   (a) $1000_4 - 1 =$;   answer in base 4

   (b) $11111_2 \div 11_2 =$;   answer in base 2

   (c) $12_8 \times 12_8 =$;   answer in base 8.   (SUJB)

13. (a) Work out the following in base 3:

   (i) $2220_3 - 1011_3$ (ii) $22_3 + 2022_3$ (iii) $22_3 \times 22_3$.

   (b) Calculate in binary:

   (i) $10111_2 + 10011_2$ (ii) $110000_2 - 111_2$

   (iii) $11011_2 + 1101_2 + 10011_2$.

14. Write the denary value 57 in

   (a) base 2   (b) base 3   (c) base 4   (d) base 8

   (e) base 12.

15. A base 7 number is written as a two-digit number, mn. In terms of m and n, what is the denary value of this number? What is the remainder when this number is divided by 7?

16. In base 12, T represents ten and E represents eleven. Show that $10T_{12}$ represents the denary value 154. Find the values of

   (a) 23_{12} (b) $2E_{12}$ (c) TT_{12}.

   Write in base 12 the denary numbers

   (d) 13   (e) 144   (f) 133.

   Work out in base 12

   (g) $9 + 5 - T$ (h) $E + 7$ (i) $TE - 1$ (j) $ET - E$.

2 FRACTIONS AND PERCENTAGES

FRACTIONS

The top of a fraction is called the *numerator*; the bottom of a fraction is called the *denominator*.

Two fractions are *equivalent* if they are of the same value. For example, $\frac{1}{2}$ is equivalent to $\frac{2}{4}$. We can find any number of equivalent fractions by multiplying the top and the bottom of a fraction by the same number (see Fig. 2.1). Thus

$$\frac{1}{2} = \frac{1 \times 2}{2 \times 2} = \frac{2}{4} \quad \text{and} \quad \frac{1}{2} = \frac{1 \times 3}{2 \times 3} = \frac{3}{6}$$

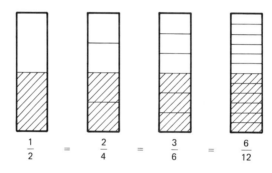

$$\frac{1}{2} = \frac{2}{4} = \frac{3}{6} = \frac{6}{12}$$

Fig. 2.1

Similarly, we can show that $\frac{3}{6}$ is the fraction $\frac{1}{2}$ by dividing the top and bottom by the same number:

$$\frac{3}{6} = \frac{3 \div 3}{6 \div 3} = \frac{1}{2}$$

This process is called *cancelling down* into *lowest terms*.

Example Write $\frac{12}{156}$ in its lowest terms.

Cancelling down in stages:

$$\frac{12}{156} = \frac{12 \div 2}{156 \div 2} = \frac{6}{78} = \frac{6 \div 2}{78 \div 2} = \frac{3}{39} = \frac{3 \div 3}{39 \div 3} = \frac{1}{13}$$

Mixed numbers, such as $7\frac{1}{2}$ and $5\frac{3}{4}$, may also be written as *top-heavy* or *improper fractions*. For example

$$7 = \frac{7}{1} = \frac{14}{2}$$

so

$$7\frac{1}{2} = \frac{14}{2} + \frac{1}{2} = \frac{15}{2}$$

$$5 = \frac{5}{1} = \frac{20}{4}$$

so

$$5\frac{3}{4} = \frac{20}{4} + \frac{3}{4} = \frac{23}{4}$$

WORKING WITH FRACTIONS

Addition and Subtraction

Fractions that are to be added together or subtracted from each other must first be written in an equivalent form so that they have the same denominator.

Example

$$\frac{1}{2} + \frac{1}{3}$$

These two fractions must be written in equivalent form, that is with the *same* denominator. The lowest common multiple of 2 and 3 is 6, and it follows that both $\frac{1}{2}$ and $\frac{1}{3}$ can be written as sixths (Fig. 2.2).

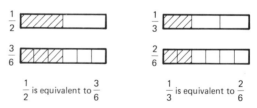

$\frac{1}{2}$ is equivalent to $\frac{3}{6}$ $\frac{1}{3}$ is equivalent to $\frac{2}{6}$

Fig. 2.2

Then:

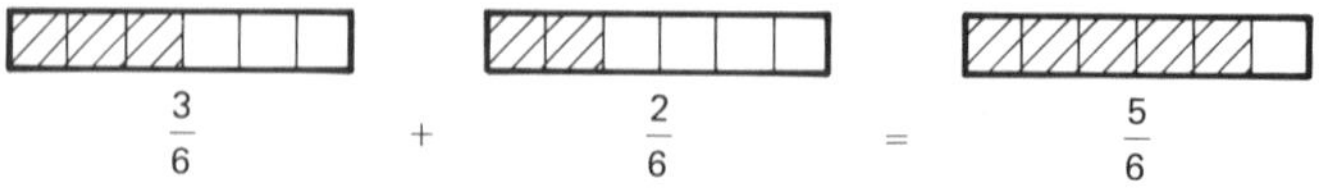

$\frac{3}{6}$ $+$ $\frac{2}{6}$ $=$ $\frac{5}{6}$

Fig. 2.3

So

$$\frac{1}{2} + \frac{1}{3} = \frac{3}{6} + \frac{2}{6} = \frac{5}{6}$$

Mixed numbers should be written as top-heavy fractions.

Example $2\frac{3}{4} - \frac{5}{6}$.

First, write $2\frac{3}{4}$ as a top-heavy fraction: $2\frac{3}{4} = \frac{11}{4}$.

Now, the LCM of 4 and 6 is 12, so

$$\frac{11}{4} = \frac{11 \times 3}{4 \times 3} = \frac{33}{12}$$

$$\frac{5}{6} = \frac{5 \times 2}{6 \times 2} = \frac{10}{12}$$

Hence

$$\frac{11}{4} - \frac{5}{6} = \frac{33}{12} - \frac{10}{12} = \frac{23}{12}$$

Multiplication

Multiplication of two fractions is relatively easy — the numerators are multiplied together and the denominators are multiplied together.

Example
$$\frac{3}{4} \times \frac{1}{2} = \frac{3 \times 1}{4 \times 2} = \frac{3}{8}$$

Sometimes it is possible to cancel out a factor that appears on the top and on the bottom *before* multiplying.

Example
$$\frac{6}{7} \times \frac{1}{9} = \frac{\overset{2}{\cancel{6}} \times 1}{7 \times \underset{3}{\cancel{9}}} = \frac{2 \times 1}{7 \times 3} = \frac{2}{21}$$

If a fraction is to be multiplied by a whole number, then the whole number should first be changed into a fraction, before proceeding in the usual way.

Example
$$\frac{3}{4} \times 5 = \frac{3}{4} \times \frac{5}{1} = \frac{3 \times 5}{4 \times 1} = \frac{15}{4}$$

Mixed numbers (such as $7\frac{1}{2}$ and $5\frac{3}{4}$) should be changed to top-heavy fractions before multiplying.

Example
$$\frac{4}{9} \times 5\frac{3}{4} = \frac{4}{9} \times \frac{23}{4} = \frac{\overset{1}{\cancel{4}} \times 23}{9 \times \underset{1}{\cancel{4}}} = \frac{23}{9}$$

Division

To divide one fraction by another, the second fraction is turned upside down and multiplied.

Examples

$$\frac{3}{5} \div \frac{7}{8} = \frac{3}{5} \times \frac{8}{7} = \frac{3 \times 8}{5 \times 7} = \frac{24}{35}$$

$$2\frac{2}{3} \div \frac{8}{9} = \frac{8}{3} \div \frac{8}{9}$$

$$= \frac{8}{3} \times \frac{9}{8}$$

$$= \frac{8 \times 9}{3 \times 8} = \frac{9}{3} = 3$$

CONVERTING FRACTIONS TO DECIMALS

A fraction can be converted into a decimal by rewriting the top as a decimal (so 1 becomes 1.0000, 3 becomes 3.0000, and so on) and then dividing it repeatedly by the denominator.

Example

$$\frac{1}{8} = \frac{1.000}{8}$$

and

$$\begin{array}{r} 0.125 \\ 8)\overline{1.000} \\ \underline{8} \\ 20 \\ \underline{16} \\ 40 \\ \underline{40} \end{array}$$

Thus $\frac{1}{8} = 0.125$

If the division is not exact, then continue to one more than the required number of decimal places and round off.

If continual division of the numerator leads to the same number or group of numbers repeating, then the decimal is said to be *recurring*, and the recurring digits are denoted by dots placed above them.

Examples

$$\frac{1}{3} = 0.333\,33\ldots = 0.\dot{3}$$

$$\frac{60}{111} = 0.540\,540\,540\ldots = 0.\dot{5}4\dot{0}$$

CONVERTING DECIMALS TO FRACTIONS

Examples

$$0.25 = \frac{25}{100} = \frac{25 \div 25}{100 \div 25} = \frac{1}{4}$$

$$0.108 = \frac{108}{1000} = \frac{108 \div 4}{1000 \div 4} = \frac{27}{250}$$

There are two steps:

(*i*) write the decimal as a whole number, divided by the appropriate power of ten;

(*ii*) cancel down if possible.

EXERCISE 2a Work out the following:

1. (a) $\frac{1}{3} + \frac{1}{4}$ (b) $\frac{1}{4} + \frac{1}{5}$ (c) $\frac{3}{4} + \frac{2}{3}$ (d) $\frac{3}{4} + \frac{3}{5}$

2. (a) $\frac{1}{2} - \frac{1}{5}$ (b) $\frac{2}{3} - \frac{2}{5}$ (c) $\frac{3}{4} - \frac{2}{7}$ (d) $\frac{5}{8} - \frac{1}{2}$

3. (a) $\frac{1}{8} \times \frac{4}{7}$ (b) $\frac{4}{5} \times \frac{3}{4}$ (c) $\frac{10}{17} \times 2$ (d) $2\frac{7}{9} \times 5\frac{2}{5}$

4. (a) $\frac{3}{8} \div \frac{3}{10}$ (b) $\frac{4}{11} \div \frac{3}{22}$ (c) $\frac{2}{5} \div 2$ (d) $2\frac{4}{7} \div 1\frac{1}{8}$

5. (a) $3\frac{1}{4} - 1\frac{1}{2}$ (b) $\frac{11}{13} \times 1\frac{6}{7}$ (c) $1\frac{4}{5} \div 2\frac{1}{4}$ (d) $1\frac{3}{4} - 3\frac{1}{3}$

6. (a) $2\frac{1}{8} + 1\frac{3}{4}$ (b) $2\frac{1}{8} - 1\frac{3}{4}$ (c) $2\frac{1}{8} \times 1\frac{3}{4}$ (d) $2\frac{1}{8} \div 1\frac{3}{4}$

7. (a) $3\frac{2}{9} + 1\frac{1}{3}$ (b) $3\frac{2}{9} - 1\frac{1}{3}$ (c) $3\frac{2}{9} \times 1\frac{1}{3}$ (d) $3\frac{2}{9} \div 1\frac{1}{3}$.

8. Convert the following fractions to decimals, rounding off to 2 d.p.:

(a) $\frac{2}{3}$ (b) $\frac{7}{20}$ (c) $\frac{5}{8}$ (d) $\frac{5}{9}$ (e) $\frac{2}{7}$.

9. Convert these decimals to fractions, written in their lowest terms:

(a) 0.2   (b) 0.75   (c) 1.6   (d) 0.16   (e) 0.55

(f) 0.05   (g) 0.48   (h) 0.125   (i) 0.375   (j) 0.008.

10. Write the following fractions as decimals, showing clearly which digits recur:

(a) $\frac{1}{9}$ (b) $\frac{4}{11}$ (c) $\frac{9}{11}$ (d) $\frac{4}{7}$ (e) $\frac{22}{7}$ (f) $\frac{1}{11}$.

PERCENTAGES

One part per hundred, i.e. the fraction $\frac{1}{100}$, is called *one percent* and is written 1%. 25% represents twenty-five parts per hundred, i.e. the fraction $\frac{25}{100}$; 40% represents $\frac{40}{100}$, and so on.

One whole unit is represented by $\frac{100}{100}$ or 100%. Amounts greater than one are represented by percentages greater than 100%. For example, if a quantity is doubled, it is 200% of its old value; if a wage is increased by, say, 6% then the new wage is 106% of the old.

Decimals and fractions are converted to percentages by multiplying by 100%. Thus

$$0.45 = 0.45 \times 100\% = 45\%$$

$$1.67 = 1.67 \times 100\% = 167\%$$

and similarly with fractions

$$\frac{1}{8} = \frac{1}{8} \times 100\% = \frac{1}{\overset{}{\underset{2}{8}}} \times \frac{\overset{25}{\cancel{100}}}{1} = \frac{25}{2} = 12\tfrac{1}{2}\%$$

$$1\frac{1}{2} = \frac{3}{2} \times 100\% = \frac{3}{\cancel{2}} \times \frac{\overset{50}{\cancel{100}}}{1} = 150\%$$

Conversely, a percentage may be converted to a decimal by dividing it by 100:

$$31\% = 0.31$$

$$16.7\% = 0.167$$

$$121\% = 1.21$$

Percentages can be rewritten as fractions by writing the denominator as 100 instead of % and cancelling down if possible:

$$32\% = \frac{32}{100} = \frac{32 \div 4}{100 \div 4} = \frac{8}{25}$$

$$125\% = \frac{125}{100} = \frac{125 \div 25}{100 \div 25} = \frac{5}{4} = 1\tfrac{1}{4}$$

$$5\tfrac{1}{2}\% = \frac{5\frac{1}{2}}{100} = \frac{5\frac{1}{2} \times 2}{100 \times 2} = \frac{11}{200}$$

To find a percentage of some amount, or to convert a part of some total to a percentage, it is best to treat the percentage as a fraction.

Examples (*i*) Find 15% of £22.

$$15\% \text{ of } £22 = \frac{15}{100} \text{ of } £22 = \frac{15}{100} \times \frac{£22}{1}$$

Converting £22 to pence gives 2200 pence. Thus

$$\frac{15 \times 2200}{100 \times 1} \text{ pence} = \frac{15 \times \overset{22}{\cancel{2200}}}{\underset{1}{\cancel{100}} \times 1} = 330 \text{ p}$$

$$= £3.30$$

(*ii*) A boy and a girl score 27 and 20 out of a possible 60 marks in a maths test. Work out their scores as percentages.

The boy scores 27 out of 60 or $\frac{27}{60}$ of the total. This is

$$\frac{27}{60} \times 100\% = \frac{\overset{9}{\cancel{27}} \times \overset{5}{\cancel{100}}}{\underset{20}{\cancel{60}} \times 1} \%$$

$$= 45\%$$

The girl scores 20 out of 60 or $\frac{20}{60}$ of the total. This is

$$\frac{20}{60} \times 100\% = \frac{\overset{1}{\cancel{20}} \times 100}{\underset{3}{\cancel{60}} \times 1} \%$$

$$= \frac{100}{3} \% = 33\tfrac{1}{3}\%$$

EXERCISE 2b Write the following decimals and fractions as percentages:

1. (a) 0.31 (b) 0.05 (c) 1.5 (d) 0.005 (e) 0.001

2. (a) $\frac{3}{5}$ (b) $\frac{2}{3}$ (c) $\frac{1}{25}$ (d) $\frac{3}{8}$ (e) $\frac{21}{200}$

3. (a) $1\frac{3}{4}$ (b) $1\frac{2}{3}$ (c) $2\frac{4}{5}$ (d) $3\frac{5}{8}$ (e) $2\frac{37}{200}$.

4. Write these percentages as decimals:
   (a) 32% (b) 89% (c) 102% (d) $67\frac{1}{2}$% (e) $88\frac{1}{2}$%.

5. Write these percentages as fractions in their lowest terms:
   (a) 75% (b) 60% (c) 32% (d) 130% (e) $1\frac{1}{2}$%
   (f) $15\frac{1}{2}$% (g) $12\frac{1}{2}$% (h) $3\frac{1}{3}$% (i) $5\frac{1}{4}$% (j) $16\frac{2}{3}$%.

6. Find
   (a) 10% of 85   (b) 15% of £60   (c) 30% of 250
   (d) 20% of £6.50   (e) 120% of £6.50   (f) $12\frac{1}{2}$% of £24.

7. A boy scores 36 out of 60 for his maths and 63 out of 90 in English. Convert these marks to percentages. Is he better at maths or English?

8. In a school of 350, 105 are boys. What percentage are girls? If 14 boys are absent, what percentage is this of
   (a) the whole school   (b) the boys.

9. I fit an attachment to my car that the advertisers claim will improve my petrol consumption by 'up to 5%'. I normally get 40 miles per gallon. What should I get now, if the advertisers' claim is valid? In fact I get 41 miles per gallon, with the attachment fitted. What is the percentage improvement?

10. In an O-level exam, 10.5% of the candidates are awarded grade 'A'. If there are 20 000 candidates for this particular exam, how many will receive a grade A? 5200 candidates were awarded grade B. What percentage is this?

TAXES

Taxes are usually expressed as percentages. For example, value added tax (VAT) is 15%. Income tax is 30%, although everyone has a 'tax allowance', that is, some part of their income upon which no income tax is charged.

Example A man earns £148 per week. He has a tax allowance of £28 per week. If income tax is 30%, how much tax is deducted and what is his 'take-home' pay?

The man earns £148. He pays tax on £120 (i.e. his weekly earnings less £28 weekly tax allowance).

$$30\% \text{ of } £120 = \frac{30}{100} \times £120 = £36$$

He pays £36 tax and takes home £148 − £36 = £112 per week.

SIMPLE INTEREST

When someone invests a sum of money, the *principal*, he receives *interest* at a *rate* quoted as a percentage.

If a principal of £P is invested for T years at an interest rate of $R\,\%$ per year, then the investor will receive interest, £I, given by the formula

$$£I = \frac{P \times R \times T}{100}$$

Example My grandmother leaves me £10 000 to be kept in trust for 8 years at 12% interest. What will the money be worth after that time?

$$P = £10\,000; \qquad R = 12\%; \qquad T = 8\,\text{years}$$

$$£I = \frac{10\,000 \times 12 \times 8}{100} = £9600$$

Thus the total amount will be £10 000 + £9600 = £19 600.

COSTS, PROFITS AND DISCOUNTS

A trader buys stock at *cost price* and sells it to his customers at a *selling price*. Normally, the selling price is higher than the cost price, so the trader makes a *profit*:

profit = selling price − cost price

Sometimes, however, the trader makes a *loss* — that is, the selling price is lower than the cost price:

loss = cost price − selling price

On other occasions, a trader may offer a *discount* on the old price of an article:

new price = old price − discount

Profits, losses, costs and discounts are often expressed as percentages.

Example A shopkeeper buys bars of chocolate of a certain size at £5.60 for a box of 35 bars. He sells them at 25% profit. What is the selling price of each bar?

The chocolate bars cost £5.60 for 35, i.e. £5.60 ÷ 35 = 16 p each.

The profit is 25% of 16 p, i.e.

$$\frac{25}{100} \times 16 = 4\,\text{p}$$

selling price = cost + profit = 16 p + 4 p = 20 p per bar

If we know the selling price of an article, and the percentage profit that is made on the sale or the discount offered, it is possible to work out the original cost of the item.

Examples (*i*) A trader makes a profit of 30% on an article for sale in his shop at £26. What is the cost price?

If the trader is selling at 30% profit, then the selling price is $100\% + 30\% = 130\%$ of cost price. Thus

$$130\% \text{ of cost} = £26$$

so $\qquad 1\%$ of cost $= £26 \div 130 \quad$ or $\quad \dfrac{2600}{130}$ pence

$$= 20\,\text{p}$$

Therefore

$$100\% \text{ of cost} = 20\,\text{p} \times 100$$

$$= £20$$

That is, the cost price of the article is £20.

(*ii*) Everything in a sale is reduced by 10% of its normal price. If I buy something in this sale for £4.86, what is the normal price and how much is the discount?

sale price $= 90\%$ of normal price $\quad = £4.86 = 486\,\text{p}$

so $\qquad 1\%$ of normal price $\quad = 486 \div 90$

$$= 5.4\,\text{p}$$

$$100\% \text{ of normal price} = 5.4 \times 100 = 540\,\text{p}$$

$$= £5.40$$

discount $= £5.40 - £4.86 = 54\,\text{p}$

EXERCISE 2c

1. How much VAT at 15% is due on goods worth:
   (a) £5.00   (b) £8.50   (c) £10.29   (d) £13.85?

2. If a woman earns £150 per week and has a tax allowance of £50 per week, how much income tax, charged at 30%, does she have to pay?

3. A man earns £132 per week and has a tax allowance of £48. How much income tax, at 30%, does he have to pay?

4. A successful salesman earns £22 000 in one year. He is allowed £4500 free of tax, and pays income tax at 30% on the first

£10 000 of taxable pay and at 40% on the rest. What is his tax bill that year?

5. A man invests £2400. What would be his interest in one year at
   (a) 6%   (b) 8%   (c) $12\frac{1}{2}$%   (d) $9\frac{1}{4}$%?

6. A man invests £5600 at 9%. What will be his simple interest after
   (a) 1 year   (b) 2 years   (c) 5 years?

7. £5000 is kept in a trust for 5 years, during which time it earns $12\frac{1}{2}$% simple interest per year. What will the trust be worth at the end of the 5 years?

8. A woman invests £2230 at 9% simple interest per year. How long before her savings have grown to £3000 or more?

9. A boy earns £44 per week in his first job. He has a tax allowance of £28 per week, but must pay income tax at 30% on the rest; he also must pay 9% National Insurance on *all* of the £44. How much will he have when he opens his pay packet? What percentage, to the nearest whole number, is this of his weekly earnings before deductions?

10. A trader buys 144 packets of soap powder for £57.60. If he makes a profit of 40% on this, what is the shop price of an individual packet of soap powder?

    They do not sell well at this price, so the trader makes a 'special offer' of 6 p off the shop price of each packet. What, now, is his percentage profit on the cost price of each packet?

11. In a sale, everything is reduced by 15%. If I buy something for £4.25, what was its original price?

12. I buy a book for £3.60. The bookseller is making a profit of 25% on his cost price. What did he pay for the book?

13. A company offers a discount of 4% if I pay my bills within 7 days.
    (a) My first bill is for £130. What is the discount worth?
    (b) I pay my second bill the day it arrives. If I actually pay £144.00, what was the original amount on the bill?

14. A man is given a mortgage of £25 500, which is 85% of the cost of a house which he hopes to buy. What is the cost of the house and how much must the man raise himself?

15. A hi-fi shop is offering a music centre at £280 which it advertises as '30% off the original price'. What was the original price?

MISCELLANEOUS EXERCISE 2

1. Work out

   (a) $\dfrac{3\frac{2}{7} \times \frac{7}{18}}{4\frac{3}{5}}$
   (b) $\dfrac{1\frac{1}{3} \times \frac{1}{4}}{\frac{2}{15}}$
   (c) $\dfrac{\frac{1}{2} - \frac{1}{3}}{\frac{5}{6}}$
   (d) $\dfrac{\frac{1}{4} + \frac{1}{3}}{\frac{1}{2} \times \frac{1}{3}}$

   (e) $\dfrac{\frac{1}{5} + \frac{5}{6}}{5\frac{1}{6}}$
   (f) $\dfrac{1\frac{1}{3} - \frac{1}{2}}{2\frac{1}{2} - 1\frac{1}{3}}$
   (g) $\dfrac{(3\frac{1}{2} \times 6) + \frac{1}{4}}{5\frac{2}{3}}$
   (h) $\dfrac{(2\frac{1}{3} \times 5) + 2\frac{1}{2}}{8\frac{1}{2} - 1\frac{5}{12}}$.

2. Find

   (a) $\frac{5}{18}$ of £450
   (b) 12% of £450
   (c) 132% of £450

   (d) $\frac{3}{7}$ of £714
   (e) $12\frac{1}{2}$% of £864
   (f) $6\frac{1}{2}$% of £202.

3. A trader makes 25% profit on his costs for articles which he sells at £400. What do these articles cost him?

4. A girl scores 33 points out of a possible 60 in her maths test. What is her percentage? Is this better or worse than $38\frac{1}{2}$ out of 70 in English and 45 out of 81 in French?

5. Two-thirds of a fence have been painted. If there are still 15 m to paint, how long is the fence?

6. After a wage increase of 8% a man's weekly earnings rise to £162. How much did he earn before the increase?

   If, at the same time, he must pay tax at 30% on all his earnings, by what percentage will his tax bill rise?

7. A wine trader buys Italian wine at a cost to him of 1800 lire per bottle. What is this in pence if £1 = 2400 lire? The trader sells the wine in the United Kingdom at £2.25 per bottle, but 40% of this is tax. What is the tax per bottle and how much profit does the trader enjoy on each bottle sold? What are the trader's profits as a percentage of his costs?

8. The value of my stocks and shares falls by 10% one week, but rises the following week by 20% of their new lower value. Show that the rise over the fortnight is 8% of the original value.

9. The menu lists the price of a meal as £8.00 before the service charge of 10% and VAT at 15% are added. Show that the final cost of the meal is £10.12, and that this is $26\frac{1}{2}$% more than the menu price. Why is the increase *not* simply 10% + 15% = 25%?

10. (a) A cassette recorder is advertised in a shop as having a list price of £35, plus VAT. The dealer offers a reduction of 18% before adding VAT at 15%.

Calculate
(i) the advertised price including VAT;
(ii) the reduction offered in pounds, before VAT is added;
(iii) the reduced final price of the recorder, to the nearest penny.

(b) A car costing £2600 loses 13% of its value at the end of each year. What is its value, to the nearest £10, after two years? (SUJB)

11. A shopkeeper made a profit of £20 by selling a suit of clothes for £92.

Write down the cost price to the shopkeeper, and calculate the percentage profit which he made on this cost price.

At a later date, the cost price to the shopkeeper was increased, but the shopkeeper still sold similar suits for £92, although his profit was reduced to 15%. Calculate the new cost price to the shopkeeper.

Later still, the cost price to the shopkeeper was increased to £90, and the shopkeeper raised his selling price so that he still made 15% profit. Calculate
(i) the new selling price to the customer,
(ii) the percentage increase in the price paid by the customer. (C)

12. A trader buys 300 kg of strawberries for £210. He begins to sell them at the rate of £1.20 per kilogram. When 180 kg have been sold, the strawberries begin to go soft and he reduces the price to 60 p per kilogram. He sells another 60 kg at this price, but the rest go bad and have to be thrown away. Calculate the percentage profit on his outlay.

Next day he buys another 300 kg for £210 and begins to sell them at £1 per kilogram. When 200 kg have been sold at this price, he decides to reduce the price. Find the price per kilogram that he must charge in order to make a profit of 25% on this day's outlay, assuming that all the strawberries are sold and none are thrown away. (O & C)

13. Two men invested money for one year in each of the following:
(A) a Building Society which paid interest at 7.5% per annum free of income tax,
(B) a Municipal Bond which paid interest at 12% per annum on which income tax at 30% was payable,
(C) the National Savings Bank which paid interest at 5% per annum. (The first £70 of interest was free of tax but on any remainder tax at 30% was payable.)

(a) The first man invested £600 in A, £2000 in B and £400 in C. Find his total net interest (after tax), and express this as a percentage of the capital invested.

(b) The second man invested £4000 in A, £7000 in B and a further sum in C. If he paid a total of £312 in income tax, find how much he invested in C, and find his total net interest. (Ox)

14. Three children, A, B and C, are sharing a bowl of food. When the bowl is passed to A, he always takes one-sixth of whatever is in it, whereas B and C always take one-fifth and one-quarter respectively, of whatever is in the bowl when it is passed to them. If the bowl, which is full at the start, is passed round in the order A, B, C,

(a) show that all the children receive equal amounts.

(b) find what fraction of the food is left when each child has taken (i) one helping, (ii) two helpings.

If, on the other hand, the bowl is passed round in the order C, B, A,

(c) show that the sizes of the helpings taken by C, B and A are in the ratio $5:3:2$,

(d) find what fraction of the bowlful each child has eaten, and what fraction is left, after each child has taken two helpings. (LU)

3 RATIO AND PROPORTION

RATIO

Fractions are sometimes written as *ratios*. For example, the ratio $1:10$ is equivalent to the fraction $\frac{1}{10}$.

Ratios may be cancelled down to lower terms, just like fractions. Thus the ratio $2:8$ would normally be cancelled down to $1:4$ just as the fraction $\frac{2}{8}$ would normally be cancelled down to $\frac{1}{4}$.

The scales of maps and models are often given as ratios. Ordnance Survey Maps, for example, are scaled $1:50\,000$. Thus a distance of 1 cm on the map represents a distance of 50 000 cm or 500 m on the ground.

Example A model aircraft is built to the scale $1:120$. If the wing-span of the model is 20 cm, what is the wing-span of the aircraft?

As the scale of the model is $1:120$, the wing-span of the actual aircraft will be 120×20 cm $= 2400$ cm $= 24$ m.

If the aircraft is 42 m long, how long is the model?

The aircraft is 42 m $= 4200$ cm long. The model is $\frac{1}{120}$ of this size:

$$4200 \times \frac{1}{120} = 35 \text{ cm}$$

Unlike a fraction, however, a ratio may show the relationship between more than two amounts.

Example (*i*) Martin, Alan and Patrick share £60 between them in the ratio $3:4:5$. How much does each receive?

The ratio apportions $3 + 4 + 5 = 12$ equal parts. Thus each part is worth $£\frac{60}{12} = £5$. Martin receives three parts, i.e. $3 \times £5 = 15$; Alan receives four parts, i.e. $4 \times £5 = £20$; and Patrick receives five parts, i.e. $5 \times £5 = £25$.

Example (*ii*) If $a:b = 4:5$ and $b:c = 6:7$ find $a:b:c$.
Multiplying both parts of the ratio $a:b$ by 6 gives
$4 \times 6:5 \times 6 = 24:30$ and similarly multiplying $b:c$ by 5
gives $6 \times 5:7 \times 5 = 30:35$. Now, as b in both ratios is the
same, i.e. 30, we can say

$$a:b:c = 24:30:35$$

EXERCISE 3a

1. Express in lowest terms the ratios
   (a) $2:4$ (b) $3:9$ (c) $12:8$
   (d) $10:20:40$ (e) $15:25:30$ (f) $16:24:32:48$.

2. Express in lowest terms the ratios
   (a) $1\,\text{cm}:1\,\text{m}$ (b) $1\,\text{m}:1\,\text{km}$ (c) $1\,\text{cm}:1\,\text{km}$
   (d) $1\,\text{cm}:4\,\text{km}$.

3. A model bridge is 30 cm long and represents a real bridge
   which is 120 m long. What is the scale of the model?
   If the model is 3 cm wide, what is the width of the actual
   bridge?
   The bridge supports are 20 m high; what is the height of the
   supports of the model bridge?

4. I draw a map for a friend so that his journey of 5 km to my
   house is represented by a road of 20 cm. What is the scale of
   this map?
   If my friend misses a turning, and his actual journey is represented on the map by a road 34 cm long, how far has he
   come?

5. Divide 12 in the ratio
   (a) $1:2$ (b) $1:2:3$ (c) $1:4:7$.

6. Divide 54 in the ratio
   (a) $3:2:1$ (b) $3:3:2:1$ (c) $3:5:4:6$.

7. Divide 108 in the ratio
   (a) $7:5$ (b) $2:3:4$ (c) $2:3:3:4$.

8. Jonathan divides £56 between himself and Janette, so that he
   keeps three times as much as he gives her. How much does
   Janette get?

9. In a game of Scrabble, Harry scores twice as many as Dick but
   half as many as Tom. Write down a ratio representing Tom,
   Dick and Harry's scores. If the three together score a total of
   567, what are their three scores?

10. A photograph has sides in the ratio $3:2$. If a standard print is $7\frac{1}{2}$ cm long, find the length of the shorter side. If the photograph is enlarged so that the longer side is $10\frac{1}{2}$ cm, what is the width?

11. The angles of an isosceles triangle are in the ratio $2:2:5$. What are its angles in degrees?

12. x, y and z are three quantities such that $x:y = 5:7$ and $y:z = 4:3$. Find the ratio $x:y:z$.

13. If $x:y = 3:5$ and $y:z = 6:7$, find $x:y:z$.

14. If $a:b = 2:3$ and $b:c = 5:4$, find $a:b:c$.

15. If $l:m = 8:5$ and $m:n = 8:3$, find $l:m:n$.

16. If $a:b = 2:1$ and $b:c = 4:1$, find $a:c$.

17. If $m:n = 2:7$ and $n:p = 2:9$, find $m:p$.

18. If $x:y = 7:2$ and $y:z = 3:1$, find $x:z$.

19. An ordnance survey map has a scale of $1:50\,000$.
    (a) How far is a journey shown as 9 cm on the map?
    (b) On the map, a reservoir is represented by a rectangle 0.2 cm by 0.5 cm. What are the length and breadth of the reservoir, and what is its area?
    (c) On another map a journey of 15 km was shown as 50 cm. What is the scale of this map?

20. A map is drawn to a scale of $1:50\,000$.
    (a) Calculate the actual distance, in kilometres, represented by 1 cm on the map.
    (b) Two towns are 24 km apart. Calculate, in centimetres, their distance apart on the map.
    (c) On the map, a farm has an area of 20 cm². Calculate, in square kilometres, the actual area of the farm.   (C)

DIRECT PROPORTION

Two quantities that increase or decrease together, always staying in the same ratio to each other (i.e. if one is doubled then so is the other; if one is halved, then so is the other; and so on), are said to be in *direct proportion* or to *vary directly*.

If y is proportional to x we write

$$y \propto x$$

Moreover, if the ratio $y:x$ is $k:1$, it follows that

$$y = kx$$

Example The height, b, of an image on a screen is in direct proportion to the distance, x, of the screen from the projector. If the image is 30 cm high when the screen is 150 cm from the projector, how far from the screen should the projector be if the image is to be reduced to 24 cm?

$$b \propto x$$

and
$$b = kx$$

We know that $b = 30$ when $x = 150$, so

$$30 = k \times 150$$

Therefore
$$k = \frac{30}{150} = \frac{1}{5}$$

We can now write a full equation between b and x replacing k with $\frac{1}{5}$, i.e.

$$b = \frac{1}{5}x$$

If $b = 24$, it follows that

$$24 = \frac{1}{5}x$$

giving
$$x = 5 \times 24 = 120$$

The projector must be placed 120 cm from the screen.

INVERSE PROPORTION

Two quantities that vary in such a way that one increases in the same proportion as the other decreases are said to be *inversely proportional* or to *vary inversely*.

$$y \propto \frac{1}{x}$$

It follows that

$$y = k\frac{1}{x} = \frac{k}{x}$$

Examples (*i*) If y is inversely proportional to the square of x and $y = 3$ when $x = 4$ find the value of y when $x = 6$.

$$y \propto \frac{1}{x^2}$$

and

$$y = \frac{k}{x^2}$$

As $y = 3$ and $x^2 = 16$ when $x = 4$

$$3 = \frac{k}{16}$$

Therefore

$$k = 3 \times 16 = 48$$

So

$$y = \frac{48}{x^2}$$

When $x = 6$, $x^2 = 36$.

$$y = \frac{48}{36} = 1\frac{1}{3}$$

(*ii*) The pressure, P, of a quantity of gas varies inversely with the volume, V, of its container. If the gas pressure is $10 \, \text{N/m}^2$ in a container of $25 \, \text{m}^3$, what will the pressure be in a container of $20 \, \text{m}^3$ volume?

Since P varies inversely with V

$$P \propto \frac{1}{V}$$

and

$$P = \frac{k}{V}$$

Now $P = 10$, when $V = 25$. Hence

$$10 = \frac{k}{25}$$

giving

$$k = 250$$

Thus

$$P = \frac{250}{V}$$

So when $V = 20$

$$P = \frac{250}{20} = 12.5 \, \text{N/m}^2$$

1. If $y \propto x$, and $y = 4$ when $x = 10$, find
   (a) y when $x = 15$ (b) x when $y = 16$.

2. If $y \propto x^2$, and $y = 3$ when $x = 2$, find
   (a) y when $x = 4$ (b) x when $y = 48$.

3. If $y \propto \dfrac{1}{x}$, and $y = 4$ when $x = 6$, find
   (a) y when $x = 8$ (b) x when $y = 2$.

4. If $y \propto \dfrac{1}{x^2}$, and $y = 4$ when $x = 6$, find
   (a) y when $x = 4$ (b) x when $y = 1$.

5. If $p \propto q^3$, and $p = 12$ when $q = 2$, find
   (a) p when $q = 3$ (b) q when $p = 324$.

6. If $r \propto \dfrac{1}{\sqrt{s}}$, and $r = 7$ when $s = 36$, find
   (a) r when $s = 49$ (b) s when $r = 10\frac{1}{2}$.

7. The thickness of a wooden barrier is directly proportional to the number of planks used to build it. If four planks make a 9 cm barrier, how thick would a barrier of six planks be?

8. The number of neighbours who complain about the noise of my record player is in direct proportion to the volume setting. If two neighbours complain when I have it set on '3', how many will complain when I turn it up to '9'?

9. The number, n, of people in the queue in the post office seems to vary inversely with the time, t, I have to spare, i.e. $n \propto \dfrac{1}{t}$. When I have 6 minutes, two people are queuing. How long is the queue likely to be when I have only 1 minute to complete my business?

10. The time it takes me to get to work in the mornings is inversely proportional to the speed at which I drive. At 40 m.p.h. it takes me 12 minutes. How long will it take me at
    (a) 30 m.p.h.   (b) 48 m.p.h.   (c) 64 m.p.h.?

11. The pressure of a gas in a container varies directly with the temperature. If it is at a pressure of 50 N/m² at $75°$ what will the pressure be at $135°$?

12. The commission earned by the Worseforware perfume sales-man varies directly with his sales. If he is paid £22 in one week, having sold £143 worth of goods, what commission can he expect in a week when he sells £208 worth? How much would he need to sell to earn £40?

13. The length of time taken to complete a job varies inversely with the number of men working on it. If 10 men take 10 days, how long will eight men take?

14. Corresponding sides of similar triangles are directly pro-portional to each other. The three triangles in Fig. 3.1 are similar. Find the lengths x, y and z.

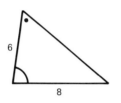 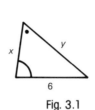 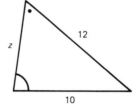

Fig. 3.1

4 POWERS

$$5 \times 5 \text{ is written } 5^2$$

Five is said to be *raised to the power two* (or *squared*) as there are *two* fives multiplied together. Similarly,

$$5 \times 5 \times 5 \text{ is written } 5^3$$

Five is said to be *raised to the power three* (or *cubed*) as there are *three* fives multiplied together.

$$5 \times 5 \times 5 \times 5 \text{ is written } 5^4$$

Five is *raised to the power four* as there are *four* fives multiplied together, and so on.

We could work out the value of these powers. Thus $5 \times 5 = 25$; hence $5^2 = 25$. $5 \times 5 \times 5 = 125$; hence $5^3 = 125$, and so on.

The power notation is convenient short-hand when strings of the same number are multiplied together. Be careful not to confuse 5×2 (which is 10) and 5^2 (which is $5 \times 5 = 25$).

COMBINING POWERS

Adding powers of a number is equivalent to multiplication. Consider $5^2 \times 5^3$.

$$5^2 \times 5^3 = (5 \times 5) \times (5 \times 5 \times 5)$$
$$= 5 \times 5 \times 5 \times 5 \times 5$$
$$= 5^5$$

Thus
$$5^2 \times 5^3 = 5^{2+3} = 5^5$$

Examples
$$2^3 \times 2^4 = 2^{3+4} = 2^7$$
$$10^2 \times 10^3 \times 10^4 = 10^{2+3+4} = 10^9$$

Subtracting powers of a number is equivalent to division. Consider $5^3 \div 5^2$.

$$5^3 \div 5^2 = \frac{5 \times \cancel{5} \times \cancel{5}}{\cancel{5} \times \cancel{5}} = 5^1$$

Thus
$$5^3 \div 5^2 = 5^{3-2} = 5^1$$

Examples

$$25 \div 22 = 2^{5-2} = 2^3$$
$$10^4 \div 10^3 = 10^{4-3} = 10^1$$

Multiplying powers of a number is equivalent to raising it to one power and then immediately to another. Consider $(5^2)^4$.

$$(5^2)^4 = 5^2 \times 5^2 \times 5^2 \times 5^2$$
$$= 5 \times 5 \times 5 \times 5 \times 5 \times 5 \times 5 \times 5$$
$$= 5^8$$

Thus $(5^2)^4 = 5^{2 \times 4} = 5^8$

Examples

$$(3^3)^2 = 3^{3 \times 2} = 3^6$$
$$(10^3)^3 = 10^{3 \times 3} = 10^9$$

EXERCISE 4a

1. Write as powers
   (a) $2 \times 2 \times 2$ (b) $3 \times 3 \times 3 \times 3$ (c) $4 \times 4 \times 4$
   (d) $7 \times 7 \times 7 \times 7 \times 7 \times 7$.

2. Work out the values of
   (a) 2^4 (b) 3^3 (c) 7^2 (d) 4^1 (e) 3^4
   (f) 4^3 (g) 2^5 (h) 6^3.

3. Simplify the following, giving your answers as powers:
   (a) $2^5 \times 2^3$ (b) $3^4 \times 3^2$ (c) $2^5 \div 2^3$ (d) $3^4 \div 3^2$
   (e) $(2^5)^3$ (f) $(3^4)^2$.

4. (a) Work out the values of
       (i) 2^2 (ii) 2^4 (iii) 2^6 (iv) 2^8.
   (b) Do the values of 2^4 and 2^2 multiplied together give 2^6?
   (c) Use your answers to show that
       (i) $2^8 \div 2^6 = 2^2$ (ii) $(2^4)^2 = 2^8$.

5. Write as powers of 10
   (a) one hundred   (b) one thousand   (c) one million.

6. Deduce from your answers to Question 5 the power of 10 that represents
   (a) one hundred thousand
   (b) one hundred million
   (c) one American billion (one thousand million)
   (d) one English billion (one million million).

45

ZERO AS A POWER

Consider $5^4 \div 5^4$. When any number is divided by itself the answer is 1. (For example $2 \div 2 = 1$; $11 \div 11 = 1$, etc.) Thus $5^4 \div 5^4 = 1$. However, if we apply the rules of powers, then

$$5^4 \div 5^4 = 5^{4-4} = 5^0$$

Hence

$$5^0 = 1$$

We could have shown the same with *any* number, not just 5. *Any* number raised to the power zero is one. Thus, for example,

$$7^0 = 1$$

$$\left(\frac{1}{4}\right)^0 = 1$$

NEGATIVE POWERS

Consider $5^2 \div 5^6$.

$$5^2 \div 5^6 = 5^{2-6} = 5^{-4}$$

But

$$5^2 \div 5^6 = \frac{5 \times 5}{5 \times 5 \times 5 \times 5 \times 5 \times 5}$$

$$= \frac{1}{5 \times 5 \times 5 \times 5}$$

$$= \frac{1}{5^4}$$

So 5^{-4} is the same as $\frac{1}{5^4}$.

In general, a negative power means the *reciprocal* of the number or 'one over the number'. Thus

$$4^{-2} = \frac{1}{4^2} = \frac{1}{16}$$

$$7^{-1} = \frac{1}{7}$$

$$10^{-3} = \frac{1}{10^3} = \frac{1}{1000}$$

FRACTIONS AS POWERS

Consider $5^{\frac{1}{2}}$. If $5^{\frac{1}{2}}$ is squared, we get

$$(5^{\frac{1}{2}})^2 = 5^{\frac{1}{2} \times 2} = 5^1$$

$$(5^{\frac{1}{2}})^2 = 5.$$

It follows that $\qquad 5^{\frac{1}{2}} = \sqrt{5}$

i.e. the *square root* of 5.

Similarly, we could show that

$$2^{\frac{1}{3}} = \sqrt[3]{2} \qquad \text{i.e. the } cube\ root \text{ of 3}$$

$$7^{\frac{1}{4}} = \sqrt[4]{7} \qquad \text{i.e. the } fourth\ root \text{ of 7}$$

and so on.

Now consider $5^{\frac{2}{3}}$.

$$5^{\frac{2}{3}} = (5^{\frac{1}{3}})^2 = (\sqrt[3]{5})^2$$

i.e. the square of the cube root of 5. Alternatively, if $5^{\frac{2}{3}}$ is cubed, we get

$$(5^{\frac{2}{3}})^3 = 5^{\frac{2}{3} \times 3} = 5^2$$

As $5^{\frac{2}{3}}$ cubed gives 5^2, it follows that $5^{\frac{2}{3}} = \sqrt[3]{5^2}$, i.e. the cube root of 5 squared. Similarly

$$8^{\frac{2}{3}} = (8^{\frac{1}{3}})^2 = (\sqrt[3]{8})^2 = (2)^2 = 4$$

or $\qquad 8^{\frac{2}{3}} = (8^2)^{\frac{1}{3}} = \sqrt[3]{64} = 4$

Examples (*i*) $\quad 4^{\frac{1}{2}} = \sqrt{4} = 2$

(*ii*) $\quad 27^{\frac{1}{3}} = \sqrt[3]{27} = 3$

(*iii*) $\quad 27^{\frac{2}{3}} = (27^{\frac{1}{3}})^2 = (3)^2 = 9$

(*iv*) $\quad 4^{\frac{3}{2}} = (\sqrt{4})^3 = 2^3 = 8$

(*v*) $\quad 4^{-\frac{2}{2}} = (\sqrt{4})^{-3} = 2^{-3} = \dfrac{1}{8}$

(*vi*) $\quad 64^{-\frac{1}{3}} = \dfrac{1}{64^{\frac{1}{3}}} = \dfrac{1}{\sqrt[3]{64}} = \dfrac{1}{4}$

EXERCISE 4b Find the values of

1. (a) 6^0 (b) 3.4^0 (c) $(\frac{1}{2})^0$ (d) $(8.35)^0$

2. (a) 2^{-1} (b) 3^{-2} (c) 10^{-2} (d) 10^{-4}

3. (a) $9^{\frac{1}{2}}$ (b) $9^{-\frac{1}{2}}$ (c) $81^{\frac{1}{4}}$ (d) $81^{\frac{3}{4}}$

4. (a) $9^{\frac{3}{2}}$ (b) $9^{-\frac{3}{2}}$ (c) $1000^{\frac{2}{3}}$ (d) $1000^{-\frac{2}{3}}$.

5. Work out the following, giving your answer both as a value and as a power of 2:

     (a) $2^4 \div 2^3$ (b) $2^2 \times 2^{-1}$ (c) $2^2 \times 2^{-4}$ (d) $2^2 \div 2^{-1}$

     (e) $2^{-2} \times 2^{-4}$ (f) $(2^{-2})^2$ (g) $2^{-2} \div 2^{-4}$ (h) $(2^{-2})^{\frac{1}{2}}$.

Find the values of

6. (a) $3^2 \times 3^{-3}$ (b) $3^2 \div 3^{-3}$ (c) $(4^2)^3$ (d) 39^0

7. (a) $9^{\frac{1}{2}}$ (b) $8^{\frac{2}{3}}$ (c) $9^{-\frac{1}{2}}$ (d) $121^{-\frac{1}{2}}$

8. (a) $16^{\frac{1}{4}}$ (b) $16^{\frac{3}{4}}$ (c) $16^{-\frac{3}{4}}$ (d) $(16^{\frac{1}{4}})^5$

9. (a) $(-5)^0$ (b) $(-5)^1$ (c) $(-5)^2$ (d) $(-5)^3$.

10. Without using tables or a calculator, find the values of p, q, r and s in the following equations:

     (a) $3^p = 81$ (b) $2^q = 1$ (c) $r^3 = \dfrac{1}{125}$ (d) $27^{\frac{1}{3}} = s$.

(SUJB)

POWERS AND ARITHMETIC IN STANDARD FORM

Multiplication and Division

Numbers written in standard or scientific form include powers of ten as part of the number. These powers of 10 multiply and divide each other just like any other powers. For this reason it is best to separate the powers of 10 and deal with them on their own.

Examples (i) $(3.9 \times 10^2) \times (1.1 \times 10^4)$.

Rearranging the problem to bracket the powers of 10 together, we have

$$(3.9 \times 1.1) \times (10^2 \times 10^4) = (3.9 \times 1.1) \times 10^{2+4}$$
$$= 4.29 \times 10^6$$

(ii) $(1.44 \times 10^{-3}) \div (7.2 \times 10^{-6}) = (1.44 \div 7.2) \times (10^{-3} \div 10^{-6})$
$$= 1.44 \div 7.2 \times 10^{-3 -(-6)}$$
$$= 0.2 \times 10^{-3+6}$$
$$= 0.2 \times 10^3$$

However, this number is not yet in standard form since 0.2 is not a number between 1 and 10. Using $0.2 = 2 \times 10^{-1}$ we continue

$$0.2 \times 10^3 = (2 \times 10^{-1}) \times 10^3 = 2 \times 10^{-1+3} = 2 \times 10^2$$

(iii)

$$\frac{(1.1 \times 10^{-3})^2}{6.05 \times 10^4} = \frac{(1.1)^2 \times (10^{-3})^2}{6.05 \times 10^4}$$

$$= \frac{1.21}{6.05} \times \frac{10^{-6}}{10^4}$$

$$= 0.2 \times 10^{-6-4}$$

$$= (2 \times 10^{-1}) \times 10^{-10}$$

$$= 2 \times 10^{-11}$$

Addition and Subtraction

Addition and subtraction of numbers written in standard form is more tricky. In fact the powers of 10 make the problem *more* difficult; it is best to convert the numbers into ordinary decimals and then add or subtract in the usual way.

Examples (i) $1.1 \times 10^2 + 2.4 \times 10^3 = 110 + 2400 = 2510$

$$= 2.510 \times 10^3$$

(ii) $9.1 \times 10^{-2} - 4.3 \times 10^{-3} = 0.091 - 0.0043 = 0.0867$

$$= 8.67 \times 10^{-2}$$

EXERCISE 4c   Without a calculator work out the following, giving your answers in standard form:

1. $(2 \times 10^4) \times (3 \times 10^5)$

2. $(5 \times 10^{-7}) \div (4 \times 10^{-3})$

3. $(8.4 \times 10^3) \times (1.1 \times 10^{-2})$

4. $(3.3 \times 10^3) \div (1.1 \times 10^{-2})$

5. $(5 \times 10^{-7}) \times (4 \times 10^{-3})$

6. $\dfrac{(5.7 \times 10^2) \times (3.5 \times 10^4)}{2.1 \times 10^{-2}}$

7. $\dfrac{(9 \times 10^{-4}) \times (4 \times 10^5)}{3.6 \times 10^{-2}}$

8. $(2.3 \times 10^3) + (2.2 \times 10^2)$

9. $(2.3 \times 10^3) - (2.2 \times 10^2)$

10. $3.2 \times 10^4 + 5.4 \times 10^3$

11. $(3.91 \times 10^{-2}) - (2.5 \times 10^{-3})$

12. $5.11 \times 10^{-2} - 9.87 \times 10^{-4}$

13. $\dfrac{0.0002 \times (0.036 \div 0.6)}{1.2 \div (0.016 \div 0.4)}$

14. $\dfrac{(4.2 \times 10^3) \times (8.1 \times 10^{-2})}{(1.8 \times 10^{-2}) \times (3.6 \times 10^5)}$

15. $\dfrac{0.0013 \times 0.21 \times 1.21}{2.31 \times 0.039}$

16. $\dfrac{(6.4 \times 10^2) \times (8.4 \times 10^8) \times (9 \times 10^2)}{(1.6 \times 10^3) \times (1.44 \times 10^{-2}) \times 7}.$

ALGEBRAIC POWERS

The rules for combining powers apply to algebraic values in exactly the same way as they apply to ordinary numbers. Thus $y \times y \times y$ would be shortened to y^3; y^4 would mean $y \times y \times y \times y$, etc.

Examples (i) $y^2 \times y^3 = y^{2+3} = y^5$

(ii) $y^5 \div y^7 = y^{5-7} = y^{-2}$, i.e. $\dfrac{1}{y^2}$

(iii) $(y^2)^3 = y^{2 \times 3} = y^6$

(iv) $y^{\frac{1}{2}} = \sqrt[2]{y}$ and $y^{\frac{3}{4}} = (\sqrt[4]{y})^3$ or $\sqrt[4]{y^3}$

(v) $y^0 = 1$.

In algebraic problems involving more than one letter, be careful not to muddle up powers of *different* letters. Thus $x^2 y^3$ cannot be simplified, though $y^2 y^3$ would be written as y^5.

Examples (vi) $p^3 q^2 \times pq = p^{3+1} \times q^{2+1} = p^4 q^3$

(vii) $p^3 q \div pq^2 = p^{3-1} \times q^{1-2} = p^2 q^{-1}$

(viii) $\sqrt{p^4 q^6} = \sqrt{p^4} \times \sqrt{q^6} = p^2 q^3.$

EXERCISE 4d   Simplify the following as far as possible:

1. (a) $p \times p \times p \times p \times p$
   (c) $(p^3)^2$

   (b) $p^3 \times p^2 \times p$
   (d) $(p^3)^{-2}$

2. (a) $\dfrac{1}{q \times q \times q \times q}$
   (c) $(q^{-2})^{-1}$

   (b) $\dfrac{1}{q} \times \dfrac{1}{q} \times \dfrac{1}{q}$
   (d) q^0

3. (a) $x^2 y \times x^3$
   (c) $x^2 y \times x^{-1} y$

   (b) $(x^2 y)^2$
   (d) $x^2 y \times x^{-2} y^{-2}$

4. (a) $yz^3 \div z^2$ (b) $y^3z \div y^4$

    (c) $y^3z^{-1} \div x$ (d) $y^3z^{-1} \div y^{-1}z^{-1}$

5. (a) $\sqrt{a} \times \sqrt{a}$ (b) $\sqrt{a} \times a^0$

    (c) $\sqrt{a^2b^2}$ (d) $(a^{\frac{1}{4}})^{-1}$

6. (a) $(a \times a^3)^2$ (b) $(a^3 \times \sqrt{a})^2$

    (c) $(a^{-\frac{1}{3}} \times a^4)^{-1}$ (d) $(\sqrt{a} \times a^2)^{\frac{1}{2}}$

7. (a) $x^0y^2 \times x^0y^0$ (b) $p^3q^2 \times pq^2r$

    (c) $\dfrac{m^2}{n} \times m^2n^2$ (d) $(mn^2)^2$

8. (a) $p^{-2} \times \dfrac{1}{p^2}$ (b) $(y^{-2})^{-3}$

    (c) $q^{-2} \div q^2$ (d) $x^{-\frac{1}{2}} \div x^{\frac{1}{2}}$

9. (a) $a^{-\frac{3}{4}} \times a^{-\frac{1}{4}}$ (b) $\sqrt{(pq^{2r})}$

    (c) $\sqrt[3]{r^{-3}q^6}$ (d) $\dfrac{tu^{-\frac{1}{2}}}{t^{\frac{1}{2}}u^{-\frac{1}{2}}}$

10. (a) $\dfrac{a^3b^2}{c} \times \dfrac{c^2}{a^2b}$ (b) $\dfrac{x^7y^3}{z^2} \times \dfrac{x^2z}{y^7}$

11. (a) $2p^0q^2r \div p^{-1}qr^2$ (b) $\dfrac{3m^2n^2}{p^2} \div pm^2n^2$.

12. Simplify $\dfrac{ab^5}{cd^4} \times \dfrac{c^2d^3}{m^4b^2} \div \dfrac{ad^2b^2}{c}$.   (SUJB)

5 SETS

SET NOTATION

Numbers or objects may be bracketed together to form a *set*. Sets are usually denoted by a capital letter and written inside curly brackets. For example, integers or whole numbers form a set, usually called Z, where

$$Z = \{\ldots, -3, -2, -1, 0, 1, 2, 3, \ldots\}$$

Or we might define a set, F, to be the factors of 6:

$$F = \{1, 2, 3, 6\}$$

The symbol $\in$ denotes that a number or object *belongs to* a set. A member of a set is often called an *element*, so $\in$ could also be translated as *'is an element of'*. $\notin$ means the opposite: *does not belong to*. Thus

$$4 \in Z \qquad \text{but} \qquad 4 \notin F$$

means that 4 belongs to the set of whole numbers, Z, but not to F, the set of factors of 6.

Some elements of a set may be grouped together to form a *subset*. For example, the set of natural numbers, $N = \{1, 2, 3, \ldots\}$ and is a subset of Z, the set of *all* whole numbers. We write

$$N \subset Z \qquad \text{or} \qquad Z \supset N$$

meaning that N *is a subset* of Z or Z *contains the set* N. Similarly

$$F \subset Z \qquad \text{and} \qquad Z \supset F$$

The opposite, *'is not a subset of'*, is written $\not\subset$.

$n(A)$ means *the number of elements in set* A. Thus $n(F) = 4$ because set F consists of 4 elements. F is a *finite* set, i.e. it has a finite number of elements. Z is an *infinite* set: the list of whole numbers runs on for ever.

The set containing no elements at all is called the *empty* or *null* set, denoted $\emptyset$ or $\{\ \}$. Thus $n(\emptyset) = 0$.

The set of all possible elements, usually defined at the beginning of each problem, is denoted by $\&$ or $\mathscr{U}$. Thus a question may begin $\& = \{x : 0 \leqslant x \leqslant 20\}$ meaning that the universal set is to be the set of all numbers, x, from 0 to 20. Numbers outside that range are not to be considered.

VENN DIAGRAMS

The relationships between sets may be illustrated by *Venn diagrams*. Each set is shown within a rectangular universal set, overlapping or containing other sets as appropriate. For example, the set of natural numbers, N is a subset of the set of all whole numbers, Z. This would be written as $N \subset Z$ in set language, and illustrated by the Venn diagram in Fig. 5.1.

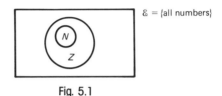

Fig. 5.1

When sets have some elements in common, they are shown to overlap each other on a Venn diagram (see Fig. 5.2). Elements in *both* sets form the *intersection* of A and B, written in set language as $A \cap B$.

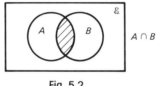

Fig. 5.2

Sets that have no elements in common appear on a Venn diagram as sets which do not overlap (Fig. 5.3).

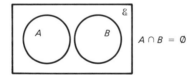

Fig. 5.3

All the elements of two sets belonging to one set or the other or to both sets make up the *union* of A and B, written in set language as $A \cup B$ (see Fig. 5.4).

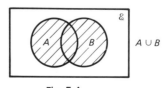

Fig. 5.4

Elements that lie outside a given set, A, form the *complement* of A, written A' (Fig. 5.5).

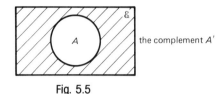

Fig. 5.5

Example Three sets, A, B, C, are defined as follows:

$$A = \{0, 1, 2, 3, 4\} \qquad B = \{1, 3\} \qquad C = \{2, 4, 6, 8\}$$

where $\mathscr{E} = \{0, 1, 2, 3, 4, 5, 6, 7, 8, 9\}$.

By looking closely at the elements in each set we can see that the two elements in B (i.e. 1 and 3) occur in A as well; thus B is a subset of A. C and B have no elements in common. A and C both contain elements 2 and 4, and so intersect. A Venn diagram makes this information clearer (Fig. 5.6).

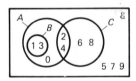

Fig. 5.6

Notice how easy it is to see from Fig. 5.6 that B is a subset of A, and that A (but not B) intersects with C. Moreover, by placing the elements of each set in their proper places on the diagram, it is possible to read off certain results:

$$A \cap C = \{2, 4\}$$
$$A \cup C = \{0, 1, 2, 3, 4, 6, 8\}$$
$$B \cap C = \emptyset \quad \text{(i.e. B and C have no elements in common)}$$
$$A \cap B' = \{0, 2, 4\}$$

EXERCISE 5a 1. Write in words the meaning of the following in set language:

   (a) $A \supset B$ (b) $2 \in C$ (c) $C \not\subset D$ (d) $n(C) = 10$.

2. Write in set language the following statements:

   (a) set X contains set Y

   (b) the set S is not empty

   (c) $\frac{1}{2}$ does not belong to set Z

(d) the number of elements in set Z is 5

(e) set A is not a subset of B

(f) use only numbers from 1 to 30.

3. If $Z = \{$whole numbers$\}$, $E = \{$even numbers$\}$,
$O = \{$odd numbers$\}$, is it true that
(a) $E \neq Z$ (b) $E \subset Z$ (c) $n(E) = 20$ (d) $Z \supset O$.

4. $\& = \{$all towns and cities in the world$\}$, $C = \{$capital cities$\}$,
$B = \{$British cities$\}$, $W = \{$Welsh cities$\}$. Is it true that
(a) $C \not\subset B$ (b) $W \in B$ (c) $W \subset B$
(d) London $\in B$ (e) Cheltenham $\subset C$
(f) Cardiff $\notin W$ (g) $n(W) < n(B)$.

5.

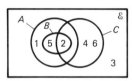

Fig. 5.7

If $\& = \{1, 2, 3, 4, 5, 6\}$, $A = \{1, 2, 5\}$, $B = \{2, 5\}$, $C = \{2, 4, 6\}$,
as shown on the Venn diagram (Fig. 5.7), list the elements of
(a) $A \cap B$ (b) $B \cup C$ (c) A' (d) $A \cap B'$
(e) $(A \cup C)'$.

6. If $E = \{$Bristol, Manchester, London, Liverpool, Edinburgh$\}$
and $C = \{$Paris, Bonn, Rome, London, Edinburgh$\}$, list the
cities in the sets
(a) $E \cap C$ (b) $E \cup C$ (c) $C' \cap E$ (d) $C \cap E'$.

7.

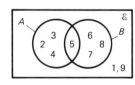

Fig. 5.8

If the universal set $\& = \{1, 2, 3, \ldots, 9\}$ and $A = \{2, 3, 4, 5\}$,
$B = \{5, 6, 7, 8\}$ (see Fig. 5.8), list the numbers in the sets
(a) $A \cap B$ (b) $A \cup B$ (c) A' (d) $(A \cup B)'$.
A third set is $C = \{2, 3\}$. Show C on a copy of the Venn
diagram in Fig. 5.8.

8.

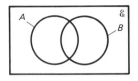

Fig. 5.9

If $\mathscr{E} = \{1, 2, 3, \ldots, 16\}$, $A = \{$multiples of 3$\}$, $B = \{$factors of 12$\}$, list the members of A and B. Copy the Venn diagram in Fig. 5.9 and show on it the numbers 1 to 16.

List the elements of

(a) $A \cap B$ (b) A' (c) $A \cup B$ (d) $A' \cap B$.

9. $\mathscr{E} = \{$letters of the alphabet$\}$, $A = \{a, b, c, d, e\}$, $V = \{a, e, i, o, u\}$, $B = \{b, c\}$. Show the sets A, V and B on a Venn diagram. Is it true that

(a) $A \cap V = \{a, e\}$ (b) $A \cup V = A$ (c) $A \supset B$

(d) $A \subset B$ (e) $A \cap B \in A$ (f) $A \cup B = A$

(g) $B' \cap A = \{a, d, e\}$ (h) $y \in V' \cap A'$.

Describe in words the letters belonging to V'.

10.

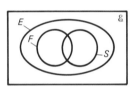

Fig. 5.10

$\mathscr{E} = \{1, 2, 3, \ldots, 11, 12\}$, $E = \{2, 4, 6, 8, 10, 12\}$, $F = \{4, 8, 12\}$, $S = \{6, 12\}$. Copy the Venn diagram in Fig. 5.10 and place the numbers 1 to 12 in appropriate regions. List the members of

(a) $E \cap F \cap S$ (b) $E \cap (F \cup S)'$ (c) $E' \cap F$.

The statement in set language $E' \cap F = \emptyset$ could be interpreted, in everyday language, to mean 'no odd number is a multiple of four'. State, in a similar fashion, the meaning of

(d) $E' \cap S = \emptyset$ (e) $E \cap S' \neq \emptyset$ (f) $F \subset E$.

11. $\mathscr{E} = \{$houses in my road$\}$, $T = \{$terraced houses$\}$, $S = \{$semi-detached houses$\}$.

(a) What in everyday language is meant by $T \cup S \neq \mathscr{E}$.

(b) Describe a house belonging to $T' \cap S'$.

If $B = \{$bungalows$\}$ write down set language statements equivalent to

(c) None of the terraced houses in my road are bungalows.

(d) Some of the bungalows in my road are semi-detached.

12.

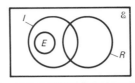

Fig. 5.11

The Venn diagram in Fig. 5.11 shows the relationship between the sets $I = \{$isosceles triangles$\}$, $E = \{$equilateral triangles$\}$, $R = \{$right-angled triangles$\}$. Is it true that

(a) all isosceles triangles are also equilateral triangles

(b) all equilateral triangles are also isosceles triangles

(c) isosceles triangles can never be right-angled triangles

(d) equilateral triangles can never be right-angled triangles?

MATCHING AREAS ON A VENN DIAGRAM

To illustrate areas on a Venn diagram that have been described in set language, make careful use of directional shading. Those parts of a diagram that have been shaded in more than one direction form areas of intersection between sets; any part that has been shaded at all is part of the union of the sets.

Examples (*i*) Find the area represented by $A' \cup B$ on a Venn diagram.

(a)

(b)

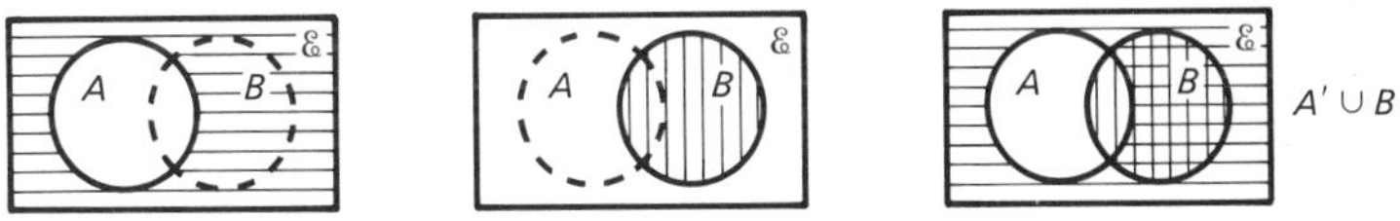

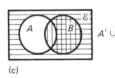
$A' \cup B$
(c)

Fig. 5.12

(a) First shade A' (i.e. everything outside of A), ignoring B altogether, and using horizontal strokes (see Fig. 5.12a).

(b) Now shade B using vertical strokes, ignoring A and the horizontal shading (Fig. 5.12b).

(c) *Any* part that has been shaded, either as part of stage (a) or as part of stage (b) is part of the union $A' \cup B$ (Fig. 5.12c).

(*ii*) Find the area represented by $A' \cap B$ on a Venn diagram.

The intersection of the two sets A' and B has been shaded *both* vertically and horizontally.

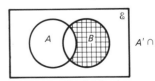
$A' \cap B$

Fig. 5.13

EXERCISE 5b

1. Illustrate on separate Venn diagrams the areas represented algebraically by
   (a) A' (b) $A \cap B'$ (c) $A \cup B'$ (d) $A' \cap B'$
   (e) $A' \cup B'$.

2. Show by shading a Venn diagram that if $A \supset B$ then $A \cap B = B$.

3. Show by shading a Venn diagram that if $A \supset B$ then $A \cup B = A$.

4.

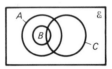

Fig. 5.14

   Copy the Venn diagram in Fig. 5.14 and shade separately the areas
   (a) $(B' \cap A) \cap C$ (b) $B \cap C'$ (c) $B' \cap (A \cap C')$.

5.

 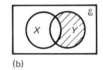 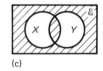

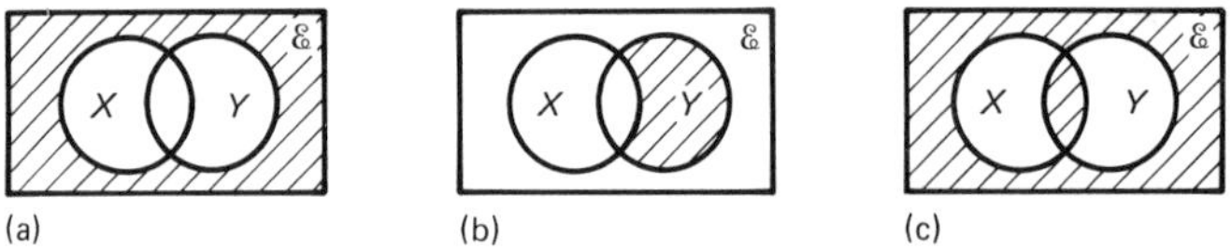

   (a)   (b)   (c)

Fig. 5.15

   Describe in set notation the shaded areas on the Venn diagrams in Fig. 5.15.

6. Draw Venn diagrams to prove that
   (a) $(X \cap Y) \cup (X \cap Y') = X$ (b) $(X' \cap Y) \cup X = X \cup Y$.

7. Copy the Venn diagram shown in Fig. 5.16. Shade
   (a) A (b) $B \cap C$ (c) $A \cup (B \cap C)$.
   On a second copy of the diagram shade
   (d) $A \cup B$ (e) $A \cup C$.
   Hence show that $A \cup (B \cap C) = (A \cup B) \cap (A \cup C)$.

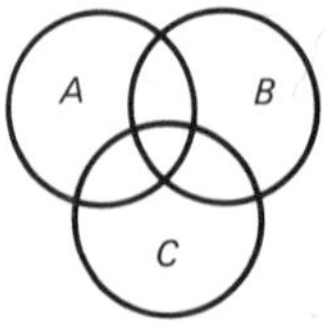

Fig. 5.16

8. Prove by shading Venn diagrams that
   $$A \cap (B \cap C) = (A \cap B) \cup (A \cap C)$$

58

NUMBER PROBLEMS

Venn diagrams are also useful in clarifying the numbers of elements in different sets.

Examples (*i*) In a class of 32, 8 do not study any languages; 20 study French and 10 study German. How many students are doing both French and German.

Since $8 + 20 + 10 = 38$, it follows that some pupils *must* be taking two languages, since there are only 32 people in the entire class.

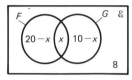

Fig. 5.17

Let there be x pupils taking both French and German. The number taking just French is then $20 - x$; the number taking just German is $10 - x$ (see Fig. 5.17). The total number of pupils in the class is

$$8 + (20 - x) + (10 - x) + x = 32$$

This gives a simplified equation

$$38 - x = 32$$

Hence

$$x = 6$$

(*ii*) In a class of 30, everybody must study at least two sciences. 10 study physics and biology; 19 study physics and chemistry; 15 study biology and chemistry. How many study all three?

This problem is more complex as there are three subjects to consider. However, the approach is identical.

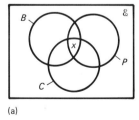

(a)

Fig. 5.18 (a)

Let the number taking all three subjects be x. Mark x on a Venn diagram (Fig. 5.18 (a)) where all three sets, B, P and C, overlap.

Since everyone must study at least two sciences, it follows that the numbers taking just biology, just physics or just chemistry are all zero. Mark these on the diagram (see Fig. 5.18 (b)).

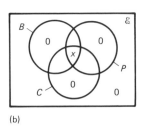

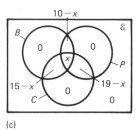

Fig. 5.18 (b) and (c)

We are told that 10 students are studying physics and biology. Of these, x are *also* taking chemistry, so the number taking physics and biology but *not* chemistry must be $10-x$. Similarly, there are $19-x$ students taking physics and chemistry but *not* biology; and $15-x$ taking biology and chemistry but *not* physics. When these are marked on the Venn diagram, it is complete (Fig. 5.18 (c)).

As there are 30 in the class, we can write

$$x + (15-x) + (10-x) + (19-x) = 30$$

Hence
$$44 - 2x = 30$$
$$2x = 14$$
$$x = 7$$

EXERCISE 5c   1.

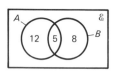

Fig. 5.19

The Venn diagram in 5.19 shows the *number* of elements in each region. Find

(a) $n(A \cap B)$ (b) $n(A)$ (c) $n(B)$ (d) $n(A \cup B)$.

If $n(\mathscr{E}) = 30$, find

(e) $n((A \cup B)')$ (f) $n(A')$.

60

2.

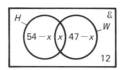

Fig. 5.20

There are 88 houses in my street. Each week 54 take *The Worplesdon Herald* magazine; another 47 take *The Worplesdon World*. 12 houses do not take a weekly magazine at all. If x houses take both, use the Venn diagram in Fig. 5.20 to form an equation in x. Find x.

3. Of the 88 families in my street, 52 have a dog. 28 families have no pet at all but there are 20 cats also living in the street. If x families have both a cat and a dog, how many (in terms of x) have *just* a dog and no cat? Draw a Venn diagram to show the numbers of families without pets, those with just a dog, those with just a cat and those with both a dog and a cat. Form an equation in x and solve it.

4. Of the 88 families living in my street, 15 have no children at all, 22 families have just boys; 21 families have just girls. How many families have both boys and girls?

5. In a class of 30, 24 students do woodwork, 16 do metalwork and 5 are taken out of craft lessons altogether (to do Latin). How many pupils do both woodwork and metalwork?

6. In a club of **25 cricketers** 2 are wicket-keepers and never play as anything else. 15 are regarded as strong batsmen and 12 as strong bowlers. How many are regarded *both* as strong bowlers and batsmen?

7. In a class of 40, all the pupils do French. 20 also study Latin and 30 are learning German. If only 3 do French and no other language, how many do all three?

8.

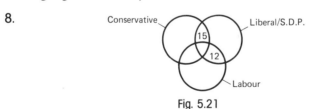

Fig. 5.21

In a sample of 100 voters, 15 said that, at some time in their lives, they had voted Conservative and Liberal/S.D.P. but never Labour. 12 said they had voted Labour and Liberal/S.D.P. but never Conservative. 2 people said they had voted on different occasions for Conservative and Labour, but never

Liberal. 25 always voted Conservative and nothing else. 27 always voted Labour. 11 always voted Liberal/S.D.P. Complete the Venn diagram in Fig. 5.21 and find out how many voters in this sample have voted for all three parties at one time or another.

MISCELLANEOUS EXERCISE 5

1. Write in set language
   (a) 2 belongs to set E but not O
   (b) 2 belongs to both sets P and E
   (c) sets O and E do not intersect.

2. $\mathscr{E} = \{$pupils who come to your school$\}$, $P = \{$pupils who bring a packed lunch$\}$, $L = \{$pupils who have a school lunch$\}$, $C = \{$pupils who come to school by car$\}$, $S = \{$pupils in the sixth form$\}$. Describe someone who is a member of

   (a) $P \cap C$ (b) $C \cup S$ (c) $C' \cap L$ (d) $(S \cup L)'$.

   Write a statement in set language to describe x who brings a packed lunch and does not come to school by car.

3. Show by shading a Venn diagram that
   (a) $A \cup A' = \mathscr{E}$
   (b) if $B \subset A'$, then
         (i) $A' \cup B = A'$ (ii) $A \cap B = \emptyset$
   (c) $(A \cup B)' = A' \cap B'$
   (d) $(A \cap B)' = A' \cup B'$.

4. In this question, P and Q are sets, and $P * Q$ means $P \cap Q'$. In a Venn diagram, $P * Q$ would be shown by the shaded area (Fig. 5.22).

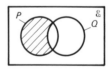

Fig. 5.22

Draw three separate Venn diagrams and shade the areas which represent
   (a) $P' * Q$,   (b) $P * Q'$,   (c) $(P * Q) \cap P$.   (LU)

5.

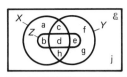

Fig. 5.23

$\& = \{a, b, c, d, e, f, g, h, j\}$. Sets X, Y and Z are as shown in Fig. 5.23. Which of the following are true?

(a) $Z \subset X \cap Y$ (b) $Z \supset X \cup Y$

(c) $Z \subset X \cup Y$ (d) $Z \cap X = \{b\}$

(e) $Z \cap X = \{b, d\}$ (f) $Z \cup (X \cap Y) = \{d, h\}$

(g) $Z' = \{a, c, f, g, h, j\}$ (h) $Z' \cap X = \{a, c, h\}$

(i) $Z' \cup Y' = \{a, c, j\}$.

6.

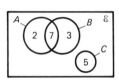

Fig. 5.24

The five statements below refer to the Venn diagram (Fig. 5.24). The figures in the diagram represent the number of elements in each subset. In each case, state whether the statement is true or false; if you think it is false, state the correct number of elements in the given set.

(a) $n(A) = 2$ (b) $n(A \cap B \cap C) = 0$

(c) $n(A \cup B \cup C) = 17$ (d) $n(A \cup B) = 5$

(e) $n(B \cap C') = 3$.   (JMB)

7.

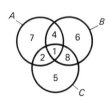

Fig. 5.25

The universal set $\&$ consists of 33 elements. A, B and C are three sets and the numbers of elements in the subsets are shown in the diagram (Fig. 5.25). Calculate

(a) $n(A \cup B)$ (b) $n(A \cap C)$ (c) $n(A')$.   (C)

8.

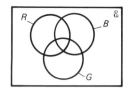

Fig. 5.26

There are 34 coloured marbles in a box that are coloured red (R), blue (B) or green (G) or any combination of these colours.

There are 3 marbles coloured red, blue and green, 6 marbles coloured red only, 5 marbles coloured blue only, 7 marbles coloured red and blue but not green.

(a) Copy the Venn diagram (Fig. 5.26) and place the numbers 3, 6, 5 and 7 in the appropriate regions.

(b) There are 16 marbles that are blue or have some blue in them. There are twice as many marbles that are green only as there are green and red but not blue marbles. Calculate how many marbles are
   (i) green and blue, but not red,
   (ii) green and red, but not blue,
   (iii) green only. (WJEC)

9. $\&$ is the set of the first twenty natural numbers, so that
   $\& = \{1, 2, 3, 4, 5, 6, 7, 8, 9, 10, 11, 12, 13, 14, 15, 16, 17, 18, 19, 20\}$.
   List the members of the following subsets:
   (a) $A = \{x : 11 < 4x - 5 \leqslant 43\}$,
   (b) $B = \{x : x$ is a prime number, $x > 1\}$,
   (c) $C = \{x : x$ is a factor of 20, $x > 1\}$,

   Draw a Venn diagram showing the relationship between $\&$, A, B and C, writing each of the members of $\&$ in the appropriate region.
   List the members of the following sets:
   (d) $A' \cap B$ (e) $(A \cup B)'$
   (f) $B' \cap C'$ (g) $(A \cup B) \cap C$. (LU)

10. Each day 45 trains leave a certain terminus. The next three stations are Aton, Beton and Ceton. Taking
    $\& = \{$all trains from the terminus$\}$,
    $A = \{$trains stopping at Aton$\}$,
    $B = \{$trains stopping at Beton$\}$,
    $C = \{$trains stopping at Ceton$\}$.

write normal English sentences (not using technical words like 'set') to express the following symbolic statements:

(a) $n(A) = 24$ (b) $C \subset B$.

Write symbolic statements to express the following sentences:

(c) Some trains stop at all three stations.

(d) 30 trains stop at Beton.

Use statements (b) and (c) to draw a Venn diagram to illustrate the relations between $\mathscr{E}, A, B$ and C.

Given that 5 trains stop at none of the three stations, find the number which stop at both Aton and Beton.

Given also that 13 trains stop at Ceton, and 18 at Aton but not at Ceton, find the number that stop at Beton only.   (LU)

6 BASIC ALGEBRA

In algebra, letters are used to represent numbers. There are several reasons why this may be convenient. For example, in Chapter 4 we proved that $5^0 = 1$ (see page 46). We could prove in exactly the same way that $2^0 = 1$ or $4^0 = 1$ or even $(3.456)^0 = 1$, for the result applies to *all* numbers. The result was written at length: *any number raised to the power zero is one.* However, the result could have been written in a shorter form using algebra. For, on the understanding that x represents any number, $x^0 = 1$ means the same thing.

Often, quite complicated ideas can be expressed quickly and easily with algebra. For example, *any number greater than one has a square-root greater than one but less than the number itself* could be written: $1 < \sqrt{x} < x$.

Another reason for replacing a number with a letter is that, often, we do not yet know the value of that number.

Example A friend thinks of a number, doubles it and adds three, He tells me the answer is nine. What number did he first think of?

Let the number be represented by the letter x:

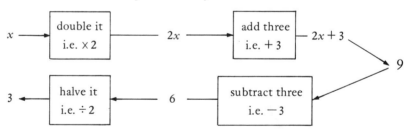

Hence $x = 3$, meaning the number my friend first thought of is three. (See Chapter 7 for a full treatment of the use of algebra in solving problems.)

SUBSTITUTING INTO FORMULAE

Perhaps the most common use of algebra is to express mathematical relationships as formulae. For example, it is usual to give the area of a circle as πr^2 rather than as *'pi times the square of the radius'*.

Working out a quantity from the values of the various letters in the formula is easy: just replace each letter by the number given for it.

Examples (*i*) If $T = a + 3b$, find T when $a = 5$ and $b = 6$

Replacing the letters a and b by their value, we get

$$T = 5 + (3 \times 6)$$
$$= 5 + \quad 18$$
$$= 23$$

(*ii*) If $P = (3x + 2y)^2$, find P when $x = 3$ and $y = 1.5$

$$P = (3 \times 3 + 2 \times 1.5)^2$$
$$= (\quad 9 \quad + \quad 3 \quad)^2$$
$$= 12^2$$
$$= 144$$

EXERCISE 6a Work out the following formula from the values given. [Take π as $\frac{22}{7}$.]

1. $P = 2a + 2b$ Find P when $a = 6$, $b = 4$

2. $F = ma$ Find F when $m = 60$ and $a = -\frac{3}{4}$

3. $E = mgh$ Find E when $m = 0.4$, $g = 10$ and $h = 3.2$

4. $A = \frac{1}{2}bh$ Find A when $b = 7$, $h = 5$

5. $p = 1 - q$ Find p when $q = \frac{3}{16}$

6. $v = u + at$ Find v when $u = 5$, $a = -2$ and $t = 2$

7. $y = mx + c$ Find y when $m = -2$, $x = 3$, $c = 5$

8. $E = \frac{1}{2}mv^2$ Find E when $m = 2.4$, $v = 2.1$

9. $r = \sqrt{x^2 + y^2}$ Find r when $x = 5$ and $y = 12$

10. $A = \left(\dfrac{a + b}{2}\right)h$ Find A when $a = 5$, $b = 12$ and $h = 2\frac{1}{2}$

11. $A = \pi r^2$ Find A when (a) $r = 14$ (b) $r = 1.4$

12. $V = \frac{4}{3}\pi r^3$ Find V when (a) $r = 3$ (b) $r = 0.3$

13. $s = ut + \frac{1}{2}at^2$ Find s when $u = 6$, $a = 5$ and $t = 3$

14. $v^2 = u^2 + 2as$ Find v when $u = 5$, $a = 6$ and $s = 2$

15. $T = 2\pi\sqrt{\dfrac{L}{g}}$ Find T when $g = 10$ and $L = 4.9$

16. $S = 2\pi(r + b)$ Find S when $r = 0.45$ and $b = 0.25$

17. $P = \dfrac{mv^2}{r}$ Find P when $m = 3$, $r = 8$ and $v = 0.4$

18. $S = \dfrac{a(1 - r^n)}{1 - r}$ Find S when $a = 3$, $r = \frac{1}{3}$ and $n = 4$

19. $s = \sqrt{np(1 - p)}$ Find s when $n = 12$, $p = \frac{1}{4}$

20. $\dfrac{1}{f} = \dfrac{1}{u} + \dfrac{1}{v}$ Find f when $u = 6$ and $v = 8$.

SIMPLIFYING ALGEBRAIC EXPRESSIONS

Sometimes a formula is written in a correct, but clumsy, form. With a little extra work it might be written in a simpler, more elegant way. For example, the perimeter, P, of a square with sides of length x could be given as the formula $P = x + x + x + x$. Such a formula is accurate but is not well written; it can be simplified to the neater and shorter form $P = 4x$.

Examples   (*i*) $8x^2 \times 2x$

$$= (8 \times 2) \times (x^2 \times x)$$

$$= 16x^3$$ Simple numbers should be multiplied or divided out; letters should be written to the lowest possible power.

(*ii*) $\dfrac{10x^3}{5x}$

$$= \dfrac{\overset{2}{\cancel{10}}\overset{x^2}{\cancel{x^3}}}{\underset{}{\cancel{5}\cancel{x}}}$$

$$= 2x^2$$

As different letters represent different numbers, it is *not* possible to combine them in a single term.

(*iii*) $3x - 2y$ This cannot be simplified any further.

(*iv*) $8x^2 \times 2y$

$$= (8 \times 2) \times (x^2 \times y)$$ Here we can simplify 8×2, but the x^2 and y stay as they are.

$$= 16x^2y$$

(v) $\dfrac{p^2q^2 \times pq}{p^2q}$

Here the letters p and q appear several times and the expression can be made shorter by cancelling out p^2 and q.

$= \dfrac{\cancel{p^2}q^2 \times p\cancel{q}}{\cancel{p^2}\cancel{q}}$

$= q^2p$

Do not try to add or subtract different powers of one letter; and do not try to cancel down just one side of an addition or subtraction sign.

(vi) $x^2 + x$

This cannot be simplified further. Although x^2 and x are related, they represent different numbers.

(vii) $\dfrac{a+b}{b}$

Trying to cancel out just one side of an addition (or subtraction) sign to give $\dfrac{a+\cancel{b}}{\cancel{b}}$ is a common error. In fact, in this case, no simplification is possible. Division and multiplication cancel with each other; division and addition do *not*.

EXERCISE 6b Simplify as far as possible; if no simplification is possible then explain why.

1. $3 \times a$

2. $5 \times b \ + \ 2 \times b$

3. $a + a + a + a + a$

4. $a \times a \times a \times a$

5. $6a + 3b + 2a + b$

6. $3x^2 + 2x^2 + x^2$

7. $2mn + mn - mn$

8. $m + m + p - m - p + 2p + m$

9. $ab + a + ab + b + ab$

10. $3(x+y) + 2x + 4y$

11. $3x^3 + 2x^2x - 3y$

12. $6 + 3xy - 4xy + x$

13. $3p^2 \times 4pq$

14. $6d^2e \times 5df$

15. $8p + qpq + 3p^2q$

16. $(m+m+m) \times (m+m+m)$

17. $\dfrac{12mn}{4}$

18. $\dfrac{25rst}{5r}$

19. $\dfrac{21j^2s^3f^2}{7js^2f}$

20. $\dfrac{jk+7}{7jk}$

21. $\dfrac{6m-2n}{mn}$

22. $\dfrac{a^2b-a^3c}{bc}$

BRACKETS

Algebra is a very precise code, demanding careful attention to detail. Small differences in the way a formula is written can completely alter its meaning. In particular, brackets are important because they change the order in which calculations are done: brackets are *always worked out first*.

Examples (*i*) $3x + 2$

means take the number x, multiply it by 3 and then add 2 to the result, but

$3(x + 2)$

means take the number x, add 2 first and *then* multiply by 3. In this case the 2 is also multiplied by 3.

$$3(x + 2) = 3x + 6$$

To illustrate the difference, let $x = 4$:

$$3x + 2 = 3 \times 4 + 2 = 12 + 2 = 14$$

but $\qquad 3(x + 2) = 3 \times (4 + 2) = 3 \times 6 = 18$

(*ii*) $3x^2$

means take the number x and square it; then multiply the result by 3, but

$(3x)^2$

means take the number x and multiply it by 3; then square the result. Thus the 3 is also squared, i.e.

$$(3x)^2 = 9x^2$$

Again, to illustrate the difference let $x = 4$:

$$3x^2 = 3 \times 4^2 = 3 \times 16 = 48$$
$$(3x)^2 = (3 \times 4)^2 = 12^2 = 144$$

EXPANDING BRACKETS

Sometimes it is useful to rewrite a formula removing the brackets. The brackets are said to have been *expanded* into a string of algebraic terms.

Examples (*i*)
$$2 + 3(x + 4) = 2 + 3 \times x + 3 \times 4$$
$$= 2 + 3x + 12$$
$$= 3x + 14$$

Notice that *both* the x and the 4 that were originally inside the the brackets are multiplied by 3.

If a negative number precedes the bracket, the sign of *both* terms inside the bracket will change.

(*ii*)
$$5 - (x + 2) = 5 - x - 2$$
$$= 3 - x$$

The sign of the 2 changes as well as the sign of the x.

(*iii*)
$$6 - (x - 4) = 6 - x + 4$$
$$= 10 - x$$

as $-(-4)$ is equivalent to $+4$.

Brackets may also be multiplied by brackets.

(*iv*) $(x + 3)(x + 2)$

$= x(x + 2) + 3(x + 2)$ Each term in the first bracket must multiply each term in the second bracket.

$= x^2 + 2x + 3x + 6$ The remaining brackets are then multiplied out. Finally, $2x + 3x$ can be

$= x^2 + 5x + 6$ simplified to $5x$.

Again, be careful with negative signs:

(*v*) $(x - 4)(2x - 3)$

$= x(2x - 3) - 4(2x - 3)$ The first bracket must multiply each term in the second bracket, but this time one of the terms is negative (i.e. -4).

$= 2x^2 - 3x - 8x + 12$ The multiplication is completed, remembering that $-4 \times (-3) = 12$.

$= 2x^2 - 11x + 12$ Finally, the string is simplified as far as possible.

Brackets may also be raised to a power. Thus $(m - 2n)^2$ means $(m - 2n)(m - 2n)$. It is best to write out the multiplication in full, and then complete it stage by stage:

$$(vi) \qquad (m-2n)^2 = (m-2n)(m-2n)$$
$$= m(m-2n) - 2n(m-2n)$$
$$= m^2 - 2mn - 2mn + 4n^2$$
$$= m^2 - 4mn + 4n^2$$

Notice that this is *not* the same as $(m)^2 - (2n)^2$.

EXERC'SE 6c Expand the following brackets, simplifying your results as far as possible.

1. $5 + 2(x + 3)$
2. $2x + x(3 + x)$
3. $5ab - a(b + 3)$
4. $4xy - 3(x + y)$
5. $2pq - p(q + q^2)$
6. $3(a + b) - a(1 + b)$
7. $5(c - d) + 3(c - d)$
8. $3mn - 2n(m - n)$
9. $7(p - 2q) - q(p - 2)$
10. $5(r - s) - 2(s - 1) - 3(1 - r)$
11. $(u + 6)(2 + u)$
12. $(v + 5)(v - 3)$
13. $(n + p)(p - 2)$
14. $(2n - m)(m - 2n)$
15. $(c - 5d)(5c - 3d)$
16. $(4e - 3f)(3e - 4f)$
17. $(a + b)^2$
18. $(a + 2b)^2$
19. $(a - b)^2$
20. $(3e - f)^2$
21. $(2e + 3f)^2$
22. $(5g - 2h)^2$
23. $a + 3(5 + a + b)$
24. $(a + 3)(5 + a + b)$
25. $(c + d)(3 + c - d)$
26. $(e - f)(2 - e - f)$
27. $c + d(3 + c - d)$
28. $e - f(2 - e - f)$.

ALGEBRAIC FRACTIONS

Algebraic fractions obey the same rules of cancelling down, adding and subtracting, multiplying and dividing as ordinary fractions.

Examples (*i*) $\dfrac{x}{2} + \dfrac{x}{3}$.

The lowest common denominator is $2 \times 3 = 6$ (as 2 and 3 have no factors in common). Over this denominator:

$$\frac{x}{2} \quad \text{has equivalent} \quad \frac{x \times 3}{2 \times 3} = \frac{3x}{6}$$

and $\dfrac{x}{3}$ has equivalent $\dfrac{x \times 2}{3 \times 2} = \dfrac{2x}{6}$

Thus $\dfrac{x}{2} + \dfrac{x}{3} = \dfrac{3x}{6} + \dfrac{2x}{6} = \dfrac{5x}{6}$

(ii) $\dfrac{2}{a} - \dfrac{3}{b}$.

This time the denominators are algebraic. As a and b represent different numbers with no factors in common, the lowest common denominator is $a \times b = ab$. Over this denominator:

$\dfrac{2}{a}$ has equivalent $\dfrac{2 \times b}{a \times b} = \dfrac{2b}{ab}$

and $\dfrac{3}{b}$ has equivalent $\dfrac{3 \times a}{b \times a} = \dfrac{3a}{ab}$

So $\dfrac{2}{a} + \dfrac{3}{b} = \dfrac{2b}{ab} + \dfrac{3a}{ab} = \dfrac{2b + 3a}{ab}$

(iii) $\dfrac{5}{2pq} + \dfrac{3}{4pr}$.

The denominators in this case *do* have factors in common (namely $2p$). The lowest common denominator is $4pqr$ as this includes all three letters that occur in the two denominators. Over this denominator:

$\dfrac{5}{2pq}$ has equivalent $\dfrac{5 \times 2r}{2pq \times 2r} = \dfrac{10r}{4pqr}$

$\dfrac{3}{4pr}$ has equivalent $\dfrac{3 \times q}{4pr \times q} = \dfrac{3q}{4pqr}$

Hence $\dfrac{5}{2pq} + \dfrac{3}{4pr} = \dfrac{10r}{4pqr} + \dfrac{3q}{4pqr} = \dfrac{10r + 3q}{4pqr}$

(iv) $\dfrac{4x - 3}{2} + \dfrac{1}{3}$.

If the top (or bottom) of the algebraic fraction is in two parts, like $4x - 3$, it is very easy to separate them incorrectly. It is a good idea to put brackets around the parts as a *first step*. Thus $4x - 3$ becomes $(4x - 3)$.

73

In this example, the lowest common denominator is 6, so we write:

$$\frac{4x-3}{2} = \frac{(4x-3)}{2} = \frac{(4x-3)\times 3}{2\times 3} = \frac{12x-9}{6}$$

So
$$\frac{4x-3}{2} + \frac{1}{3} = \frac{12x-9}{6} + \frac{2}{6} = \frac{12x-7}{6}$$

(v) $\dfrac{3a^2b^2}{c} \div \dfrac{6b^2c}{d}.$

$$\frac{3a^2b^2}{c} \div \frac{6b^2c}{d} = \frac{3a^2b^2}{c} \times \frac{d}{6b^2c}$$

Cancelling down by 3 and by b^2 we get

$$\frac{\cancel{3a^2b^2}}{c} \times \frac{d}{\cancel{6b^2c}_{2}} = \frac{a^2d}{2c^2}$$

EXERCISE 6d Work out the following, expressing your answers as single fractions in their lowest terms.

1. $\dfrac{a}{3} + \dfrac{a}{5}$

2. $\dfrac{2b}{3} + \dfrac{b}{6}$

3. $\dfrac{c}{3} + \dfrac{2d}{7}$

4. $\dfrac{3e^2}{4} - \dfrac{f}{2}$

5. $\dfrac{g}{4} \times \dfrac{g^2}{3}$

6. $\dfrac{g}{4} - \dfrac{g^2}{3}$

7. $\dfrac{g}{4} \div \dfrac{g^2}{3}$

8. $\dfrac{2b-1}{3} - \dfrac{b}{2}$

9. $\dfrac{3b+2}{2} + \dfrac{b}{3}$

10. $\dfrac{5j+2}{3} - \dfrac{j}{2}$

11. $\dfrac{2k-2}{3} + \dfrac{3k}{4}$

12. $\dfrac{7k-1}{2} - \dfrac{k}{3}$

13. $\dfrac{m+1}{2} + \dfrac{m+2}{3}$

14. $\dfrac{n+1}{4} + \dfrac{n+2}{3}$

15. $\dfrac{3p-2}{4} - \dfrac{p+3}{2}$

16. $\dfrac{q-r}{2} + \dfrac{q+r}{3}$

17. $\dfrac{s-t}{4} - \dfrac{t+u}{5}$

18. $\dfrac{1}{j} + \dfrac{1}{k}$

19. $\dfrac{2}{l} - \dfrac{3}{m}$

20. $\dfrac{4n}{p} + \dfrac{5p}{q}$

21. $\dfrac{6q}{r^2} - \dfrac{2}{3q}$

22. $\dfrac{5q}{r} - \dfrac{2rs}{q}$

23. $\dfrac{6q}{r^2} \times \dfrac{2r}{3q}$

24. $\dfrac{11s}{3t} - \dfrac{3s}{ut}$

25. $\dfrac{11s}{3t} \div \dfrac{3s}{ut}$ 26. $\dfrac{r}{2s} + \dfrac{s}{r}$ 27. $\dfrac{r}{2s} \times \dfrac{s}{r}$

28. $p^2 m^2 \times \dfrac{p}{mq}$ 29. $p^2 m^2 \div \dfrac{p}{mq}$ 30. $p^2 m^2 + \dfrac{p}{mq}$

31. $\dfrac{u}{3v} + \dfrac{v}{6}$ 32. $\dfrac{x}{y^2} + \dfrac{x}{y}$ 33. $\dfrac{2u}{3vw} + \dfrac{v}{6w}$

34. $\dfrac{x}{y^2 x} + \dfrac{x}{yz}$ 35. $\dfrac{a^2}{12bc^2} - \dfrac{3}{4bc}$ 36. $\dfrac{4}{5d^2 e} - \dfrac{3}{4de^2}$

37. $\dfrac{2u}{3vw} \div \dfrac{v}{6w}$ 38. $\dfrac{x}{y^2 z} \div \dfrac{x}{yz}$ 39. $\dfrac{a^2}{12bc^2} \div \dfrac{3}{4bc}$

40. $\dfrac{4}{5d^2 e} \div \dfrac{3}{4de^2}$ 41. $\dfrac{a^2 b^2}{c^2} \times \dfrac{cbd}{a^3}$ 42. $\dfrac{6m^4 p^5}{q} \times \dfrac{1}{2pq}.$

FACTORISING

Just as it is sometimes helpful to rewrite a formula so that the brackets are eliminated, so on other occasions it might be easier to deal with a long string of algebraic terms if they are grouped into brackets. This process, the reverse of expanding brackets, is called *factorising*.

Factorising by Grouping Terms

Examples (*i*) $3xy + 2x$

$= x(3y + 2)$

The two terms have x in common.

Thus x can be written outside a bracket such that it multiplies the terms inside the bracket to give $3xy + 2x$.

(*ii*) $4y^2 z + yz$

$= yz(4y + 1)$

Similarly, the two terms in this example contain the factors yz which can be written outside a bracket as shown.

(*iii*) $ac - ad + bc - bd$

There is nothing common to *all four* terms in this case. So we look for *pairs* with common factors. Here

$$ac - ad = a(c - d)$$

$= a(c - d) + b(c - d)$ and

$$bc - bd = b(c - d)$$

$= (c - d)(a + b)$ $(c - d)$ is now a common factor that can be written outside a *second* bracket.

(iv) $pr - 2qr + 2qs - ps$

Again, there is nothing common to all four terms so we take pairs with common factors as in Example (iii).

$$= r(p - 2q) + s(2q - p)$$

This time, however, we cannot continue as simply for $(p - 2q) \neq (2q - p)$. We must adjust the signs, as shown, using $(2q - p) = -(p - 2q)$

$$= r(p - 2q) - s(p - 2q)$$

$$= (p - 2q)(r - s)$$

Now we can proceed as before.

EXERCISE 6e   Factorise the following:

1. $6 + 2m$

2. $3 + 12e$

3. $15 + 36p$

4. $5f - 15fg$

5. $16q - 8qr$

6. $7x - 21x^2$

7. $5q - q^2$

8. $11x - 121xy$

9. $21m^2n + 28mn$

10. $lm^2n - lmn$

11. $y^2z + yz^2$

12. $2a^2b + 6a^2$

13. $3mp + 6mq - 3mr^2$

14. $nm + n + 2m + 2$

15. $pq + p + 2q + 2$

16. $15 + 3l + 5k + kl$

17. $4j + 8 - ij - 2i$

18. $6 + 2d - cd - 3c$

19. $fh + fi + gh + gi$

20. $ac + ad + bc + bd$

21. $tv + 2tw + uv + 2uw$

22. $2eg + eh + 2fg + fh$

23. $ru + rt - su - st$

24. $2jl - jm + 2kl - km$

25. $2wx + 2wz - 3yx - 3yz$

26. $3nq + 3nr - pr - pq$

27. $2a^3y - by - 2a^3z + bz$

28. $s^2u - vt + tu - s^2v$

29. $9pm^2 - 6pn - 6qm^2 + 4qn$

30. $2w^2y - zx + 2yx - w^2z$

31. $6(tv + uw) + 4uv + 9tw$

32. $8ac + 2ad + 12bc + 3bd$

33. $6x(xz - y) - 4yz + 9x^3$

34. $10e^2 - 5eh + 12fe - 6fh$

35. $ab + bc + bd$

36. $3a^3 + 6a^2b + 3a^2c^2$

37. $2p + 2q + mp + mq + n^2p + n^2q$

38. $3d + 3e + f^2d + ef^2 + gd + ge$

39. $xy + xz + 2x - y^2 - yz - 2y$ 40. $hj + hk - 4h - ij - ik + 4i$.

Factorising Quadratic Expressions

A *quadratic* expression is a string of three algebraic terms of the form $ax^2 + bx + c$. For example, $x^2 + 5x + 6$ is a quadratic expression. This may be factorised by rewriting $5x$ as $3x + 2x$, and grouping terms:

$$x^2 + 5x + 6 = x^2 + 3x + 2x + 6$$
$$= x(x + 3) + 2(x + 3)$$
$$= (x + 3)(x + 2)$$

Notice that 3 and 2 not only add up to 5 (so $5x = 3x + 2x$) but also multiply to give 6. Other quadratics can be factorised if the number at the end has a pair of factors which add up to the number of x's.

Examples (*i*) $x^2 - 6x + 8$

We need to find a factor pair of $+8$ whose sum is -6. The possibilities are

+8	*possible* *factor pairs*	*sum*	
	$+1, +8$	$+9$	✗
	$-1, -8$	-9	✗
	$+4, +2$	$+6$	✗
	$-4, -2$	-6	✓

Thus we can rewrite the quadratic:

$$x^2 - 6x + 8 = x^2 - 2x - 4x + 8$$
$$= x(x - 2) - 4(x - 2)$$
$$= (x - 2)(x - 4)$$

(*ii*) $x^2 + 3x - 18$.

This time we need to find a factor pair of -18 whose sum is $+3$.

-18	*possible* *factor pairs*	*sum*	
	$+1, -18$	-17	✗
	$-1, +18$	$+17$	✗
	$+2, -9$	-7	✗
	$-2, +9$	$+7$	✗
	$+3, -6$	-3	✗
	$-3, +6$	$+3$	✓

Hence

$$x^2 + 3x - 18 = x^2 - 3x + 6x - 18$$
$$= x(x-3) + 6(x-3)$$
$$= (x-3)(x+6)$$

Quadratics such as $2x^2 + 5x - 3$ which begin with more than one x^2 are factorised in much the same way, although there is an extra step: the first number must be multiplied with the last, and factor pairs of *that product* considered as before.

Example $2x^2 + 5x - 3$

$2 \times (-3) = -6$

Find the factor pair of $2 \times (-3) = -6$ which has a sum of $+5$.

	possible factor pairs	sum	
	$+1, -6$	-5	✗
	$-1, +6$	$+5$	✓
-6	$+2, -3$	-1	✗
	$-2, +3$	$+1$	✗

Thus
$$2x^2 + 5x - 3 = 2x^2 - x + 6x - 3$$
$$= x(2x-1) + 3(2x-1)$$
$$= (2x-1)(x+3)$$

If the x^2 term in the quadratic is negative, then the procedure is no different, although care must be taken with signs. Remember that $-x^2$ means $-1x^2$ and be sure to rearrange the terms into the usual order if necessary.

Example $2x - x^2 + 3$.

Rearranging the order and remembering that $-x^2 = -1x^2$:
$$-x^2 + 2x + 3$$

$-1 \times (+3) = -3$

So we must find a factor pair of -3 that has a sum of $+2$, i.e. $+3$ and -1.

$$-x^2 + 2x + 3 = -x^2 + 3x - x + 3$$
$$= x(-x + 3) + 1(-x + 3)$$
$$= (-x + 3)(x + 1)$$

The term $(-x + 3)$ is correct, but clumsy; it is better to change the order putting the positive term first, i.e. $(3 - x)$. So

$$2x - x^2 + 3 = (3 - x)(x + 1)$$

Some quadratics, for example $6x^2 - 31xy + 5y^2$ contain *two* variables (in this case, x and y). The procedure for factorising these is virtually identical.

Example $6x^2 - 31xy + 5y^2$

$6 \times (+5) = +30$

Find the factor pair of $6 \times (+5) = +30$ which has a sum of -31: clearly -30 and -1 will work. Thus

$$6x^2 - 31xy + 5y^2 = 6x^2 - xy - 30xy + 5y^2$$
$$= x(6x - y) - 5y(6x - y)$$
$$= (6x - y)(x - 5y)$$

Two important quadratic factorisations that should be remembered are:

(i) $x^2 + 2xy + y^2 = (x + y)^2$
(ii) $x^2 - 2xy + y^2 = (x - y)^2$.

EXERCISE 6f   Factorise these quadratics:

1. $x^2 + 6x + 8$

2. $x^2 + 10x + 16$

3. $x^2 + 12x + 27$

4. $x^2 + 8x + 15$

5. $x^2 + 7x + 10$

6. $x^2 + 3x - 18$

7. $x^2 + 3x - 10$

8. $x^2 - 11x + 28$

9. $x^2 + 4x + 3$

10. $x^2 - 6x + 5$

11. $24 + 11x + x^2$

12. $20 + 9x + x^2$

13. $y^2 + 19y + 34$

14. $y^2 + 18y + 65$

15. $z^2 - 7z - 44$

16. $x^2 + x - 30$

17. $n^2 + 5n - 36$

18. $p^2 - 5pq - 66q^2$

19. $x^2 - 11xy + 18y^2$

20. $x^2y^2 - 11xy + 24$

21. $2x^2 + 7x + 6$

22. $6x^2 + 13x + 5$

23. $2x^2 + 15x + 7$

24. $3x^2 + 7x + 2$

25. $2x^2 + 11x + 15$

26. $3x^2 + 22x - 16$

27. $4x^2 + 19x - 5$

28. $5x^2 - 21x + 4$

29. $7x^2 - 9x + 2$

30. $12v^2 - 145v + 12$

31. $6c^2 + 13c + 6$

32. $21r^2 - 32r - 5$

33. $10t^2 - 9t - 7$

34. $3l^2 - 8l + 4$

35. $10p^2 - 29p - 21$

36. $4s^2 + 35s + 24$

37. $2f^2 - 21f + 54$

38. $3m^2 + 13m - 10$

39. $8e^2 + 43e - 30$

40. $6d^2 + d - 22$

41. $-6x^2 - x + 1$

42. $-6x^2 - 5x + 6$

43. $2 + x - 10x^2$

44. $5 - 17x - 12x^2$

45. $1 + x - 2x^2$

46. $6 + x - 2x^2$

47. $12 + 5x - 3x^2$

48. $7 + 34x - 5x^2$

49. $33x - 4x^2 - 8$

50. $35x - 6 - 11x^2$

51. $13x - 3x^2 - 14$

52. $17x - 4x^2 - 13$

53. $46g - 7g^2 + 21$

54. $15 - 2b^2 - 7b$

55. $37k + 55 + 6k^2$

56. $15 - 4l^2 - 17l$

57. $4 - 36m^2 + 7m$

58. $m^2 - 24n^2 + 10mn$

59. $p^2 - 24q^2 - 5pq$

60. $12p^2 - 49q^2 - 28pq.$

Difference of two squares

Consider $(a - b)(a + b)$.

$$
\begin{aligned}
(a - b)(a + b) &= (a - b)a + (a - b)b \\
&= a^2 - ba + ab - b^2 \\
&= a^2 - b^2
\end{aligned}
$$

Thus it follows that

$$a^2 - b^2 = (a - b)(a + b)$$

where a and b are *any* numbers.

Examples (i) $25 - x^2 = 5^2 - x^2$

$$= (5 - x)(5 + x)$$

(ii) $\quad 4a^2 - b^2 = (2a)^2 - b^2$

$$= (2a - b)(2a + b)$$

(iii) $\quad 3p^2 - 12q^2 = 3(p^2 - 4q^2)$

$$= 3(p^2 - (2q)^2)$$

$$= 3(p - 2q)(p + 2q)$$

(iv) $\quad 6.3^2 - 3.7^2 = (6.3 - 3.7)(6.3 + 3.7)$

$$= 2.6 \times 10$$

$$= 26$$

EXERCISE 6g   Using the difference of two squares rule, factorise the following:

1. $3^2 - y^2$
2. $p^2 - q^2$
3. $r^2 - s^2$

4. $p^2 - (3q)^2$
5. $(mn)^2 - p^2$
6. $u^2 v^2 - 3^2$

7. $25 - y^2$
8. $121 - w^2$
9. $81 - r^2$

10. $144 - 25x^2$
11. $81s^2 - t^2$
12. $36y^2 - x^2$

13. $9t^2 - 4u^2$
14. $121f^2 - 49j^2$
15. $64s^2 - 49t^2$

16. $18r^2 - 2s^2$
17. $8d^2 - 2e^2$
18. $20a^2 - 80b^2$

19. $12d^2 - 48e^2$
20. $50c^2 - 98$
21. $200 - 32z^2$.

Without using long multiplication, work out

22. $97^2 - 3^2$
23. $81^2 - 19^2$
24. $123^2 - 23^2$

25. $300^2 - 290^2$
26. $51.6^2 - 48.4^2$
27. $0.009^2 - 0.001^2$

28. $1257^2 - 743^2$
29. $998^2 - 4$
30. $1009^2 - 81$.

7 ALGEBRAIC EQUATIONS AND PROBLEM SOLVING

LINEAR EQUATIONS

The two sides of an equation are in a state of balance. For example

$$2 + 3 = 4 + 1$$

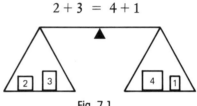

Fig. 7.1

(see Fig. 7.1). Balance is preserved *only* if both sides are treated in *exactly* the same way. Thus, we may

(*i*) Add the same amount to both sides (Fig. 7.2(a)):

$$2 + 3 + 1 = 4 + 1 + 1$$

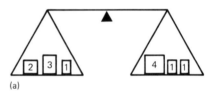

(a)

(*ii*) Subtract the same amount from both sides (Fig. 7.2(b)):

$$2 + 3 + 1 = 4 + 1 + 1$$
$$- 2 \qquad\quad - 2$$

giving

$$3 + 1 = 4$$

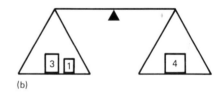

(b)

(*iii*) Multiply the *whole* of both sides by the same amount (Fig. 7.2(c)):

$$2 \times (3 + 1) = 2 \times 4$$

giving

$$(2 \times 3) + (2 \times 1) = 2 \times 4$$

or $\qquad 6 + 2 = 8$

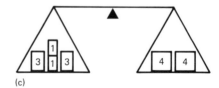

(c)

Fig. 7.2

(*iv*) Divide the *whole* of both
sides by the same amount
(Fig. 7.2(d)):

$$\frac{6}{2} + \frac{2}{2} = \frac{8}{2}$$

giving

$$3 + 1 = 4$$

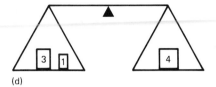

(d)

Fig. 7.2 (continued)

We may also square (or square root) the *whole* of both sides. Thus,
for example

$$3 + 1 = 4$$
$$\Rightarrow \quad (3 + 1)^2 = 4^2$$

Do *not* square individual items, however, for then each term is
multiplied by something *different*; balance is lost (Fig. 7.3) and the
resulting equation is *false*.

$$3^2 + 1^2 = 9 + 1 = 10$$

but $\quad 4^2 = 16$

So $\quad 3^2 + 1^2 \neq 4^2$

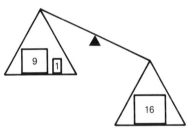

Fig. 7.3

Examples (*i*) Solve $6x + 7 = 5 - 2x$.

Add $2x$ to both sides:

$$6x + 7 + 2x = 5 - 2x + 2x$$
$$8x + 7 = 5$$

Subtract 7 from both sides:

$$8x + 7 - 7 = 5 - 7$$
$$8x = -2$$

Finally, divide both sides by 8:

$$\frac{8x}{8} = \frac{-2}{8}$$

giving

$$x = -\tfrac{1}{4}$$

83

(ii) Solve $2(3x - 2) = 20 - 3(x + 2)$.

The brackets make the problem more complicated so multiply them out as the first step, taking care with the negative signs:

$$6x - 4 = 20 - (3x + 6)$$
$$6x - 4 = 20 - 3x - 6$$
$$6x - 4 = 14 - 3x$$

Add $3x$ to both sides:

$$6x - 4 + 3x = 14 - 3x + 3x$$

Simplify and add 4 to both sides:

$$9x - 4 + 4 = 14 + 4$$
$$9x = 18$$

Finally, divide both sides by 9:

$$\frac{9x}{9} = \frac{18}{9}$$
$$x = 2$$

(iii) Solve $\dfrac{x - 2}{3} - \dfrac{x + 1}{6} = \dfrac{x - 1}{10}$.

In this case, it is the algebraic fractions that make the equation difficult to solve. Remember that the algebraic parts $x - 2$, $x + 1$ and $x - 1$ must be treated as single terms, so as a first step, write three brackets as follows:

$$\frac{(x - 2)}{3} - \frac{(x + 1)}{6} = \frac{(x - 1)}{10}$$

Now the lowest common multiple of the denominators 3, 6 and 10 is 30. So as the next step, multiply the whole of both sides by 30:

$$30 \times \frac{(x - 2)}{3} - 30 \times \frac{(x + 1)}{6} = 30 \times \frac{(x - 1)}{10}$$

Cancel down: $\qquad 10(x - 2) - 5(x + 1) = 3(x - 1)$

Multiply out: $\qquad 10x - 20 - 5x - 5 = 3x - 3$

Simplify: $\qquad\qquad\quad 5x - 25 = 3x - 3$

Subtract $3x$ and add 25 to both sides:

$$2x = 22$$

$$x = 11$$

EXERCISE 7a   Find x from the following equations. Show each step in your reasoning.

1. $3x + 7 = 19$

2. $5x - 2 = 13$

3. $3 - 2x = 1$

4. $5 - 7x = -9$

5. $11 - 3x = 6x + 2$

6. $x^2 - 8 = 1$

7. $2x^3 - 7 = 9$

8. $18 - x^2 = 9$

9. $5x - 3 = 11 - 2x$

10. $\dfrac{12}{x} = 4$

11. $\sqrt{x} + 6 = 10$

12. $17 - \sqrt{x} = 7 + \sqrt{x}$

13. $3(x - 2) = 12$

14. $2(x + 1) - 1 = 17$

15. $5(2x - 4) = 4$

16. $4(2 - x) = 3(x - 9)$

17. $8 - (x + 3) = 4$

18. $5 + (2x + 1) = 0$

19. $3 - 2(x + 1) = 8$

20. $14 - 3(2x + 3) = 2$

21. $12 - \frac{2}{3}(2x + 1) = 6$

22. $11 - \frac{1}{4}(5x + 2) = 8$

23. $9 - \frac{1}{2}(x + 3) = 3$

24. $3 - \frac{1}{5}(x + 3) = 1$

25. $15 - 3(2x - 1) = 9$

26. $1 - 5(2x - 3) = 6$

27. $5 + 3(x - 1) = 2(x + 3)$

28. $6 + 4(x - 1) = 12x + 2$

29. $11 - 7(x - 1) = 3(x + 1) - 9$

30. $17 - 3(x - 1) = 24 + x$

31. $12 - 2(2x - 1) = \frac{1}{2}(x + 1)$

32. $11(x + 2) + 3(x + 1) = 17(2x - 1) + 2$

33. $\dfrac{x + 2}{3} = 4$

34. $\dfrac{x - 3}{5} = 1$

35. $\dfrac{3x + 5}{8} = x$

36. $\dfrac{2x - 16}{3} = 2x$

37. $\dfrac{2x + 6}{5} = 3x - 4$

38. $\dfrac{5x - 7}{2} = 4$

39. $\dfrac{7x - 1}{2} = 13 - x$

40. $\dfrac{2x - 5}{3} = 25 - x$

41. $\dfrac{x-2}{3} = \dfrac{x+4}{5}$

42. $\dfrac{3x-5}{6} = \dfrac{9-x}{9}$

43. $\dfrac{x+1}{6} = \dfrac{1-x}{4}$

44. $\dfrac{x-2}{7} = 2 + \dfrac{3-x}{14}$

45. $\dfrac{x-1}{2} + \dfrac{x+1}{3} = \dfrac{2x+5}{6}$

46. $\dfrac{2x-4}{2} + \dfrac{x+1}{10} = \dfrac{2x+1}{5}$

47. $\dfrac{2x+1}{2} - \dfrac{x+2}{4} = \dfrac{x+10}{8}$

48. $\dfrac{2x-1}{3} - \dfrac{2x+1}{4} = \dfrac{x-4}{12}$

49. $\dfrac{3x-1}{2} - \dfrac{x-1}{6} = \dfrac{x+8}{3}$

50. $\dfrac{x+1}{3} - \dfrac{x-1}{9} = \dfrac{x+8}{18}.$

REARRANGING FORMULAE

Formulae may be rearranged in precisely the same way as simple equations — that is, each side must be added to, subtracted from, multiplied or divided *exactly* as the other.

Examples (*i*) Rearrange the formula $y = mx + c$ to express x in terms of y, m and c.

$$y = mx + c$$

Subtract c from both sides:

$$y - c = mx$$

Divide each side by m:

$$\dfrac{y-c}{m} = \dfrac{mx}{m}$$

Hence

$$\dfrac{y-c}{m} = x$$

(*ii*) Rearrange the formula $q = \sqrt{\dfrac{2r}{p}}$ to make p the subject.

Square both sides:

$$q^2 = \left(\sqrt{\dfrac{2r}{p}} \right)^2$$

giving

$$q^2 = \dfrac{2r}{p}$$

Multiply both sides by p:

$$p \times q^2 = p \times \frac{2r}{p}$$

$$pq^2 = 2r$$

Divide both sides by q^2:

$$\frac{pq^2}{q^2} = \frac{2r}{q^2}$$

Hence

$$p = \frac{2r}{q^2}$$

EXERCISE 7b Rearrange the formulae below to make the given letter the subject. Show each step in your reasoning.

1. $P = 4a$; a

2. $V = ir$;   (a) i (b) r

3. $F = ma$; m

4. $A = 2\pi r$; π

5. $E = mgh$; h

6. $I = \dfrac{Prt}{100}$; r

7. $A = \frac{1}{2}ab$; b

8. $V = \frac{1}{3}abh$; h

9. $p = 1 - q$; q

10. $s = \dfrac{o}{h}$;   (a) o (b) h

11. $v = u + at$;   (a) u (b) a

12. $v^2 = u^2 + 2as$;   (a) a (b) u

13. $S = 2\pi(r + h)$; h

14. $E = \frac{1}{2}mv^2$;   (a) v^2 (b) v

15. $A = \pi r^2$; r

16. $y = mx + c$;   (a) c (b) x

17. $V = \frac{4}{3}\pi r^3$; r

18. $r = \sqrt{x^2 + y^2}$;   (a) y^2 (b) y

19. $P = \dfrac{mv^2}{r}$;   (a) r (b) v

20. $s = ut + \frac{1}{2}at^2$;   (a) u (b) a

21. $A = \left(\dfrac{a + b}{2}\right)h$;   (a) h (b) a

22. $s = \sqrt{np(1 - p)}$; n

23. $T = 2\pi\sqrt{\dfrac{l}{g}}$;   (a) l (b) u

24. $\dfrac{1}{f} = \dfrac{1}{u} + \dfrac{1}{v}$;   (a) $\dfrac{1}{u}$ (b) u

PROBLEMS LEADING TO SIMPLE EQUATIONS AND FORMULAE

Examples (*i*) The perimeter of a rectangle is 36 cm. If it is twice as long as it is wide, what is its area?

As we do not yet know the lengths of the rectangle's sides we must use letters. Let the width be w. Then the length must be twice this, i.e. $2w$.

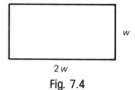

Fig. 7.4

The perimeter is

$$2w + w + 2w + w = 6w$$

But we are told that the perimeter is 36 cm. So now we can make the simple equation:

$$6w = 36$$

giving $w = 6$ cm.

Thus the rectangle is 6 cm wide, and, therefore, 12 cm long.

$$\text{area} = \text{length} \times \text{breadth} = 12 \text{ cm} \times 6 \text{ cm} = 72 \text{ cm}^2$$

(*ii*) This year, a man is four times the age of his son. In five years' time he will be three times as old as his son. How old is the man now?

Let the son's current age be x years. His father is four times as old or $4x$ years. In five years' time, *both* father and son will be five years older. So the son's future age is $x + 5$ years and the father's is $4x + 5$ years. But in five years, the father is three times his son's age. That is

$$4x + 5 = 3(x + 5)$$

Expanding the bracket, we get the equation

$$4x + 5 = 3x + 15$$

Subtracting $3x$ and 5 from both sides gives

$$4x + 5 - 3x - 5 = 3x + 15 - 3x - 5$$

$$x = 10$$

Thus the son is currently 10 years old and his father is therefore 40. (And in five years, the son will be 15 and his father 45 — three times as old.)

(*iii*) A taxi company charges a minimum fare of m pence for a journey up to 1 mile and then q pence per mile after that. In terms of m and q, what would be the cost of a journey of (a) 2 miles (b) 8 miles (c) x miles?

(a) A journey of 2 miles incurs the basic charge of m pence but I must also pay q pence for the extra mile:

$$\text{Total} = m + q \text{ pence}$$

(b) For a journey of 8 miles, again I pay the basic charge of m pence but this time the journey is 7 miles over the 1 mile limit. So I must pay $7q$ pence extra:

$$\text{Total} = m + 7q \text{ pence}$$

(c) A journey of x miles will cost m pence plus an extra charge for journeying beyond the 1 mile limit (assuming $x > 1$). The extra mileage is $x - 1$ miles. Thus the extra charge is $(x - 1)q$ pence:

$$\text{Total} = m + (x - 1)q \text{ pence}$$

EXERCISE 7c

1. (a) I ask a friend to think of a number, double it and add four. He tells me his answer is 18. Show that this can be written algebraically as $2x + 4 = 18$. What number did my friend think of?

   (b) Another friend, playing the same game, tells me his answer is 66. What number did he first think of?

2. My friend now asks me to think of a number, add 5 to it, double the result and then take away 7. If my answer is 13, what number did I first think of?

3. I think of another number, treble it, subtract 14, multiply by 10 and divide by two. If my answer is -100, what (negative) number did I think of?

4. Three consecutive numbers (i.e. like $3, 4, 5$) are n, $n + 1$ and $n + 2$. If the sum of the three numbers is 42, form an equation and find the three numbers.

5. Three consecutive *even* numbers are n, $n + 2$ and $n + 4$. What is the fourth? If the sum of the first and the fourth of these numbers is 26, what are the four numbers?

6. The perimeter of a rectangle is 28 cm. If the length is 10 cm more than the width, find the sides of the rectangle.

7. The perimeter of a rectangle is 64 cm. If the length of the rectangle is three times the width, find the area of the rectangle.

8. The perimeter of an isosceles triangle is 35 cm. If the two sloping sides are both twice the length of the base, find the length of the base.

9. Find, in terms of l, the perimeter of the shape in Fig. 7.5. If the perimeter is 60 cm, find the area.

Fig. 7.5

10. A young girl is one-third of her mother's age. In ten years' time, she will be one-half her mother's age; how old will the girl be then?

11. The elder of two brothers is exactly twice the age of the other. Three years ago, the elder brother was three times the other's age. How old are the boys now?

12. At the greengrocer's, carrots cost q pence per kilogram, potatoes cost $q + 5$ pence per kilogram and Brussels sprouts cost $2q + 3$ pence per kilogram. If I buy 2 kg of carrots, 5 kg of potatoes and 1 kg of sprouts, find, in terms of q, how much I have spent.

The bill comes to £1.54. What is the cost of the sprouts?

13. At the newsagent I buy a copy of *The Worplesdon Times* for t pence, a chocolate bar for $t - 5$ pence and two magazines for $2t + 3$ pence each. If the bill comes to £1.27, what is the cost of my newspaper?

14. I drive for t hours at s kilometres per hour and for T hours at S kilometres per hour. How far have I travelled?

15. A bus company charges a minimum fare of m pence for a journey of up to one fare stage, and then an extra q pence for each fare stage reached (so that a journey passing one fare stage costs $m + q$ pence). Find, in terms of m and q, the cost of a journey that passes

(a) 2 (b) 5 (c) x

fare stages.

16. The same bus company proposes to revise the fares by raising the minimum fare by 5 pence and charging $3q$ pence for the

first fare stage, $2q$ pence for the second and then q pence for each subsequent fare stage. Find, in terms of m and q, the revised fare for journeys of

(a) 2 (b) 5 (c) x (where $x > 2$)

fare stages.

SIMULTANEOUS EQUATIONS

It is only possible to solve equations for *two* unknown values if there are *two* equations to work on simultaneously.

Example Find x and y if

$$2x + y = 8 \tag{1}$$

and

$$3x - y = 7 \tag{2}$$

If we add together the left-hand sides of the two equations, then the result must equal the two right-hand sides added together. Moreover, if we add the two left-hand sides, then $+y$ and $-y$ will cancel, leaving an equation that contains only one unknown quantity, x.

$$2x + y = 8$$
$$3x - y = 7$$

Adding gives

$$5x = 15$$

Hence

$$x = \frac{15}{5} = 3$$

Now, if $x = 3$, we can say that, from Equation (1)

$$(2 \times 3) + y = 8$$

or

$$6 + y = 8$$

Therefore

$$y = 2$$

Thus the solution to Equations (1) and (2) is $x = 3$, $y = 2$.

Sometimes it is necessary to multiply one or both equations so that the number of ys in each equation is the same. Also, if the signs of the ys in both equations are the same, then the equations must be *subtracted* (not added).

Example Find x and y if

$$3x - 2y = 1 \tag{1}$$

$$x - 5y = 9 \tag{2}$$

First, we must multiply Equation (1) by 5 and Equation (2) by 2 so that both equations then contain $10y$.

Multiplying Equation (1) by 5 gives

$$15x - 10y = 5$$

Multiplying Equation (2) by 2 gives

$$2x - 10y = 18$$

Subtracting Equation (2) from Equation (1) leaves

$$13x = -13$$

Hence

$$x = -1$$

Putting $x = -1$ in Equation (1) gives

$$(3 \times -1) - 2y = 1$$
$$-3 - 2y = 1$$

Adding 3 to both sides:

$$-2y = 4$$

Dividing by -2:

$$y = \frac{4}{-2} = -2$$

Thus the solution to Equations (1) and (2) is $x = -1$, $y = -2$.

EXERCISE 7d Solve the following pairs of simultaneous equations:

1. $x + y = 5$
   $x - y = 3$

2. $2x + y = 12$
   $4x - y = 6$

3. $2x + 3y = 17$
   $4x - 3y = 7$

4. $5x + y = 10$
   $3x - y = 2$

5. $2a + b = 12$
   $a + b = 7$

6. $3p - q = 8$
   $3p - 2q = 7$

7. $2y + z = 7$
   $y + z = 5$

8. $p - 7q = 5$
   $p - 5q = 9$

9. $y + x = 8$
   $x - y = 2$

10. $3m - n = 11$
    $3m - 2n = 13$

11. $p + 2q = 7$
    $3p - 4q = 21$

12. $c + d = 4$
    $3d - c = 16$

13. $5x + 2y = 19$
    $7x - y = 19$

14. $x + 4y = 3$
    $2x - 8y = -2$

15. $3x + y = 7$
    $y + x = 5$

16. $2y + 7z = -13$
    $4y + 5z = -8$

17. $4g - 5h = 3$
    $6g - 7h = 4$

18. $12f - 6e = -2$
    $7e - 3f = 6$

19. $3m - 5n = -2.5$
    $9m + 8n = -5.2$

20. $4p - 2q = -7$
    $3p - q = 5$

PROBLEMS LEADING TO SIMULTANEOUS EQUATIONS

Examples (*i*) The two points $(3, 11)$ and $(2, 8)$ lie on the line $y = mx + c$. Find m and c.

As the point $(3, 11)$ lies on the line, so the equation of the line $y = mx + c$ must work for $y = 11$ and $x = 3$, i.e. $11 = 3m + c$. Similarly, since the point $(2, 8)$ lies on the line, $y = 8$ and $x = 2$ must also satisfy the equation $y = mx + c$, hence $8 = 2m + c$. Now we have two equations that can be solved simultaneously:

$$11 = 3m + c \tag{1}$$

$$8 = 2m + c \tag{2}$$

Subtracting Equation (2) from Equation (1) gives

$$3 = m$$

Substituting back into the first equation gives

$$11 = 3 \times 3 + c$$

Hence $\qquad\qquad c = 2$

(*ii*) A taxi company charges a minimum fare of m pence for any journey up to 1 mile and then q pence per mile after that. If a journey of 2 miles costs £1.10 and a journey of 8 miles costs £2.90, what is the minimum charge and the cost per mile outside the 1 mile limit?

A journey of 2 miles costs $m + q$ pence and a journey of 8 miles costs $m + 7q$ pence (see page 89). We are told that the 2 mile journey costs £1.10 (110 pence) and that the 8 mile journey costs £2.90 (or 290 pence). Thus

$$m + q = 110 \tag{1}$$

and $\qquad\qquad m + 7q = 290 \tag{2}$

93

Subtracting Equation (1) from Equation (2):

$$6q = 180$$

$$q = 30 \text{ pence}$$

Substituting the value of q back into Equation (1):

$$m + 30 = 110$$

$$m = 80 \text{ pence}$$

Thus the taxi firm's minimum charge is 80 p and the cost per mile after the first mile is 30p.

EXERCISE 7e

1. Two numbers, x and y, have a sum of 15 and a difference of 3. Find x and y.

2. Find two numbers which have a difference of 12 and a sum of 24.

3. Two apples and a banana cost 36p. Just one apple and a banana cost 26p. What is the cost of an apple? What is the cost of a banana?

4. Five tins of peas and three cans of beans cost £1.53; one can of peas and two cans of beans cost 60 pence. Find the cost per tin of peas and beans.

5. Two adults' tickets and one child's ticket to the theatre cost £7.50. Two children's and one adult's tickets cost £6.00. Find the cost of the tickets.

6. I buy 30 stamps at the post office. Some are second-class (costing $12\frac{1}{2}$p each) and the rest are first-class (costing 16p each). If the total cost is £4.10, how many first-class stamps did I buy?

7. I have in my pocket a total of 82p in loose change, made up of x 5p pieces and y 2p pieces. If the numbers were the other way round — that is, if I had x 2p pieces and y 5p pieces — I would have only 58p. Write down two equations in x and y and solve them simultaneously.

8. A man normally works at £x per hour for a 35 hour week. He is paid £y per hour of overtime. One week he works 38 hours and receives £120; the next week he works 41 hours and receives £135. What are his normal and overtime rates of pay?

9. A bus company charges a basic fare of m pence, and q pence for each fare stage passed. One journey takes me past three

fare stages and costs 40p; another journey, passing five fare stages, costs 56p. What is the minimum fare? How much would a journey passing eight fare stages cost?

10. (a) A line has the equation $y = mx + c$. If the points $x = 2$, $y = 13$ and $x = 3$, $y = 18$ lie on this line, find m and c.

    (b) Another line, also of the form $y = nx + d$, goes through the points $(2, 1)$ and $(5, 7)$. Find n and d.

    (c) A line passes through the points $(1, 5)$ and $(3, 17)$. Find the equation of this line.

11. The value, T, of a term in a series is given by the formula $T = a + (n - 1)d$ where a and d are constants. When $n = 2$, $T = 9$ and when $n = 4$, $T = 17$. Find a and d.

12. The velocity of a particle is given by the formula $v = u + at$. When $t = 3$, $v = 17$ and when $t = 5$, $v = 25$. Find a and u.

QUADRATIC EQUATIONS

Quadratics that Factorise

The solution of quadratic equations that factorise depends upon a peculiar property of zero, namely that if the product of two numbers is zero then one of the numbers must be zero.

Examples (*i*) $x^2 + 4x = 0$.

Factorising: $x(x + 4) = 0$.

So *either* $x = 0$

or $(x + 4) = 0$ i.e. $x = -4$

Thus there are two possible answers: $x = 0$ or $x = -4$.

(*ii*) $x^2 + 5x + 6 = 0$.

Since the left-hand side of the equation is a quadratic expression that factorises to $(x + 3)(x + 2)$ (see page 76), we may say

$$x^2 + 5x + 6 = 0$$

$$(x + 3)(x + 2) = 0$$

But if these two expressions, $(x + 3)$ on the one hand and $(x + 2)$ on the other, multiply to give zero, then one of them *must* be zero.

95

So *either* $(x + 3) = 0 \Rightarrow x = -3$

or $(x + 2) = 0 \Rightarrow x = -2$

The equation has *two* possible solutions: $x = -3$ or -2.

(*iii*) $2x^2 + 5x - 3 = 0$

Factorising the left-hand side (see page 78):

$$(2x - 1)(x + 3) = 0$$

Hence, *either*

$$2x - 1 = 0 \Rightarrow 2x = 1 \Rightarrow x = \tfrac{1}{2}$$

or $x + 3 = 0 \Rightarrow x = -3$

The two solutions are $x = \tfrac{1}{2}$ or $x = -3$.

It may be necessary to rearrange the equation to give zero on the right-hand side.

Example $6x^2 - 11x + 8 = 3$.

Subtracting 3 from both sides:

$$6x^2 - 11x + 8 - 3 = 3 - 3$$

Hence $6x^2 - 11x + 5 = 0$

Factorising: $(6x - 5)(x - 1) = 0$

So either $6x - 5 = 0 \Rightarrow 6x = 5 \Rightarrow x = \tfrac{5}{6}$

or $x - 1 = 0 \Rightarrow x = 1$

The solutions are $x = \tfrac{5}{6}$ or $x = 1$.

Sometimes, considerable rearranging is necessary.

Example Solve the equation $x = \dfrac{7}{6 + x}$.

Multiplying both sides by $(6 + x)$:

$$x(6 + x) = 7$$

Multiplying the bracket out and subtracting 7 from both sides:

$$6x + x^2 - 7 = 0$$

Rearranging into the usual order:

$$x^2 + 6x - 7 = 0$$

Hence
$$x^2 - x + 7x - 7 = 0$$
$$x(x-1) + 7(x-1) = 0$$
$$(x-1)(x+7) = 0$$

So either $x = 1$ or $x = -7$.

EXERCISE 7f   Write down the solutions to the following:

1. $(x-2)(x-3) = 0$ 2. $(x+4)(x-3) = 0$

3. $(p+3)(p+2) = 0$ 4. $x(x-2) = 0$

5. $xy = 0$

6. $x(x-1)(x-2) = 0$. (*Note*: there are *three* possible answers.)

Solve these equations by factorising (rearrange Questions 12 to 16 first):

7. $x^2 + 3x = 0$ 8. $x^2 - 2x = 0$

9. $z^2 - 4z = 0$ 10. $5z - z^2 = 0$

11. $p^3 - p^2 = 0$ 12. $2x^2 = x$

13. $r^2 = 5r$ 14. $s^2 = 3s$

15. $r^5 = -3r^4$ 16. $r^3 = -r^2$.

Solve the following quadratic equations by factorising them first:

17. $x^2 + 6x + 8 = 0$ 18. $a^2 + 6a - 16 = 0$

19. $b^2 - 2b - 15 = 0$ 20. $x^2 - 7x + 10 = 0$

21. $2x^2 + 5x - 3 = 0$ 22. $4c^2 - 12c + 5 = 0$

23. $11c^2 + 8c - 3 = 0$ 24. $12x^2 + 13x + 3 = 0$

25. $5x^2 - 3x - 2 = 0$ 26. $5d^2 + 2d - 7 = 0$

27. $12x^2 - 23x - 9 = 0$ 28. $14q^2 + 61q + 42 = 0$.

Rearrange these equations to give zero on the right-hand side and solve them by factorising:

29. $x^2 + 6x = 27$ 30. $x^2 + x = 2$

31. $6x^2 + x = 2$ 32. $3x^2 + 14x = 5$

33. $a^2 - 11a + 30 = 2$ 34. $2x^2 + 13x - 2 = -20$

35. $6x^2 + 9x - 5 = 1$ 36. $17x = 10x^2 + 3$

37. $15 - x^2 = 23x + 3x^2 + 30$ 38. $2x^2 + 5x + 3 = 12x$

39. $21b^2 + 2b = 24b + 8$

40. $6x^2 - 5 = 13x$

41. $20w^2 = 28 - 19w$

42. $x^2 - 6x = 3x + 2x - 24$

43. $y(2y + 7) = -6$

44. $q(5q + 14) = 3$

45. $a = \dfrac{2}{(a+1)}$

46. $x = \dfrac{3}{(x-2)}$

47. $b = \dfrac{6}{b-5}$

48. $y = \dfrac{1}{2y-1}$

49. $c = \dfrac{15}{7+2c}$

50. $z = \dfrac{4}{15z+4}$.

Quadratics that do not Factorise

If the quadratic will not factorise, then there is a formula to use. If

$$ax^2 + bx + c = 0$$

then
$$x = \frac{-b \pm \sqrt{b^2 - 4ac}}{2a}$$

Examples (*i*) Solve $7x^2 + 4x - 1 = 0$.

Putting $a = 7$, $b = 4$ and $c = -1$ in the above formula:

$$x = \frac{-4 \pm \sqrt{4^2 - (4 \times 7 \times -1)}}{2 \times 7}$$

$$= \frac{-4 \pm \sqrt{16 - (-28)}}{14}$$

So either $x = \dfrac{-4 + \sqrt{44}}{14} = 0.188$ (3 d.p.)

or $x = \dfrac{-4 - \sqrt{44}}{14} = -0.760$ (3 d.p.)

(*ii*) $4z^2 - 2 = 3z + 11$.

First, we must ensure that the right-hand side is zero and that the terms are in order (z^2 first, then z and then the number).

Subtracting $3z + 11$ from both sides and arranging into order gives:

$$4z^2 - 3z - 13 = 0$$

Comparing with the form $az^2 + bz + c$ we see that $a = +4$, $b = -3$ and $c = -13$. Substituting these values into the formula gives

$$z = \frac{-(-3) \pm \sqrt{(-3)^2 - (4 \times 4 \times -13)}}{2 \times 4}$$

Now, $-(-3) = +3$ and $(-3)^2 = (-3) \times (-3) = +9$, so

$$z = \frac{+3 \pm \sqrt{+9 + 208}}{8}$$

$$= \frac{+3 \pm \sqrt{217}}{8} = \frac{+3 \pm 14.731}{8}$$

Hence

$$z = \frac{+3 + 14.731}{8} = 2.22 \quad \text{(2 d.p.)}$$

or

$$z = \frac{+3 - 14.731}{8} = -1.47 \quad \text{(2 d.p.)}$$

It is worth remembering that the square-root of a negative number does not exist, so $b^2 - 4ac$ *must always* be a positive quantity. If you make it negative, do not ignore the minus sign: go back and check your arithmetic. Remember, too, that *any* number squared is positive, so b^2 is always positive, even if b is negative (as in this example).

EXERCISE 7g   Use the formula $x = \dfrac{-b \pm \sqrt{b^2 - 4ac}}{2a}$ to solve the following quadratic equations, giving your answers to 2 d.p. where appropriate:

1. $x^2 + 3x + 2 = 0$
2. $2x^2 + 5x + 2 = 0$
3. $3x^2 + 7x + 2 = 0$
4. $2x^2 + 2x - 3 = 0$
5. $x^2 + x - 5 = 0$
6. $x^2 - 8x + 5 = 0$
7. $x^2 - 6x + 3 = 0$
8. $x^2 - 4x - 4 = 0$
9. $x^2 - 3x - 2 = 0$
10. $3x^2 - 2x - 7 = 0$
11. $-2y^2 - 5y + 2 = 0$
12. $-y^2 - 2y + 5 = 0$
13. $-z^2 - 3z + 6 = 0$
14. $p - p^2 + 3 = 0$.

Rearrange these equations to make the right-hand side zero and then solve by formula:

15. $a^2 + a - 2 = 1$
16. $2a - a^2 = -2$
17. $m^2 - 2m = 3 - 4m$
18. $3z^2 - 2z = z^2 + 1$

19. $2b^2 + 3 = 2 - 5b$

20. $3a^2 - 12a = -3 - 19a$

21. $3y(y + 1) = 1$

22. $2x^2 + 10x = x - 3$

23. $4 - y = \dfrac{2}{y}$

24. $y = \dfrac{2}{(2y + 1)}.$

PROBLEMS LEADING TO QUADRATIC EQUATIONS

Examples (*i*) Two consecutive *even* numbers have a product of 168. What are they?

Let the first number be x. Then the next (i.e. consecutive) even number is $x + 2$. The product of these two numbers is $x \times (x + 2)$ and is to be 168, i.e.

$$x(x + 2) = 168$$

or
$$x^2 + 2x - 168 = 0$$

Factorising in the usual way:

$$(x + 14)(x - 12) = 0$$

giving

$x = -14$ so that the second number is -12

or $x = +12$ so that the second number is $+14$.

(*ii*) A rectangular, open-topped water tank is to be made out of 14 m² of sheet metal so that it is 4 m long and has a square cross-section, as shown in Fig. 7.6(a). If the tank is x metres high and x metres wide, find x and the volume of the tank.

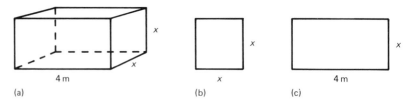

(a)   (b)   (c)

Fig. 7.6

The area of each of the two square ends is $x \times x = x^2$ (Fig. 7.6(b)). So the area of the two of them is $2x^2$. The area of the rectangle bottom and of each of the two rectangular sides is $4 \times x = 4x$ (Fig. 7.6(c)). So the area of these three sides together is $12x$. Thus the area of all five sides of the tank is $2x^2 + 12x$ square metres.

But the area of the sides must equal the area of sheet metal required to build the tank, i.e. $14\,\text{m}^2$. Thus

$$2x^2 + 12x = 14$$

$$2x^2 + 12x - 14 = 0$$

Dividing both sides by 2:

$$x^2 + 6x - 7 = 0$$

and factorising in the usual way:

$$(x + 7)(x - 1) = 0$$

giving $\qquad\qquad x = -7 \quad\text{or}\quad +1$

But x represents the side length of a water tank which cannot be a negative quantity, so the answer $x = -7$ cannot be allowed. Therefore x must be 1 m. The volume of the tank is $4\,\text{m} \times 1\,\text{m} \times 1\,\text{m} = 4\,\text{m}^3$.

EXERCISE 7h *In most of these questions there are two answers; if one answer is not allowable, say why.*

1. I think of a number, square it and add the original number to the result. The total is 42. What two numbers could I have thought of?

2. A friend thinks of a number, squares it, doubles the result and then adds the original number to make a total of 36. What could the original number have been? He then tells me that his original number was *not* a whole number. What is his number?

3. A girl thinks of a number, squares it and then adds three times the original number to give a total of 40. What could her number have been? What must it be if she says she chose a a positive number?

4. If the area of the rectangle shown in Fig. 7.7 is $54\,\text{cm}^2$, find x.

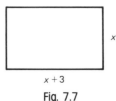

$x + 3$

Fig. 7.7

5.

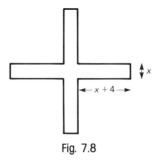

Fig. 7.8

If the area of the cross shape shown in Fig. 7.8 is 93 cm², find x.

6. A rectangular garden is laid out with lawns and paths as shown in Fig. 7.9. If the paths are both x metres wide, and the garden is 20 m by 15 m, show that the area of the lawn is given by $(20-x)(15-x)$ m². If, in fact, the area of the lawn is 234 m², find x.

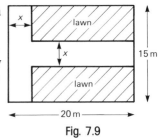

Fig. 7.9

7. The living room in my house is 3 ft longer than its width. If the area of the room is 304 square feet, work out its length and width.

8. A rectangular tank is 2 m high and $1\frac{1}{2}$ m longer than it is wide. If the volume of the tank is 9 m³, find the length and breadth.

9. A small closed tank has a square cross-section of side length x cm and is 30 cm high (Fig. 7.10). If the surface area of the tank (including the top) is 3200 cm², find x.

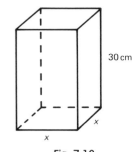

Fig. 7.10

10. The hypotenuse of a right-angled triangle is 8 cm longer than the shortest side (see Fig. 7.11). If the third side is 7 cm longer than the shortest side, find the length of the hypotenuse (using Pythagoras' theorem).

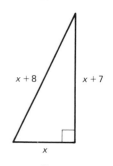

Fig. 7.11

11. In another right-angled triangle, the second side is 3 cm longer than the shortest side and the hypotenuse is 6 cm longer than the shortest side. Find the lengths of the three sides.

12. A man journeys 18 km at x km/h. Show that this takes him $\dfrac{18}{x}$ h. He then travels a further 7 km at $(x-1)$ km/h. How long would this take him? Form an expression for the total journey time (using the terms x and $(x-1)$). If the total journey time is 6 h, form an equation and show that it leads to the equation $18(x-1)+7x = 6x(x-1)$. Simplify this further to form a quadratic equation and solve it to find x.

13. A man walks 8 km uphill at x km/h; he walks down again at $(x+2)$ km/h. If the journey there and back takes him 6 h, find x.

14. A light aircraft flies 240 km, with the wind, at x km/h. It flies against the wind on the return journey and can only make headway at $(x-40)$ km/h. If the total journey time there and back is 5 h, show that

$$\frac{240}{x} + \frac{240}{x-40} = 5$$

Find x.

15. With the current a boy can swim 180 m at a speed of x m/min. Against the current he can only swim at $(x-5)$ m/min. If it takes him 30 min to swim the 180 m and back again, find x.

FACTOR THEOREM

The factor theorem says that $(x-a)$ is a factor of a function if substituting $x = a$ into the function gives zero.

Examples (i)   Show that $(x-2)$ is a factor of $2x^2 - 3x - 2$.

Put $x = 2$ into the function:

$$2x^2 - 3x - 2 = 2(2)^2 - 3(2) - 2$$
$$= 8 - 6 - 2$$
$$= 0$$

So, by the factor theorem, $(x-2)$ is a factor of $2x^2 - 3x - 2$.

103

Suppose we try some other value, say $x = 1$. Then

$$2x^2 - 3x - 2 = 2(1)^2 - 3(1) - 2 = 2 - 3 - 2 = -3$$

$2x^2 - 3x - 2 \neq 0$ when $x = 1$, so $(x - 1)$ is *not* a factor.

In fact, $2x^2 - 3x - 2$ is a quadratic function which factorises to $(x - 2)(2x + 1)$. This confirms that $(x - 2)$ is a factor and that $(x - 1)$ is not. As $(2x + 1)$ is the other factor, putting $x = -\frac{1}{2}$ (which makes $2x + 1 = 0$) into the function $2x^2 - 3x - 2$ will also give zero.

The factor theorem, however, applies to *all* functions, not just to quadratics.

(*ii*) Find the factors of $x^3 - 2x^2 - x + 2$.

Try $x = 1$:

$$x^3 - 2x^2 - x + 2 = (1)^3 - 2(1)^2 - (1) + 2$$
$$= 1 - 2 - 1 + 2 = 0$$

Hence $(x - 1)$ is a factor. Similarly, by trial and error, we can show that putting $x = -1$ or $x = 2$ into the function gives zero. So the complete set of factors is $(x - 1)(x + 1)(x - 2)$.

(*iii*) Find the value of k in $x^4 - 5x^3 + 2x^2 - kx + 6$ given that $(x - 1)$ is a factor.

As $(x - 1)$ is a factor, it follows from the factor theorem that putting $x = 1$ into the function will give zero:

$$x^4 - 5x^3 + 2x^2 - kx + 6 = (1)^4 - 5(1)^4 + 2(1)^2 - k(1) + 6$$
$$= 1 - 5 + 2 - k + 6$$
$$= 4 - k$$

As this is to be zero $k = 4$.

EXERCISE 7i

1. Show that $(x - 2)$ is a factor of $x^3 + x^2 - 4x - 4$. Show that $(x + 2)$ and $(x + 1)$ are factors too.

2. Show that $(x - 3)$ is a factor of $x^3 - 3x^2 + x - 3$. Is $(x + 3)$ a factor?

3. Show that $(x - 1)$ is a factor of $x^4 - x^3 + x - 1$. Can you find another factor?

4. Show that $(x + 2)$ is a factor of $x^3 + 2x^2 - x - 2$. Find two other factors.

5. Show that $(x - \frac{1}{2})$ is a factor of $2x^2 - 7x + 3$, but that $(x + \frac{1}{2})$ is not.

6. If $(x - 3)$ is a factor of $x^2 + 5x - k$, find k.

7. If $(x - 2)$ is a factor of $x^3 + kx^2 - 3x + 1$, find k.

8. If $(x - 1)$ is a factor of $x^3 + x^2 - kx + 7$, find k.

9. Given that the equation $x^3 - 4x^2 + x + 6 = 0$ has integer solutions only, find the three factors.

10. The equation $x^3 - 13x + k$ has $(x + 4)$ as a factor. Find k. Hence find two other factors.

11. Show that $(x - 2)$ is a factor of $4x^3 - 8x^2 - x + 2$.

    Find the values of $4x^3 - 8x^2 - x + 2$ when $x = +\frac{1}{2}$ and when $x = -\frac{1}{2}$. Hence write down the solution set to the equation $4x^3 - 8x^2 - x + 2 = 0$ if

    (a) x is an integer (b) x is a rational number.

12. Show that $(x - \frac{1}{3})$ is a factor of $x^3 - 2\frac{1}{3}x^2 - 2\frac{1}{3}x + 1$.

    Given that the equation $x^3 - 2\frac{1}{3}x^2 - 2\frac{1}{3}x + 1 = 0$ has two integer roots, factorise the expression completely.

13. If $(x - 1)$ and $(x - 2)$ are *both* factors of $x^3 + x^2 + px + q$, find p and q.

14. If $(x - 1)$ and $(x + 2)$ are *both* factors of $x^3 - ax^2 + bx - 3$, find a and b.

15. Show that $(x + 1)$ is a factor of $x^3 + x^2 - 4x - 4$ but that $(x - 1)$ is not. The two remaining factors are $(x - a)$ and $(x + a)$; find a.

16. $x^3 - 2x^2 + 3x - k$ has $(x - 2)$ as a factor. Find k.

17. $x^3 - px^2 + q$ has both $(x - 2)$ and $(x + 1)$ as factors. Find p and q.

18. If $x^4 - px^2 + q$ has $(x - 2)$ and $(x - 1)$ as factors, find p and q. Find the two other factors.

MISCELLANEOUS EXERCISE 7

1. (a) Use the formula $T = a + (n - 1)d$ to find
   (i) T when $a = 2$, $d = 3$ and $n = 5$;
   (ii) n when $a = 3$, $d = 4$ and $T = 31$.

(b) Use the equation $T - mg = mf$ to find
(i) the value of T when $m = 10$, $g = 32$ and $f = 15$;
(ii) the value of f when $m = 4$, $g = 32$ and $T = 140$.

(SUJB)

2. (a) Simplify

(i) $(3p - 5q)(2p + 3q)$ (ii) $\dfrac{a-3}{2} - \dfrac{a-4}{3}$.

(b) Factorise
(i) $15ab^2 - 5a^2b + 25ab$ (ii) $4x - 4y - xy + y^2$
(iii) $3ab^2 - 6a^2b$ (iv) $x^2 - 6x + 5$.

(SUJB)

3. Solve the following pairs of simultaneous equations:

(a) $4x + y = 9$ (b) $3x - 4y = -6$ (c) $5x + 7y = -1$
    $7x - y = 2$ $5x + 2y = 16$ $4x + 3y = 7$

4. Factorise

(a) $6xy + 2x$ (b) $3x^2 + 2x^3y$ (c) $12x^2y^2 + 4xy$
(d) $mn + 2m^2 + 2pm + pn$ (e) $2rt - st - 2rv^2 + sv^2$
(f) $x^2 + 5x - 14$ (g) $2x^2 + x - 21$.

5. Solve the following quadratic equations (to 3 s.f., if necessary):

(a) $x^2 + 9x + 20 = 0$ (b) $x^2 - x = 6$
(c) $3x^2 = x + 2$ (d) $3x^2 - x - 5 = 0$
(e) $2x^2 + 3x - 11 = 0$ (f) $x^2 - 3x - 1 = 2$

6. (a) Solve the equation $4.3 - 1.4x = 0.8$.

(b) Solve the simultaneous equations $\begin{cases} 5x + 3y = 7 \\ 2x - 7y = 11 \end{cases}$

(c) Solve the quadratic equation $2x^2 + 7x - 15 = 0$ (JMB)

7. (a) Solve the equations $\begin{cases} 3x + 6y = 4 \\ 2x - 3y = 5. \end{cases}$

(b) Consider the formula $L = \dfrac{(X + 3)(1 - 2X)}{X}$.

(i) What is the value of L when $X = 2$?
(ii) What values of X will make $L = 0$?

(iii) If the formula is written in the form $L = \dfrac{aX^2 + bX + C}{X}$

what is the value of b?

(SUJB)

8. (a) (i) Simplify $2x(x - 1) - (x + 3)^2$.
(ii) Factorise $x^2 - 7x - 8$.

(b) For each of the following relations express m in terms of y, x and c.

(i) $y = \dfrac{mc}{x}$ (ii) $y = mx + c$

(c) Solve the simultaneous equations

$$\begin{aligned} y &= 4x + 7, \\ 2y &= 3x + 4. \end{aligned} \qquad \text{(JMB)}$$

9. Give the solution sets of the following:

(a) $(x - 4)^2 = x^2 - 8x + 16$ (b) $(x - 4)^2 = x^2$

(c) $(x - 4)^2 = -8x$ (d) $(x - 4)^2 = 16$

Explain why the equation $(x - 4)^2 = -x^3$ cannot have a positive root. Given that this equation has a root which is a negative integer, find this root. (LU)

10. It is given that $x = 1 - 2p$ and $y = 2 + 3p$.

(a) Calculate the value of
    (i) x when $p = -3$, (ii) p when $y = 3$.

(b) Find a formula for p in terms of x.

(c) Given that $xy = -\frac{1}{2}$, show that $12p^2 + 2p - 5 = 0$.

(d) Solve the equation $12p^2 + 2p - 5 = 0$, giving each answer correct to two decimal places. (AEB '82)

11. It is stated that you can find the temperature by counting the chirps of the snowy tree cricket: the relation is given as

$$T = 40 + \frac{N}{4}$$

where T is the temperature in degrees Fahrenheit and N is the number of chirps per minute.

(a) State the temperature if the chirping rate is 60 per minute.

(b) What chirping rate would you expect if $T = 65$?

(c) At what temperature will the cricket cease to chirp?

(d) The relation between T, temperature in degrees Fahrenheit, and C, temperature in degrees Centigrade, is

$$T = 32 + \tfrac{9}{5}C$$

Find a formula for C in terms of N, giving your answer as simply as you can. (O & C)

12. I buy n boxes of sweets, each of which contains x sweets. The sweets are divided equally between y children.

(a) How many sweets in total did I buy?

(b) How many sweets did each child receive?

107

13. In a shop, apples cost 8 pence each, oranges cost x pence each and baskets cost 12 pence each.

   (a) Find
      (i)   the cost of 7 apples in a basket,
      (ii) the cost, in terms of y, of y apples in a basket,
      (iii) the cost, in terms of x, of 6 oranges in a basket,
      (iv) the cost, in terms of a, b and x, of a apples and b oranges in a basket.

   (b) Express in terms of y, the number of apples that can be bought in a basket for y pence.   (WJEC)

14. A man buys x boxes of tea at a cost of £z for each box. He takes all of this tea and divides it into n packets each of mass y grams.

   (a) What is the mass of tea in each of the original boxes in grams.

   (b) How much has the tea in each packet cost him?   (Ox)

15. If I buy x kg of oranges at 60p/kg and y kg of lemons at 75p/kg, my bill would be £1.95. In fact, I buy y kg of oranges and x kg of lemons so my bill comes to £2.10. Form two equations, each in terms of x and y, and solve them to find x and y.

16. Two workmen compare their weekly wages. Their rates of pay are £b per hour for the basic wage and £c per hour for overtime.

   One man works a basic week of 35 hours and 10 hours overtime and receives £122.50. The other man works a basic week of 40 hours and 5 hours overtime and receives £117.50.

   Write down two equations, each in terms of b and c, and solve them simultaneously to find the two rates of pay.   (SUJB)

17. (a) Given that x is a positive whole number and that the total cost of $(3x-8)$ metres of ribbon at $(x-4)$ pence per metre is 39 pence, write down an equation in x and show that it reduces to

$$3x^2 - 20x - 7 = 0$$

   Solve this equation and write down the cost of 1 metre of ribbon.

   (b) Solve, giving your answers correct to 2 decimal places,

$$x^2 = 9x - 11$$ (C)

18. A rectangular piece of paper ABCD is $(x-2)$ cm by $(x+1)$ cm. A corner piece, BEF, 4 cm by 9 cm, is removed, as shown in Fig. 7.12.

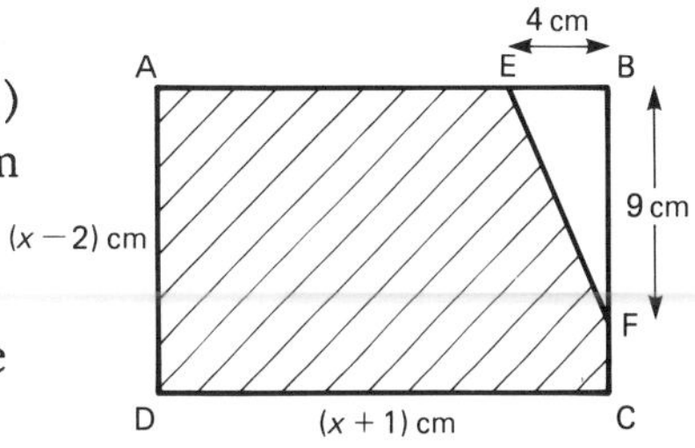

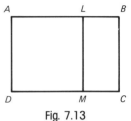

Fig. 7.12

(a) What, in terms of x, was the area of the original rectangular piece of paper?

(b) What is the area of the triangular piece removed?

(c) Show that the area of the remaining paper, AEFCD, (shown shaded in Fig. 7.12) is $x^2 - x - 20$.

(d) If, in fact, the area of the shaded part is 190 cm², find the length and breadth of the original paper.

19. In the rectangle $ABCD$ (Fig. 7.13), $AB = x$ cm and $BC = 1$ cm. The line LM is drawn so that $ALMD$ is a square.

Write down, in terms of x,

(a) the length LB,

(b) the ratios $\dfrac{AB}{BC}$ and $\dfrac{BC}{LB}$.

Fig. 7.13

(c) If $\dfrac{AB}{BC} = \dfrac{BC}{LB}$, obtain a quadratic equation in x. Hence find x correct to two decimal places. (LU)

20. A racing cyclist completes the uphill section of a mountainous course of 75 km at an average speed of V km/h. Write down, in terms of V, the time taken for the journey.

He then returns downhill along the same route at an average speed of $(V+20)$ km/h. Write down the time taken for the return journey.

Given that the difference between the times is one hour, form an equation in V and show that it reduces to

$$V^2 + 20V - 1500 = 0.$$

Solve this equation and calculate the time taken to complete the uphill section of the course.

Calculate also the cyclist's average speed over the 150 km. (C)

8 BINARY OPERATIONS

OPERATIONS

A rule for combining numbers together is called an *operation*. A *binary operation* is a rule for combining two numbers together.

The four *basic operations* are addition, subtraction, multiplication and division; for these we invariably use the symbols $+, -, \times, \div$. Other operations may be defined differently.

Example The operation $*$ is defined by the rule

$$\boxed{a * b = a - b + (a \times b)}$$

Find (a) $3 * 5$ (b) x if $3 * x = 11$.

(a) To find the value of $3 * 5$, we must substitute $a = 3$ and $b = 5$ into the given formula:

$$3 * 5 = 3 - 5 + (3 \times 5)$$
$$= 3 - 5 + 15$$
$$= 13$$

(b) Substituting $a = 3$ and $b = x$ in the formula, we get

$$3 * x = 3 - x + 3x$$
$$= 3 + 2x$$

But this is equal to 11, so

$$3 + 2x = 11$$

Subtracting 3 from both sides gives

$$2x = 8$$

Hence $$x = 4$$

EXERCISE 8a

1. If $a * b = 3a - b$, find
   (a) $2 * 1$ (b) $3 * 1$ (c) $3 * 4$ (d) $4 * 3$
   (e) $5 * 0$ (f) $0 * 5$.

2. If $a @ b = a + ab$, find
   (a) $1 @ 3$ (b) $4 @ 5$ (c) $3 @ 4$ (d) $4 @ 3$
   (e) $5 @ 4$ (f) $3 @ 1$.

3. If $a * b = \dfrac{a+b}{2}$, find

   (a) $1 * 1$ (b) $2 * 1$ (c) $1 * 2$ (d) $3 * 4$
   (e) $4 * 3$.

4. The operation $\square$ is defined by $a \square b = (a+1)(b+2)$. Show that $4 \square 5$ is $5 \times 7 = 35$. Find

   (a) $1 \square 1$ (b) $2 \square 5$ (c) $4 \square -1$ (d) $-1 \square 4$
   (e) $-1 \square 0$ (f) $0 \square -1$.
   Find

   (g) x if $7 \square x = 56$ (h) y if $6 \square y = 49$
   (i) z if $z \square 3 = 40$.

5. If $a * b = 3a - b$, solve the following equations:

   (a) $3 * x = 7$ (b) $4 * x = 7$ (c) $6 * x = 18$
   (d) $8 * x = 30$.

6. If $a @ b = a + ab$, solve the following equations:

   (a) $4 @ x = 16$ (b) $3 @ x = 18$ (c) $7 @ x = 21$
   (d) $x @ 2 = 6$.

7. If $a * b = 2a + b - 3$, find the values of

   (a) $3 * 4$ (b) $4 * 3$.
   Solve the following equations:
   (a) $3 * x = 12$ (d) $x * 4 = 7$.

8. If $a \otimes b = ab - a - b$, find

   (a) $3 \otimes 6$ (b) $4 \otimes 5$ (c) $0 \otimes 9$.
   Solve the equations
   (d) $0 \otimes x = -8$ (e) $0 \otimes x = +8$ (f) $x \otimes 3 = 7$.

9. If $a \sim b = 4a - 3b$, find the values of

   (a) $4 \sim 5$ (b) $5 \sim 4$ (c) $2 \sim -1$.
   Solve the equations
   (d) $3 \sim x = 9$ (e) $x \sim 3 = 11$ (f) $x \sim x = 6$.

10. If $a * b = a^2 - b^2$, find

    (a) $4 * 3$ (b) $5 * 2$.
    Solve the equations
    (c) $5 * x = 24$ (d) $13 * x = 25$.
    What is the value of
    (e) $5 * 5$ (f) $x * x$.

11. If $a * b = ab + a + b$, find

    (a) $3 * 5$ (b) $3 * 0$ (c) $3 * -5$.

    Solve the equations

    (d) $3 * x = 19$ (e) $3 * y = 10$ (f) $z * 3 = 0$.

12. If $x @ y = (x - y)(x + y)$, work out

    (a) $3 @ 4$ (b) $4 @ 3$ (c) $2 @ 2$ (d) $2 @ -2$.

    If $5 @ a = 0$, find two possible values of a.

LAWS OF COMBINATION

Commutative Law

An operation $*$ is *commutative* if $a * b = b * a$, that is, if for *any* two numbers, the operation gives the same answer regardless of the order of the numbers. Addition and multiplication, for example, are commutative:

$$2 + 3 = 3 + 2 = 5$$

$$2 \times 3 = 3 \times 2 = 6$$

but subtraction and division are not commutative:

$$2 - 3 = -1 \quad \text{but} \quad 3 - 2 = +1$$

$$2 \div 3 = \tfrac{2}{3} \quad \text{but} \quad 3 \div 2 = 1\tfrac{1}{2}$$

Associative Law

An operation $*$ is *associative* if $a * (b * c) = (a * b) * c$, that is if, in two applications of the operation upon *any* three numbers, it does not matter how the numbers are bracketed into pairs. Again, addition and multiplication are associative:

$$2 + (3 + 4) = (2 + 3) + 4 = 9$$

$$2 \times (3 \times 4) = (2 \times 3) \times 4 = 24$$

but subtraction is not associative,

$$2 - (3 - 4) = 2 - (-1) = 2 + 1 = 3$$

whereas $(2 - 3) - 4 = (-1) - 4 = -5$

Nor is division associative:

$$2 \div (3 \div 4) = 2 \div \tfrac{3}{4} = \tfrac{8}{3}$$

whereas $(2 \div 3) \div 4 = \tfrac{2}{3} \div 4 = \tfrac{1}{6}$

Example

$$a \oplus b = a - b + (a \times b)$$

Find whether or not the operation $\oplus$ is (a) commutative, (b) associative.

(a) If the operation $\oplus$ is commutative, $a \oplus b = b \oplus a$. Let $a = 2$ and $b = 3$:

$$2 \oplus 3 = 2 - 3 + (2 \times 3) = 5$$

$$3 \oplus 2 = 3 - 2 + (3 \times 2) = 7$$

Thus $2 \oplus 3 \neq 3 \oplus 2$ so the operation is *not* commutative.

(b) If the operation $\oplus$ is associative, $(a \oplus b) \oplus c = a \oplus (b \oplus c)$. Let $a = 2$, $b = 3$ and $c = 4$. We already know (from (a) above) that $2 \oplus 3 = 5$. Hence

$$(2 \oplus 3) \oplus 4 = 5 \oplus 4 = 5 - 4 + (5 \times 4) = 21$$

Now $\quad 3 \oplus 4 = 3 - 4 + (3 \times 4) = 11$

So $\quad 2 \oplus (3 \oplus 4) = 2 \oplus 11 = 2 - 11 + (2 \times 11) = 13$

Thus $(2 \oplus 3) \oplus 4 \neq 2 \oplus (3 \oplus 4)$ so the operation is *not* associative.

EXERCISE 8b

1. If $a @ b = a + ab$, find

   (a) $2 @ 4$ (b) $4 @ 2$ (c) $3 @ 5$ (d) $5 @ 3$.

   Is operation @ commutative?

2. If $a * b = \dfrac{a + b}{2}$, find

   (a) $2 * 4$ (b) $4 * 2$ (c) $3 * 5$ (d) $5 * 3$.

   Do your results suggest that operation $*$ is commutative?

3. The operation $\odot$ is defined by $\sqrt{a^2 + b^2}$. Find

   (a) $3 \odot 4$ (b) $4 \odot 3$ (c) $5 \odot 12$ (d) $12 \odot 5$.

   Do you think this operation is commutative?

4. If $a \square b = (a + 1)(b + 2)$, find

   (a) $4 \square 2$ (b) $2 \square 4$.

   Is this operation commutative?

5. The operation $\odot$ is defined by $a \odot b = 2a^2 - b$. Devise a simple test of your own to prove that this operation is *not* commutative.

6. If $a * b = \dfrac{a+b}{2}$, find

(a) $(2 * 4) * 1$ (b) $2 * (4 * 1)$.

Do your results suggest that operation $*$ is associative?

7. If the operation $**$ is defined by $a ** b = 4ab$ find

(a) $3 ** 4$ (b) $4 ** 5$ (c) $(3 ** 4) ** 5$
(d) $3 ** (4 ** 5)$.

Are your results to (c) and (d) the same? Does this suggest that operation $**$ is associative?

8. If $a \sim b = a + b + 2$, find

(a) $5 \sim 2$ (b) $2 \sim 3$ (c) $(5 \sim 2) \sim 3$
(d) $5 \sim (2 \sim 3)$.

Do you think that operation $\sim$ is associative?

9. The operation $\triangle$ is defined by the rule $a \triangle b = a + b - 5$. Find

(a) $3 \triangle 4$ (b) $4 \triangle 5$ (c) $(3 \triangle 4) \triangle 5$
(d) $3 \triangle (4 \triangle 5)$.

Do you think this operation is associative?

10. If $a \oplus b = a^2 + 2a - b$, find

(a) $(1 \oplus 2) \oplus 3$ (b) $1 \oplus (2 \oplus 3)$.

Is this operation associative?

11. If $a \odot b = \sqrt{a^2 + b^2}$, find

(a) $(3 \odot 4) \odot 12$ (b) $3 \odot (4 \odot 12)$.

Is this operation associative?

12. Use the numbers 2, 3 and 4 to test for yourself whether or not the operation @ defined by the rule $a @ b = a + ab$ obeys the associative law.

IDENTITY

The *identity element, i*, under an operation $*$ is the element which combines with any other number to leave that number unaltered, that is

$$i * a = a * i = a$$

Under addition, the identity element is zero:

$$a + 0 = 0 + a = a$$

Under multiplication, the identity element is 1:

$$a \times 1 = 1 \times a = a$$

(*Note* Some operations do not have an identity element.)

Example

$$a \triangle b = a + b - 5$$

Find the identity element under the operation $\triangle$.

Let the identity element be i, then:

$$a \triangle i = a \qquad \text{by definition of the identity element.}$$

But also $\quad a \triangle i = a + i - 5$

So $\qquad a + i - 5 = a$

Hence $\qquad i = 5$

Check $\ 2 \triangle 5 = 2 + 5 - 5 = 2 \qquad$ Both 2 and 3 have been left unaltered

$\qquad\qquad 5 \triangle 3 = 5 + 3 - 5 = 3 \qquad$ when combined with 5 under operation $\triangle$.

INVERSE

If a given operation has an identity element, then the *inverse* of a number x is written x^{-1} and combines with x to give the identity:

$$x * x^{-1} = i$$

Under addition, for example, the inverse of 2 is -2 as $2 + (-2) = 0$ and 0 is the identity element under addition. Similarly the inverse of 3 is -3, the inverse of 4 is -4, and so on.

Under multiplication, which has identity 1, the inverse of 2 is $\frac{1}{2}$ since $2 \times \frac{1}{2} = 1$. Similarly, the inverse of 3 is $\frac{1}{3}$ since $3 \times \frac{1}{3} = 1$, the inverse of 4 is $\frac{1}{4}$, and so on.

There will be different inverses for different numbers under different operations; some may not have an inverse; others may be their own inverse. If no identity element exists under an operation then the inverse of an element does not exist either.

Example

$$a \triangle b = a + b - 5$$

Under the operation $\triangle$ the identity element is 5 (see above). Find the inverse of (a) 3 (b) 0.

(a) The inverse of 3 combines with 3 under $\triangle$ to give the identity element, 5. If the inverse of 3 is x, then

$$3 \triangle x = 5$$

So $\qquad 3 + x - 5 = 5$

or $\qquad x = 5 + 5 - 3$

$$= 7$$

Check $3 \triangle 7 = 3 + 7 - 5 = 5$.

(b) Similarly, the inverse of 0 under $\triangle$ combines with 0 to give 5. If we call this inverse y, then

$$0 \triangle y = 5$$

So $\qquad 0 + y - 5 = 5$

giving $\qquad\qquad y = 10$

Check $0 \triangle 10 = 0 + 10 - 5 = 5$.

EXERCISE 8c

1. (a) If $a * b = a + b - 3$, find the values of
   (i) $4 * 3$ (ii) $6 * 3$ (iii) $7 * 3$ (iv) $\frac{1}{2} * 3$ (v) $-1 * 3$
   (vi) $x * 3$.
   (b) State the identity element for operation $*$.
   (c) Work out $5 * 1$. What is the inverse of 5 under the operation $*$?
   (d) Solve the equation $4 * y = 3$ to find the inverse of 4.
   (e) Solve the equation $8 * z = 3$ to find the inverse of 8.

2. If $a \square b = a + b - 2$, find the values of
   (a) $5 \square 2$ (b) $7 \square 2$ (c) $-1 \square 2$.
   State the identity element for operation $\square$.
   Solve the equations
   (d) $4 \square x = 2$ (e) $y \square 1 = 2$ (f) $z \square 9 = 2$.
   What are the inverses of 4, 1 and 9 under this operation?

3. The operation $\triangle$ is defined by $a \triangle b = \frac{1}{2}ab$. Work out the values of
   (a) $5 \triangle 1$ (b) $5 \triangle 2$ (c) $5 \triangle 4$.
   (d) State the identity element under the operation $\triangle$.
   (e) Solve the equation $6 \triangle x = 2$. What is the inverse of 6?
   (f) Solve the equation $y \triangle 8 = 2$. What is the inverse of 8?

4. Find the identity element i under operation @ where
   $x @ y = x + y + 4$ by solving the equation $x @ i = x$.

5. Solve the equation $a \odot i = a$ to find the identity element i under the operation $\odot$ where $a \odot b = a + b - 11$.

6. The operation $*$ is defined by $a * b = 4ab$.

   (a) By solving the equation $x * i = x$, prove that i, the identity element, is $\frac{1}{4}$.

   (b) Solve the equation $2 * y = \frac{1}{4}$ to show that the inverse of 2 is $\frac{1}{32}$.

   (c) Show that the inverse of 3 is $\frac{1}{48}$. Can you find the inverse of 5?

7. Show that 4 is the identity element under the operation @, where $a @ b = a + b - 4$. What are the inverses of

   (a) 4   (b) 0   (c) 2   (d) 3   (e) 10.

8. If $x \otimes y = 2 + (x - 2)(y - 2)$, show that the identity element under the operation $\otimes$ is 3. Find the inverses of

   (a) 3   (b) 1   (c) 4   (d) 5   (e) 6.

9. If $a ** b = \sqrt{a^2 + b^2}$, show that the identity element under $**$ is 0. Is it possible to find an inverse for 4 under operation $**$?

10. Show that, if $a * b = a^2 + b^2$, then there is no identity element under $*$.

11. Find the identity element for the operation $\odot$ where $x \odot y = x + xy + y$. Find the inverse of

    (a) 1   (b) 4.

    Can you find an inverse for -1?

12. (a) Multiply the matrices $\begin{pmatrix} 3 & 4 \\ 4 & 5 \end{pmatrix}\begin{pmatrix} 1 & 0 \\ 0 & 1 \end{pmatrix}$. Why is $\begin{pmatrix} 1 & 0 \\ 0 & 1 \end{pmatrix}$

    known as the *identity matrix*?

    (b) Multiply the two matrices $\begin{pmatrix} 2 & 3 \\ 3 & 5 \end{pmatrix}\begin{pmatrix} 5 & -3 \\ -3 & 2 \end{pmatrix}$. Why is

    $\begin{pmatrix} 5 & -3 \\ -3 & 2 \end{pmatrix}$ known as the *inverse of* $\begin{pmatrix} 2 & 3 \\ 3 & 5 \end{pmatrix}$?

COMBINATION TABLES

To show how any pair of numbers drawn from a set combine under a given operation, it is often helpful to draw up a *combination table*. A combination table is exactly like a multiplication table except, of course, the operation need not be multiplication. Combination tables may be used to find the identity element and inverses without complicated algebra.

Example Numbers drawn from the set $\{1, 2, 3, 4\}$ are multiplied together under *modulo* 5, that is, two numbers are multiplied together, the result divided by 5, and only the remainder recorded. Thus $3 \times 4 = 12 = 2 \pmod{5}$ since 12 divided by 5 gives a remainder 2.

The combination table for the set $\{1, 2, 3, 4\}$ under multiplication (mod. 5) is:

$\times$ (mod. 5)	1	2	3	4
1	1	2	3	4
2	2	4	1	3
3	3	1	4	2
4	4	3	2	1

(You are advised to check this for yourself so that you are sure you understand the operation.)

From the combination table we can see at once that 1 is the identity element under this operation, since it operates with $1, 2, 3$ and 4 to give, in turn, $1, 2, 3$ and 4. Reading across the 2 line, we can see that the inverse of 2 is 3 since the identity element, 1, appears under column 3. Similarly, the inverse of 1 is 1; the inverse of 3 is 2 and the inverse of 4 is 4.

Notice that the table uses only the numbers $1, 2, 3$ and 4, i.e. the numbers of the original set and no others. The set $\{1, 2, 3, 4\}$ is said to be *closed* under multiplication in modulo 5.

EXERCISE 8d

1. Numbers drawn from the set $\{1, 2, 3, 4, 5\}$ are multiplied in modulo 6; that is, two numbers are multiplied and the result is divided by 6, only the remainder being recorded. For example, $4 \times 5 = 20 = 2 \pmod{6}$.

$\times$ (mod. 6)	1	2	3	4	5
1	1	2	.	.	.
2	2	4	0	2	4
3	.	0	3	.	.
4	.	.	.	4	.
5	.	.	.	.	1

The partially finished combination table is shown. Copy and complete the table and use it to answer the following questions.

(a) Is the set closed under this operation?

(b) What is the identity element under this operation? What are the inverses of
   (i) 5   (ii) 1   (iii) 3.

(c) If $x * 2 = 2$, where $*$ represents this operation, what are the two possible values of x?

2. Copy and complete the combination table for addition in modulo 9 on the set $\{0, 3, 6\}$.

$+(\text{mod. } 9)$	0	3	6
0	0	·	·
3	·	·	0
6	·	·	·

(a) What is the identity element?

(b) What is the inverse of each element?

(c) Is the set closed under this operation?

3. Repeat Question 2 for the set $\{0, 3, 6, 7\}$.

4. Draw up a combination table for multiplication in modulo 7 for the set $\{1, 2, 3, 4, 5, 6\}$. Is the set closed under this operation? What is the identity element? Find the inverses of
   (a) 2   (b) 3   (c) 5.

Use your table to solve the following equations in which $*$ represents this operation:
   (d) $4 * x = 5$ (e) $y * 3 = 4$.

5. Draw up a combination table for multiplication in modulo 4 for the set $1, 2, 3$. What is the identity element? What are the inverses of
   (a) 1   (b) 3.

Explain why the set is *not* closed under this operation and why there is no inverse for 2.

MISCELLANEOUS EXERCISE 8

1. If $a * b = 2a^2 + ab$,
   (a) calculate $3 * 2$

119

(b) write down an expression for $b * a$.

(c) If $3 * x = 0$, calculate x. (SUJB)

2. The operation $*$ is defined by $a * b = 2a^2 - 3b$.

   (a) Calculate $3 * 2$.

   (b) Write down an algebraic expression for $b * a$.

   (c) If $a * a = a$, find possible values of a. (SUJB)

3. The operation @ is defined by $a @ b = \dfrac{1}{a} + \dfrac{1}{b}$.

   Find the values of

   (a) $2 @ 4$ (b) $1 @ 5$.

   Solve the equations

   (c) $1 @ x = 1\frac{1}{3}$ (d) $y @ 2 = \frac{5}{8}$.

   Find the values of

   (e) $2 @ (4 @ 3)$ (f) $(2 @ 4) @ 3$.

   What does this suggest about the operation?

4. If operation $\odot$ is defined by $a \odot b = 2a^2 - b$, find

   (a) $2 \odot 3$ (b) $8 \odot 3$ (c) $5 \odot 4$ (d) $4 \odot 9$

   (e) $2 \odot 6$ (f) $4 \odot 4$.

   Find

   (g) x if $3 \odot x = 14$ (h) y if $y \odot 3 = 29$

   (i) z if $z \odot 5 = -3$.

5. The operation $\oplus$ is defined by $a \oplus b = a^2 + 2a - b$. Find

   (a) $7 \oplus 6$ (b) $2 \oplus -1$ (c) $-3 \oplus 1$ (d) $-2 \oplus -3$

   (e) $6 \oplus -2$ (f) $-1 \oplus -1$.

   (g) Find x if $4 \oplus x = 20$.

   (h) Find two possible values of y if $y \oplus 0 = 0$.

   (i) Find two possible values of z if $z \oplus 3 = 0$.

6. The operation $*$ is defined on the set of positive rational numbers by $a * b = \dfrac{ab}{a + b}$.

   (a) Express as fractions in their simplest form

       (i) $2 * 3$ (ii) $(3 * 4) * 5$ (iii) $\frac{1}{2} * \frac{1}{4}$.

   (b) Express, as simply as possible, in terms of x
       (i) $x * x$ (ii) $(x * x) * (x * x)$.

   (c) Solve the equation $7 * x = 2$. (JMB)

7. S is the set of all rational numbers (positive and negative, including zero). An operation $*$ is defined by
$$x * y = x + y - xy \quad \text{for} \quad x, y \in S$$
   (a) Evaluate $2 * 3$.
   (b) Show that the identity element for $*$ is 0.
   (c) Find inverses of $2, 3$ and 4.
   (d) If $z = x * y$, find a formula for y in terms of x and z.
   (e) State the inverse of y.   (LU)

8. An operation $\otimes$ is defined on the set of natural numbers as follows: $a \otimes b$ is the remainder when the product of a and b is divided by 10. For example $4 \times 8 = 32$, so $4 \otimes 8 = 2$.
   (a) Copy and complete the operation table shown, adding a fourth element to obtain a set P that is closed under this operation.

$\otimes$	2	4	8	·
2	4	·	·	·
4	·	·	2	·
8	·	2	·	·
·	·	·	·	·

   (b) For the set P under this operation
      (i) state the identity element,   (ii) find the inverse of 2.
           (O & C)

9. The operation $*$ is defined on the set $\{1, 2, 3, 4, 0\}$ as follows: the value of $a * b$ is the remainder when $a^2 + b^2$ is divided by 5. For example, to find $2 * 3$, first find $2^2 + 3^2$ $(= 13)$, then find the remainder when 13 is divided by 5 (i.e. 3). So $2 * 3 = 3$.
   (a) State whether the operation $*$ is commutative.
   (b) Copy and complete the table:

$*$	1	2	3	4	0
1	2	0	·	·	1
2	0	·	3	·	4
3	·	·	·	·	·
4	·	·	·	·	·
0	1	4	·	·	·

(c) Find the solution sets of the equations

(i) $4 * x = 1$, (ii) $2 * y = 3$, (iii) $1 * z = 4$.

(d) The operation $*$ is not associative on this set. Illustrate this fact by suitable calculations involving elements from the set. (O & C)

10. (a) $P = \begin{pmatrix} 1 & 2 \\ -1 & -1 \end{pmatrix}$; $I = \begin{pmatrix} 1 & 0 \\ 0 & 1 \end{pmatrix}$; $Q = P^2$; R is the inverse of P.

Find the matrices Q and R and show that $PQ = R$. Hence copy and complete the table.

×	I	P	Q	R
I	.	.	.	.
P	.	.	.	.
Q	.	.	.	.
R	.	.	.	.

(b) Write out the table for $\{1, 3, 7, 9\}$ under multiplication modulo 10, with the border elements of the table so arranged that the pattern of the table corresponds exactly with the pattern of the table in (a). (O & C)

9 FUNCTIONS AND MAPPINGS

FUNCTIONS

The relationship between the members of one set, called the *domain*, and those of another, called the *co-domain* or the *range*, can be shown on an *arrow diagram*. For example, Fig. 9.1 links members of the set $\{0, 1, 2\}$ with their *images* after squaring, in the set $\{0, 1, 2, 3, 4, 5\}$.

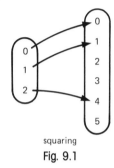

squaring
Fig. 9.1

The arrow diagram illustrates the *mapping* $x \to x^2$. Other algebraic processes or *functions* can be defined as mappings. For example,

$$f: x \to 2x + 3$$
$$f: x \to y, \quad y = 2x + 3$$

both describe the operation (*the function f*) such that a number, x, is doubled and then 3 added. A third (and very useful) way of writing this is

$$f(x) = 2x + 3$$

Under this function, 1 is mapped on to 5 (as $2 \times 1 + 3 = 5$); a short way of writing this is $f(1) = 5$. Similarly, 2 is mapped on to 7 (as $2 \times 2 + 3 = 7$); we might write $f(2) = 7$. 3 is mapped on to 9, i.e. $f(3) = 9$, and so on (Fig. 9.2).

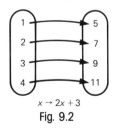

$x \to 2x + 3$
Fig. 9.2

Manipulating functions is exactly like rearranging equations.

123

Example $f(x) = 3 + x$ and $g(x) = 5 - x$. Find x if

    (a) $f(x) = 6$ (b) $f(x) = g(x)$.

    (a) $f(x) = 6$ implies $3 + x = 6$. Subtracting 3 from both sides gives $x = 3$.

    (b) $f(x) = g(x)$ implies

$$3 + x = 5 - x$$

    Rearranging: $x + x = 5 - 3$

$$2x = 2$$

$$x = 1$$

EXERCISE 9a

1. Find the images of the following, using the mapping $x \rightarrow 2x$:
   (a) 1   (b) 3   (c) 4   (d) $\frac{1}{3}$ (e) 0
   (f) -5 (g) $-\frac{1}{4}$.

2. Find the images of the following under the mapping $x \rightarrow 4x + 3$:
   (a) 0   (b) 4   (c) -2 (d) $\frac{1}{2}$ (e) $-\frac{1}{2}$
   (f) $\frac{3}{4}$ (g) $-\frac{3}{4}$.

3. Copy and complete the following arrow graphs:

  (a)   (b)   (c)

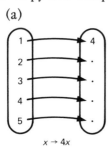 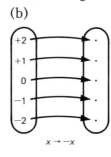 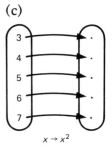

  (d)   (e)   (f)

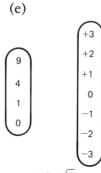 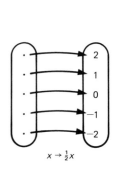

4. Draw arrow graphs to show the images of each member of the given domain under the given function.

   (a) $f: x \rightarrow 3x + 1$ $\{-2, -1, 0, +1, +2\}$

   (b) $g: x \rightarrow y, \ y = 1 - \frac{1}{2}x$ $\{-4, -2, 0, +2, +4\}$

   (c) $h(x) = 3x + 2$ $\{-2, -1, 0, +1, +2\}$

   (d) $j(x) = 10 - \sqrt{x}$ $\{0, 1, 4, 9, 16\}$.

5. If the function g is defined by $g: x \rightarrow y, \ y = \dfrac{1}{x}$, what are the images of

   (a) 2   (b) 3   (c) 1   (d) -2 (e) -1

   (f) $\frac{1}{2}$ (g) $\frac{1}{3}$ (h) $\frac{1}{4}$.

6. The function f is defined by $f(x) = 2x^2 + 4$. Find

   (a) $f(1)$ (b) $f(2)$ (c) $f(-1)$ (d) $f(-2)$ (e) $f(-3)$

   (f) $f(\frac{1}{2})$.

7. If $f: x \rightarrow 3x - 1$, solve the following equations:

   (a) $f(x) = 5$ (b) $f(x) = 14$ (c) $f(x) = -4$

   (d) $f(x) = 0$ (e) $f(x) = \frac{1}{2}$.

8. If $f: x \rightarrow \frac{1}{2}x$ and $g: x \rightarrow 2x + 3$, solve the following:

   (a) $f(x) = 0$ (b) $g(x) = 0$ (c) $f(x) = -2$

   (d) $g(x) = -2$ (e) $f(x) = g(2)$ (f) $f(x) = g(5)$

   (g) $f(2) = g(x)$ (h) $f(5) = g(x)$ (i) $f(-1) = g(x)$.

9. Solve the following equations, given that $f: x \rightarrow x - 1$ and $g: x \rightarrow 2x + 2$:

   (a) $f(x) = 3$ (b) $g(x) = 3$ (c) $f(x) = -1$

   (d) $g(x) = -1$ (e) $f(x) = g(1)$ (f) $f(x) = g(0)$

   (g) $g(x) = f(-1)$ (h) $g(x) = f(x)$.

10. If $f: x \rightarrow 5 - 2x$ and $g: x \rightarrow 3x$, solve the following equations:

   (a) $f(x) = g(0)$ (b) $g(x) = f(0)$ (c) $f(-1) = g(x)$

   (d) $f(x) = g(x)$.

11. (a) If $f(x) = x^2$ and $g(x) = (x + 1)^2$, solve the equation $f(x) = g(x)$.

   (b) If $h: x \rightarrow x^2$ and $j: x \rightarrow 2x^2 - 3$, find, to two decimal places, the solutions to the equation $h(x) = j(x)$.

12. If $f(x) = (x - 1)^2$ and $g(x) = (2x - 1)^2$, find the solution set to the equations

   (a) $f(x) = 9$ (b) $g(x) = x$ (c) $f(x) = g(x)$.

COMPOUND FUNCTIONS

If *two* functions act together, they are said to form a *compound* or *composite* function.

Example Two functions are defined as follows:

$$f: x \rightarrow 2x$$

$$g: x \rightarrow x - 2$$

Find the image of 3 when (a) f acts first, followed by g, (b) g acts first, followed by f.

(a) The image of 3 under the function f is

$$f(3) = 2 \times 3 = 6$$

Now the image of 6 under g is

$$g(6) = 6 - 2 = 4$$

In summary

Notice that we could write this process as $g[f(3)]$ or $gf(3)$. Thus gf represents the function f *followed by* g. (This is often a source of great confusion, so take careful note. You may find it helpful to draw square brackets of your own whenever you are asked to evaluate a compound function, i.e. $gf(x)$ becomes $g[f(x)]$.

(b) If g acts first upon 3, then

$$g(3) = 3 - 2 = 1$$

Then, in turn $\qquad f(1) = 2 \times 1 = 2$

In summary

$$\begin{array}{ccc} & g & f \\ 3 & \longrightarrow 1 & \longrightarrow 2 \end{array}$$

Clearly, the order in which the functions operate is crucial. This time we have found the composite function $f[g(3)]$ or $fg(3)$, where fg represents the function g *followed by* f.

Algebraically, the effect of the compound function gf acting on x is

$$gf(x) = g[f(x)] = g[2x] = 2x - 2$$

and the effect of fg is

$$fg(x) = f[g(x)] = f[x-2] = 2(x-2) = 2x-4$$

Example If $f(x) = x^2$ and $g(x) = x - 2$, find the following:

(a) $gf(3) = g[f(3)] = g(9) = 9 - 2 = 7$

(b) $fg(3) = f[g(3)] = f(1) = 1^2 = 1$

(c) $gf(x) = g[f(x)] = g(x^2) = x^2 - 2$

(d) $fg(x) = f[g(x)] = f(x-2) = (x-2)^2$.

EXERCISE 9b

1. If $f(x) = 5x$ and $g(x) = 2x + 1$, find

    (a) $f(1)$ (b) $g(1)$ (c) $f(2)$ (d) $g(2)$

    (e) $g[f(1)]$ (f) $f[g(1)]$ (g) $g[f(2)]$ (h) $f[g(2)]$.

2. If $f(x) = \dfrac{1}{x}$ and $g(x) = x^2$, find

    (a) $f(2)$ (b) $g(2)$ (c) $f(3)$ (d) $g(3)$

    (e) $f[g(2)]$ (f) $f[g(3)]$ (g) $g[f(2)]$ (h) $g[f(3)]$.

3. Two functions are defined as $f: x \rightarrow 3x$ and $g: x \rightarrow -1$. Find

    (a) $f(3)$ (b) $g(3)$ (c) $f(2)$ (d) $g(9)$

    (e) $g[f(3)]$ (f) $f[g(3)]$.

    Show that the composite function $gf(x) = 3x - 1$.

    Find a similar algebraic expression for the composite function $fg(x)$.

4. Two functions are defined as follows: $h: x \rightarrow 4x$ and $j: x \rightarrow x + 2$. Find

    (a) $h(1)$ (b) $j(1)$ (c) $hj(1)$ (d) $jh(1)$.

    Show that the composite function $hj(x) = 4x + 8$, and find $jh(x)$.

5. Three functions are $f: x \rightarrow 2x,$ $g: x \rightarrow -x$ and $h: x \rightarrow x + 4$. Find

    (a) $fg(1)$ (b) $gf(1)$ (c) $fh(1)$ (d) $hf(1)$

    (e) $gh(1)$ (f) $hg(1)$.

    Show that $fg(x) = gf(x) = -2x$.

6. Four functions are $f: x \rightarrow x^2,$ $g: x \rightarrow x - 2,$ $h: x \rightarrow \sqrt{x},$ and $j: x \rightarrow x + 2$. Find

    (a) $fg(2)$ (b) $gf(2)$ (c) $ff(2)$ (d) $fh(4)$

    (e) $fh(x)$ (f) $fg(x)$.

7. If $f: x \rightarrow 2x + 1$ and $g: x \rightarrow \frac{1}{2}(x-1)$, find

   (a) $fg(2)$ (b) $gf(4)$.

   Show that $fg: x \rightarrow x$.

8. If $f: x \rightarrow x^2$, $g: x \rightarrow x - 3$ and $h: x \rightarrow \frac{1}{2}x$, find algebraic expressions for

   (a) fg (b) gf (c) fh (d) hf

   (e) gh (f) hg.

9. Two functions are defined by $f: x \rightarrow x^3$ and $g: x \rightarrow x^4$. Find algebraic definitions for the composite functions

   (a) fg (b) gf.

   Hence show that $fg(x) = gf(x)$.

10. If $f: x \rightarrow 4x$ and $g: x \rightarrow 5x$, show that $fg(x) = gf(x)$.

INVERSE FUNCTIONS

Suppose a function f maps x on to a value y. Then the *inverse function*, f^{-1}, will reverse the process, that is, map the value y back on to x.

By definition, the composite function $f^{-1}f$ maps x back on to itself, so $f^{-1}f$ is an *identity function*, $f^{-1}f: x \rightarrow x$.

Finding the inverse of a function depends upon tracing it back step by step.

Examples (*i*)   Find the inverse of $f: x \rightarrow 2x + 3$.

The upper flow diagram shows each stage of the function f. First, multiply by 2 to get $2x$, then add three. Working the process in reverse, that is starting from the right-hand side and working leftwards doing the exact opposite at each stage, we first subtract 3 and then halve the result. Hence

$$f^{-1}: x \rightarrow \tfrac{1}{2}(x - 3)$$

Check $f(4) = 2 \times 4 + 3 = 11,$

$$f^{-1}(11) = \tfrac{1}{2}(11 - 3)$$
$$= 4.$$

(*ii*) Find the inverse of $g: x \rightarrow \dfrac{2x-3}{5}$.

$$g: \xrightarrow{x} \boxed{\times 2} \xrightarrow{2x} \boxed{-3} \xrightarrow{2x-3} \boxed{\div 5} \xrightarrow{\quad} \dfrac{2x-3}{5}$$

$$\dfrac{5x+3}{2} \xleftarrow{\quad} \boxed{\div 2} \xleftarrow{5x+3} \boxed{+3} \xleftarrow{5x} \boxed{\times 5} \xleftarrow{x} : g^{-1}$$

Thus $g^{-1}: x \rightarrow \dfrac{5x+3}{2}$.

Check $g(4) = \dfrac{2 \times 4 - 3}{5} = \dfrac{8-3}{5} = \dfrac{5}{5} = 1$

$g^{-1}(1) = \dfrac{5 \times 1 + 3}{2} = \dfrac{8}{2} = 4$

EXERCISE 9c

1. Complete the following flow diagram to find the inverse of the function, $f: x \rightarrow 2x + 4$

$$f: \xrightarrow{x} \boxed{\times 2} \xrightarrow{2x} \boxed{+4} \xrightarrow{\quad} \dots$$

$$\dots \xleftarrow{\quad} \boxed{\dots} \xleftarrow{\dots} \boxed{-4} \xleftarrow{x} : f^{-1}$$

2. The flow charts illustrate the functions $f: x \rightarrow \dfrac{x}{3} - 1$ and $g: x \rightarrow \dfrac{3x+2}{4}$. Trace them back to find f^{-1} and g^{-1}.

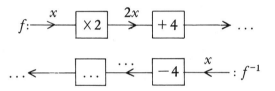

(a) $f: \xrightarrow{x} \boxed{\div 3} \xrightarrow{x/3} \boxed{-1} \xrightarrow{\quad} \dfrac{x}{3} - 1$

(b) $g: \xrightarrow{x} \boxed{\times 3} \xrightarrow{3x} \boxed{+2} \xrightarrow{3x+2} \boxed{\div 4} \xrightarrow{\quad} \dfrac{3x+2}{4}$

Find the inverses of the following functions defining them in the style $f: x \rightarrow 2x$. In each case, find (a) $f(4)$ and (b) $f^{-1}[f(4)]$.

3. $f: x \rightarrow 2x$ 4. $f: x \rightarrow 4x$

5. $f: x \rightarrow 5x + 6$ 6. $f: x \rightarrow 3x + 5$

7. $f: x \rightarrow 6x - 2$ 8. $f: x \rightarrow \frac{1}{2}x + 1$

9. $f: x \to \frac{1}{4}x - 2$

10. $f: x \to \frac{x+2}{3}$

11. $f: x \to \frac{x-5}{2}$

12. $f: x \to \frac{x-4}{8}$

13. $f: x \to \frac{1}{x}$

14. $f: x \to \frac{4}{x}$

15. $f: x \to -x$

16. $f: x \to x^2 - 1$

17. $f: x \to 2x^2 + 1$

18. $f: x \to 3x^2 + 2$

19. $f: x \to (x-1)^2$

20. $f: x \to \sqrt{2x+1}$.

21. If $g: x \to 3x + 1$, find
   (a) g^{-1} (b) $g(2)$ (c) $g^{-1}(7)$

22. If $h: x \to 5 - 2x$, find
   (a) h^{-1} (b) $h(-1)$ (c) $h^{-1}(7)$.

23. If $j: x \to (1 - \frac{1}{3}x)$, find
   (a) j^{-1} (b) $j(6)$ (c) $j^{-1}(-1)$.

24. If $s: x \to \frac{1}{2}(1 - x)$, find
   (a) s^{-1} (b) $s^{-1}(\frac{1}{4})$ (c) $s(\frac{1}{2})$.

25. If $f: x \to \frac{1}{4}(1 - \frac{1}{2}x)$, find
   (a) f^{-1} (b) $f^{-1}(\frac{-1}{8})$ (c) $f(3)$.

MISCELLANEOUS EXERCISE 9

1. If $x \in \{$positive odd numbers$\}$, describe the image set of x under the following functions:
   (a) $f: x \to -x$ (b) $g: x \to 2x$ (c) $h: x \to x + 1$.

2. If $x \in \{$negative integers$\}$, describe the image set of x under the following functions:
   (a) $f: x \to -x$ (b) $g: x \to x^2$ (c) $h: x \to \frac{x}{x-1}$.

3. $f(x) = 2x; \quad g(x) = x + 2; \quad h(x) = x^2$.
   Find the solution sets to the following equations:
   (a) $f(x) = \frac{1}{2}$ (b) $g(x) = -\frac{1}{2}$ (c) $f(x) = x$
   (d) $g(x) = x$ (e) $f(x) = g(x)$ (f) $h(x) = x$
   (g) $h(x) = f(x)$ (h) $h(x) = g(x)$.

4. Functions f and g are defined for all values of x by
$$f: x \rightarrow (x-2)^2$$
$$g: x \rightarrow 5(x-2)$$
(a) Find the values of x for which $f(x) = \frac{1}{9}$.

(b) Factorise $(x-2)^2 - 5(x-2)$. Hence, or otherwise, find the values of x for which $f(x) = g(x)$.

(c) Solve the equation $f(x) = 2x$, giving your answers correct to 2 decimal places. (AEB '82)

5. $f(x)$ denotes the remainder when an integer x is divided by 10. Given that $x > 10$, find a possible value of x in each of the following cases.

(a) $f(x) = 4$ (b) $2f(x) = f(x)$ (c) $f(x^2) > 2 + f(x)$.
(C)

6. A function S is defined on two-digit numbers as the sum of the digits of the number. For example $S(26) = 2 + 6 = 8$; $S(97) = 9 + 7 = 16$. Find

(a) $S(22)$ (b) $S(45)$ (c) $S(56)$.

Given that $x < 20$, find possible values of x in the following cases:

(d) $S(x) = 3$ (e) $S(x) = 4x$ (f) $S(x) = \frac{1}{2}x$.

7. The function f is defined as follows for any positive integer n:
$$\text{if } n \text{ is even, } f(n) = \tfrac{1}{2}n$$
$$\text{if } n \text{ is odd, } f(n) = n + 1$$
(a) Write down the values of f(9), ff(9) and fff(9).

(b) Find the value of n for which $f(n) = 7$, and two values of n for which $f(n) = 8$.

(c) Name the set of values of n for which $f^{-1}(n)$ has two values, and the set for which it has only one value.

(d) Explain why, for any value of n except 1 or 2, $ff(n) < n$.

(e) A computer is programmed so that when any positive integer n is set into it, it finds and prints f(n), then sets f(n) into itself, finds and prints ff(n), then sets ff(n) into itself, and so on indefinitely. Show that if $n = 9$ the computer will eventually print 2, and describe what happens after that. (LU)

8. $f: x \rightarrow 2x + 1$. Given that two simple functions, h and g, are equivalent to f, i.e. $f(x) = hg(x)$, suggest definitions of h and g.

131

9. Two functions are defined by
$$f: x \rightarrow 4-x^2 \quad \text{and} \quad g: x \rightarrow (4-x)^2.$$

(a) Find $f(2)$ and $g(2)$ and hence show that $f(x) \neq g(x)$.

(b) If h and i are two (simple) functions such that $f(x) = hi(x)$, which is first to act on x, h or i?

(c) Define the functions h and i algebraically.

(d) Suggest a composite function, in terms of h and i, equivalent to g.

10. (a) If $f: x \rightarrow 2x-1$ show that $f^{-1}: x \rightarrow \frac{1}{2}(x+1)$.

(b) Find, expressed in a similar fashion, g^{-1} if $g: x \rightarrow 3x$.

(c) Find the composite functions
   (i) $f^{-1}g^{-1}$ (ii) gf (iii) $(gf)^{-1}$.

What can you say about $f^{-1}g^{-1}$ and $(gf)^{-1}$?

10 STRAIGHT LINE GRAPHS

PLOTTING A LINE

Frequently, the relationship between two quantities is shown on a graph. Points on a graph have *coordinates* (x, y) where x measures the distance along the horizontal axis and y measures the distance up the vertical axis (Fig. 10.1). The point $(0, 0)$ is called the *origin*.

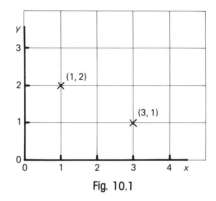

Fig. 10.1

If a series of points are plotted so that their y-coordinates are related to their x-coordinates according to some function, then they will trace out a path (or *locus*).

Example Draw the graph of $y = 3x + 4$ (for $0 \leqslant x \leqslant 4$).

Taking a series of values for x, we can find a number of coordinates by working out (from the relationship $y = 3x + 4$) a series of related values for y:

x	0	1	2	3	4
$y = 3x + 4$	4	7	10	13	16

Figure 10.2 shows the points $(0, 4)$, $(1, 7)$, $(2, 10)$, $(3, 13)$ and $(4, 16)$. The points have been plotted carefully and joined up. Clearly they lie on a straight line.

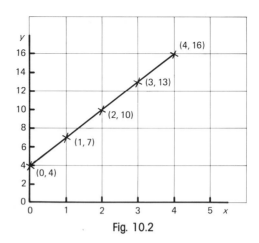

Fig. 10.2

Every point on the line has coordinates that satisfy the relationship $y = 3x + 4$. For example, $(1\frac{1}{2}, 8\frac{1}{2})$ lies on the line and $8\frac{1}{2} = (3 \times 1\frac{1}{2}) + 4$.

We can use the graph to read off values of x and y that are associated with each other. For example, if $x = 2\frac{1}{2}$, we can see from the graph (Fig. 10.3) that $y = 11\frac{1}{2}$; equally if $y = 14$, we can see that $x = 3\frac{1}{3}$.

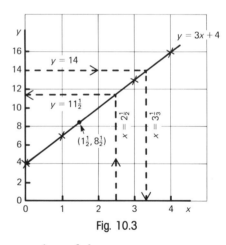

Fig. 10.3

In general, any equation of the sort

$$y = mx + c$$

(or any equation that can be rearranged into this form) can be represented on a graph by a straight line. Moreover, a line is fully defined by *two points*; so we need only find *two* pairs of coordinates to draw the graph of a line. It is simplest to find the y value associated with $x = 0$ and the x value associated with $y = 0$. It is sensible to find a third point as a check, but it is a waste of time and effort to find more than three points.

Example On the same diagram, draw graphs of the lines

$$2x + y = 8$$

$$3x - y = 7$$

(These both represent lines since they both may be rearranged to the form $y = mx + c$, i.e. $y = -2x + 8$ and $y = 3x - 7$.)

$2x + y = 8$. At $x = 0$, $y = 8$ and at $y = 0$, $2x = 8$, hence $x = 4$. Also, at $x = 1$, $y = 6$. We could tabulate this:

x	y
0	8
4	0
1	6

$3x - y = 7$. Since the results are fairly simple, we could go directly to the table:

x	y
0	-7
$\frac{7}{3}$	0
1	-4

The two lines are plotted in Fig. 10.4.

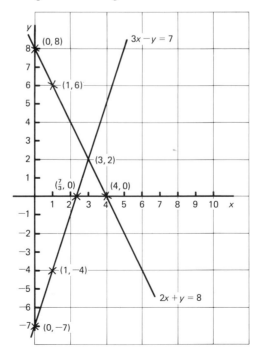

Fig. 10.4

135

Notice that the two lines meet at the point $(3, 2)$. This is the solution to the pair of simultaneous equations

$$2x + y = 8$$
$$3x - y = 7$$

(see page 91).

EXERCISE 10a

1. Plot the points $(0, 1)$, $(1, 3)$, $(2, 5)$, $(3, 7)$. Join up the points. What do you notice? Is the point $(-1, -1)$ on your line? Is the point $(1\frac{1}{2}, 3)$ on your line?

2. Plot the following points on the same graph as you used in Question 1: $(1, 3)$, $(0, 4)$, $(5, -1)$, $(-1, 5)$, $(4, 4)$, $(2, 2)$. Join them up to form a straight line. Which point does *not* lie on the line?

3. Complete the following table:

x	0	1	2	3	4	5	6	7	8
$y = 2x + 1$	1	3	5	...	...	...	...	...	...

Plot the points $(0, 1)$, $(1, 3)$, $(2, 5)$, $(3, ...)$, etc. on a graph and show that they lie on a straight line. Do you need to find so many points to plot the graph? How many do you need?

4. Complete the following tables and plot the lines on *one* graph:

   (a) $y = 5 - x$ (b) $y = x + 3$ (c) $y = x - 1$

x	y
0	5
	0
1	

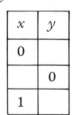

x	y
0	
	0
1	

x	y
2	

What can you say about lines (a) and (b)? Where do they intersect?

What can you say about lines (b) and (c)? Where do they intersect?

5. Which of the following equations would be represented by straight line graphs?

   (a) $y = 3x + 8$ (b) $y = 4x - 5$ (c) $y = 2x$
   (d) $y = 5 - 2x$ (e) $y = x^3$ (f) $y = x^2 + 2x + 1$
   (g) $5x + 4y = 6$ (h) $y = 4$.

6. Complete the following tables and plot the lines on one graph:

(a) $y = 7 - 2x$

x	y
0	
	0
1	

(b) $y = 2x - 1$

x	y
0	
	0
1	

What is their point of intersection? How is this related to the pair of simultaneous equations

$$y = 7 - 2x$$
$$y = 2x - 1$$

7. Use a graphical method to solve the following simultaneous equations:

(a) $x + y = 5$
    $x - y = 3$

(b) $2x + y = 12$
    $4x - y = 6$

(c) $2x + 3y = 17$
    $4x - 3y = 7$

(d) $5x + y = 10$
    $3x - y = 2$

(e) $3x + y = 7$
    $y + x = 5$

(f) $5x + 2y = 19$
    $7x - y = 19$

GRADIENTS AND INTERCEPTS

The *gradient* of a line measures its *slope*, i.e. how steep it is. The gradient can be found from two points known to lie on the line using the ratio

$$\text{gradient} = \frac{\text{distance up}}{\text{distance along}} \quad \text{or} \quad \frac{\text{change in } y \text{ value}}{\text{change in } x \text{ value}}$$

In the equation of a straight line, $y = mx + c$, the gradient is given by m (see Fig. 10.5).

The *intercept* of a line determines where the line cuts the y-axis. In the equation $y = mx + c$, the intercept is given by c (Fig. 10.5).

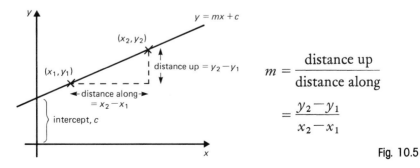

Fig. 10.5

137

Note that

(*i*) lines of the same gradient but different intercepts are parallel (Fig. 10.6(a)),

(*ii*) lines of the same intercept meet on the *y*-axis (Fig. 10.6(b)).

(*iii*) downward sloping lines have a negative gradient (Fig. 10.6(c)).

(*iv*) horizontal lines have zero gradient (Fig. 10.6(d)).

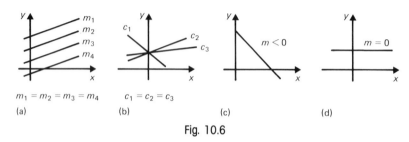

$m_1 = m_2 = m_3 = m_4$ $c_1 = c_2 = c_3$

(a)   (b)   (c)   (d)

Fig. 10.6

Examples (*i*) What is the gradient of the line $2y + 3x - 7 = 0$?

Since we have the equation of the line in full, it should be possible to 'read off' the gradient by rearranging the equation into conventional $y = mx + c$ format:

Add 7 and subtract $3x$ from both sides:

$$2y = -3x + 7$$

Divide both sides by 2:

$$y = \frac{-3}{2}x + \frac{7}{2}$$

Hence the gradient is $\frac{-3}{2}$.

(*ii*) From the graph in Fig. 10.7, find the gradient of the line and where it cuts the *y*-axis. Hence write down the equation of the line.

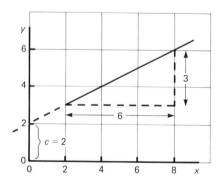

Fig. 10.7

138

The line passes through the points $(2, 3)$ and $(8, 6)$. The 'distance up' between these points is $6 - 3 = 3$, and the 'distance along' is $8 - 2 = 6$. Hence the gradient

$$m = \frac{\text{distance up}}{\text{distance along}} = \frac{3}{6} = \frac{1}{2}.$$

By extending the line back to the y-axis, we can see that the intercept $c = 2$.

As $m = \frac{1}{2}$ and $c = 2$, the equation of the line is $y = \frac{1}{2}x + 2$.

(*iii*) Find the equation of the line passing through the points $(-1, 4)$ and $(5, 1)$.

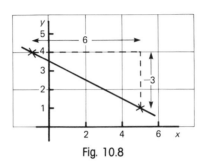

Fig. 10.8

From the graph in Fig. 10.8, it is obvious that this is a downward sloping line, with a *negative* gradient. The point $(-1, 4)$ lies above the point $(5, 1)$. But the gradient formula still applies, for the 'distance up' proves to be a negative quantity:

$$m = \frac{\text{distance up}}{\text{distance along}} = \frac{1 - 4}{5 - (-1)} = \frac{-3}{+6} = -\frac{1}{2}$$

Given this value for m, the equation of the line must be $y = -\frac{1}{2}x + c$. As the point $(5, 1)$ lies on the line, $x = 5$ and $y = 1$ will solve the equation:

$$1 = -\frac{1}{2} \times 5 + c$$
$$c = 3\frac{1}{2}$$

As $m = -\frac{1}{2}$ and $c = 3\frac{1}{2}$, the equation of the line is $y = -\frac{1}{2}x + 3\frac{1}{2}$.

EXERCISE 10b

1. What are (i) the gradients and (ii) the intercepts of the following lines:

(a) $y = 4x + 3$ (b) $y = -x + 2$ (c) $y = 5 - 4x$

(d) $y = 4 + 5x$ (e) $y - x = 3$ (f) $3y = 4 - 2x$.

2. Rearrange the equation $4y + 5x - 3 = 0$ into the usual $y = mx + c$ format. What is the gradient of this line? What is its intercept?

3. Rearrange the equation $6y - 2x + 5 = 0$ into the usual $y = mx + c$ format. What is the gradient of this line? What is its intercept?

4. Find (i) the gradients and (ii) the intercepts of the following lines:

   (a) $2y + 7x = 5$ (b) $9y + 3x - 5 = 0$
   (c) $5x + 9y = 8$ (d) $3x - 2y + 6 = 4$
   (e) $x - y = 0$ (f) $2y + 3 + 4x = 8$.

5. Three of the following lines are parallel to each other. Which?

   (a) $2y = 3x - 4$ (b) $3y = 2x - 4$ (c) $4y = 6x + 1$
   (d) $3y + 2x = 6$ (e) $2 + y = 4 + 1\frac{1}{2}x$
   (f) $y + x = 0$.

6. Which of the following statements are true?

   (a) $y = 3x - 1$ and $y = 2x - 1$ are parallel.
   (b) $y = 5x + 6$ and $5y = x + 6$ have the same intercept.
   (c) $y = 5x + 6$ and $5y = x + 6$ are parallel.
   (d) The gradient of $5y = x + 6$ is $\frac{1}{5}$.
   (e) $2y + 3x = 4$ and $2y - x = 4$ meet on the x-axis.
   (f) $2y + 3x = 4$ and $2y - x = 4$ meet on the y-axis.
   (g) $y = 4$ is a horizontal line.
   (h) $y = 4x$ goes through the point $(4, 1)$.
   (i) $x = 4$ is a vertical line.
   (j) The slope of $4x = 3y$ is $\frac{3}{4}$.

7. Find the equations of the following lines:

(a)

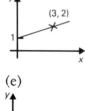

(b)

(c)

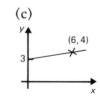

(d)

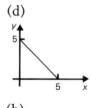

(e)

(f)

(g)

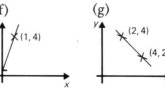

(h)

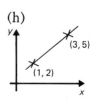

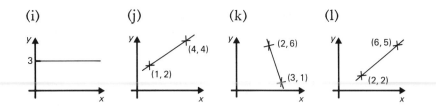

(i)   (j) (4,4) (1,2)   (k) (2,6) (3,1)   (l) (6,5) (2,2)

8. Find the gradients of the lines that pass through the points:

(a) $(1,1)$ and $(4,4)$ (b) $(3,4)$ and $(5,6)$
(c) $(3,9)$ and $(9,3)$ (d) $(0,0)$ and $(5,3)$
(e) $(-1,3)$ and $(3,-1)$ (f) $(-2,-3)$ and $(2,3)$
(g) $(2,3)$ and $(5,3)$ (h) $(3,0)$ and $(0,3)$.

9. Find the equations of the lines that pass through the points:

(a) $(0,1)$ and $(5,6)$ (b) $(0,7)$ and $(6,4)$
(c) $(2,7)$ and $(7,2)$ (d) $(4,1)$ and $(1,4)$
(e) $(0,0)$ and $(3,2)$ (f) $(0,7)$ and $(5,7)$
(g) $(-1,3)$ and $(-3,8)$ (h) $(3,-1)$ and $(4,1)$.

10. Match these six equations with the graphs shown in Fig. 10.9.

(i) $y = 3x + 1$ (ii) $y = x - 2$ (iii) $y = 7 - x$
(iv) $y = 6$ (v) $y = x^2 - 1$ (vi) $y = 20x$.

(a)   (b)   (c)

(d)   (e)   (f)

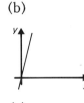

Fig. 10.9

11. A line of gradient $+2$ and another of gradient -2 meet at the point $P(3, 6)$, as shown in Fig. 10.10. Find the area of the triangle OPQ.

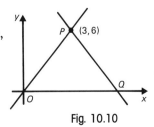

Fig. 10.10

MISCELLANEOUS EXERCISE 10

1. Figure 10.11 shows three lines. The equations of these lines are

   (a) $y = 2$ (b) $y = 2x - 2$ (c) $y = 10 - x$.

   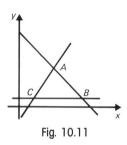

   Fig. 10.11

   Copy the diagram and indicate to which line each equation applies.

   Find the coordinates of the points A, B and C and find the area of triangle ABC.

2. Write down the gradients of lines (a) to (h) in Fig. 10.12.

   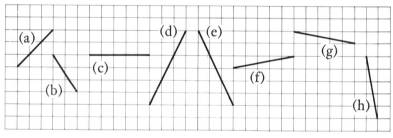

   Fig. 10.12

3. The lines $y = 2x$ and $y = 5 - \frac{1}{2}x$ meet at right angles at a point P. Find the coordinates of P. If Q is the point $(4, 8)$, show that Q lies on the line $y = 2x$. Draw an 8×8 grid; plot the points P and Q and the given two lines on your graph. Find the coordinates of two points R and S such that PQRS is a square. Find the equations of the lines QR and RS.

4. The lines AB and DE intersect at F (Fig. 10.13). The equation of AB is $4y - 3x = 12$ and the equation of DE is $2y + 3x = 24$.

   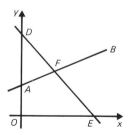

   Fig. 10.13

(a) Write down the coordinates of the points A and D which lie on the y-axis and hence the length of AD.

(b) By drawing graphs of the two lines AB and DE, or otherwise, find the coordinates of the point F.

(c) Calculate the areas of the triangle ADF and the quadrilateral $OAFE$, given that E is on the x-axis.   (WJEC)

5. The diagram (Fig. 10.14) shows the two lines
$$3x + 4y = 12,$$
$$2x - y = 2.$$

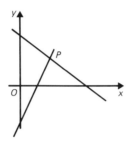

Fig. 10.14

Sketch a copy of this diagram and mark clearly which equation belongs to which line.

Calculate the coordinates of P, the point of intersection of the two lines.

Shade on your diagram the region defined by

$\{(x, y): y > 0\} \cap \{(x, y): 3x + 4y < 12\} \cap \{(x, y): 2x - y > 2\}.$
(LU)

6. Find, graphically or otherwise, the solution set of the simultaneous equations
$$2x - y + 1 = 0$$
$$x - 4y + 18 = 0 \qquad \text{(SUJB)}$$

7. Draw a grid with axes marked from -3 to $+8$. Plot the points $A(-2, -1)$, $B(3, 4)$ and $C(7, 6)$. Draw the line AB and find its mathematical equation. Draw the line BC and find its equation. Find the coordinates of the point D so that ABCD is a parallelogram. *Write down* the gradients of the lines AD and DC.

8. The conversion of degrees Centigrade to degrees Farenheit can be shown as a line graph.

Plot the three points given in the table below on a graph (put °F on the vertical axis).

°C	0	10	20
°F	32	50	68

Join up the points to make a straight line. From your graph, estimate the Centigrade equivalents to

(a) 40°F   (b) 60°F.

Estimate the Farenheit equivalents to

(c) 15°C   (c) 32°C.

What is the gradient of the straight line? Where does it cut the vertical axis? Suggest an equation relating y °F to x °C.

9. In an experiment, the results of measuring x and y are as follows:

x	1	2	3	4	5
y	5	7	10	11	13

Plot these points on a graph and show that all but one of them lie on a straight line. Measure the gradient and intercept of the line and suggest an equation relating x and y.

11 INEQUALITIES AND LINEAR PROGRAMMING

The statement 'nine is greater than seven' is written mathematically as $9 > 7$. Similarly, 'seven is less than nine' is written as $7 < 9$. Statements such as these are known as *inequations* or *inequalities*.

They may be combined with an 'equals' sign; thus $\geqslant$ means 'greater than or equal to' and $\leqslant$ means 'less than or equal to'.

INEQUALITIES ON THE NUMBER LINE

Simple inequalities (and sets defined in terms of inequalities) can be shown on a number line. Figure 11.1 illustrates the range $5 \leqslant x < 9$. Notice that 5 itself *is* included in the range; this is indicated by the solid circle ($\bullet$). However, 9 is *not* included and its exclusion is indicated by the open circle ($\circ$).

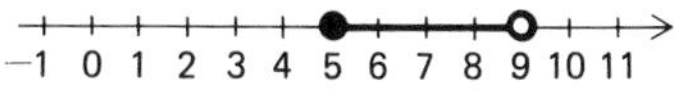

Fig. 11.1

Example If $A = \{-2 \leqslant x \leqslant 4\}$ and $B = \{1 < x < 8\}$, illustrate on the number line the set $A \cap B$.

As a member of B, x must be greater than 1: as a member of A, x must be less than or equal to 4. Thus, if $x \in A \cap B$ then $1 < x \leqslant 4$. Figure 11.2 illustrates $A \cap B$ on the number line.

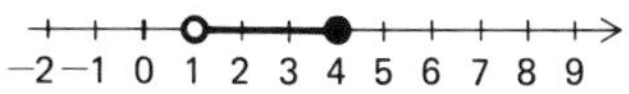

Fig. 11.2

SIMPLIFYING INEQUALITIES

Inequalities behave in a similar fashion to equations. For example, we may add or subtract convenient numbers from both sides. Thus, to solve $x - 3 \geqslant 7$ we should proceed as follows

$$x - 3 \geqslant 7$$

$$x - 3 + 3 \geqslant 7 + 3$$

$$x \geqslant 10$$

However, it is only possible to multiply or divide *by positive numbers*. If we multiply both sides of the inequality $9 > 7$ by $+10$, we get $90 > 70$, which is true. But if we multiplied both sides by -10, the result '$-90 > -70$' is *false*. The effect of multiplying (or dividing) by a negative number is to reverse the inequality, for $-90 < -70$.

Example $-6x < -12$.

Divide both sides by -6 and *reverse the inequality*:

$$x > 2$$

On some occasions it is simpler to solve an inequality by trial and error.

Example $x \in \{1, 2, 3, 4, 5, 6, 7, 8\}$ and $f(x) = x^2 - 10x + 25$. Find the solution set to $f(x) > 4$.

Putting $x = 1$ gives

$$f(1) = (1)^2 - 10(1) + 25 = 1 - 10 + 25 = 16$$

i.e. $f(1) > 4$, so $x = 1$ is a solution. Similarly, we can show that $f(2) = 9$, so $x = 2$ is also a solution. However, putting $x = 3$ gives

$$f(3) = (3)^2 - 10(3) + 25 = 4$$

i.e. $f(3)$ is *not* greater than 4, and $x = 3$ is *not* a solution.

We can show in the same way that $x = 4, 5, 6$ and 7 gives values that are not greater than 4. However, $x = 8$ gives

$$f(8) = (8)^2 - 10(8) + 25 = 9$$

Thus the completed solution set is $x \in \{1, 2, 8\}$.

EXERCISE 11a

1. Use $>, <, \geqslant$ and $\leqslant$ signs to define the ranges indicated:

(a) (b) (c)

2. Illustrate the following ranges on a number line:

(a) $-3 \leqslant x \leqslant 2$ (b) $4 < x < 6$ (c) $3 < x \leqslant 5$
(d) $x > 4$.

3. If $A = \{-3 \leqslant x \leqslant 2\}$ and $B = \{0 \leqslant x < 4\}$ define the following sets:

(a) $A \cap B$ (b) $A \cup B$ (c) A' (d) $A' \cap B$.

4. The number lines shown in Fig. 11.3 illustrate the sets A and B. Illustrate in a similar manner the sets

   (a) $A \cap B$ (b) $A \cup B$.

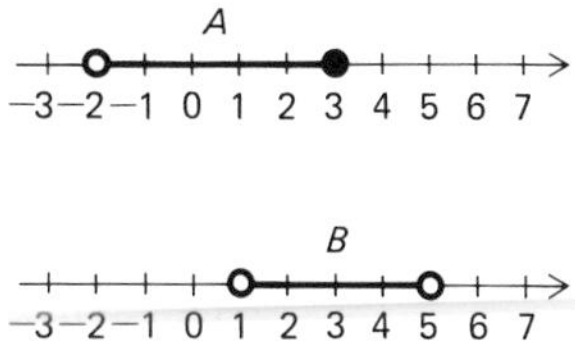

Fig. 11.3

5. Figure 11.4 shows the two parts of the range A'. Illustrate on the number line the range A.

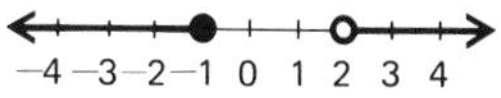

Fig. 11.4

Simplify:

6. $x + 3 < 8$

7. $x - 4 \geqslant -2$

8. $3x + 2 \geqslant 7$

9. $4(x - 6) < 3x$

10. $3 < 2(x + 1)$

11. $(x - 2) > 4(x + 2)$

12. $2(x - 3) \geqslant 4x$

13. $\frac{1}{2}x - 5 \geqslant 3$

14. $\frac{1}{3}x - 4 < 3 - \frac{2}{3}x$

15. $-5x < -40$

16. $-2x > 5$

17. $3 - x < 3$

18. $-\frac{1}{3}x > -5$

19. $\frac{x + 3}{2} > 4$

20. $\frac{x - 3}{4} > \frac{x + 2}{5}$

21. $\frac{x - 1}{6} \leqslant \frac{1 - x}{4}$

22. $\frac{x - 2}{3} \geqslant \frac{2x + 1}{5}$

23. $x(x - 1) > x^2$

24. $2x(x + 1) < 2x^2 - 3$

25. $3x^2 \leqslant (3x - 1)(x - 2)$

26. $(2x - 1)(2x + 3) > 4x^2$

27. $3x(x - 1) \geqslant (3x - 1)x + 3$

28. $x^2 > 4$

29. $3x^2 < 75$

30. $2x^2 \geqslant 4\frac{1}{2}$

31. $1 + 2x^2 > 33$

32. $3x^3 < 81$.

33. If $x \in \{1, 2, 3, 4, 5, 6\}$, find the solution sets to the following inequalities:

   (a) $(x - 2)(x - 4) < 0$ (b) $(x + 2)(x - 3) < 0$
   (c) $x(x - 2) < 3$.

34. If x is a positive integer, find the solution set to $x(x + 1) \leqslant 6$.

147

35. Given that $f(x) = x^3 - 7$, find the set of integers such that $f(x) > 0$.

36. $x \in \{1, 2, 3, 4, 5, 6, 7, 8\}$. Find the solution sets to the following:

   (a) $x^2 + 14 \geqslant 9x$ (b) $x^2 > 80$ (c) $x(3 - x) \geqslant 2$.

GRAPHICAL REPRESENTATION OF INEQUALITIES

An inequality is represented by an *area* on a graph. For example, all the points to the right of the line $x = 3$ satisfy the inequation $x > 3$ (Fig. 11.5). The *unwanted* region is shaded out, leaving the required area clear. As $x > 3$, points *on* the vertical line $x = 3$ are *not* included; this exclusion is indicated by the dotted line. If points on the line are included, i.e. $x \geqslant 3$, then a solid, unbroken line is used instead.

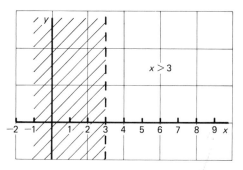

Fig. 11.5

If a number of inequalities are plotted on one graph, then the unshaded part will be limited to points which meet *all* the different inequalities.

Example Illustrate on one graph $x > 4$, $y > 2$ and $2x + y < 20$. Find the lowest value of $x + y$ subject to these inequalities, given that x and y are integers.

First, plot the lines represented by the equations $x = 4$, $y = 2$ and $2x + y = 20$ (see Fig. 11.6). Find, for each line, which side is the required region. You can do this by testing whether the origin $(0, 0)$ does or does not satisfy the inequation. For example, $2x + y < 20$ is satisfied by $x = 0$, $y = 0$, so the origin and all points to the left of the line $2x + y = 20$ lie in the required region; points to the right of the line are excluded. Shade out the unwanted regions.

Within the unshaded region there are 16 points (indicated as dots) with integer coordinates: $(5, 3), (5, 4), (5, 5), \ldots, (8, 3)$. (Points on the line are *not* included in this case.) Given these choices, the least value of $x + y$ is $5 + 3 = 8$.

148

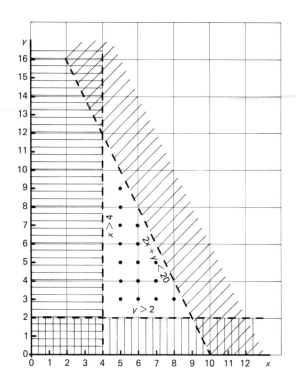

Fig. 11.6

EXERCISE 11b
1. Write down the inequalities represented by the *unshaded* areas:

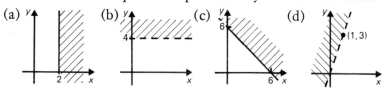

2. Illustrate on *separate* diagrams, shading out the unwanted regions:

   (a) $x > 5$ (b) $y \leqslant 7$ (c) $x + y \leqslant 8$ (d) $x > 2y$.

3. Which area on the graph in Fig. 11.7 satisfies *both* the following inequalities:
$$y \leqslant 1 \qquad x + y \geqslant 5.$$

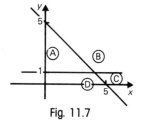

Fig. 11.7

4. Which area on the graph in Fig. 11.8 satisfies *all* the following inequalities:
$$x \geqslant -2 \qquad y \leqslant 4 \qquad x + y \leqslant 5.$$

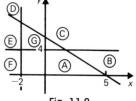

Fig. 11.8

5. Which area on the graph in Fig. 11.9 satisfies *all* the following inequalities:

$$x \leqslant 4 \qquad y \geqslant 2 \qquad 3x \leqslant y.$$

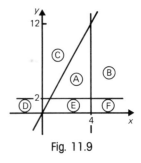

Fig. 11.9

6. Illustrate on a single graph the following inequalities:

$$x \leqslant 10 \qquad y \leqslant 5 \qquad x + y \leqslant 12.$$

7. Illustrate on a single graph the inequalities:

$$x \geqslant 0 \qquad y \geqslant 0 \qquad x + y < 9 \qquad x + 2y < 12.$$

8. Illustrate on one graph the following inequalities:

$$x \leqslant 6 \qquad y \geqslant \tfrac{1}{2}x \qquad y \leqslant 2x.$$

9. Illustrate on one graph the following inequalities, shading out the unwanted region:

$$y > 0 \qquad y < 3x \qquad x + y < 4.$$

List the coordinates (x, y) that satisfy all three inequalities, given that x and y are whole numbers.

10. Using a scale of 1 cm to represent 1 unit on both axes, draw, for positive values only of x and y, the graphs of the straight lines

$$2x + y = 22 \qquad 11x + 16y = 176 \qquad y = 2x.$$

Mark clearly on your graph paper all the points with co-ordinates (x, y) such that x and y are whole numbers which satisfy simultaneously all the three inequalities

$$2x + y < 22 \qquad 11x + 16y > 176 \qquad y < 2x.$$

By listing the coordinates of these points, or otherwise, state the (whole-number) coordinates of the points which satisfy the inequalities above and are such that

(a) $x + y$ has its greatest value,

(b) $x^2 + y^2$ has its least value. (O & C)

11. Indicate on squared paper the region for which

$$x \geqslant 2, \quad y \geqslant 0, \quad 3x + y \geqslant 12, \quad 2x + 3y \geqslant 12$$
$$\text{and} \quad 10x + 6y \geqslant 51.$$

Use a scale of 2 cm for 1 unit and note that there is no need to allow for negative values of x or y.

(a) Find the least values of $x + y$ and $2x + y$ subject to these inequalities. Give also the coordinates of the points at which these occur.

(b) If x and y are required to be whole numbers, find the new least values of $x+y$ and $2x+y$ still subject to the original restrictions. Again give the coordinates of the points which give these least values. (Ox)

12. (a) The set of points with coordinates (x, y) satisfies the five inequalities

$$x \geqslant 0, \qquad y \geqslant 0, \qquad y + 2x \geqslant 8,$$
$$4y + 3x \leqslant 24 \qquad \text{and} \qquad 3y \leqslant 2x.$$

(i) Using 2 cm to represent 1 unit on each axis, construct accurately on graph paper, and clearly indicate by shading the unwanted regions, the region in which the set of points (x, y) must lie.

(ii) Using your graph, find the least value of $(x-y)$ for points in the region.

(b) The owner of a large piece of land plans to divide it into not more than 36 plots and to build either a house or a bungalow on each plot. He decides that he will build at least 20 houses and that there will be at least twice as many houses as bungalows.

Taking b to represent the number of houses and b the number of bungalows, write down three inequalities, other than $b \geqslant 0$ and $b \geqslant 0$, which satisfy the above conditions. (C)

LINEAR PROGRAMMING

Example A local cabinet-maker has two designs: the standard sells for £150 and takes 4 hours to build; the deluxe version takes 8 hours to build and sells for £250. If the manufacturer has 10 men working for him for 8 hours a day and contracts with local shops that require him to supply at least four deluxe and two standard cabinets per day, what is his maximum revenue per day?

The difficulty in this type of problem is translating the written information into algebraic form. Always begin by defining x and y.

Let the manufacturer make x deluxe cabinets and y standard cabinets each day.

He is under contract to make four of the deluxe type, so $x \geqslant 4$, and two of the standard type, so $y \geqslant 2$.

Ten men work 8 hours each day, providing 80 man-hours of work. It takes 8 hours to make one deluxe cabinet, so it must take $8x$ man-hours to make x of them. It takes 4 hours to make a standard cabinet, so it must take $4y$ hours to make y of them. Thus the total work done in one day is $8x + 4y$ hours and this, obviously, cannot be more than the 80 hours of work his men do each day. Thus we have a third condition:

$$8x + 4y \leqslant 80$$

or (dividing both sides by 4)

$$2x + y \leqslant 20$$

Finally, he takes £250 for each deluxe cabinet, so he must take £250x for x of them and, similarly, £150y on the y standard cabinets. Thus his daily receipts, $R = £250x + £150y$.

The three conditions are therefore $x \geqslant 4$, $y \geqslant 2$ and $2x + y \leqslant 20$ and the manufacturer aims to maximise $R = 250x + 150y$.

Since these are similar inequalities to the example on page 148, the graphical illustration is much the same. However, we must add to the graph the lines represented by $R = 250x + 150y$.

Suppose R is £1500: we can find two points on the line $1500 = 250x + 150y$ and add the line R_1 to the graph. Suppose instead that the revenue is £2250. In the same way, we can find two points that lie on the line $2250 = 250x + 150y$ and add line R_2 to the graph.

R_1:	x	y
	0	10
	6	0

R_2:	x	y
	0	15
	9	0

Lines R_1 and R_2 are shown on the graph in Fig. 11.10. It is clear that they are parallel — as are all the revenue lines represented by $R = 250x + 150y$. It is not necessary to plot further lines accurately: the highest revenue line achievable (represented by R_{max}) is the line parallel to R_1 and R_2 that just touches the unshaded region (at the point $(4, 12)$). Higher revenues are not possible; lower revenues are possible but undesirable. So, to maximise revenue, the cabinet-maker should produce four deluxe cabinets and twelve standard cabinets each day. His revenue will be

$$\begin{aligned} R_{max} &= 250x + 150y \quad \text{where } x = 4 \text{ and } y = 12 \\ &= 250(4) + 150(12) \\ &= 1000 + 1800 \\ &= £2800 \end{aligned}$$

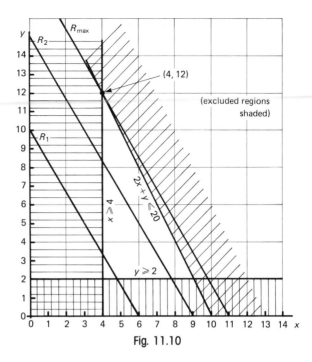

Fig. 11.10

EXERCISE 11c

1. A manufacturer makes x whichits and y whatsits per week. Each whichit takes 3 machine hours and four units of raw materials to make; each whatsit takes 2 hours on the machine and one unit of raw materials.

   (a) Show that the total machine time used is $3x + 2y$ hours.

   (b) Show that the total of raw materials used is $4x + y$ units.

   (c) If the manufacturer has only 42 machine hours per week and 36 units of raw materials, write down two inequalities that he must satisfy (other than $x \geqslant 0$ and $y \geqslant 0$).

   (d) Illustrate these two inequalities on a graph.

   (e) If the manufacturer makes £50 profit on each whichit and £30 on each whatsit, write down an expression, in terms of x and y, for his total profit, £P, per week.

   (f) By choosing various levels of profit, draw a series of profit lines on your graph. How many whichits and whatsits should the manufacturer make to maximise his profit, and what is his maximum possible profit?

2. A baker takes 1 hour to prepare a batch of pies and 2 hours to prepare a batch of cakes.

   (a) If she makes x batches of pies and y batches of cakes, how long must she work (in terms of x and y)?

   (b) If the baker never works more than 10 hours in a day, write down an inequality that must be met by the baker.

153

(c) The bakery has storage space for only nine batches of pies or cakes. Write down another inequality that must be met.

(d) Illustrate these inequalities on a graph.

(e) The baker makes £12 profit on a batch of pies and £18 on a batch of cakes. Show that her profit, £P, is given by the equation $P = 12x + 18y$.

(f) By choosing various levels of profit, draw a series of profit lines on your graph. Find the number of batches of cakes and pies she should bake each day to make maximum profit.

3. A new book is to be published in both a hardback and a paperback edition. A bookseller agrees to purchase
   (i)   15 or more hardback copies,
   (ii) more than 25 paperback copies,
   (iii) at least 45, but fewer than 60, copies altogether.

Using h to represent the number of hardback copies and p to represent the number of paperback copies, write down the inequalities which represent these conditions.

The point (h, p) represents h hardback copies and p paperback copies. Using a scale of 2 cm to represent 10 books on each axis, construct, and indicate clearly by shading the *unwanted* regions, the region in which (h, p) must lie.

Given that each hardback copy costs £5 and that each paperback copy costs £2, calculate the number of each sort that the bookseller must buy if he is prepared to spend between £180 and £200 altogether and he has to buy each sort in packets of five. (C)

4. An outing is to be organised for x children and y adults.
   Write down inequalities to express the following conditions:
   (a) the number of children must be greater than the number of adults;
   (b) the number of children must be less than three times the number of adults;
   (c) the total number of tickets (a child needs a half ticket and an adult needs a whole ticket) must be less than 60.

Using a scale of 2 cm to 10 people, draw straight line graphs and indicate clearly the region containing points corresponding to values of x and y satisfying all three conditions at the same time.

Hence find:

(d) the largest number of adults who can go on the outing;

(e) the largest total number of people who can go.   (O & C)

5. Instant coffee is sold in large jars costing £1.60 each and small jars costing £1 each. A customer receives tokens with his purchase of coffee, provided that he buys at least one large jar and more than two small jars. He can afford to spend up to £8 on coffee. He buys y large and x small jars.

   (a) Write down which two of the following inequalities are true:

   $$x \geqslant 2, \quad x > 2, \quad y \geqslant 1, \quad y > 1.$$

   (b) Prove that $5x + 8y \leqslant 40$.

   (c) If $x - y > 0$, does he buy more large or more small jars?

   (d) Draw a linear programming diagram showing all the constraints, including $x - y > 0$.

   (e) Indicate all the points on the diagram which satisfy the problem. (Use a cross or a circle.)

   (f) If he receives 5 tokens with a small jar and 7 tokens with a large jar, find the maximum number of tokens he could receive.   (SUJB)

6. Fred decides to stock two types of wine at his shop. He buys Plonko for £1.50 a bottle and Sofistiko for £2.50 a bottle. He has £1800 available for the purchase of this stock and wishes to buy at least 800 bottles. He buys x bottles of Plonko and y bottles of Sofistiko. Write down two inequalities, apart from $x \geqslant 0$ and $y \geqslant 0$, which correspond to the above conditions.

   Fred also decides that at least one-third of the bottles he buys should be Sofistiko. Using this information write down a further inequality and show that it simplifies to

   $$y \geqslant \tfrac{1}{2}x.$$

   Taking 2 cm to represent 100 units on both axes, draw a graph to illustrate these three inequalities.

   From your graph find the largest number of bottles of Plonko that Fred could buy.

   He sells the Plonko at a profit of 30 pence a bottle and the Sofistiko at a profit of 60 pence a bottle. Assuming that he is able to sell all his stock find how many bottles of each type of wine he should buy in order to maximize his profit, and calculate that profit.   (Ox)

12 FURTHER GRAPHS

The graphs of equations involving powers of x and y (i.e. those not of the style $y = mx + c$) will *not* be straight lines. In particular, a quadratic equation (of the type $y = ax^2 + bx + c$) will have the shape shown in Fig. 12.1(a). If the x^2 term is negative, the graph will be the same shape, but upside down (see Fig. 12.1(b)).

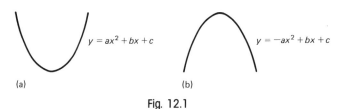

(a)　　　　　　　　　(b)

Fig. 12.1

PLOTTING THE GRAPH

To be sure of the exact path traced out by the function, it is necessary to find many coordinates that lie on the graph: two or three will *not* be enough.

Example　Draw the graph of $y = x^2 - 2x - 8$ over the domain $-4 \leqslant x \leqslant +6$.

Putting $x = -4$ gives

$$y = x^2 - 2x - 8$$
$$= (-4)^2 - 2(-4) - 8$$
$$= 16 + 8 - 8$$
$$= 16$$

So the point $(-4, 16)$ lies on the graph.

We must now repeat this for a series of values over the given domain. It is obviously simplest to use $x = -3, -2, -1$, etc., up to $+6$, and to set out the calculation of the y-coordinates as a table:

x	-4	-3	-2	-1	0	1	2	3	4	5	6
x^2	16	9	4	1	0	1	4	9	16	25	36
$-2x$	$+8$	$+6$	$+4$	$+2$	0	-2	-4	-6	-8	-10	-12
-8	-8	-8	-8	-8	-8	-8	-8	-8	-8	-8	-8
y	16	7	0	-5	-8	-9	-8	-5	0	7	16

From the table, we can see that the points $(-4, 16), (-3, 7)$, $(-2, 0), \ldots, (6, 16)$ all lie on the graph $y = x^2 - 2x - 8$. The graph of these points, joined by a *smooth* curve is shown in Fig. 12.2.

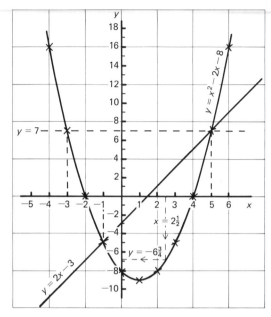

Fig. 12.2

The points $(-2, 0)$ and $(4, 0)$ where the graph crosses the x-axis, are of special importance for solving the equation $x^2 - 2x - 8 = 0$. They are called the *roots* of the equation. (We could have found them algebraically using the techniques described in Chapter 7.)

READING THE GRAPH

We can read off points from the graph without further calculation. For example, at $x = 2\frac{1}{2}$ (reading down to the curve and along to the y-axis) we can see that $y = -6\frac{3}{4}$ (Fig. 12.3).

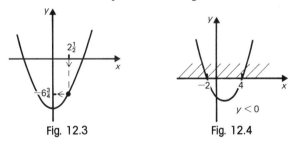

Fig. 12.3   Fig. 12.4

Similarly, we can read off various inequalities from the graph. For example, $x^2 - 2x - 8$ is negative when the curve falls below the x-axis. So, reading off the graph, $x^2 - 2x - 8 < 0$ implies that $-2 < x < 4$ (Fig. 12.4).

157

In the same way, we can read off the ranges for which

$$x^2 - 2x - 8 > 2x - 3$$

The line $y = 2x - 3$ is already plotted on the graph in Fig. 12.2; the curve is above this line when $x < -1$ and when $x > 5$ (see Fig. 12.5).

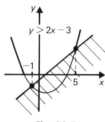

Fig. 12.5

SOLVING RELATED EQUATIONS

Other equations can be solved using this graph of $y = x^2 - 2x - 8$ provided they can be rearranged to read $x^2 - 2x - 8 = \ldots$.

Examples (*i*) Use the graph in Fig. 12.2 to solve the equation $x^2 - 2x - 15 = 0$.

If we add 7 to both sides of this new equation we get

$$x^2 - 2x - 15 + 7 = 0 + 7$$

i.e. $\qquad x^2 - 2x - 8 = 7$

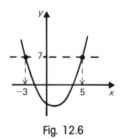

Fig. 12.6

From the graph (see also Fig. 12.6), we can see that $x^2 - 2x - 8 = 7$ at $x = -3$ and at $x = +5$.

(*ii*) Use the graph in Fig. 12.2 to solve the equation $x^2 - 4x - 5 = 0$.

Again, we must first rearrange the new equation to read $x^2 - 2x - 8 = \ldots$. So, we add $2x$ to both sides and subtract 3:

$$x^2 - 4x - 5 + 2x - 3 = 0 + 2x - 3$$

i.e. $$x^2 - 2x - 8 = 2x - 3$$

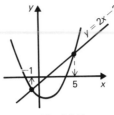

Fig. 12.7

If we plot the line $y = 2x - 3$ on the original graph (see Fig. 12.2), we find that it intersects with the original curve at $x = -1$ and at $x = +5$ (see also Fig. 12.7). These values are the solutions to the equation

$$x^2 - 2x - 8 = 2x - 3$$

and hence to the problem

$$x^2 - 4x - 5 = 0$$

TANGENTS AND GRADIENTS

The gradient of a curve is continually changing. However, we can find its value at a particular point from the tangent drawn at that point.

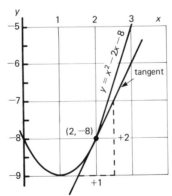

Fig. 12.8

Figure 12.8 shows the graph of $y = x^2 - 2x - 8$ for the limited domain $0 \leqslant x \leqslant 3$. The gradient of the curve at the point $(2, -8)$ is equal to the gradient of the tangent drawn at that point. Using the formula

$$\text{gradient} = \frac{\text{distance up}}{\text{distance along}} = \frac{+2}{+1} = 2$$

we see that the gradient of the tangent, and hence of the curve, at $(2, -8)$, is 2.

159

MISCELLANEOUS EXERCISE 12

1. Complete the following table:

x	-4	-3	-2	-1	0	1	2	3	4
x^2	16	9			0			9	16
-4	-4	-4			-4			-4	-4
$y = x^2 - 4$	12				-4				

Draw the graph of $y = x^2 - 4$ for $-4 \leqslant x \leqslant 4$.

(a) What are the roots of the equation $x^2 - 4 = 0$?

(b) What is the minimum possible value of $x^2 - 4$?

(c) *Use your graph* to solve the equations
   (i) $x^2 = 8$ (ii) $x^2 = 10$

(d) Draw on your graph the line $y = 3x$. What are the x-coordinates of the points of intersection with the curve? Show that these are the solution to the equation $x^2 - 3x - 4 = 0$.

(e) Draw another line on the graph that will enable you to read off the solutions to the equation $x^2 - 2x - 3 = 0$; write down these solutions.

(f) Draw the tangent to the curve at $(2, 0)$ and hence determine the gradient of the curve at that point.

2. Complete the following table and use it to draw the graph of $y = x^2 - x - 6$ over the domain $-4 \leqslant x \leqslant 5$.

x	-4	-3	-2	-1	0	1	2	3	4	5
x^2	$+16$	$+9$					4	9	16	25
$-x$	$+4$	$+3$						-3		-5
-6	-6	-6	-6	-6				-6	-6	-6
y	14	6						0		14

Use your graph to find

(a) the roots of the equation $x^2 - x - 6 = 0$

(b) the value of y when $x =$
   (i) -1.2 (ii) $+1.2$ (iii) 2.4

(c) the values of x when $y =$
   (i) 10   (ii) -5 (iii) 8

(d) the range of values of x for which
(i) $y < 0$ (ii) $y \leqslant 8$

(e) the range of values of x for which
(i) $y > 9$ (ii) $y > -2$

(f) the gradient of the curve at the points $(-1, -4)$ and $(2, -4)$ (you will need to draw the tangent at each point).

Solve the following equations by drawing appropriate lines on your graph:

(g) $x^2 - x - 6 = 3 - x$

(h) $x^2 - 3x = 4$.

3. Show that if $y = 9 - x^2$ then $y = -16$ when $x = +5$ *and* when $x = -5$. Construct a table of values of y for $x = -5, -4, -3, -2, -1, 0, 1, 2, 3, 4, 5$ where $y = 9 - x^2$.

Draw the graph of $y = 9 - x^2$ over the given domain and use it to find

(a) the roots of the equation $9 - x^2 = 0$

(b) the value of y when
(i) $x = -2.8$ (ii) $x = +3.7$

(c) the values of x when
(i) $y = 2$ (ii) $y = 4.5$

(d) the range of values of x for which $y > 0$

(e) the range of values of x for which
(i) $y < 3$ (ii) $y < -1$

(f) the gradient of the curve at the points $(-1, 8)$ and $(2, 5)$ (you will need to draw the tangent at each point).

Solve the following equations by drawing appropriate lines on your graph:

(g) $9 - x^2 = 5$

(h) $10 - 2x - x^2 = 2$.

Draw the line $y = 3x$ on your graph and hence solve the inequality $9 - x^2 < 3x$.

4. Copy and complete the table below for $y = 7x - x^3$.

x	-3	-2.5	-2	-1.5	-1	-0.5
y		-1.875		-7.125		-3.375

x	0	0.5	1	1.5	2	2.5	3
y		3.375		7.125		1.875	

161

Draw the graph of $y = 7x - x^3$ for the range of values of x from -3 to 3, and from your graph determine for what values of x in this range $7x - x^3 > 4$.

By drawing the appropriate straight line on your graph, find three solutions of the equation

$$6x - x^3 = 0. \tag{Ox}$$

5. Construct a table of values of y for $x = -1, -0.5, 0, 0.5, 1, 1.5, 2, 2.5,$ where

$$y = 20x^2 - x^3.$$

Plot the graph of $y = 20x^2 - x^3$, taking a scale of 4 cm to 1 unit on the x-axis and 2 cm to 10 units on the y-axis.

(a) Estimate from your graph the solutions of the equation
$$20x^2 - x^3 = 5.$$

(b) Estimate from your graph the solution of the equation
$$20x^2 - x^3 = 20.$$

(c) The equation $20x^2 - x^3 = k$ has just one solution. Find, from your graph, the set of values that k can take.

(O & C)

6. Functions f and g are defined by

$$f(x) = \frac{1}{x}, \qquad g(x) = 4 - x.$$

(a) Using a scale of 4 cm to 1 unit on each axis, plot and draw with the same axes the graphs of these two functions for $0.2 \leqslant x \leqslant 4.0$.

(b) From your graphs, estimate the two values of x for which $f(x) = g(x)$.

(c) Write down an equation of which these two values are the roots and simplify it. (LU)

7. (a) If $y = x - 5 + \dfrac{10}{x}$, copy and complete the table below:

x	1	1.5	2	3	4	5	6
y		3.17	2	1.33			2.67

(b) Taking 2 cm to represent 1 unit on the x-axis and 2 cm to represent 1 unit on the y-axis, draw the graph of $y = x - 5 + \dfrac{10}{x}$, for values of x from $x = 1$ to $x = 6$.

(c) From your graph write down the range of values of x for which y is less than 2.5.

(d) On the same axes draw the straight line $x + y = 5$.

(e) By drawing a suitable parallel line estimate the value of x on the graph of $y = x - 5 + \dfrac{10}{x}$, where the gradient of the tangent is -1.　　　　　　　　　　　(AEB '81)

8. (a) If $y = 2^x$, calculate y when $x = 0, 1, 2, 3, 4, 5, 6$.

(b) Draw the graph of $y = 2^x$ for values of x lying between 0 and 6.

(c) Use the graph to find N, if $2^N = 20$.

(d) Find the gradient of the chord joining the point where $x = 1$ to the point where $x = 5$.

(e) Find the gradient of the curve at the point where $x = 4$.　　　　　　　　　　　(SUJB)

13 CALCULUS

DIFFERENTIATION

The gradient of a straight line is a constant — the value of m in the equation $y = mx + c$.

The gradient of a *curve* is continuously changing, so is a different value at different points on the curve.

The gradient at any one particular point is taken to be the gradient of the tangent drawn at that point (see Fig. 13.1 and page 159).

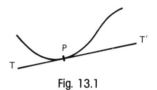

Fig. 13.1

However, it is possible to find the gradient of a curve algebraically using a special formula. For example, on the curve given by the equation $y = x^n$, the gradient, now to be denoted $\dfrac{dy}{dx}$, is given by the formula $\dfrac{dy}{dx} = nx^{n-1}$.

Examples (i) On the curve $y = x^3$, $\dfrac{dy}{dx} = 3x^{(3-1)} = 3x^2$. So at the point $(2, 8)$ on the curve the gradient is $3(2)^2 = 12$ (by substituting $x = 2$ into the gradient formula).

(ii) On the curve $y = x^4$, $\dfrac{dy}{dx} = 4x^{(4-1)} = 4x^3$. So at a point on the curve, say $(-1, 1)$, the gradient is $4(-1)^3 = -4$ (by substituting $x = -1$ into the gradient formula).

The process of finding the gradient formula is called *differentiation*. The quantity $\dfrac{dy}{dx}$ is called the *derivative* or *differential coefficient*.

More complicated equations can be differentiated, for the formula $\frac{dy}{dx} = nx^{n-1}$ applies regardless of whether the power, n, in $y = x^n$ is positive or negative, a whole number or a fraction. Moreover, multiplying x^n by some other number simply multiplies the derivative by the same number, that is, if

$$y = kx^n$$

then

$$\frac{dy}{dx} = knx^{n-1}$$

Note that if $y = k$ then $\frac{dy}{dx} = 0$. That is, the derivative of a constant is zero. (Remember that the graph of $y = k$ is a horizontal line, parallel to the x-axis and, clearly, of zero gradient.)

The derivative of a series of terms added or subtracted is simply the derivative of each term, added or subtracted. But the formula $\frac{dy}{dx} = nx^{n-1}$ *does not apply to terms multiplying or dividing each other* — brackets, etc., must be expanded to simple powers of x *before* you differentiate.

Remember that $\frac{1}{x} = x^{-1}$ and that $\sqrt{x} = x^{1/2}$ (see Chapter 4).

Examples

y	$\dfrac{dy}{dx}$
7	0
x	$x^0 = 1$
$3x$	$3x^0 = 3$
x^2	$2x$
$3x^2$	$3 \times 2x = 6x$
$-16x^3$	$-16 \times 3x^2 = -48x^2$
$\sqrt{x} = x^{1/2}$	$\frac{1}{2}x^{-1/2}$
$x^{1/3}$	$\frac{1}{3}x^{-2/3}$
$\dfrac{1}{x^2} = x^{-2}$	$-2x^{-3}$

y	$\dfrac{dy}{dx}$
$3x^{-4}$	$3 \times -4x^{-5} = -12x^{-5}$
$3x^{-1/2}$	$3 \times -\frac{1}{2}x^{-3/2} = -\frac{3}{2}x^{-3/2}$
$6x^2 + 2x - 1$	$12x + 2$
$3x^{-1} - 2x^{-2}$	$-3x^{-2} + 4x^{-3}$
$(x+2)(x-1) = x^2 + x - 2$	$2x + 1$
$(x+2)^2 = x^2 + 4x + 4$	$2x + 4$

EXERCISE 13a Differentiate the following i.e. find $\dfrac{dy}{dx}$:

1. x^2 　　　　2. $2x^2$ 　　　　3. x^3

4. $3x^3$ 　　　　5. $3x^2$ 　　　　6. x

7. $5x$ 　　　　8. 3 　　　　9. -8

10. x^{-1} 　　　　11. x^{-4} 　　　　12. $3x^{-2}$

13. $-5x^{-3}$ 　　　　14. $x^{1/3}$ 　　　　15. $x^{2/5}$

16. $x^{-1/2}$ 　　　　17. $4x^{3/4}$ 　　　　18. $-3x^{1/2}$

19. $\dfrac{1}{x}$ 　　　　20. $\dfrac{3}{x^3}$ 　　　　21. $\dfrac{8}{x^4}$

22. $\dfrac{-1}{5x^5}$ 　　　　23. $\sqrt{x}$ 　　　　24. $\dfrac{4}{\sqrt{x}}$

25. $x\sqrt{x}$ 　　　　26. $3x - 1$ 　　　　27. $5x + 2$

28. $3 - x$ 　　　　29. $5 - 2x$ 　　　　30. $3x^2 - 2$

31. $3x^2 - 2x + 1$ 　　　32. $5x^2 + 6x - 2$ 　　　33. $4x^3 - 2x + 1$

34. $5\sqrt{x} - \dfrac{1}{x}$ 　　　35. $7x^{2/5} - x^{-1/3}$ 　　　36. $x(x-1)$

37. $3x^2(2x + 1)$ 　　　38. $(x-1)(x+1)$ 　　　39. $(2x-3)^2$

40. $(3x-1)^2$.

41. If $y = x^2 - 1$, find $\dfrac{dy}{dx}$ and use it to calculate the gradient of the curve at the points

(a) $(1,0)$ 　　　(b) $(2,3)$ 　　　(c) $(-3,8)$ 　　　(d) $(0,-1)$.

42. If $y = 3x^2 - 2x + 1$, find $\dfrac{dy}{dx}$ and use it to calculate the gradient of the curve at the points
    (a) $(1, 2)$ (b) $(2, 9)$ (c) $(0, 1)$ (d) $(-1, 8)$.

43. If $y = x^3$, find $\dfrac{dy}{dx}$ and use it to calculate the gradient of the curve at the points
    (a) $(-2, -8)$ (b) $(-1, -1)$ (c) $(0, 0)$ (d) $(1, 1)$
    (e) $(2, 8)$.

44. If $y = 4x^3 + 2x - 1$, find $\dfrac{dy}{dx}$ and use it to calculate the gradient of the curve at the points
    (a) $(1, 5)$ (b) $(-1, -7)$ (c) $(0, -1)$.

45. Find the gradient of the curve $y = 3x^4 - 2x^2 + 6$ at the points
    (a) $(1, 7)$ (b) $(2, 46)$ (c) $(-2, 46)$.

46. Find the gradient of the curve $y = \sqrt{x}$ at the points
    (a) $(1, 1)$ (b) $(9, 3)$ (c) $(\tfrac{1}{4}, \tfrac{1}{2})$.

47. Find the gradient of the curve $y = \dfrac{1}{x^2}$ at the points
    (a) $(1, 1)$ (b) $(-1, 1)$ (c) $(\tfrac{1}{2}, 4)$ (d) $(2, \tfrac{1}{4})$.

48. Find the gradient of the curve $y = \dfrac{1}{\sqrt{x}}$ at the points
    (a) $(1, 1)$ (b) $(\tfrac{1}{4}, 2)$ (c) $(2, 0.7)$.

FINDING A POINT OF GIVEN GRADIENT

Just as we can find the gradient of a curve at a given point, so we can use differentiation to find a point at which the gradient is a particular value.

Example Find the point on the curve $y = 4x^2 - 6x + 5$ at which the gradient is 2.

Differentiating $4x^2 - 6x + 5$:

$$\frac{dy}{dx} = 8x - 6$$

Now, at the required point the gradient is to be 2, i.e. at this point $\frac{dy}{dx} = 2$, or

$$8x - 6 = 2$$
$$8x = 8$$
$$x = 1$$

The point has the x-coordinate 1, and the y-coordinate is given by

$$y = 4x^2 - 6x + 5$$
$$y = 4(1)^2 - 6(1) + 5$$
$$= 4 - 6 + 5$$
$$= 3$$

Thus the point at which the gradient is 2 is $(1, 3)$.

FINDING TURNING POINTS

Consider the curve shown in Fig. 13.2. It shows two *turning points,* that is a local *maximum* and a local *minimum.* At these turning points, the tangents are parallel to the x-axis, that is, their slopes are zero. So at a maximum or minimum point, the gradient of the curve, and hence $\frac{dy}{dx}$, is zero. This is a very important result that leads to the solution of many practical problems.

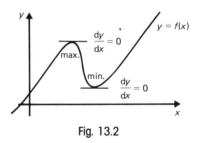

Fig. 13.2

Example Find the minimum point on the curve $y = x^2 - 4x + 16$.

Differentiating $x^2 - 4x + 16$ gives $\frac{dy}{dx} = 2x - 4$

For a minimum, $\frac{dy}{dx} = 0$. Therefore $2x - 4 = 0$ and $x = 2$.
$y = (2)^2 - 4(2) + 16 = 12$. So the minimum point is $(2, 12)$.

To decide whether the turning point is a maximum or a minimum, the sign of $\dfrac{dy}{dx}$ just before and just after the turn must be considered. If the point is a minimum, then $\dfrac{dy}{dx}$ is negative before the turn and positive after (Fig. 13.3). If the point is a maximum, then the reverse holds, i.e. $\dfrac{dy}{dx}$ is positive before and negative after the turn.

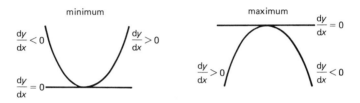

Fig. 13.3

Example Find the maximum and minimum points on the curve $y = x^3 - 4\frac{1}{2}x^2 + 2$.

Differentiating:

$$\frac{dy}{dx} = 3x^2 - 9x = 3x(x - 3)$$

For a turning point $\dfrac{dy}{dx} = 0$. Therefore

$$3x(x - 3) = 0$$

giving $\qquad\qquad\qquad x = 0 \quad \text{or} \quad x = 3$

Now, at $x = -1$ $\quad \dfrac{dy}{dx} = 3(-1)(-4) = +12$

at $x = +1$ $\quad \dfrac{dy}{dx} = 3(+1)(-2) = -6$

at $x = +4$ $\quad \dfrac{dy}{dx} = 3(+4)(+1) = +12$

So the curve has a positive gradient until $x = 0$, then a negative gradient; so the point $(0, 2)$ is a maximum. The gradient is positive again after $x = 3$, so the point $(3, -11\frac{1}{2})$ is a minimum.

1. $y = 4x^2 - 12x - 5$. Find $\dfrac{dy}{dx}$ and use it to find the x-coordinate of the point at which the gradient of the curve is 4. What is the y-coordinate at that point?

2. $y = 3x^2 - 12x + 15$. Find $\dfrac{dy}{dx}$ and use it to find the x-coordinate of the point at which the gradient of the curve is 6. What is the y-coordinate at that point?

3. $y = 2x^2 + x + 7$. Find $\dfrac{dy}{dx}$ and use it to find the x-coordinate of the point at which the gradient of the curve is 5. What is the y-coordinate at that point?

4. Find the points (x,y) on the curve $y = 3x^2 - 5x + 4$ at which the gradient is
   (a) 1   (b) -2 (c) 4.

5. Find the points (x, y) on the curve $y = \frac{1}{2}x^4 - 6$ at which the gradient is
   (a) 2   (b) -2 (c) $\frac{1}{4}$ (d) $-\frac{1}{4}$ (e) 0.

6. Find the *two* points on the curve $y = x^3 - x + 7$ at which the gradient is $+2$, and show there is *no* point at which the curve has a gradient of -2.

7. Find the coordinates of the turning points on these curves:

(a)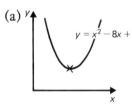
$y = x^2 - 8x + 26$

(b)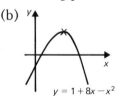
$y = 1 + 8x - x^2$

(c)
$y = x^2 + 3x$

(d)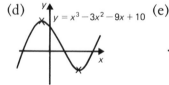
$y = x^3 - 3x^2 - 9x + 10$

(e)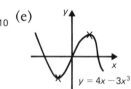
$y = 4x - 3x^3$

(f)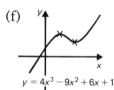
$y = 4x^3 - 9x^2 + 6x + 1$

8. $y = 8x^3 - 6x + 5$. Find $\dfrac{dy}{dx}$ and show that there are two points at which the gradient is zero. Find these points. Which is the minimum and which the maximum?

9. Find the coordinates of the two turning points on the curve $y = x^3 - 6x^2 + 9x + 3$. Which is the minimum and which the maximum?

10. Find the turning points on the curve $y = 2x^3 - 24x + 5$. Which is the minimum and which the maximum?

11. The graph of $y = 15x^2 - 2x^3 - 36x + 23$ is shown in Fig. 13.4. Find the coordinates of the points marked P, Q, R and S.

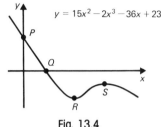

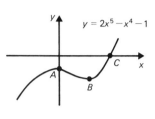

Fig. 13.4   Fig. 13.5

12. A portion of the graph $y = 2x^5 - x^4 - 1$ is shown in Fig. 13.5. Find the coordinates of the points A, B and C.

PROBLEMS

Example A farmer has 24 sections of fencing, each 1 m long. What is the maximum area of a rectangular field that he can enclose?

Suppose the farmer encloses a rectangular field using x sections of fence for the length and y sections of fence for the breadth (Fig. 13.6).

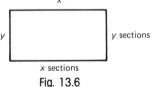

Fig. 13.6

Then the farmer will use $x + y + x + y = 2x + 2y$ sections of fence.

As he has just 24 sections to use, $2x + 2y = 24$.

Dividing both sides by 2 and rearranging gives $y = 12 - x$.

The *area* of the field, A, is length $\times$ breadth, i.e. $A = xy$. Now, we want an equation relating A to x alone, without the complication of a second variable, y; otherwise we cannot differentiate. However, if we replace y with $(12 - x)$ then the equation for A becomes

$$A = x(12 - x)$$

or $$A = 12x - x^2$$

171

Hence $\dfrac{dA}{dx} = 12 - 2x$

For a maximum $\dfrac{dA}{dx} = 0$, so

$$12 - 2x = 0$$

$$x = 6$$

If the length x is 6 then the breadth, $y = 12 - x = 12 - 6 = 6$. So the farmer maximises the area he can fence off by making the field a square of 6 m by 6 m, enclosing 36 m².

EXERCISE 13c

1. A man intends to make a dog pen by fencing off part of his garden, using his back wall as one of the sides. He uses 20 m of fencing to enclose an area x m deep and y m wide, as shown in Fig. 13.7. Show that $y = 20 - 2x$ and that the area, A, of the enclosed pen is given by $A = 20x - 2x^2$.

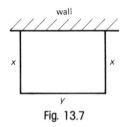

wall

x x

y

Fig. 13.7

Find the maximum area that the man can fence off.

2. The area of a rectangular field is 400 m². If the field is x m wide, write down the length of the field in terms of x.

Show that the perimeter, P, of the field is given by $P = 2x + 800x^{-1}$.

Find $\dfrac{dP}{dx}$ and so prove that the minimum length of fencing required is 80 m.

3.

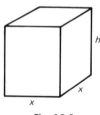

h

x

x

Fig. 13.8

The volume of a closed, square-based oil tank is 64 m³. If the base has side length x m and the height of the tank is h m

(Fig. 13.8), show that $b = \dfrac{64}{x^2}$.

The tank is to be manufactured to have the least possible surface area. Show that the surface area of the tank, A, is given by $A = 2x^2 + \dfrac{256}{x}$.

Find $\dfrac{dA}{dx}$ and hence find the minimum surface area of the tank.

4. Two positive integers, x and y, add up to 32. Find the maximum possible value of their product.

5. Two numbers, x and y, have a product of 40. Find, to 2 d.p., their least possible sum.

6. The cost of running a coach depends partly upon various overheads and partly upon the speed at which it is driven. The cost *per hour*, $£y$, is given by $y = 16 + \dfrac{x^2}{400}$ where x is the speed in km/h.
   (a) How long does a journey of 200 km take at an average speed of x km/h?
   (b) Use your answer to (a) to write down a formula for the *total* cost of a journey of 200 km made at x km/h.
   (c) Find the most economical speed for this coach journey.

7.

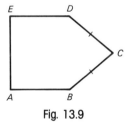

Fig. 13.9

A piece of wire 48 cm long, is bent into the shape of the pentagon $ABCDE$ shown in the diagram (Fig. 13.9), where $ABDE$ is a rectangle and triangle BDC is isosceles. Given that $AE = 6x$ cm, $BC = CD = 5x$ cm and $AB = y$ cm, find an expression for y in terms of x. Hence, or otherwise, show that the area A of the figure, measured in cm², is given by $A = 144x - 36x^2$.

Find the value of x which gives the maximum value of A, and hence find the maximum value of A. (JMB)

173

8. A rectangular box, made of thin sheet metal and without a lid, is of length $2x$ cm, width x cm, and height h cm. Write down an expression, in terms of x and h, for the area of sheet metal required to make the box.

Given that this area is 600 cm², show that

$$h = \frac{600 - 2x^2}{6x}.$$

Hence show that the volume, V cm³, of the box is given by the formula

$$V = 200x - \frac{2x^3}{3}.$$

Find $\dfrac{dV}{dx}$ and hence find the value of x for which V is a maximum. Calculate the volume of the largest such box which can be constructed using exactly 600 cm² of sheet metal.   (LU)

9.

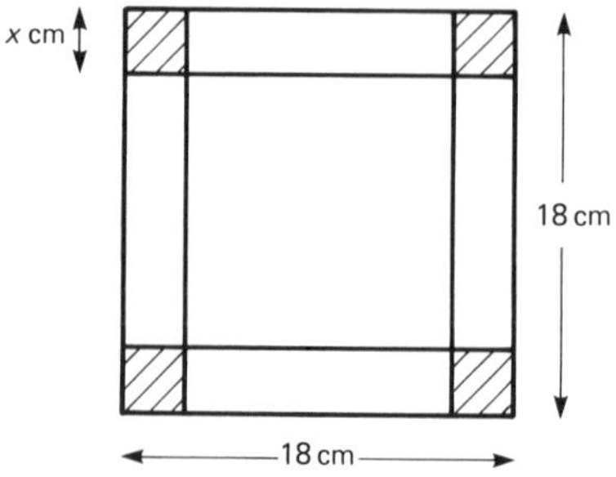

x cm

18 cm

18 cm

Fig. 13.10

The diagram (Fig. 13.10) represents a square sheet of metal 18 cm by 18 cm. At each corner a square x cm by x cm is cut away and the four rectangular flaps are folded upwards to form an open box with a square base and height x cm. Write down

(a) the length of the square base,
(b) the area of the square base,
(c) the volume of the box.

Given that the volume of the box is V cm³, show that

$$V = 4x^3 - 72x^2 + 324x$$

By differentiating this expression, prove that the maximum volume of the box is 432 cm³.   (JMB)

INTEGRATION

Integration is the reverse of differentiation. For example, if we are given $\dfrac{dy}{dx} = 5x^4$, can we find y? We might guess $y = x^5$, since this would give $\dfrac{dy}{dx} = 5x^4$. However, $y = x^5 + 56$ or $y = x^5 - 107$ are also solutions since they, too, give $\dfrac{dy}{dx} = 5x^4$. In general, we say the *integral* of $5x^4$ is $x^5 + C$, where C is some number — the *constant of integration*. As a short-hand notation, we write $\int 5x^4 \, dx = x^5 + C$.

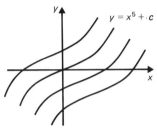

Fig. 13.11

This general solution, $y = x^5 + C$, represents a family of possible solutions which all have the same gradient for any given value of x (Fig. 13.11). More generally, if $\dfrac{dy}{dx} = x^n$, then $y = \int x^n \, dx$, where

$$\int x^n \, dx = \frac{1}{n+1} x^{n+1} + C \quad (n \neq -1)$$

Remember, dx is as much part of the notation as $\int$ and the constant, C, as much a part of the answer.

This formula works for all values of n, whether positive or negative, whole numbers or fractions, *except* $n = -1$ (which would make the denominator of $\dfrac{1}{n+1}$ zero).

Multiplying x^n by a number simply multiplies the integral by the same number. So

$$\int kx^n \, dx = \frac{k}{n+1} x^{n+1} + C$$

Note the integral of a constant k:

$$\int k \, dx = kx + C$$

175

Integrating a series of terms is, like differentiation, simply a matter of integrating each term. However, the formula applies to *powers of x only*, and does not apply to terms multiplied together — so brackets, etc., must be multiplied out *before* you integrate.

Examples Using $\int kx^n \, dx = \dfrac{k}{n+1} x^{n+1} + C.$

(i) $\int 2x^3 \, dx = \dfrac{2}{3+1} \times x^{3+1} + C = \dfrac{2}{4} x^4 + C = \dfrac{1}{2} x^4 + C$

(ii) $\int x^{1/3} \, dx = \dfrac{1}{\frac{1}{3}+1} x^{1/3+1} + C = \dfrac{1}{\frac{4}{3}} x^{4/3} + C = \dfrac{3}{4} x^{4/3} + C$

(iii) $\int 6x^{-2} \, dx = \dfrac{6}{-2+1} x^{-2+1} + C = \dfrac{6}{-1} x^{-1} + C = -6x^{-1} + C$

The results given in the table below were obtained using the same formula. You are advised to work through them all before proceeding to Exercise 13d.

y	$\int y \, dx$
7	$7x + C$
$3x^2$	$x^3 + C$
$x^{1/2}$	$\frac{2}{3}x^{3/2} + C$
$3x^{-4}$	$-x^{-3} + C$
$3x^{-1/2}$	$6x^{1/2} + C$
$6x^2 + 2x - 1$	$2x^3 + x^2 - x + C$
$3x^{-2} - 2x^{-3}$	$-3x^{-1} + x^{-2} + C$
$(x+2)(x-1) = x^2 + x - 2$	$\frac{1}{3}x^3 + \frac{1}{2}x^2 - 2x + C$
$(x+2)^2 = x^2 + 4x + 4$	$\frac{1}{3}x^3 + 2x^2 + 4x + C$

EXERCISE 13d Integrate the following:

1. x^2 2. $3x^2$ 3. x^3 4. $4x^3$

5. 6 6. 2 7. 0 8. $6x^5$

9. $5x^6$ 10. x^{-2} 11. x^{-4} 12. $3x^{-2}$

13. $-5x^{-3}$ 14. $x^{1/3}$ 15. $x^{2/5}$ 16. $x^{-1/3}$

17. $4x^{3/4}$ 18. $-3x^{1/2}$ 19. $\dfrac{3}{x^2}$ 20. $\dfrac{-4}{x^3}$

21. $\dfrac{-12}{x^5}$ 22. $\dfrac{-3}{x^4}$ 23. $\sqrt{x}$ 24. $\dfrac{4}{\sqrt{x}}$

25. $x\sqrt{x}$ 26. $3x-1$ 27. $5x+2$ 28. $3-x$

29. $5-2x$ 30. $3x^2-2$ 31. $3x^2-2x+1$

32. $5x^2+6x-2$ 33. $4x^3-2x+1$ 34. $6x^{1/2}-x^{-1/2}$

35. $7x^{2/5}-x^{-1/3}$ 36. $x(x-1)$ 37. $2x^2(2x+1)$

38. $(x-1)(x+1)$ 39. $(2x-3)^2$ 40. $(3x-1)^2$.

EVALUATING THE CONSTANT OF INTEGRATION

Example The gradient of a curve is given by the formula $\dfrac{dy}{dx} = 2x-6$. If the curve passes through the point $(3,4)$, find the formula for y and the value of y at $x=5$.

If $\dfrac{dy}{dx} = 2x-6$, then

$$y = \int(2x-6)\,dx$$
$$= x^2 - 6x + C$$

But when $x=3$, $y=4$. Therefore

$$4 = (3)^2 - 6(3) + C$$
$$4 = 9 - 18 + C$$

Hence $C = 4 + 18 - 9 = 13$

So $y = x^2 - 6x + 13$

When $x=5$: $y = (5)^2 - 6(5) + 13$
$$= 25 - 30 + 13$$
$$= 8$$

EXERCISE 13e   1. The gradient of a curve is given by the formula $\dfrac{dy}{dx} = 2x+1$.

If the curve passes through the point $(1,7)$, find y when $x=4$.

2. The gradient of a curve passing through the point $(1,10)$ is given by the formula $\dfrac{dy}{dx} = 4x^3 + 2x - 3$. Find y when $x=2$.

3. The gradient of a curve passing through the point $(2, 6)$ is given by the formula $\frac{dy}{dx} = 3x^2$. Find y when $x = 1$.

4. The gradient of a curve passing through the point $(4, 1)$, is given by the formula $\frac{dy}{dx} = 8x^{-2}$. Find y when $x = 1$.

5. The gradient of a curve that passes through the point $(\frac{1}{2}, \frac{1}{2})$ is given by the formula $\frac{dy}{dx} = -2x$. Find y when $x = 0$.

6. A curve meets the x-axis at $x = 3$. If $\frac{dy}{dx} = (3-x)^2$, find the equation for y.

7. The gradient of a curve is given by $\frac{dy}{dx} = kx^2$. If the curve passes through the points $(1, -2)$ and $(2, 5)$, find k and the formula for y.

8. The gradient of a curve is given by $\frac{dy}{dx} = kx^3 - 2x$. If the curve passes through the points $(1, -\frac{1}{2})$ and $(2, 11\frac{1}{2})$, find k and the formula for y.

DEFINITE INTEGRATION

Differentiating a function gives the gradient of the curve. Integration gives the *area between the curve and the x-axis.* Finding the area below the curve, however, requires that *two* values of x are specified (for the sides). These values, $x = a$ and $x = b$ in Fig. 13.12 are called *limits* and are written at the top and bottom of the integral sign.

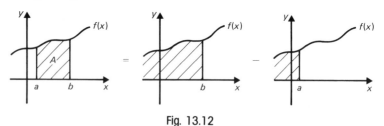

Fig. 13.12

If $\int f(x)\, dx = F(x)$

$$A = \int_a^b f(x)\, dx = [F(x)]_a^b = F(b) - F(a)$$

So to find the area under the curve between $x = a$ and $x = b$, integrate the function, work out the values of the integral, $F(x)$, for $x = a$ and $x = b$, and find the difference between them. (Incidentally, the constant of integration will always disappear with this subtraction, so may be dropped from the calculation — the *only* time you may leave it out.)

Notice the notation above, in particular the positions of the upper and lower limits and the square brackets.

This process of integrating between limits is called *definite integration*, and the result is *always* a value and *never* a function of x.

Examples (*i*) Find the area between the x-axis and the line $y = 4x$ between $x = 1$ and $x = 3$ (a) by integration (b) by geometry (see Fig. 13.13).

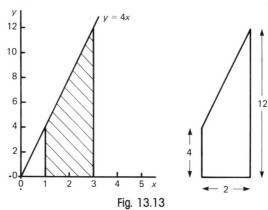

Fig. 13.13

(a) $\displaystyle\int_1^3 4x\,dx = [2x^2]_1^3 = (2(3)^2) - (2(1)^2)$

$$= 18 - 2 = 16 \text{ square units}$$

(b) The area of a trapezium is given by *base length* × *average length of parallel sides*, i.e.

$$A = 2 \times \left(\frac{4 + 12}{2}\right) = 16 \text{ square units}$$

(*ii*) Evaluate the area of the 'cap' formed by the x-axis and $y = (x + 3)(5 - x)$.

The curve is a parabola, with roots at $x = -3$ and $x = +5$, as shown in Fig. 13.14.

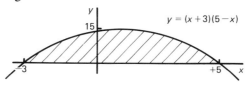

Fig. 13.14

179

$$A = \int_{-3}^{+5} (x+3)(5-x)\,dx = \int_{-3}^{+5} (15+2x-x^2)\,dx$$

$$= \left[15x + x^2 - \frac{x^3}{3} \right]_{-3}^{+5}$$

$$= \left(15 \times (5) + (5)^2 - \frac{(5)^3}{3} \right) - \left(15 \times (-3) + (-3)^2 - \frac{(-3)^3}{3} \right)$$

$$= \left(75 + 25 - \frac{125}{3} \right) - (-45 + 9 + 9)$$

$$= 58\tfrac{1}{3} - (-27)$$

$$= 85\tfrac{1}{3} \text{ square units}$$

EXERCISE 13f Evaluate the following definite integrals:

1. $\int_0^1 3x^2\,dx$

2. $\int_0^1 2x^3\,dx$

3. $\int_1^2 3x\,dx$

4. $\int_2^4 3\,dx$

5. $\int_0^1 6\,dx$

6. $\int_1^2 x^{-2}\,dx$

7. $\int_1^2 x^{-4}\,dx$

8. $\int_3^9 3x^{-2}\,dx$

9. $\int_1^2 -5x^{-3}\,dx$

10. $\int_4^9 x^{1/2}$

11. $\int_1^8 x^{1/3}\,dx$

12. $\int_1^{16} 14x^{3/4}\,dx$

13. $\int_9^{16} x^{-1/2}\,dx$

14. $\int_1^{81} 18x^{-1/4}\,dx$

15. $\int_0^2 (3x^2 - 2x)\,dx$

16. $\int_{-3}^5 (5x+2)\,dx$

17. $\int_1^3 (3-x)^2\,dx$

18. $\int_{-5}^{+5} (5-x)^2\,dx$

19. $\int_0^2 (4x^3 - 3x - 1)\,dx$

20. $\int_1^4 2\sqrt{x}\,dx$

21. $\int_{-1}^2 \frac{32}{x^2}\,dx$

22. $\int_1^{16} \frac{4}{\sqrt{x}}\,dx$

23. $\int_0^1 x\sqrt{x}\,dx$

24. $\int_{-2}^{+2} (x-2)^2\,dx.$

25. Find the area between the x-axis and the curve $y = 3x(x-2)$ between the limits $x = 2$ and $x = 4$.

26. Find the area between the curve $y = x^2 - 3x - 4$ and the x-axis between the limits $x = 4$ and $x = 6$.

27.

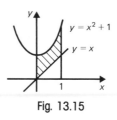

Fig. 13.15

Figure 13.15 shows the graphs of $y = x^2 + 1$ and $y = x$. Find the area of the shaded portion.

28. Draw a *sketch* of the graph $y = x(3 - x)$ for $-1 \leqslant x \leqslant 4$. Find the area that lies beneath the curve and above the x-axis.

29.

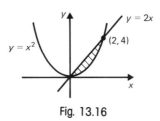

Fig. 13.16

Figure 13.16 shows the curve $y = x^2$ and the line $y = 2x$. Find the area of the shaded portion.

30.

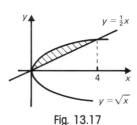

Fig. 13.17

Find the area between the line $y = \dfrac{x}{2}$ and the curve $y = \sqrt{x}$, shown as the shaded area in Figure 13.17.

31. Show that the line $y = x - 1$ and the curve $y = 4x - x^2 - 3$ intersect at the points $(1, 0)$ and $(2, 1)$. Find the area enclosed by the line and the curve.

32. Show that the line $y = x - 2$ and the curve $y = 7x - x^2 - 10$ intersect at the points $(2, 0)$ and $(4, 2)$. Find the area enclosed by the line and the curve.

33.

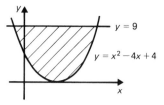

Fig. 13.18

Find the two points at which the line $y = 9$ intersects the curve $y = x^2 - 4x + 4$.

Copy the sketch in Fig. 13.18.

Label clearly the line, the curve and the points of intersection.

Find by integration the shaded area enclosed by the line and curve.

34. Repeat Question 33 for the following lines and curves. In each case illustrate the problem with a sketch.

(a) $y = x^2 + 2x + 3$; $y = 6$

(b) $y = x^2 - 6x + 9$; $y = 4$

(c) $y = x^2 - 7x + 15$; $y = 5$

(d) $y = x^2 - 8x + 16$; $y = x - 2$

(e) $y = x^2 - 2x + 1$; $y = x + 5$.

35.

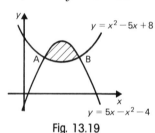

Fig. 13.19

Figure 13.19 shows the curves $y = x^2 - 5x + 8$ and $y = 5x - x^2 - 4$. Find the coordinates of the points A and B where the two curves intersect and use integration to find the area enclosed between them.

36. Repeat Question 35 for the following curves:

(a) $y = x^2 - 4x + 4$ and $y = 10x - x^2 - 16$

(b) $y = x^2 - 5x + 7$ and $y = 7x - x^2 - 9$

(c) $y = x^2 - 3x + 4$ and $y = 4 - x^2$.

14 TRAVEL GRAPHS

DISTANCE–TIME GRAPHS

A journey can be illustrated graphically by plotting the distance travelled away from some starting point against the time taken. For example, Fig. 14.1 shows the distance–time graph for a journey of 12 km made by a cyclist. For the first 20 min, the cyclist makes good progress, covering a lot of ground quickly. Unfortunately, at A, he has a puncture, which he stops to repair. So for the next 15 min he does not travel any further: the portion AB of the distance–time graph is completely flat. Having made his repair, the cyclist continues his journey, but at a slower pace, until he arrives at C.

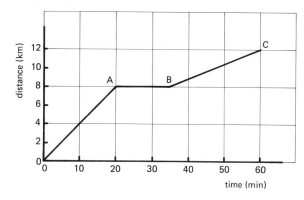

Fig. 14.1

The speed of the traveller can be found from the *slope* of the distance–time graph; the steeper the graph the faster the rate of travel. The cyclist in this example travels 8 km in the first 20 min of his journey, so his speed is $\dfrac{\text{distance}}{\text{time}} = \dfrac{8}{20} = 0.4$ km/min or $0.4 \times 60 = 24$ km/h. In the last 25 min of his journey he only covers another 4 km. So his speed is $\dfrac{4}{25} = 0.16$ km/min or $0.16 \times 60 = 9.6$ km/h.

More than one journey can be represented on the same graph. And a *return* journey is represented by a downward sloping graph (for, as time goes by, so the traveller gets nearer to his starting point).

Example Caroline sets out at 12 noon to drive from her lodgings in London to her parents' home in Chichester (a distance of 100 km). She drives at an average speed of 50 km/h. Her sister Susan decides to meet her. She sets out from Chichester at 12.30 p.m., cycling up the London Road at 20 km/h for the first half hour. She rests for 20 min and then continues at the same speed. When do the sisters meet, and how far are they from Chichester?

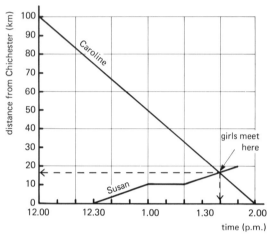

Fig. 14.2

Figure 14.2 shows the distance–time graph of the girls' journeys. Caroline's journey is shown as the *downward sloping* line, for she is *approaching* Chichester. It will take her 2 h to drive 100 km at 50 km/h. So she will arrive at Chichester at 2.00 p.m. Susan's outward but slower journey is shown as the gently rising line. Her rest period is shown by the flat portion of the graph. From the graph, it is clear that they meet at 1.40 p.m., about 17 km from Chichester.

EXERCISE 14a

1. A boy sets out on a cycle ride. He cycles for half an hour at 20 km/h, stops for 10 minutes and then sets out again, this time at 15 km/h, for another 40 m. He stops for 15 min and then cycles home at a steady 20 km/h. How far is his complete journey? Illustrate the journey on a distance–time graph.

2. A motorist sets out on a journey of 100 km. He drives for the first half hour at an average speed of 40 km/h. Then he reaches the motorway and his speed increases to an average of 100 km/h. He drives for another half hour on the motorway, then stops for 15 min at a service station before completing his journey by an 'A'-road at an average speed of 60 km/h. How long does the journey take him? Illustrate the journey with a distance–time graph.

3.

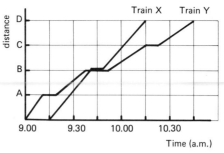

Fig. 14.3

Two trains, X and Y, set out at different times from the same station and for the same destination, D, passing through towns A, B and C along the way. The journeys are illustrated by the distance–time graph in Fig. 14.3. Describe, in words, the journeys of each train. When does the second train catch up with the first?

4. Two men agree to meet at a point between their respective home-towns. Mr A sets out at 9.30 a.m. from Ayton, driving at a steady 60 km/h, half an hour after Mr B has left Beetown which is 120 km away. Mr B drives at 75 km/h but stops for 20 min on the way. Illustrate the men's journeys on a distance–time graph and use it to find the time at which the men meet and the distance of their rendezvous from Ayton.

5.

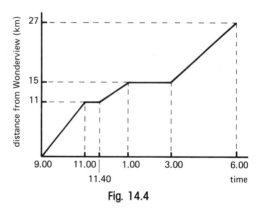

Fig. 14.4

The distance–time graph shown in Fig. 14.4 represents the progress made by a rambler journeying from Wonderview Youth Hostel to Longrest, 27 km away.

(a) What is the rambler's average speed for the whole journey?

(b) What is his fastest speed? How far did he walk at this speed?

(c) What is his slowest speed (not counting rest periods)?

6.

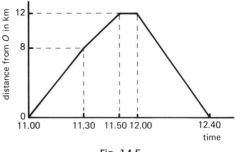

Fig. 14.5

The graph (Fig. 14.5) which consists of straight line segments represents the distance of a cyclist from his starting point (*O*) plotted against time. Draw the graph accurately on squared paper using scales of 1 cm for 5 minutes and 1 cm for 1 kilometre. Find the average speeds in kilometres per hour of the cyclist:

(a) between 11.00 and 11.30

(b) on his outward journey

(c) on his return journey.

At 11.30 a pedestrian was 12 km from *O* and walked towards *O* at a steady speed of 6 km/h. Plot the straight line graph of his path, and hence find the times of the two occasions when he met the cyclist. (Ox)

7. A motorist travels at an average speed of 60 m.p.h. on a motorway.

At 1.00 p.m. he is at a point A on a motorway, and is travelling towards a service station B, which is 20 miles away. When he gets there he rests for 10 minutes before leaving the motorway to travel to C which is 40 miles *from B*, arriving there at 2.50 p.m. At C he joins another motorway and travels at 60 m.p.h. on to D, which is 50 miles *from C*.

D is therefore 110 miles from A.

(a) Draw a graph of the motorist's journey from A to D, using 6 cm to represent one hour and 2 cm to represent 10 miles.

At 2.00 p.m. a lorry driver leaves D to travel to C on the motorway, and passes the motorist at 3.00 p.m.

(b) Using the same graph paper, draw a graph of the lorry driver's journey.

(c) (i) What time does the motorist arrive at D?

(ii) What is the motorist's speed when not on the motorway?

(iii) What is the lorry driver's speed?

(iv) At what time does the lorry driver arrive at C?

(WJEC)

8. *ABCD* are four stations on a railway line. *B* is 40 miles from
A, *C* is 80 miles from *A* and *D* is 120 miles from *A*. All trains
travelling between *A* and *B* and between *C* and *D* travel at
60 miles per hour, but between *B* and *C* they can only travel
at 40 miles per hour because of repairs being made to the
track. All trains stop at *B* and *C* and wait at both stations for
6 minutes before proceeding on their way.

(a) (i) Draw a graph of the train that starts from *A* at
12.00 noon and proceeds to *D*, using 6 cm to represent one hour (on the short side of the graph paper)
and 2 cm to represent 10 miles (on the long side of
of the graph paper).

(ii) Use your graph to find the time the train LEAVES *B*.

(b) (i) On the same graph paper, draw a graph of the train
that starts from *D* at 12.20 p.m. and proceeds to *A*.

(ii) Use your graph to find at what time this train
ARRIVES at *B*.

(iii) Use your graph to find when and where the two
trains pass each other. (WJEC)

VELOCITY–TIME GRAPHS

Instead of plotting the distance covered, we might instead plot a
traveller's *speed* against time.

The total distance covered can be found from the area underneath
the graph (see Fig. 14.6). The acceleration of the traveller at any
time can be found from the slope of the graph.

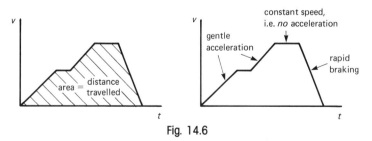

Fig. 14.6

Note: the average velocity $= \dfrac{\text{total distance covered}}{\text{total time taken}}$.

187

Example The velocity–time graph for a school race run by a young boy is shown in Fig. 14.7. Find

(a) his acceleration during each phase of the run

(b) the length of the race

(c) the boy's average speed over the whole race.

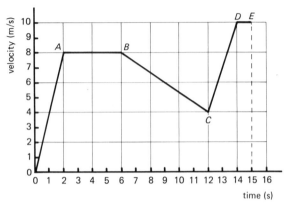

Fig. 14.7

(a) In the first 2 s the boy accelerates smoothly to 8 m/s.

$$\text{acceleration} = \frac{\text{increase in velocity}}{\text{time}} = \frac{8}{2} = 4 \text{ m/s}^2$$

For 4 s the boy maintains this pace, so he is not accelerating.

But for the next 6 s, from B to C on the graph, the boy tires and steadily loses speed.

$$\text{deceleration} = \frac{\text{decrease in velocity}}{\text{time}} = \frac{8-4}{6} = \frac{4}{6} = \frac{2}{3} \text{ m/s}^2$$

In the next phase, from C to D on the graph, the boy makes his final spurt. His speed increases from 4 m/s to 10 m/s in 2 s:

$$\text{acceleration} = \frac{10-4}{2} = \frac{6}{2} = 3 \text{ m/s}^2$$

In the final second, the velocity–time graph is flat, i.e. there is no acceleration.

(b) The length of the race, that is the distance run by the boy, can be found from the area underneath the graph. Figure 14.8 shows the graph divided into various triangular, rectangular and trapezoidal sections. By finding the area of each section and totalling them, we see the boy runs

$$8 + 32 + 36 + 14 + 10 = 100 \text{ m}$$

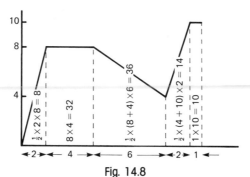

Fig. 14.8

(c) The boy's average speed $= \dfrac{\text{total distance run}}{\text{total time taken}} = \dfrac{100}{15}$

$= 6.67$ m/s.

EXERCISE 14b   1. Figure 14.9 shows the velocity–time graph for a cycle ride.

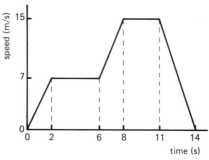

Fig. 14.9

(a) What is the cyclist's greatest speed?

(b) What is his greatest acceleration?

(c) How far does the cyclist ride?

(d) What is his average speed?

2.

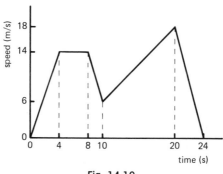

Fig. 14.10

Figure 14.10 shows the velocity–time graph for a certain journey.

(a) What is the greatest speed reached?

(b) What is the initial acceleration?

(c) What is the deceleration in the last phase of the journey?

(d) How long is the journey?

(e) What is the average speed?

3. In the first 20 s of his journey, a motorist accelerates from rest to v m/s, as shown in Fig. 14.11. How far, in terms of v, does he travel in this time.

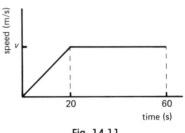

Fig. 14.11

The motorist continues at this speed; if he has travelled exactly 1 km in the first minute of his journey, calculate the value of v.

4. Figure 14.12 shows a sketch of the velocity–time graph for the first 80 s of a car journey. How far does the car travel in the first 10 s?

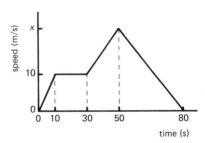

Fig. 14.12

If the car covers 1100 m in the 80 s, what is the value of x?

5.

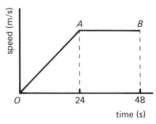

Fig. 14.13

The speed–time graph of a car during the first 48 seconds of its motion consists of two straight lines OA and AB (Fig. 14.13)

The car starts from rest, travels 360 metres in the first 24 seconds and it then travels at a constant speed for the remaining 24 seconds.

Calculate

(a) the distance travelled in the first 12 seconds,

(b) the distance travelled in the last 24 seconds,

(c) the average speed for the 48 seconds.   (C)

6. A car is travelling at 36 km/h. What is this speed converted into m/s? The car accelerates from rest to 36 km/h in 5 s. It travels at this speed for 10 s before accelerating again to 108 km/h over a further 10 s. Sketch the velocity–time graph for these 25 s. How far does the car travel in this time?

7. A bus accelerates smoothly away from a bus-stop to 54 km/h in 20 s. It travels at this speed for 30 s, when the driver has to brake sharply, decelerating the vehicle from 54 km/h to 18 km/h in 2 s. The driver accelerates again, up to 36 km/h in 8 s and then coasts gently to a halt, over a further 30 s, at the next bus-stop. Sketch the velocity–time graph for this journey (showing speeds in m/s). What is the distance between the two bus-stops?

8. A car accelerates from rest and readings are taken of the speed, in metres per second, and the time, in seconds.

Speed	0	5.2	10.1	14.2	17.1	18.9	20.2	21.1	21.7	22.0	22.2
Time	0	1	2	3	4	5	6	7	8	9	10

Choose suitable scales to plot the readings on a graph, taking speed as the y-axis.

Use your graph to estimate:

(a) the speed after 3.5 seconds;

(b) the time when the speed is 8.0 m/s;

(c) the rate at which the speed was changing (i.e. acceleration) at 6 seconds;

(d) the distance travelled in the first ten seconds, to the nearest 5 m.   (SUJB)

9. A particle moves along a straight line AB so that, after t seconds, the velocity v m/s in the direction **AB** is given by

$$v = 2t^2 - 9t + 5.$$

Corresponding values of t and v are given in the table below:

t	0	1	2	3	4	5	6	7
v	5		-5	-4	1	10	23	

Calculate the value of v when $t = 1$ and the value of v when $t = 7$.

Taking 2 cm to represent 1 second on the horizontal axis and 2 cm to represent 5 m/s on the vertical axis, draw the graph of

$$v = 2t^2 - 9t + 5 \quad \text{for the range } 0 \leqslant t \leqslant 7.$$

Use your graph to estimate
(a) the values of t when the velocity is zero,
(b) the time at which the acceleration is zero.
(c) the acceleration after 6 seconds. $\hspace{2cm}$ (C)

DIFFERENTIATION AND TRAVEL

Velocity, $\dfrac{ds}{dt}$

If the distance travelled by a moving object is s m and s can be defined in terms of the time, t s, we can find the velocity using differentiation (instead of drawing a graph and measuring gradients):

$$\text{velocity} = \text{gradient of distance–time graph} = \frac{ds}{dt}$$

Acceleration, $\dfrac{dv}{dt}$

Similarly, once we know the velocity we can find the acceleration using differentiation a second time:

$$\text{acceleration} = \text{gradient of velocity–time graph} = \frac{dv}{dt}$$

Note: when tackling problems of this sort, it is worth remembering that the moving object is
(a) 'at the starting point' or 'at the beginning' when $t = 0$ and $s = 0$
(b) 'at rest' when $v = 0$
(c) 'moving steadily' when $a = 0$.

Example A particle travels a distance s m from its starting point in time t s where $s = t^3 - 3t^2 - 9t$. Find the velocity and acceleration of the particle after 2 s. When is the particle at rest?

$$\text{velocity,} \quad v = \frac{ds}{dt} = 3t^2 - 6t - 9$$

$$\text{acceleration,} \quad a = \frac{dv}{dt} = 6t - 6$$

At $t = 2$ s,

$$v = 3(2)^2 - 6(2) - 9 = 12 - 12 - 9 = -9 \text{ m/s}$$

(The negative sign indicates that the particle is moving backwards.)

$$a = 6(2) - 6 = 12 - 6 = 6$$

So after 2 s, the particle is reversing at 9 m/s and accelerating at 6 m/s².

The particle is at rest when $v = 0$. We know that $v = 3t^2 - 6t - 9$. So the particle is at rest when

$$3t^2 - 6t - 9 = 0$$

$$3(t + 1)(t - 3) = 0$$

The two possible solutions to this equation are $t = -1$ (which is not possible: time is always positive) or $t = +3$. Thus the particle is momentarily at rest after 3 s.

EXERCISE 14c A particle is a distance s m from its starting point after t s of motion. Find

(a) a formula for the velocity, v,

(b) a formula for the acceleration, a, of the particle, and

(c) the values of s, v and a after 3 s if

1. $s = t^2 + 4t + 12$ 2. $s = t^3 - 3t^2$

3. $s = 4t^2 - 3t + 6$ 4. $s = 2t^3 + 3t^2 + 4t - 1$

5. $s = 100 - t^2$ 6. $s = 5t + 6$

7. $s = -4t + \frac{1}{2}t^2$ 8. $s = 4\sqrt{t}$.

9. The velocity of a particle is given by the formula $v = t^2 - 25$. Find

(a) the velocity when $t = 0$

(b) the velocity when $t = 10$

(c) the acceleration when $t = 0$

(d) the acceleration when $t = 10$.

Find also the time when the particle is at rest.

10. The distance, s m, of a particle from its starting point, O, after t s is given by the formula $s = 2t^3 - 9t^2 + 12t$. Find a formula for the velocity of the particle after t s and show that it is momentarily at rest at $t = 1$ and $t = 2$.

Find the distance of the particle from O and its acceleration at these times.

11. A particle is s m from its starting point, O, after t s where $s = 4t^3 - 3t^2 - 6t$. Find

(a) a formula for its velocity, v, after t s

(b) the moment when it is at rest

(c) a formula for its acceleration, a

(d) the moment when there is no acceleration.

12. A particle is s m from a reference point, O, after t s where $s = t^3 - 6t^2 + 9t + 2$.

(a) How far from this reference point is the particle at the start?

(b) When is the particle at O?

(c) Find the velocity, v, of the particle after 2 s.

(d) When is the particle at rest?

13. A stone is thrown out of a window. Its height above the ground (in metres) after t s of flight is given by $h = 8 + 3t - 5t^2$.

(a) What is the height of the window above the ground?

(b) What was the speed of the stone the moment it was thrown?

(c) When is the stone at its maximum height above the ground and what is this maximum height?

(d) When does the stone hit the ground, and how fast is it travelling at that instant?

14. Repeat Question 13 for a second stone which has a height, h m, given by $h = 24 + 37t - 5t^2$.

INTEGRATION AND TRAVEL

Since integration is the reverse of differentiation, we can use it to find velocity and distance travelled from an acceleration formula:

$$v = \int a \, dt \qquad \text{and} \qquad s = \int v \, dt$$

When using integration in this way be sure to find any constants of integration.

Example A particle travels from its starting point with an initial velocity of 6 m/s and an acceleration given by $a = 3t$ m/s². Find (a) its velocity and (b) its distance from its starting point after 3 s.

(a) $v = \int 3t \, dt = \dfrac{3t^2}{2} + C.$

We are told that $v = 6$ at $t = 0$: thus

$$6 = \frac{3(0)^2}{2} + C$$

i.e. $C = 6$. So

$$v = \frac{3t^2}{2} + 6$$

After 3 s

$$v = \frac{3(3)^2}{2} + 6 = 19.5 \text{ m/s}$$

(b) $s = \int v \, dt = \int \dfrac{3t^2}{2} + 6 \; dt$

$$= \frac{t^3}{2} + 6t + k$$

At $t = 0$, the particle is at its starting point, i.e. $s = 0$. So the constant of integration, k, is also zero. Hence

$$s = \frac{t^3}{2} + 6t$$

After 3 s

$$s = \frac{3^3}{2} + 6(3) = 31.5 \text{ m}$$

EXERCISE 14d A particle moves away from its starting point with initial velocity u m/s and acceleration a m/s². Find (a) the formula for its velocity, v m/s, after t s (b) the formula for its distance, s m, from the starting point and (c) the values of a, v and s after 3 s if

1. $a = 4t; u = 2$ m/s   2. $a = 3t; u = 3$ m/s

3. $a = -\frac{1}{2}t; u = 6$ m/s   4. $a = 6 - t^2; u = 2$ m/s

5. $a = 4; u = 7$ m/s

6. $a = -1; u = 3$ m/s

7. $a = 100 - t^2; u = 5$ m/s

8. $a = 4\sqrt{t}; u = 4$ m/s

9. $a = -\sqrt{t^3}; u = 6$ m/s

10. $a = \dfrac{2}{\sqrt{t}}; u = 2$ m/s.

11.

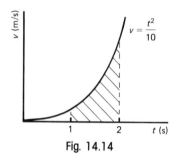

Fig. 14.14

Figure 14.14 shows the velocity–time graph for a certain car journey. Use integration to find the shaded area underneath the curve and thus the distance travelled between $t = 1$ and $t = 2$.

12.

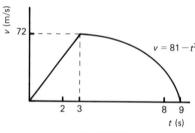

Fig. 14.15

A particle accelerates uniformly from rest to a velocity of 72 m/s in 3 s. It then decelerates so that its velocity follows the formula $v = 81 - t^2$ (see Fig. 14.15). Show that the particle is at rest again after a further 6 s.

(a) What is the deceleration when $t = 4$?

(b) Find the distance the particle travels between $t = 2$ and $t = 8$.

15 ANGLES AND PARALLELS

ANGLES

A complete turn is divided into 360°. A quarter turn, or *right angle*, is 90°. An angle of less than 90° is called an *acute* angle. An angle between 90° and 180° is called *obtuse*. An angle greater than 180° is called a *reflex* angle. (See Fig. 15.1.)

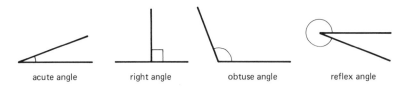

| acute angle | right angle | obtuse angle | reflex angle |

Fig. 15.1

Angles on a straight line add up to 180°; two angles that add up to 180° are said to be *supplementary*. For example, 73° and 107° are supplementary angles, and could be two angles on a straight line (see Fig. 15.2).

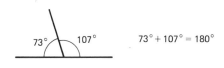

$73° + 107° = 180°$

Fig. 15.2

Complementary angles add up to 90°; for example 23° and 67° are complementary.

When two lines cross then *opposite* angles are equal (Fig. 15.3).

Fig. 15.3

Two lines that meet at right angles are said to be *perpendicular* to each other.

When a straight line cuts across two parallel lines then various angles are equal.

Corresponding angles are equal (Fig. 15.4).

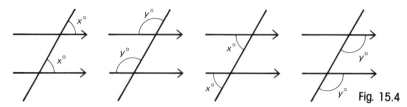

Fig. 15.4

Alternate angles are also equal (Fig. 15.5).

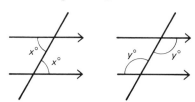

Fig. 15.5

EXERCISE 15a

1. Name the following types of angles:

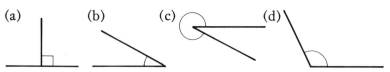

(a)   (b)   (c)   (d)

2. Give a reason for the angles shown being equal:

(a)   (b)   (c)

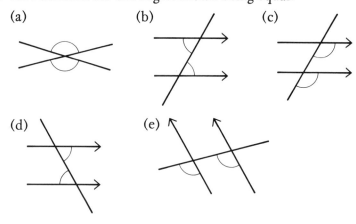

(d)   (e)

3. Work out the value of angle x in each of the following, giving reasons for your answer:

(a)   (b)   (c)

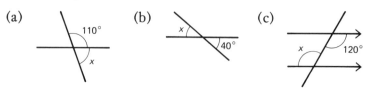

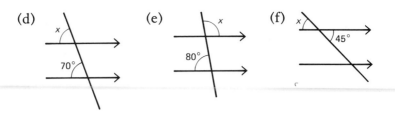

(d) x 70° (e) 80° x (f) x 45°

4. Prove that the lines AB and CD in Fig. 15.6 are parallel. Give your reasons.

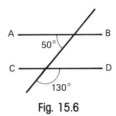

A —————— B
    50°
C —————— D
    130°

Fig. 15.6

In Questions 5 to 18, find the angles marked with letters. Be sure to give your reasons for every step.

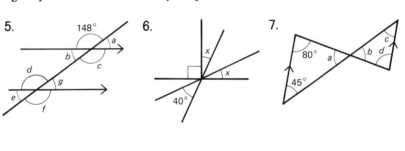

5. 148° a b c d g e f

6. x x 40°

7. 80° a b d c 45°

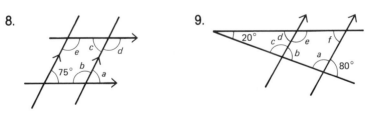

8. e c d 75° b a

9. 20° c d e f b a 80°

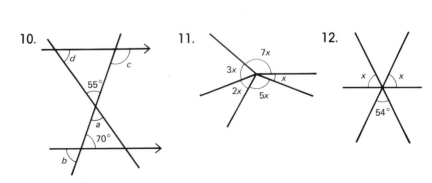

10. d c 55° a 70° b

11. 7x 3x x 2x 5x

12. x x x x 54°

13.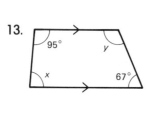

14.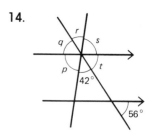

15.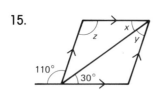

16.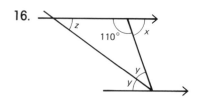

17.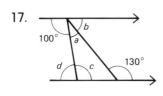

18.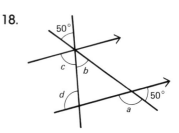

SIMPLE CONSTRUCTIONS

Any work involving accurate construction requires a sharp, medium grade pencil, an efficient eraser, an undamaged ruler marked in millimetres, a pair of compasses and set-squares. Do *not* rub out the marks you make in the process of a correct construction.

To draw one line parallel to another

(*i*) Place the longest edge of the set-square along the given line (see Fig. 15.7).

(*ii*) Place a ruler along another edge of the set square.

(*iii*) Slide the set-square down the edge of the ruler until it reaches the required position.

(*iv*) Draw the parallel line.

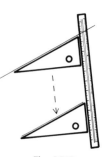

Fig. 15.7

200

To bisect a line

(*i*)   Set the compasses to a convenient radius, greater than half the length of the given line, AB.

(*ii*) Mark arcs, centred on A and B, above and below the line, in the middle region (Fig. 15.8(a)).

(*iii*) Draw a line through the points of intersection of these arcs. This line will bisect AB and be perpendicular to it (Fig. 15.8(b)).

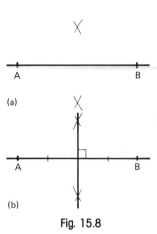

Fig. 15.8

To construct a right angle at a point on a line

(*i*)   Set the compasses to any convenient radius and mark two points, A and B, on the line on either side of the point, P (Fig. 15.9).

(*ii*) Bisect the line AB, following the procedures above.

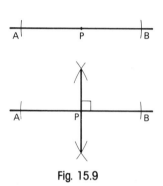

Fig. 15.9

To bisect an angle

(*i*)   Set the compasses to any convenient radius; mark arcs centred on O on both lines, as shown in Fig. 15.10(a) at A and B.

(*ii*) Draw an arc centred on A, and another centred on B, using the same radius, so that they intersect at C (Fig. 15.10(b)).

(*iii*) Draw the line OC which bisects the angle AOB (Fig. 15.10(c)).

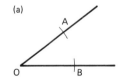

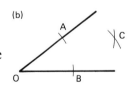

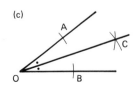

Fig. 15.10

201

EXERCISE 15b   *In these constructions, use a pencil, ruler, set-square and compasses only. Use your protractor to check the accuracy of your drawing.*

1. Draw a line. Mark on it two points, A and B, 6 cm apart. Set a pair of compasses to a radius of 5 cm and draw above the line AB a wide arc, centred on A; change the radius to 7.5 cm and draw a second arc, centred on B, to intersect with the first at C. Draw the lines AC and BC to complete a triangle with sides 6 cm, 5 cm and 7.5 cm.

   Measure the three angles $\widehat{A}$, $\widehat{B}$ and $\widehat{C}$ with a protractor and check that they total 180°.

2. Follow the procedure of Question 1 to construct accurately a triangle with sides 7 cm, 5 cm and 4 cm.

3. Follow the procedure of Question 1 to construct an equilateral triangle with sides of 6 cm.

4. Construct an isosceles triangle with sides of 8 cm, 8 cm and 4 cm.

5. Construct an equilateral triangle with sides of any convenient length. Bisect one of the angles of the triangle to make an angle of 30°; bisect the 30° angle to make another angle of 15°.

6. Construct a right angle at any convenient point P on a line. Bisect the right angle to construct an angle of 45°.

7. Draw two lines, the second line parallel to the first and 4 cm from it. Set a pair of compasses to a radius of 5 cm and from a convenient point, A, on the first line mark a point B, 5 cm from A on the same line; now mark a third point, C, 5 cm from A on the *second* line. Join A to C. Complete the construction of a rhombus ABDC.

8. Construct a square of side length 6 cm.

9. Construct a parallelogram with sides 7 cm and 8 cm.

10. Construct a triangle of any convenient size. Bisect the three angles. These angle bisectors should all meet at a point.

11. Construct another triangle of any convenient size. Construct the perpendicular bisectors of the three sides. These, too, should meet at a point.

12. Construct a third triangle of any convenient size. Bisect each side. Join the mid-point of each side to the corner opposite. These three lines (the *medians*) also meet at a single point.

ANGULAR DIRECTION

Angles are used not only in the course of geometric problems and proofs but also as precise measures of direction, in which case certain conventions must be observed.

Mathematicians measure direction in an anticlockwise sense from the horizontal x-axis. For example, directions of $75°$, $110°$ and $330°$ are measured as illustrated in Fig. 15.11.

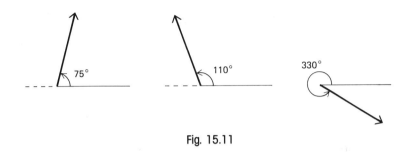

Fig. 15.11

If an angle is measured in the clockwise sense, then it is shown as a negative angle (see Fig. 15.12).

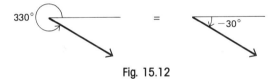

Fig. 15.12

BEARINGS

Navigators measure direction as three-figure *bearings*, angles measured *clockwise* from north (see Fig. 15.13).

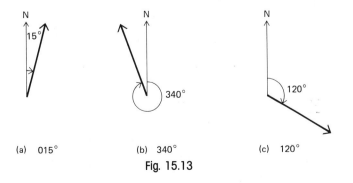

(a) 015°   (b) 340°   (c) 120°

Fig. 15.13

Alternatively, a navigator may measure from North or South in degrees east or west (Fig. 15.14).

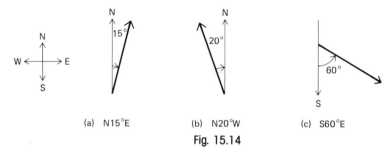

(a) N15°E   (b) N20°W   (c) S60°E

Fig. 15.14

In all, we have three formal ways of measuring a given direction. For example, a direction of 75° measured in a mathematician's way (Fig. 15.15(a)) is equivalent to the navigator's bearing of 015° (Fig. 15.15(b)) or N15°E (Fig. 15.15(c)).

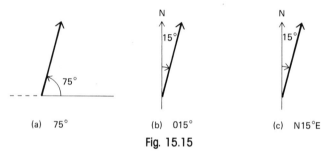

(a)   75°   (b)   015°   (c)   N15°E

Fig. 15.15

Note: Although the directions may be equivalent, it would be inappropriate to use navigational bearings in the course of a mathematical problem or vice versa.

BACK-BEARINGS

Given the bearings of a point B from a starting point A, then the bearing of A from B is known as the *back-bearing*.

Examples (*i*) Carlisle lies on a bearing of 334° from Penrith. From Fig. 15.16, it should be clear that the back-bearing, i.e. the bearing of Penrith from Carlisle, is

$$334° - 180° = 154°$$

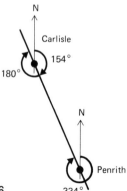

Fig. 15.16

(*ii*) Dundee lies on a bearing of 128° from Blairgowrie. From Fig. 15.17, we can see that the bearing of Blairgowrie from Dundee is

$$128° + 180° = 308°$$

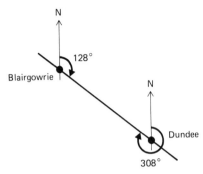

Fig. 15.17

In general, if the forward-bearing is *less* than 180°, then *add* 180° to find the back-bearing; if the forward-bearing is *greater* than 180°, then *subtract* 180° to find the back-bearing.

EXERCISE 15c

1. Write as three-figure bearings the following directions (measured by the mathematicians' convention, anticlockwise from the *x*-axis):

   (a) 64°   (b) 72°   (c) 99°   (d) 195°   (e) 282°
   (f) 343°.

2. Write the following three-figure bearings as angles measured anticlockwise from the *x*-axis:

   (a) 050°   (b) 085°   (c) 125°   (d) 186°   (e) 222°
   (f) 333°

3. Write the following directions as three-figure bearings:

   (a) N35°E   (b) N35°W   (c) S35°E   (d) S35°W.

4. Write as three-figure bearings the directions known as

   (a) due south   (b) south-east   (c) south-west
   (d) north-west.

5. The bearing of Kilmarnock from the centre of Dumfries is 318°. Find the bearing of Dumfries from Kilmarnock.

6. The bearing of Armagh from the centre of Londonderry is 147°. Find the bearing of Londonderry from Armagh.

7. The bearing of Newport from Cardiff is 049°. Find the bearing of Cardiff from Newport.

8. Plymouth lies on a bearing 234° from Exeter. Find the bearing of Exeter from Plymouth.

9. The bearing of Ipswich from Colchester is 039°; what is the bearing of Colchester from Ipswich?

10. The centre of Norwich is 26 km due west of the race-track at Great Yarmouth. The race-track, in turn, is 26 km due north of a light-house at Southwold. What is the bearing of the light-house from the centre of Norwich?

11.

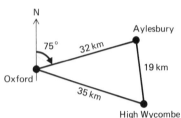

Fig. 15.18

Figure 15.18 (not drawn to scale) shows the distances between Oxford, High Wycombe and Aylesbury. Aylesbury lies on a bearing of 075° from Oxford. By drawing the triangle accurately to scale, use your protractor to find the bearing of High Wycombe:

(a) from Oxford

(b) from Aylesbury

Give your answers to the nearest degree.

12. Standing at the top of Snowdon, I can make out Conway Castle 30 km away on a bearing of 036°, and the cathedral at Bangor 15 km away on a bearing of 348°. By scale-drawing find, to the nearest whole number,

(a) the distance from Bangor to Conway

(b) the bearing of Bangor from Conway.

13. Two aircraft set out simultaneously from Heathrow. One sets course for Paris on a bearing of 115° and travels at 330 km/h; the other sets course for Madrid on a bearing of 194° and travels at 420 km/h. By scale-drawing, find the distance between the two aircraft and the bearing of the first aircraft from the second after 20 min.

14. I run at 16 km/h for 15 min on a bearing of 342°, then walk for 20 min at 6 km/h on a bearing of 032°. I then jog for a further 30 min at 10 km/h on a bearing of 165°. Find, by scale-drawing, the course I must set to return directly to my starting point. How far will I have to travel, and how long will it take me at 10 km/h?

15. A party of explorers sets out from a point A to reach a point B which lies 120 km from A on a bearing of 330°. In order to avoid some difficult country the party first travels on a bearing of 030° for a distance of 60 km to a point P, and then on a bearing of 300° for a distance of 40 km to a point Q. By accurate drawing *on squared paper* or by calculation, find the bearing and distance of B from Q.

On their actual route the party average a speed of 4 km/h, whereas if they had travelled directly from A to B they would only have averaged a speed of 2 km/h. Calculate the time saved by taking the longer route. (O & C)

16 TRIANGLES

TYPES OF TRIANGLES

A *scalene* triangle has no sides or angles equal (Fig. 16.1(a)).

An *isosceles* triangle has two sides and two angles equal (Fig. 16.1(b)). The line that cuts the third angle in half also cuts the base line in half, and meets it at right angles.

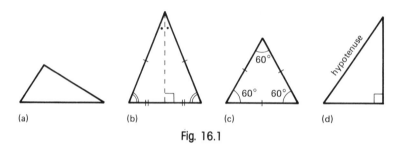

Fig. 16.1

An *equilateral* triangle has all sides equal and all angles equal to 60° (Fig. 16.1(c)).

A *right-angled* triangle contains one right angle and two acute angles (Fig. 16.1(d)). It may also be an isosceles triangle, but is never equilateral. The side opposite the right-angle (the longest side) is called the *hypotenuse*.

The relationship between the different types of triangle can be shown on a Venn diagram (see Fig. 16.2).

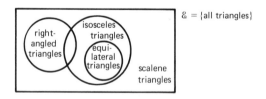

Fig. 16.2

PROPERTIES OF TRIANGLES

For *all* triangles, the following conditions must hold:

(*i*)   The sum of the three interior angles is 180°.

(*ii*) The angle formed by extending one of the sides (the *exterior* angle) is equal to the sum of the two interior angles opposite.

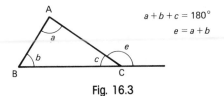

$$a + b + c = 180°$$
$$e = a + b$$

Fig. 16.3

(*iii*) The area A of a triangle is given by

$$A = \tfrac{1}{2} \text{ base} \times \text{height}$$

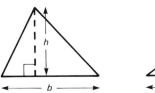 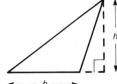

Fig. 16.4

There is nothing special about which way up a triangle is drawn; *any* side can be taken as the base simply by rotating the paper; the height will then be the perpendicular line through the opposite corner (Fig. 16.5).

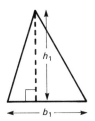 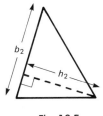 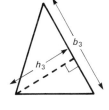

Fig. 16.5

If the area of the triangle is known, then it may be possible to deduce the length of the base or the height using

$$\text{base} = \frac{2 \times \text{area}}{\text{height}} \quad \text{or} \quad \text{height} = \frac{2 \times \text{area}}{\text{base}}$$

EXERCISE 16a   1. Find the angles x and y in the following triangles:

(a)

(b)

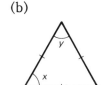

(c)

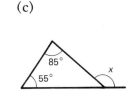

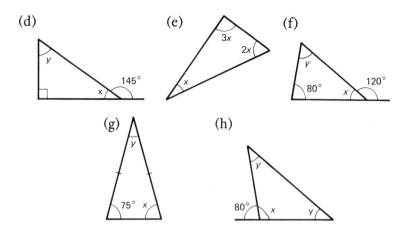

2. Find the area of a triangle of base length 5 cm and height 4 cm.

3. A triangle has area 18 cm² and height 3 cm. What is its base length?

4. A triangle has area 36 cm². If its base is 9 cm, what is its height?

5.

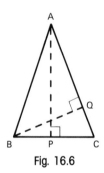

Fig. 16.6

In the triangle shown in Fig. 16.6, BC = 9 cm, BQ = 6 cm. Find the lengths of AP and AC, given that the area of the triangle is 54 cm².

6.

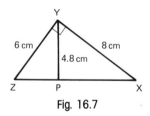

Fig. 16.7

In the triangle XYZ, $\widehat{Y} = 90°$, XY = 8 cm and YZ = 6 cm. If YP = 4.8 cm, find the length of XZ.

7.

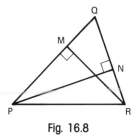

Fig. 16.8

In triangle PQR (Fig. 16.8), PQ = 12 cm, MR = 6 cm and PN = 9 cm. Find the length of QR.

SIMILAR TRIANGLES

If two triangles are the same basic shape, but one is an enlargement of the other, they are said to be *similar*. Any pair of triangles with two corresponding angles equal must be similar. The lengths of corresponding sides of similar triangles are proportional to each other. For example, triangles ABC and DEF in Fig. 16.9 are similar.

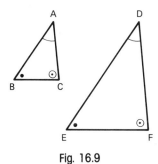

Fig. 16.9

$$\hat{A} = \hat{D}; \qquad \hat{B} = \hat{E}; \qquad \hat{C} = \hat{F}$$

and
$$\frac{AB}{DE} = \frac{AC}{DF} = \frac{BC}{EF} = k \quad \text{(the scale factor)}$$

Note that the *areas* of the triangles differ by k^2.

Examples (*i*) Two triangles, ABC and XYZ (Fig. 16.10), are similar. If XY = 20 cm, find the lengths of the other two sides of XYZ.

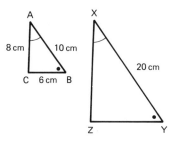

Fig. 16.10

211

Since $\dfrac{XY}{AB} = \dfrac{20}{10} = 2$ it follows that $\dfrac{YZ}{BC} = \dfrac{ZX}{CA} = 2$ (because $\triangle ABC$ is similar to $\triangle XYZ$), i.e. the other sides of XYZ are twice the length of the corresponding sides in ABC. Thus $YZ = 12$ cm and $ZX = 16$ cm.

(*ii*) Two lines, AB and CD, are parallel (Fig. 16.11). The diagonals, AD and CB, meet at X. Prove that the triangles AXB and CXD are similar. If $CD = 6$ cm, $AB = 4$ cm, $CX = 4\frac{1}{2}$ cm and $AX = 2$ cm, find BX and DX. If the area of triangle AXB is 4 cm², write down the area of CXD.

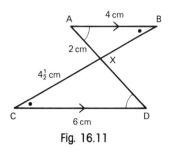

Fig. 16.11

$\hat{A} = \hat{D}$ (alternate) and $\hat{B} = \hat{C}$ (alternate).

So because the two triangles have two equal corresponding angles, AXB and DXC must be similar.

Redraw the triangles to make the correspondence between them clear. (Triangle AXB must be rotated by $180°$ to make obvious the correspondence between sides AX and DX, and between sides XC and BX — see Fig. 16.12).

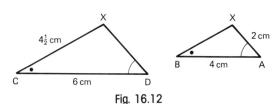

Fig. 16.12

$$\dfrac{CD}{AB} = \dfrac{6}{4} = \dfrac{3}{2}$$

Thus the scale factor, $k = \frac{3}{2}$. Hence

$$\dfrac{CX}{BX} = \dfrac{4\frac{1}{2}}{BX} = \dfrac{3}{2} \quad \text{giving} \quad BX = \dfrac{4\frac{1}{2} \times 2}{3} = 3 \text{ cm}$$

and $\quad \dfrac{DX}{AX} = \dfrac{DX}{2} = \dfrac{3}{2} \quad \text{giving} \quad DX = 2 \times \dfrac{3}{2} = 3 \text{ cm}$

Now if the scale factor is $\frac{3}{2}$, then the areas differ by a factor $(\frac{3}{2})^2 = \frac{9}{4}$. So if the smaller triangle has an area of 4 cm², then the larger one, CXD, has an area $\frac{9}{4} \times 4 = 9$ cm².

Note that similarity can be established with shapes other than triangles. The corresponding lengths will differ by a scale factor k, the areas by k^2 (*not k*) and, in the case of similar *bodies*, the *volumes* will differ by k^3 (see Chapter 21).

EXERCISE 16b
1. Triangles ABC and PQR are similar. Given the lengths shown in Fig. 16.13, find the scale factor and hence calculate the lengths x and y.

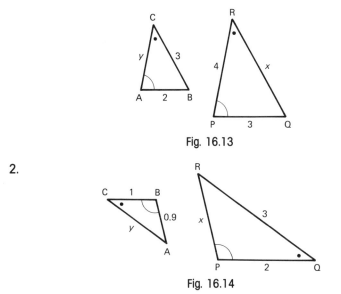

Fig. 16.13

2.

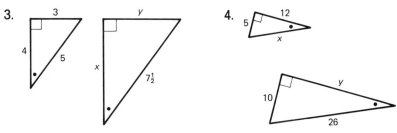

Fig. 16.14

The two triangles, ABC and PQR, shown in Fig. 16.14, are similar. First, redraw the triangles so that the positions of corresponding sides match each other. Find the scale factor and hence calculate x and y.

In Questions 3 to 12, the pairs of triangles are similar. In each case find the scale factor and calculate the lengths x and y. (Remember, it may be necessary to redraw the triangles so that the positions of corresponding sides match each other.)

3.

4.

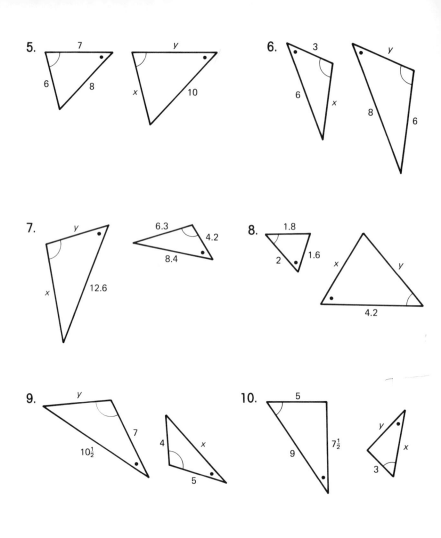

5.

6.

7.

8.

9.

10.

11.

12.

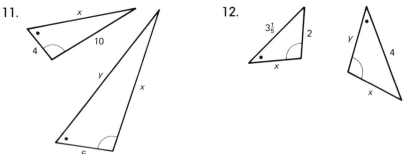

13. The scale factor between two similar triangles is 1 : 3. What is the ratio of their areas?

14. Two similar triangles have areas in the ratio 16 : 9. What is the ratio of the lengths of their corresponding sides?

15.

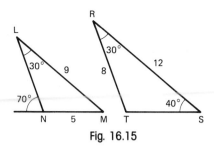

Fig. 16.15

Prove that the triangles LMN and RST in Fig. 16.15 are similar, with a scale factor of 3:4. Find the lengths of LN and ST. Find the area of triangle RST, given that the area of LMN is 18 square units.

16.

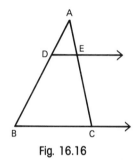

Fig. 16.16

Prove that triangles ADE and ABC, shown in Fig. 16.16, are similar. If AD = 3 cm, AE = $2\frac{3}{4}$ cm, DB = 6 cm and BC = 6 cm, find the lengths of DE and EC.

Given that the area of ADE is $2\frac{3}{4}$ cm^2 find the area of ABC. Hence show that the area of the quadrilateral, DBCE is 22 cm^2.

17.

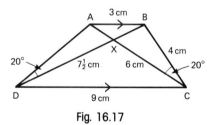

Fig. 16.17

Figure 16.17 shows a trapezium, ABCD, with AB∥CD. Prove that the triangles ABX and DXC are similar. Name another pair of similar triangles. Calculate the lengths of AX, BX and AD.

18.

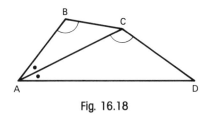

Fig. 16.18

In the quadrilateral ABCD shown in Fig. 16.18, the diagonal AC bisects $B\widehat{A}C$ and $A\widehat{B}C = A\widehat{C}D$. If AB = 8 cm, BC = 6 cm and AC = 12 cm, find the lengths of CD and AD.

The area of triangle ACD is 90 cm²; what are the areas of the triangle ABC and the quadrilateral ABCD?

CONGRUENT TRIANGLES

Congruent triangles are the same shape (as are similar triangles) but they are also the same *size* as each other. (Congruent triangles can be considered a special case of similar triangles in which the scale factor, k, is one.) There are four conditions that will prove a pair of triangles to be congruent (see Fig. 16.19).

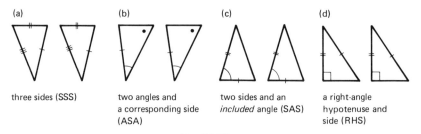

(a)	(b)	(c)	(d)
three sides (SSS)	two angles and a corresponding side (ASA)	two sides and an *included* angle (SAS)	a right-angle hypotenuse and side (RHS)

Fig. 16.19

Example Use congruent triangles to prove that the bisector of the odd angle of an isosceles triangle meets the opposite side at its mid-point and at right angles. (A 'bisector' cuts a line or an angle in half.)

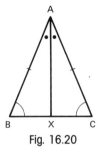

Fig. 16.20

In triangles BAX and CAX (Fig. 16.20), $B\widehat{A}X = C\widehat{A}X$ (AX is the angle bisector), $\widehat{B} = \widehat{C}$ (△ABC is an isosceles triangle) and AX is a

216

common side. Thus triangles BAX and CAX are congruent (by condition (b) in Fig. 16.19 – ASA).

Hence BX = CX, so X is the mid-point of BC. Also, $B\hat{X}A = C\hat{X}A$ but $B\hat{X}A + C\hat{X}A = 180°$ (angles on a straight line), so $B\hat{X}A = C\hat{X}A = 90°$.

EXERCISE 16c

1. Give reasons for the following pairs of triangles to be congruent:

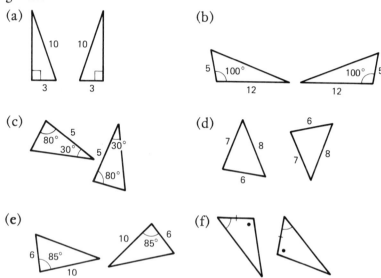

2. OAB and OCD are two triangles drawn within a circle, centre O, as shown in Fig. 16.21. Prove that the triangles are congruent.

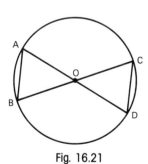

Fig. 16.21

3. A rectangle, ABCD, is divided by the diagonal AC and then by diagonal BD. Prove that triangle ABC is congruent to triangle BCD. Hence deduce that the diagonals of a rectangle are equal in length.

217

4.

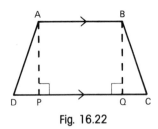

Fig. 16.22

In Fig. 16.22, ABCD is an isosceles trapezium, with AB ∥ CD and AD = BC. AP and BQ are drawn perpendicular to DC. Prove that triangles APD and BCQ are congruent and hence deduce that $\widehat{D} = \widehat{C}$.

5.

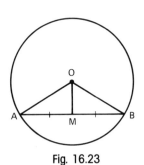

Fig. 16.23

AB is a chord of a circle, and the mid-point of the chord, M, is joined to the centre O of the circle (Fig. 16.23). Prove that triangles OAM and OBM are congruent and hence deduce that OM cuts AB at right angles.

6.

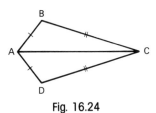

Fig. 16.24

Figure 16.24 shows a kite, ABCD, with AB = AD and CB = CD. Show that triangles ABC and ADC are congruent, and hence deduce that $\widehat{B} = \widehat{D}$.

7.

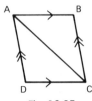

Fig. 16.25

ABCD is a parallelogram, cut by the diagonal AC, as shown in Fig. 16.25. By proving that triangles ABC and ADC are congruent, deduce that, in a parallelogram

(a) opposite sides are equal

(b) opposite angles are equal.

8.

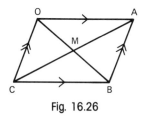

Fig. 16.26

The parallelogram OABC shown in Fig. 16.26 is divided into four triangles by its diagonals OB and AC. The diagonals meet at M. Show that triangles OMA and CBM are congruent and so deduce that M is the mid-point of OB.

9.

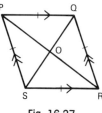

Fig. 16.27

PQRS is a rhombus, that is PQ∥RS, QR∥SP and all four sides are equal (Fig. 16.27). Show that the four triangles OPQ, OQR, ORS and OSP are all congruent. Hence deduce that the diagonals, PR and SQ, cut at right angles.

10.

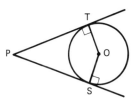

Fig. 16.28

Two lines are drawn from a point P to touch a circle, centre O, at T and S (see Fig. 16.28). The radius OT meets PT at right angles, and the radius OS meets PS at right angles. Use congruent triangles to prove that PT = PS.

MISCELLANEOUS EXERCISE 16

1.

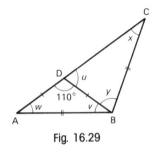

Fig. 16.29

ABC is an isosceles triangle with AB = BC. D is a point on AC such that AD = DB and $A\hat{D}B = 110°$. Calculate the sizes of the angles marked, u, v, w, x, y.   (WJEC)

2.

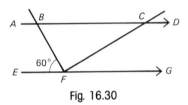

Fig. 16.30

ABCD and EFG are two parallel straight lines with BF and FC two transversals (Fig. 16.30). $B\hat{F}E = 60°$ and $B\hat{C}F : F\hat{C}D = 1:5$.
Calculate the value of $A\hat{B}F$, $B\hat{C}F$, $C\hat{F}G$ and $B\hat{F}C$.   (WJEC)

3.

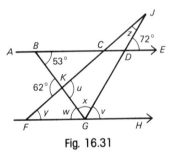

Fig. 16.31

ABCDE and FGH are two parallel straight lines with transversals BKG, FKCJ and GDJ (Fig. 16.31). $J\hat{D}E = 72°$, $K\hat{B}C = 53°$ and $B\hat{K}F = 62°$. Calculate the size of the angles marked u, v, w, x, y and z.   (WJEC)

4.

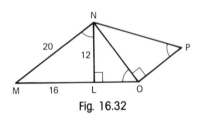

Fig. 16.32

220

Triangles LMN, LNO and NOP in Fig. 16.32 are all similar. Write down the ratios

(a) MN : NO : NP

(b) area LMN : area LNO : area NOP.

5.

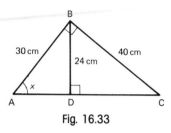

Fig. 16.33

In triangle ABC (Fig. 16.33), $\hat{B} = 90°$. A perpendicular is dropped from B to a point D on AC, as shown. Show that triangles ABC, ABD and BDC are all similar to each other.

Use similarity to find the lengths AD and DC, given that AB = 30 cm, BC = 40 cm and BD = 24 cm.

6. Two lines, AB and CD, intersect at X such that AX = CX and BX = DX. Prove that AC ∥ DB.

7.

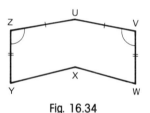

Fig. 16.34

UVWXYZ is an irregular hexagon, as shown in Fig. 16.34. UV = UZ; VW = YZ; $U\hat{Z}Y = U\hat{V}W$. Prove that UY = UW.

If, further, $X\hat{U}W = X\hat{U}Y$, show that WX = XY, and that UX is a line of symmetry.

8. P, Q and R are three points on a circle, centre O, such that PQ = QR. Prove that $O\hat{Q}P = O\hat{Q}R$.

9.

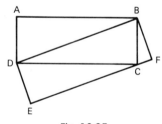

Fig. 16.35

ABCD and BDEF are rectangles (Fig. 16.35). ECF is a straight line. Prove that

(a) angle ADB = angle CDE;

(b) triangles ABD, ECD, FBC are similar;

(c) the rectangles are equal in area;

(d) $\dfrac{EC}{CF} = \dfrac{AB^2}{AD^2}$.   (Ox)

10.

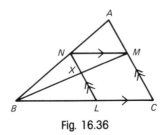

Fig. 16.36

In the diagram (Fig. 16.36), NM is parallel to BC, and NL is parallel to AC. Prove that $\triangle ANM$ is similar to $\triangle NBL$.

Given that $\dfrac{AN}{NB} = \dfrac{2}{3}$, calculate the numerical value of the ratios

(a) $\dfrac{\text{area of } \triangle ANM}{\text{area of } \triangle NBL}$,

(b) $\dfrac{NM}{BC}$,

(c) $\dfrac{\text{area of trapezium } BNMC}{\text{area of } \triangle ABC}$

(d) $\dfrac{NX}{MC}$.   (C)

11.

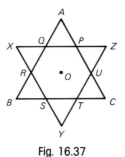

Fig. 16.37

The diagram (Fig. 16.37) shows a six-pointed star which is formed by drawing an equilateral triangle on each side of the regular hexagon $PQRSTU$. The centre of the hexagon is O.

(a) Prove that $\triangle XYZ$ is congruent to $\triangle ABC$.

(b) Show that the area of the six-pointed star is twice the area of the hexagon $PQRSTU$.

(c) If ON is drawn from O perpendicular to QP to meet QP at N, find the value of the ratio $\dfrac{ON}{OA}$.

(d) Find the value of the ratio

$$\frac{\text{area of circle } AXBYCZ}{\text{area of circle inscribed in hexagon } PQRSTU}.$$

(The inscribed circle is that which touches each side of the hexagon.) (LU)

12.

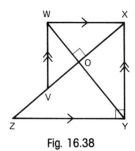

Fig. 16.38

In Fig. 16.38, VW∥XY and WX∥YZ. $\widehat{WOX} = \widehat{XYZ} = 90°$.

(a) Show that the six triangles OVW, OWX, OXY, OYZ, XYZ and VWX are all similar to each other.

(b) If OY = 48 cm and OZ = 64 cm, find the area of triangle XYZ and the length of OV.

223

17 QUADRILATERALS AND OTHER POLYGONS

Any four-sided figure is a *quadrilateral*. For any quadrilateral the sum of the interior angles is 360° (Fig. 17.1).

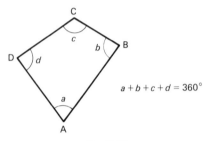

$$a + b + c + d = 360°$$

Fig. 17.1

Some quadrilaterals have special properties — usually because one pair (or both pairs) of sides are parallel.

TRAPEZIUMS

A trapezium has *one* pair of parallel sides (see Fig. 17.2). The area of a trapezium is the *average* of the parallel sides × the perpendicular distance between them.

$$A = \left(\frac{a + b}{2}\right) \times h$$

An *isosceles* trapezium has one pair of parallel sides and the other pair of sides equal in length (Fig. 17.3). The upper pair of interior angles are equal and so are the lower pair. Moreover, an upper and a lower angle add up to 180°, and the diagonals are equal in length.

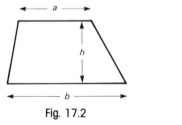

Fig. 17.2

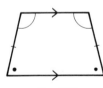

Fig. 17.3

PARALLELOGRAMS

A parallelogram is a quadrilateral with *both* pairs of sides parallel (Fig. 17.4). Its properties are:

− opposite sides are parallel
− opposite sides are equal in length
− opposite angles are equal
− the diagonals bisect each other but are *not* of equal length
− each diagonal bisects the area (into two congruent triangles)
− the area of a parallelogram is given by

$$A = \text{base} \times \text{perpendicular height}$$

Fig. 17.4

Rectangles

A rectangle is a special parallelogram in which pairs of sides are at right angles to each other (Fig. 17.5). The properties of a rectangle are those of a parallelogram *plus*

− the diagonals are of equal length.

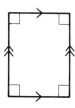

Fig. 17.5

Rhombuses

A rhombus (Fig. 17.6) is a special parallelogram in which all sides are equal in length. Its properties are those of a parallelogram *plus*

− the diagonals cut at right angles
− the diagonals bisect the interior angles but the diagonals are *not* of equal length.

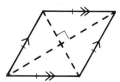

Fig. 17.6

Squares

A square is a parallelogram that is both a rectangle *and* a rhombus (Fig. 17.7). It has all the properties of those shapes (except that the diagonals *are* equal in length, unlike the rhombus). Its area is, of course, the square of one side.

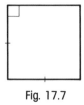

Fig. 17.7

The Venn diagram in Fig. 17.8 illustrates the relationships between these special parallelograms.

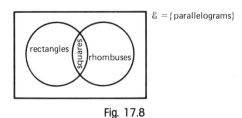

Fig. 17.8

KITES

A kite has *no* parallel sides but has two pairs of adjacent sides of equal length (Fig. 17.9).

The diagonals of a kite meet at right angles.

The area of a kite can be found by multiplying together the lengths of the two diagonals and dividing by 2.

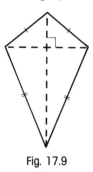

Fig. 17.9

CYCLIC QUADRILATERALS

Any figure that fits exactly inside a circle is called *cyclic*. *All* triangles are cyclic, but *not* all quadrilaterals are. For a

quadrilateral to be cyclic, its opposite angles must add up to 180°
(Fig. 17.10).

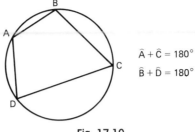

$\hat{A} + \hat{C} = 180°$

$\hat{B} + \hat{D} = 180°$

Fig. 17.10

All rectangles, squares and isosceles trapeziums are cyclic. Parallelo
grams and ordinary trapeziums are not. A kite may or may not be
cyclic; if it is, then it must contain two right angles opposite each
other, as shown in Fig. 17.11.

Cyclic

triangles

rectangles

squares

isosceles
trapeziums

some kites

Non-cyclic

parallelo-
grams

trapeziums

some kites

Fig. 17.11

EXERCISE 17a In Questions 1 to 9, find the angles marked x and y.

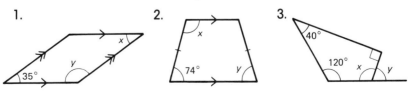

1.

2.

3.

227

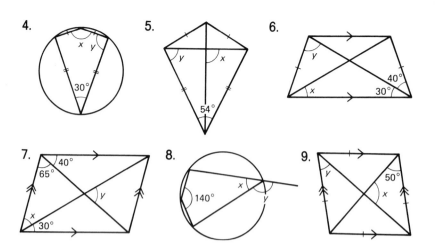

4.
5.
6.

7.
8.
9.

10. The table gives the characteristics of special quadrilaterals that have opposite sides equal and parallel. In each case, write down the type of quadrilateral. (WJEC)

Diagonals	Adjacent sides	Name of quadrilateral
unequal	unequal	
equal	unequal	
unequal	equal	
equal	equal	

11. Find the areas of the following quadrilaterals:

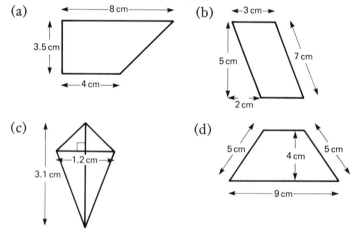

(a) 8 cm / 3.5 cm / 4 cm

(b) 3 cm / 5 cm / 7 cm / 2 cm

(c) 1.2 cm / 3.1 cm

(d) 5 cm / 4 cm / 5 cm / 9 cm

12. A parallelogram has an area of 18 cm²; its base is 6 cm long. What is the height of the parallelogram? Is it possible to find the slant height of the parallelogram from this information?

13. A quadrilateral is formed by joining the points A(2, 1), B(8, 4) C(8, 7) and D(5, 7). Plot the points A, B, C and D and identify the type of quadrilateral. Calculate the area ABCD.

14.

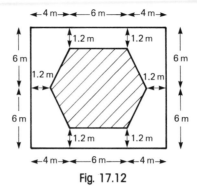

Fig. 17.12

In Fig. 17.12, which is not drawn to scale, the shaded area represents a flower bed surrounded by a path. Find the area of the flower bed.   (Ox)

15.

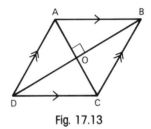

Fig. 17.13

The diagonals of a parallelogram ABCD meet at right angles at O (Fig. 17.13).

Use congruent triangles to prove that AD = AB, and hence that ABCD is a rhombus.

16. If, in Fig. 17.13, AO = OD, prove that ABCD is a square.

17.

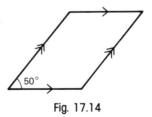

Fig. 17.14

A parallelogram includes an angle of 50° as shown in Fig. 17.14. Prove that the parallelogram cannot be cyclic.

18. Prove that a cyclic rhombus must be a square.

19.

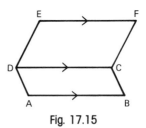

Fig. 17.15

Figure 17.15 shows two parallelograms, ABCD and CDEF, that share the side CD. Copy the diagram and add the diagonals AF and BE. Prove that these diagonals bisect each other.

20. In a quadrilateral, PQRS, it is known that PQ∥RS. If the diagonal PR bisects the angle SPQ and other diagonal, SQ, bisects angle PSR, prove that PQRS is a rhombus.

21. $\&$ = {all quadrilaterals}, P = {parallelograms}, C = {cyclic quadrilaterals}. Name and draw a member of

(a) $P \cap C$ (b) $P' \cap C$ (c) $P' \cap C'$

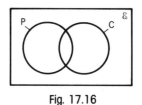

Fig. 17.16

Figure 17.16 shows a Venn diagram with sets P and C. Copy the diagram and add to your figure the sets S = {squares} and K = {kites}.

OTHER POLYGONS

A five-sided figure is called a *pentagon*; a six-sided figure is a *hexagon*; an eight-sided figure is an *octagon*. Many-sided figures are referred to in general as *polygons*. A *regular* polygon is one with all its sides equal in length and its angles equal to one another.

The sum of all the exterior angles of a polygon is 360° (Fig. 17.17).

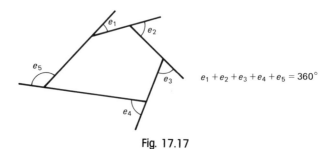

$$e_1 + e_2 + e_3 + e_4 + e_5 = 360°$$

Fig. 17.17

230

The sum of all the interior angles depends upon the number of sides, n, and is $2n - 4$ right angles. If the polygon is regular, then each of the n equal angles must be $\dfrac{2n - 4}{n}$ right angles.

Example Find the interior angle of a regular decagon.

A decagon has ten sides; hence $n = 10$. Each angle is

$$\frac{(2 \times 10) - 4}{10} \times 90° = \frac{16}{10} \times 90° = 144°$$

EXERCISE 17b

1. Figure 17.18 shows an irregular pentagon ABCDE divided into three triangles ABC, ACD and ADE. What is the sum of the interior angles of each triangle? Deduce the sum of the interior angles of the pentagon.

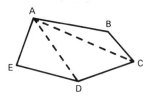

Fig. 17.18

2. Draw an irregular hexagon and divide it into triangles like the pentagon in Question 1. How many triangles are there? Deduce the sum of the interior angles of the hexagon.

3. What is the sum of all seven interior angles of a heptagon? If the heptagon is regular, what is the size of each angle?

4. What is the sum of all eight interior angles of an octagon? If the octagon is regular, what is the size of each angle?

5. By what name is a regular quadrilateral better known?

6.

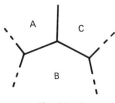

Fig. 17.19

Figure 17.19 shows the meeting point of three regular polygons, A, B and C, that form part of an interlocking pattern. A and B have the same number of sides.

(a) If A and B both have eight sides, how many sides has C?

(b) If C has ten sides, how many sides each have A and B?

7. The interior angles of an irregular pentagon are in the ratio 3 : 4 : 5 : 7 : 8. What are its interior angles, in degrees?

8. The interior angles of an irregular hexagon are in the ratio 4 : 3 : 2 : 4 : 3 : 4.

   (a) What are its interior angles?

   (b) What is the ratio of its *exterior* angles?

9. The interior angles of a straight-sided shape make a total of 1980°. How many sides does it have?

10. A regular figure has an interior angle equal to 156°. How many sides does it have?

18 SYMMETRY

LINE SYMMETRY

If a figure can be drawn on paper in such a way that if the paper is folded in half the two halves of the figure exactly cover each other, then the shape is symmetric. The line of fold is called the *axis of symmetry*. For example, a kite can be folded down the middle; the two halves cover each other exactly (Fig. 18.1).

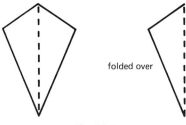

Fig. 18.1

Alternatively, we might imagine a mirror has been placed along the axis of symmetry. The image in the mirror looks exactly like the hidden half; with the half still showing, we can still 'see' the original shape (Fig. 18.2).

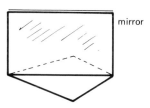

Fig. 18.2

It follows that irregular figures with no equal sides or angles cannot possibly have symmetry.

The kite shown in Fig. 18.1 has one axis of symmetry. An isosceles triangle also has one axis of symmetry, whereas an equilateral triangle has three axes of symmetry (see Fig. 18.3).

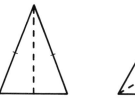

Fig. 18.3

233

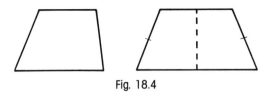

Fig. 18.4

Trapeziums generally have no axis of symmetry, although isosceles trapeziums have one (Fig. 18.4). Parallelograms generally have no axis of symmetry either, although a rectanlge has two, a rhombus has two (the diagonals) and a square (being both a rhombus and a rectangle) has four (Fig. 18.5).

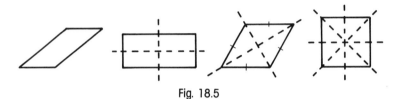

Fig. 18.5

PLANE SYMMETRY

Three-dimensional objects may also display reflection symmetry. But as they are objects, they cannot be reflected in a line: they *must* be reflected in a plane mirror — hence *plane symmetry* — that would 'slice' through their centre. For example, the pyramid shown in Fig. 18.6 has plane symmetry.

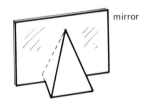

mirror

Fig. 18.6

ROTATIONAL SYMMETRY

If a shape can be twisted round and yet appear not to have been changed in any way, it is said to have *rotational symmetry*. For example, an equilateral triangle could be twisted around its centre by $120°$ and appear to be in the same position (Fig. 18.7(a)). Of course, if we label the corners A, B and C, then the change is apparent (Fig. 18.7(b)).

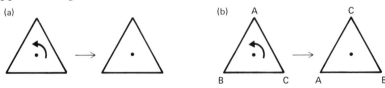

Fig. 18.7

We could rotate the triangle through 120° twice more (making three possible twists) before the triangle resumes its original position. Thus an equilateral triangle is said to have *rotational symmetry of order three* (Fig. 18.8).

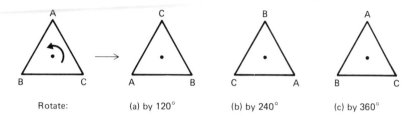

Rotate: (a) by 120°   (b) by 240°   (c) by 360°

Fig. 18.8

Parallelograms (including rectangles and rhombuses) can be rotated by 180° and appear unchanged. Again, if we label the corners, the change is apparent, as in Fig. 18.9. A shape that can be twisted by 180° and still look the same is said to have *point symmetry*. Notice that a second twist of 180° (i.e. a total turn of 360°) restores the parallelogram to its original position. Thus the parallelogram has rotational symmetry of order two (Fig. 18.10).

Fig. 18.9

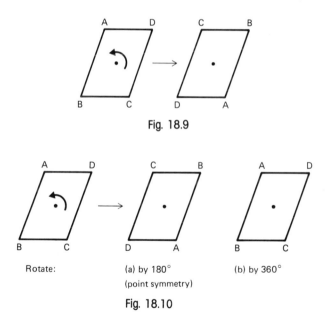

Rotate: (a) by 180°   (b) by 360°
                  (point symmetry)

Fig. 18.10

A square has rotational symmetry of order four (Fig. 18.11). Kites and trapeziums have no point symmetry (they are clearly 'upside down' when rotated by 180° – see Fig. 18.12). However, they appear unchanged if rotated by 360° (as does any figure) so they have rotational symmetry of order one.

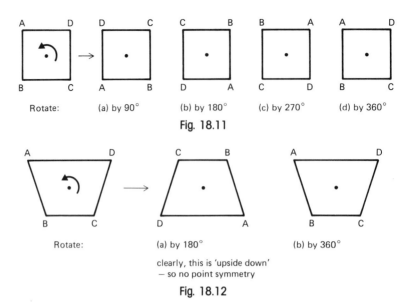

Rotate: (a) by 90°   (b) by 180°   (c) by 270°   (d) by 360°

Fig. 18.11

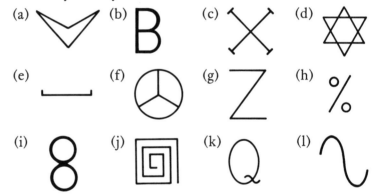

Rotate: (a) by 180°   (b) by 360°

clearly, this is 'upside down'
— so no point symmetry

Fig. 18.12

MISCELLANEOUS EXERCISE 18

1. Copy the following figures and show with broken lines any axes of symmetry.

   (a)   (b) B   (c)   (d)

   (e)   (f)   (g) Z   (h) %

   (i) 8   (j)   (k) Q   (l)

2. Which of the figures in Question 1 have rotational symmetry (other than rotation by 360°). For each shape write down its order of rotational symmetry.

3. Which shapes in Question 1 have point symmetry?

4. Name and draw two quadrilaterals with exactly one axis of symmetry.

5. Name and draw two quadrilaterals with exactly two axes of symmetry.

6. A quadrilateral has two pairs of equal sides but no axis of symmetry. What must it be?

7. A quadrilateral has two pairs of equal sides and two axes of symmetry. What must it be?

8. In the drawings below, lines of symmetry are shown as broken lines. Copy and complete the figures.

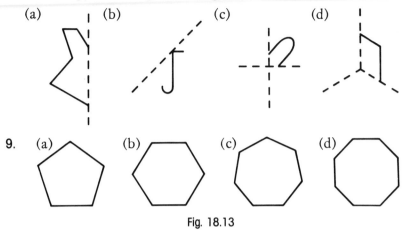

(a)   (b)   (c)   (d)

9. (a)   (b)   (c)   (d)

Fig. 18.13

Figure 18.13 shows the outlines of

(a) a regular pentagon

(b) a regular hexagon

(c) a regular heptagon

(d) a regular octagon.

For each shape:

(i) copy the outline and mark on it, as a broken line, all the axes of symmetry

(ii) write down the number of sides, the number of axes of symmetry, and the order of rotational symmetry.

(iii) Which of these shapes have point symmetry?

10. (a) From the word

E X A C T

write down all the letters that have

(i) a vertical line of symmetry

(ii) a horizontal line of symmetry

(iii) point symmetry.

Fig. 18.14

(b) Draw all the lines of symmetry for this square (Fig. 18.14) in the plane of the paper.   (AEB '81)

11. The sets C, P and S are given as follows:

$$C = \{\text{cyclic quadrilaterals}\}$$
$$P = \{\text{quadrilaterals with point symmetry}\}$$
$$S = \{\text{quadrilaterals with exactly two axes of symmetry}\}$$

Name and draw a shape that is a member of

(a) $C \cap S$ (b) $C \cap S'$ (c) $C' \cap P$ (d) $C \cap P$

(e) $P \cap S$.

12. How many planes of symmetry has a

(a) cube   (b) cuboid   (c) cone.

19 PYTHAGORAS' THEOREM AND TRIGONOMETRY

The longest side in a right-angled triangle is always opposite the right-angle; it is called the *hypotenuse*.

PYTHAGORAS' THEOREM FOR RIGHT-ANGLED TRIANGLES

The square of the hypotenuse of a right-angled triangle is equal to the sum of the squares of the other two sides.

$$h^2 = a^2 + b^2$$

Fig. 19.1

Remember, Pythagoras' theorem *only* applies to *right-angled triangles*: it is *not true* of other triangles.

Examples (*i*) Find the hypotenuse of a right-angled triangle with sides of length 3 cm and 5 cm (Fig. 19.2).

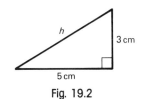

Fig. 19.2

$$h^2 = a^2 + b^2$$
$$= 3^2 + 5^2$$
$$= 9 + 25$$
$$= 34$$

So $h = \sqrt{34} = 5.83$ cm

(*ii*) A right-angled triangle has a hypotenuse of length 13 cm and a second side of length 5 cm. What is the length of the third side?

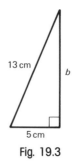

Fig. 19.3

Using Pythagoras' theorem (refer also to Fig. 19.3):

$$b^2 = a^2 + b^2$$
$$13^2 = 5^2 + b^2$$
$$169 = 25 + b^2$$

So
$$b^2 = 169 - 25 = 144$$
$$b = 12 \text{ cm}$$

The third side is 12 cm long.

EXERCISE 19a   1. Use Pythagoras' theorem to find the length of the side marked x in the following triangles:

(a)   (b)   (c)   (d)

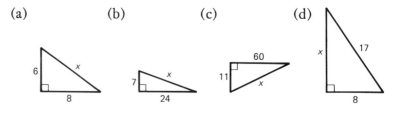

(e)   (f)   (g)   (h)

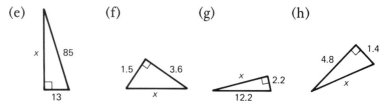

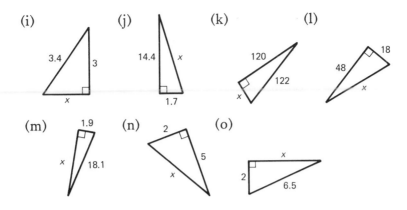

(i) 3.4, 3, x

(j) 14.4, x, 1.7

(k) 120, 122, x

(l) 18, 48, x

(m) 1.9, x, 18.1

(n) 2, 5, x

(o) x, 2, 6.5

2. A rectangle ABCD has side lengths AB = 6.3 cm and AD = 8.4 cm. Find the length of the diagonal AC.

3. A square has sides of 5 cm. Find, to three significant figures, the length of the diagonals.

4. The diagonals of a rectangle are 6.5 cm long. If one pair of sides are 2.5 cm long, how long are the other two sides?

5.

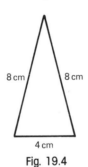

8 cm   8 cm

4 cm

Fig. 19.4

An isosceles triangle has sides 8 cm, 8 cm and 4 cm (Fig. 19.4). Use Pythagoras' theorem to find its height, and hence find its area, to 3 s.f.

6.

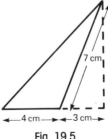

7 cm

←4 cm→ ←3 cm→

Fig. 19.5

A triangle ABC has sides of length 4 cm and 7 cm as shown in Fig. 19.5. If it overhangs its base by 3 cm, find its area to the nearest square centimetre.

7. A tent pole is supported by two guy ropes, one each side. If the pole is 1 m high and the ropes are each 150 cm long when fully stretched, how far from the foot of the pole must they be fixed into the ground? Give your answer to the nearest centimetre.

8. A dustbin is 1 m high and 60 cm across. What is the length, in centimetres, of the longest stick that can be put in it, if the lid is to fit on top?

9. A line is drawn on a graph between the points $(-13, 7)$ and $(11, 14)$. What is the length of the line?

10.

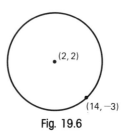

Fig. 19.6

A circle is drawn on graph paper. If its centre is at the point $(2, 2)$ and it passes through the point $(14, -3)$ (see Fig. 19.6), what is its radius?

11. A quadrilateral ABCD is formed by joining the points A$(-5, -3)$, B$(4, 9)$, C$(19, 9)$ and D$(10, -3)$. Prove that the four sides are of equal length and hence that ABCD is a rhombus.

12.

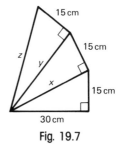

Fig. 19.7

Calculate the distances x, y and z in Fig. 19.7. Give your answers in centimetres to 1 d.p.

SINES, COSINES AND TANGENTS

All right-angled triangles with a second angle, say x, in common must be similar to each other (see Chapter 16) though they may be quite different in size (Fig. 19.8).

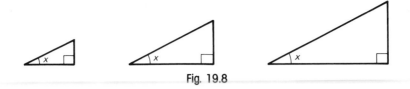

Fig. 19.8

The ratios of corresponding sides in all such right-angled triangles will be equal. Taking the side next to the angle x as the 'adjacent', the other side as the 'opposite', and the longest side the hypotenuse (see Fig. 19.9), we can define three ratios:

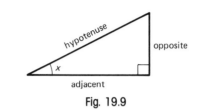

Fig. 19.9

$$sine = \frac{opposite}{hypotenuse} \qquad cosine = \frac{adjacent}{hypotenuse}$$

$$tangent = \frac{opposite}{adjacent}$$

We write for short:

$$\sin x = \frac{o}{h} \qquad \cos x = \frac{a}{h} \qquad \tan x = \frac{o}{a}$$

These ratios must be memorised. It might help to run the letters, $s = \frac{o}{h}$, $c = \frac{a}{h}$, $t = \frac{o}{a}$, together to make the word SOH-CAH-TOA (pronounced 'so-car-toe-ah'), reputedly the name of an Indian Chief!

The actual value of these ratios depends upon the angle x; for different values of x, the ratios will be different.

For any given angle the values of the sine, cosine and tangent can be found from tables or from a scientific calculator. For example, $\sin 30° = 0.5$. This means that, in any *right-angled* triangle that contains an angle of 30° (and therefore a 60° angle, too), the side opposite the 30° angle is half the length of the hypotenuse (see Fig. 19.10).

So if the opposite side is 1 cm long, the hypotenuse is 2 cm; if the opposite side is 2 cm, the hypotenuse is 4 cm; if the opposite side is $2\frac{1}{2}$ cm, the hypotenuse is 5 cm, and so on.

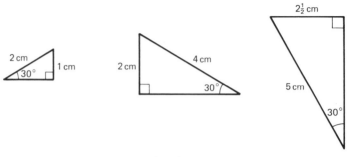

Fig. 19.10

SOLUTION OF RIGHT-ANGLED TRIANGLES

Examples (*i*) In the right-angled triangle ABC in Fig. 19.11, A = 30° and AB = 8 cm. Find the length of BC.

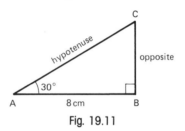

Fig. 19.11

To find the length of the opposite side, i.e. BC, given the length of the adjacent side, AB, we need to use the ratio that links the two, i.e.

$$\text{tangent} = \frac{\text{opposite}}{\text{adjacent}}$$

Thus $\qquad \tan 30° = \dfrac{\text{o}}{\text{a}} = \dfrac{BC}{AB}$

From a calculator, $\tan 30° = 0.577\,35$; we also know that AB = 8 cm. So, substituting these values in the equation above gives:

$$0.577\,35 = \frac{BC}{8}$$

$$BC = 8 \times 0.577\,35 = 4.6188$$

Rounding off, $BC = 4.62$ cm (3 s.f.)

244

(*ii*) Find the angle CAB in the triangle ABC (Fig. 19.12), given that $\widehat{B} = 90°$, AC = 13 cm and BC = 5 cm.

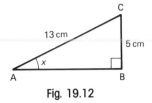

Fig. 19.12

BC is opposite the angle CAB, and AC is the hypotenuse, so we shall use the sine:

$$\sin x = \frac{o}{h} = \frac{BC}{AC} = \frac{5}{13} = 0.384\,62$$

Using the *inverse* sine function on a calculator, or from tables, we get

$$x = 22.620°$$
$$= 22.6° \quad (3\text{ s.f.})$$

Notes:

(*i*) When using one of these ratios, define it anew *every time* you use it. Do not skip steps, but write the full process, e.g. $\sin x = \frac{o}{h} = \frac{BC}{AC} = \frac{5}{13}$, etc. This will help you to understand and solve the problem.

(*ii*) Avoid, if you can, using your answers to earlier parts of a problem in subsequent calculations (you may be carrying forward a complete mistake). When it is not possible to avoid using earlier answers, use the *unrounded* figures, i.e. all four figures if you are using tables, five (or more) if you are using a calculator.

(*iii*) The *angle of elevation* is the angle between the horizontal and the line of sight for an observer on the ground of some object above him. The equivalent for an object below him is called an *angle of depression.*

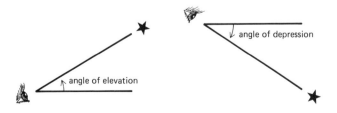

Fig. 19.13

1. Find the lengths of the sides marked x in the following:

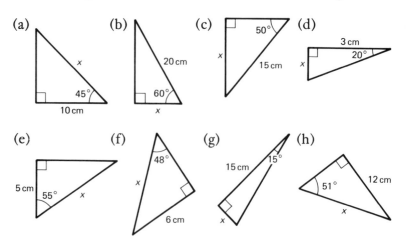

2. Find the angles marked x in the following:

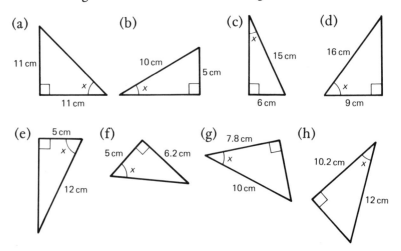

3. Find the lengths and angles indicated in the following:

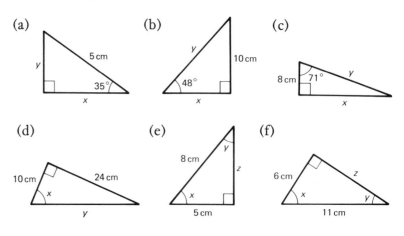

4.

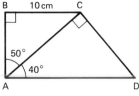

Fig. 19.14

In Fig. 19.14, $\widehat{ABC} = \widehat{ACD} = 90°$. BC = 10 cm. Find the lengths of AC and CD, giving your answers to 3 s.f.

5.

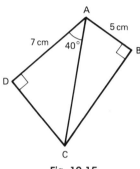

Fig. 19.15

A quadrilateral ABCD has right angles at B and D (Fig. 19.15). Given that $\widehat{DAC} = 40°$, AD = 7 cm and AB = 5 cm, find

(a) the length of the diagonal AC

(b) $\widehat{ACB}$.

6.

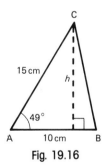

Fig. 19.16

In triangle ABC, $\widehat{CAB} = 49°$, AB = 10 cm and AC = 15 cm (Fig. 19.16). Find the height of the triangle and hence its area.

7. In triangle XYZ, $\widehat{ZXY} = 25°$, XY = 14.2 cm and XZ = 9.8 cm. Find the area of XYZ.

8. In the parallelogram PQRS, PQ = 4.9 cm, QR = 5.6 cm and $\widehat{PQR} = 38°$. Find the perpendicular distance between the sides PS and QR and the area of the parallelogram.

9. A man stands 25 m from a tall building and measures the angle of elevation of the top as 36°. What is the height of the building?

10. Standing at the top of a vertical cliff, a man spots a buoy out at sea. He knows this buoy to be 250 m from the beach and he observes the angle of depression to be 10.5°. How high is the cliff?

11. A 5 m ladder rests against a wall, with the foot of the ladder 1.2 m from the bottom of the wall. What angle does the ladder make with the ground and how far off the ground is the top?

12. An observer in a sailing dinghy 50 m out from the shore notices that the angle of elevation of the cliff top is 60° and that of a climber making his way up the vertical rock-face is exactly half, i.e. 30°. Show that the climber is *not* simply half-way up, but still has two-thirds of his climb to complete.

DROPPING A PERPENDICULAR

If a triangle does not contain a right angle, then neither Pythagoras' theorem nor sines, cosines and tangents can be simply applied to it. Sometimes, however, it is possible to solve a problem by dividing the triangle into two right-angled portions by dropping a perpendicular from one corner to the side opposite.

Example In triangle ABC (Fig. 19.17), A = 37°, B = 63°, AC = 5 cm. Find the base length AB.

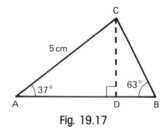

Fig. 19.17

Since the angles in a triangle must add up to 180°, we know that angle C must be given by

$$\hat{C} = 180° - 37° - 63° = 80°$$

There is no right angle in this triangle. However, if we drop a perpendicular from C to meet the base AB at D, we create two right-angled triangles that we *can* solve.

In triangle ACD

$$\cos 37° = \frac{a}{h} = \frac{AD}{AC}$$

So $AD = AC \times \cos 37° = 5 \times 0.798\,64 = 3.9932\text{ cm}$

Similarly

$$\sin 37° = \frac{o}{h} = \frac{CD}{AC}$$

So $CD = AC \times \sin 37° = 5 \times 0.601\,82 = 3.0091\text{ cm}$

Then in triangle CDB

$$\tan 63° = \frac{o}{a} = \frac{CD}{DB}$$

So $DB = \dfrac{CD}{\tan 63°} = \dfrac{3.0091}{1.9626} = 1.5332\text{ cm}$

Now, $AB = AD + DB = 3.9932 + 1.5332 = 5.5264$

$$= 5.53\text{ cm (3 s.f.)}$$

EXERCISE 19c   1. Find the lengths indicated in the following triangles:

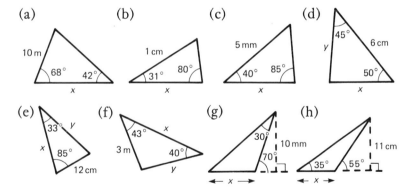

(a)   (b)   (c)   (d)

(e)   (f)   (g)   (h)

2. In triangle ABC, $\hat{A} = 64°$, $\hat{B} = 54°$, $AC = 10$ cm. Find the base length AB and the area of the triangle.

3. In triangle XYZ, $\hat{X} = 32°$, $\hat{Y} = 45°$, $XZ = 2$ m. Find the base length XY and the area of the triangle.

4. In triangle PQR, $\hat{P} = 38°$, $\hat{Q} = 32°$, $PR = 5$ m. Find the area of PQR.

5. Triangle EFG is obtuse-angled, with $\hat{F} = 132°$. If $EF = 6$ cm, $FG = 4$ cm, find the height of G above the base line EF, and hence the area of the triangle.

The three dimensions – length, breadth and height – are all perpendicular to each other, and problems set in three dimensions mainly involve finding right-angled triangles within the more complicated three-dimensional structure. It is good practice to keep one 'master' diagram to represent the full structure and show extracted right-angled triangles separately.

Example Figure 19.18 represents a wedge of cheese. It is cut with wire vertically through the diagonal CF, so that the wire passes through the cheese down the side CD (which is also vertical) and finally through the diagonal DF. Calculate the length DF and the angle CFD.

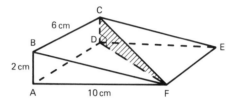

Fig. 19.18

To find DF, consider the triangle DAF which lies flat on the horizontal table (Fig. 19.19).

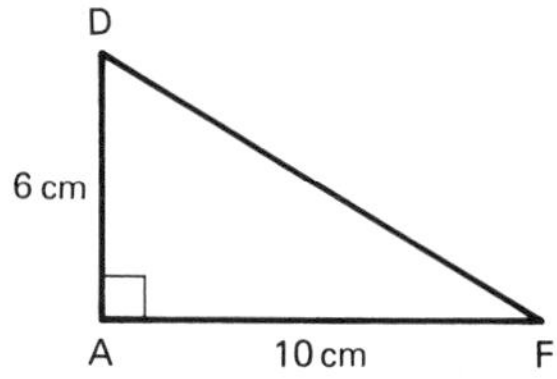

$$D\hat{A}F = 90°$$

$$DA = BC = 6 \text{ cm}$$

$$AF = 10 \text{ cm}$$

Fig. 19.19

Using Pythagoras' theorem:

$$DF^2 = DA^2 + AF^2$$

$$= 6^2 + 10^2 = 136$$

$$DF = \sqrt{136} = 11.662 = 11.7 \text{ cm} \quad (3 \text{ s.f.})$$

To find CFD, consider the triangle CDF which stands upright, in the vertical plane (Fig. 19.20).

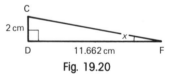

Fig. 19.20

$$CDF = 90°$$

$$DF = 11.662 \text{ cm} \quad (\text{from above})$$

$$CD = BA = 2 \text{ cm}$$

$$\tan x = \frac{o}{a} = \frac{CD}{DF} = \frac{2}{11.662} = 0.171\,50$$

Hence $\qquad x = 9.73°$ (3 s.f.)

EXERCISE 19d

1. Calculate the length of the diagonal AC (Fig. 19.21) that divides the bottom of a shoe box measuring 36 cm × 15 cm × 12 cm. Hence find the length of the diagonal AG and the angle GAC.

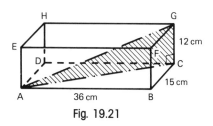

Fig. 19.21

2. A pyramid, 4 m high, stands on a 2 m square base, ABCD (Fig. 19.22). Its topmost point, O, is directly above the centre, M, of the square. Find the distance AM (halfway along the diagonal of the square) and hence find the slant height, OA, of the pyramid, and the angle OAM.

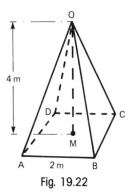

Fig. 19.22

3. The apex, O, of a pyramid with square base ABCD lies vertically above the centre, M, of the square. Each of the triangular faces is equilateral, with sides of 6 m. E is the mid-point of BC. Calculate

(a) the height OM

(b) the angle BOM

(c) the angle EOM

(d) the angle between the faces BOC and AOD.

251

4.

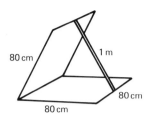

Fig. 19.23

A trapdoor, 80 cm square, is held in the open position by a supporting bar of 1 m length, as shown in Fig. 19.23. Find the angle the bar makes with the opened trapdoor and the angle the door makes with the horizontal.

5. A vertical radio mast is sited 1 km due north of an observer at O, who notes the angle of elevation of the top of the mast to be 5°. Another observer is at P, 1.4 km due east of O. Find

(a) the height of the radio mast

(b) the bearing of the radio mast from P

(c) the distance of the radio mast from P

(d) the angle of elevation of the top of the mast to the observer at P.

6.

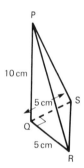

Fig. 19.24

A pointed, triangular-based arrow head, PQRS, measures 10 cm × 5 cm × 5 cm (as shown in Fig. 19.24). Given that P lies directly above Q and that $SQR = 90°$, calculate the lengths

(a) SR   (b) PR.

Find also the angle between the face PRS and the horizontal plane QRS.

SINE AND COSINE RULES

For triangles without a right angle, two formulae apply

(i) $$\frac{a}{\sin \widehat{A}} = \frac{b}{\sin \widehat{B}} = \frac{c}{\sin \widehat{C}}$$ (the *sine rule*) (*ii*) $a^2 = b^2 + c^2 - 2bc \cos \widehat{A}$ (the *cosine rule*)

where *a* is the length of the side opposite the corner A (i.e. BC); *b* is the length of the side opposite B; and *c* the length of the side opposite C (Fig. 19.25).

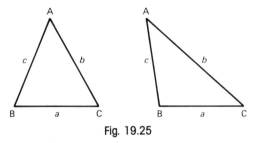

Fig. 19.25

The cosine rule also applies to the other sides:

$$b^2 = a^2 + c^2 - 2ac \cos \widehat{B} \quad \text{and} \quad c^2 = a^2 + b^2 - 2ab \cos \widehat{C}$$

Furthermore, the cosine rule can be rearranged to give a required angle when all three sides of the triangle are known:

$$\cos \widehat{A} = \frac{b^2 + c^2 - a^2}{2bc}$$

The sine and cosine rules apply not only to acute-angled triangles but also to obtuse-angled triangles (i.e. those that contain an angle of more than 90°). To find the sine and cosine of obtuse angles from tables use:

$$\sin x = \sin(180 - x) \quad \text{and} \quad \cos x = -\cos(180 - x)$$

Example In the triangle ABC (Fig. 19.26), AC = 10 cm, BC = 12 cm and $\widehat{C} = 110°$.

(a) Use the cosine rule to find the length of AB.

(b) Use the sine rule to find $\widehat{A}$.

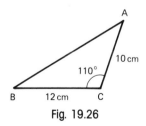

Fig. 19.26

(a) To find AB (= *c*):

$$c^2 = a^2 + b^2 - 2ab \cos \widehat{C}$$

$$= 12^2 + 10^2 - 2 \times 12 \times 10 \cos 110°$$

Finding $\cos 110°$ is a simple matter with a calculator, which will give the answer directly: $\cos 110° = -0.3420$. But finding $\cos 110°$ from four-figure tables requires an extra step:

$$\cos 110° = -\cos(180-110)° = -\cos 70° = -0.3420$$

Then, continuing with the cosine rule:

$$c^2 = 12^2 + 10^2 - 2 \times 12 \times 10 \cos 110°$$
$$= 144 + 100 - 240 \times (-0.3420)$$
$$= 326.08$$

Hence

$$AB = \sqrt{326.08} = 18.06 = 18.1 \text{ cm} \quad (3 \text{ s.f.})$$

(b) To find $\widehat{A}$:

$$\frac{a}{\sin \widehat{A}} = \frac{c}{\sin \widehat{C}}$$

Rearranging:

$$\frac{a \sin \widehat{C}}{c} = \sin \widehat{A}$$

Hence

$$\sin \widehat{A} = \frac{12 \sin 110°}{18.06} = \frac{12 \times 0.9397}{18.06} = 0.6244$$

and so $\widehat{A} = 38.6°$ (3 s.f.)

EXERCISE 19e

1. Use the sine rule to find the given angles and sides of the following triangles:
   (a) $\widehat{A} = 43°$, BC = 12 m, AB = 11 m. Find $\widehat{C}$
   (b) $\widehat{B} = 62°$, AC = 9 cm, BC = 8 cm. Find $\widehat{A}$
   (c) $\widehat{C} = 54°$, AB = 7 mm, CA = 4.1 mm. Find $\widehat{B}$
   (d) $\widehat{A} = 67°$, BC = 11.1 m, $\widehat{B} = 32°$. Find AC
   (e) $\widehat{Q} = 110°$, RP = 8 cm, $\widehat{R} = 21°$. Find PQ
   (f) $\widehat{X} = 20°$, ZY = 3 cm, XY = 8 cm. Find $\widehat{Z}$.

2. Use the cosine rule to find the missing side in these triangles:
   (a) $\widehat{A} = 32°$, AB = 54 mm, AC = 45 mm
   (b) $\widehat{B} = 67°$, BC = 34 cm, BA = 41 cm
   (c) $\widehat{C} = 27°$, CA = 73 cm, CB = 48 cm

(d) $\hat{P} = 111°$, PQ = 4 cm, PR = 5.3 cm

(e) $\hat{Y} = 123°$, YZ = 4.1 cm, YX = 7.2 cm.

3. Use the cosine rule to find the interior angles of these triangles, in which all three side lengths are known:

(a) AB = 32 cm, BC = 45 cm, CA = 38 cm

(b) PQ = 4.2 mm, QR = 2.8 mm, RP = 3.5 mm

(c) MN = 3 cm, NO = 11 cm, OM = 9 cm

(d) RS = 8.2 km, ST = 16.3 km, TR = 11.5 km.

4. Find all the missing sides and angles in the following triangles:

(a) AB = 13 cm, AC = 11 cm and $\hat{C} = 65°$

(b) AB = 15 cm, BC = 13 cm and $\hat{A} = 48°$

(c) XY = 12 cm, YZ = 9.8 cm and $\hat{Y} = 103°$

(d) PQ = 17 mm, QR = 34 mm and $\hat{Q} = 110°$

(e) RS = 3.81 m, ST = 5.32 m and TR = 6.4 m

(f) MN = 4.4 km, NO = 5.6 km and OM = 7.5 km.

MISCELLANEOUS EXERCISE 19

1.

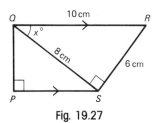

Fig. 19.27

In the figure (Fig. 19.27), the trapezium PQRS has PS parallel to QR, QR = 10 cm, RS = 6 cm, QS = 8 cm and angle QSR = angle QPS = 90°. Write down

(a) $\sin x°$,   (b) $\cos x°$,

and hence calculate

(c) the length PQ,   (d) the length PS.

(e) the area of the trapezium PQRS.   (AEB '82)

2. ABC is a triangle with D a point on BC and E a point on AC such that DE is parallel to BA (Fig. 19.28).

    EC = 16 cm,   DE = 12 cm   and   AB = 30 cm.

(a) Calculate the length of AC, and hence the length of AE.

255

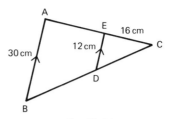

Fig. 19.28

(b) Given also that $\hat{DEC} = 90°$,
    (i)   name the other angle equal to 90°.
    (ii) Calculate the length of DC.
    (iii) Calculate the length of BD.   (WJEC)

3.

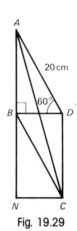

Fig. 19.29

$ABCD$ is a parallelogram (Fig. 19.29) in which $\hat{ABD} = 90°$, $\hat{ADB} = 60°$ and $AD = 20$ cm. ABN is a straight line and NC is parallel to BD. Calculate

(a) BD,   (b) AN,   (c) $\hat{ACN}$.   (C)

4.

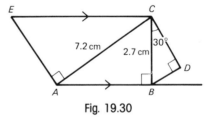

Fig. 19.30

The line AB (Fig. 19.30) is parallel to the line EC, and angles EAC, ABC and BDC are right angles. $\hat{BCD} = 30°$, and the lengths of AC and BC are 7.2 cm and 2.7 cm respectively. Calculate

(a) angle ACB,   (b) the length of BD,

(c) the length of EA.   (Ox)

5. *AB* is a building 16 metres high and *MT* a vertical mast, with *BT* representing level ground (Fig. 19.31).

The angle of elevation of the top of the mast from the top of the building is 16°42' and the angle of depression of the bottom of the mast from the top of the building is 21°48'.

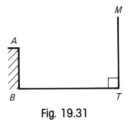

Fig. 19.31

(a) Make a sketch showing clearly the angles of elevation and depression given above.

(b) Calculate
   (i)   the length of *BT* (to the nearest metre),
   (ii) the height of the mast (by using your answer to (i)),
   (iii) the angle of elevation of the top of the mast from the bottom of the building. (WJEC)

6.

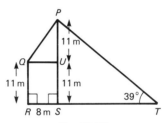

Fig. 19.32

The diagram (Fig. 19.22) represents a quadrilateral *PQRT* in which angles *QRT*, *PUQ* and *PSR* are right angles, angle *PTS* is 39°, *QR* = *PU* = *US* = 11 m and *RS* = 8 m.

Calculate

(a) angle *PQU*,   (b) the length of *PT*,

(c) the length of *RT*,   (d) the area of *PQRT*,

(e) angle *PTQ*.   (JMB)

7. *ABCD* is a rectangle with *AB* = 20 cm and *BC* = 15 cm. The points *X*, *Y*, *Z* lie on *AB*, *BC*, *CD* respectively such that *BX* = 5 cm, *BY* = 12 cm and *CZ* = 13 cm.

Calculate

(a) the lengths of the sides of the triangle *XYZ*,

(b) the size of angle *ZXY*,

(c) the area of triangle *XYZ*.   (JMB)

8.

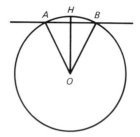

Fig. 19.33

A cylinder is floating in water with its axis horizontal. The diagram (Fig. 19.33) shows a vertical cross-section through the cylinder. O is the centre of the cross-section; A and B are points where the cross-section meets the water-surface. $OA = OB = 20$ cm, $AB = 16$ cm.

(a) Calculate, correct to two significant figures, the height above the water-level of H, the highest point of the cross-section.

(b) Show that angle AOH is, to the nearest degree, $24°$. Assuming that $\angle AOH = 24°$ and taking π as 3.14, calculate, correct to two significant figures,
    (i) the area of sector $OAHB$,
    (ii) the area of triangle AOB.

Find also, to the nearest whole number, the percentage of the volume of the cylinder which is above the water-level. (LU)

9.

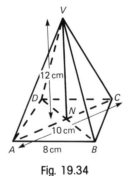

Fig. 19.34

The diagram (Fig. 19.34) shows a pyramid with a rectangular base $ABCD$ and vertex V.

The slant edges VA, VB, VC and VD are all equal and the diagonals of the base intersect at N.

$AB = 8$ cm, $AC = 10$ cm and $VN = 12$ cm.

(a) Calculate BC.

(b) Calculate VC.

(c) Write down the tangent of the angle between VN and VC.

(C)

10.

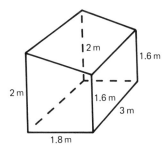

Fig. 19.35

A lean-to shed with a rectangular base stands on horizontal ground. The internal dimensions of the shed are as shown on the diagram (Fig. 19.35). Calculate the angle of slope of the roof and the area of the roof.

The shed contains a thin rigid rectangular sheet of metal 3 m long and 2.5 m wide. Calculate the smallest angle that the sheet can make with the horizontal.

Calculate also the length of the longest thin straight rod that the shed can contain (when the sheet of metal is not in it) and the angle that the rod makes with the horizontal.   (O & C)

11.

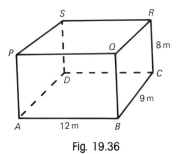

Fig. 19.36

The diagram (Fig. 19.36) represents a cuboid 12 m long, 9 m wide and 8 m high. Calculate

(a) the length of AC,   (b) the length of AR,

(c) the size of the angle between the planes $ABCD$ and $ADRQ$,

(d) the size of the angle between the line AR and the plane $ABCD$.   (JMB)

12.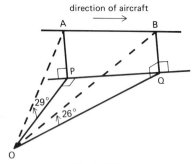

Fig. 19.37

O is the position of an observer on the horizontal plane OPQ (Fig. 19.37). The observer is watching an aircraft which is flying due east at a constant speed of 400 km/h and at a constant height of 2000 m.

When the aircraft is at A, it is due north of O and its angle of elevation from O is 29°.

Calculate the distance OP.

Later, when the aircraft is at B, its angle of elevation from O is 26°. Calculate the bearing of the aircraft from O at this instant.

Find the distance AB and hence deduce the time, in seconds to the nearest second, between the two observations.

(AEB '81)

20 CIRCLES

CIRCUMFERENCE AND AREA

The circumference and the area of a circle depend upon the radius, r, of the circle and the constant, π. The circumference is given by

$$\text{circumference} = 2\pi r$$

and the area is given by

$$\text{area} = \pi r^2$$

π is an irrational number. It cannot be written as an exact value for it continues for ever: a non-terminating, non-recurring decimal. Suitable working approximations are 3.142, 3.1416 or $\frac{22}{7}$.

Example Find the circumference and the area of a circle of radius 4 cm.

$$\text{circumference} = 2\pi r = 2 \times 3.1416 \times 4 = 25.13 \text{ cm}$$

$$\text{area} = \pi r^2 = 3.1416 \times 4^2 = 50.27 \text{ cm}^2$$

Arcs

An *arc* is part of the circumference of a circle, and is $\dfrac{x}{360}$ of its length, where x is the angle at the centre (Fig. 20.1).

Fig. 20.1

$$\text{length of arc} = \frac{x}{360} \times \text{length of circumference}$$

$$= \frac{x}{360} \times 2\pi r$$

Sectors

The area of a *sector* (part of the circle shaped rather like a slice of pie) is $\dfrac{x}{360}$ of the whole area, where x is the angle at the centre.

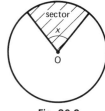

Fig. 20.2

$$\text{area of sector} = \frac{x}{360} \times \text{area of circle}$$

$$= \frac{x}{360} \times \pi r^2$$

Example Find the length of the circumference and the area of a circle of radius 5 cm. What is the length of an arc and the area of a sector of this circle formed by two radii at an angle of 72°?

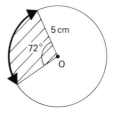

Fig. 20.3

The circumference of the circle is given by

$$2\pi r = 2 \times 3.1416 \times 5 = 31.416 \text{ cm}$$

The area of the circle is

$$\pi r^2 = \pi \times 5^2 = 3.1416 \times 25 = 78.54 \text{ cm}^2$$

The arc length is

$$\frac{72}{360} \times 31.416 = 6.2832 \text{ cm}$$

The area of the sector is

$$\frac{72}{360} \times 78.54 = 15.71 \text{ cm}^2$$

Chords

A straight line joining two points on the circumference is called a *chord*. The longest chord that it is possible to draw is the *diameter*, which passes through the centre of the circle and is twice the radius (Fig. 20.4).

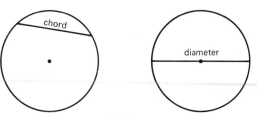

Fig. 20.4

A chord cuts the circle into *segments*, that is, portions of the circle shaped rather like a piece of an orange (Fig. 20.5).

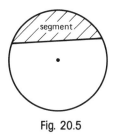

Fig. 20.5

Tangents

A *tangent* to a circle is a line that just touches it. The tangent forms a right angle with a radius drawn from the centre to the point of contact (Fig. 20.6).

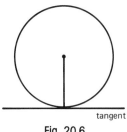

Fig. 20.6

If two tangents touch the circle at points T and S, and themselves meet at a third point, P, then PT = PS (Fig. 20.7).

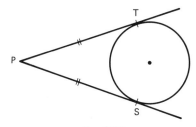

Fig. 20.7

Find the area and perimeter of the shapes in Questions 1 to 4.

1.

2.
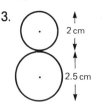

3.
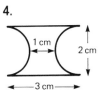

4.

Find the area of the shaded parts in Questions 5 to 8.

5.
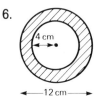

6.

7.

8.

9. Find the arc length and area of a sector of a circle if
   (a) the radius is 5 cm and the centre angle 72°
   (b) the radius is 8 cm and the centre angle is 135°
   (c) the radius is 15 cm and the centre angle is 156°.

10. Find the radius of a circle that has a circumference of
    (a) 15.7 cm   (b) 169.6 cm   (c) 78.5 cm
    (d) 37.3 cm.

11. Find the radius of a circle that has an area of
    (a) 78.5 cm²   (b) 706.9 cm²   (c) 125 700 cm²
    (d) 31.4 cm².

12. A bicycle wheel has a radius of 32 cm. How far will it have travelled when it has made 100 revolutions? How many revolutions will the wheel complete in a journey of 1 km?

13. The wheels of a car revolve 750 times for every kilometre travelled. What is their radius (to the nearest centimetre)?

14. The circumference of a circle is 785.5 mm. What is its area in cm²?

15.
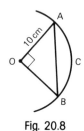

Fig. 20.8

Figure 20.8 shows part of a circle, radius 10 cm. If $A\hat{O}B = 90°$, find the area of

(a) triangle AOB   (b) sector AOB   (c) segment ACB.

16. Find the area of a segment between the minor arc of a circle and a chord 10 cm long if the radius of the circle is

(a) 10 cm   (b) 13 cm.

17.

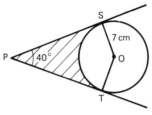

Fig. 20.9

Two tangents drawn from a point, P, meet a circle, centre O, at S and T (Fig. 20.9). If the radius of the circle is 7 cm and $T\hat{P}S = 40°$, find the shaded area.

FOUR COMMON CIRCLE THEOREMS

Centre angle double that at circumference

The angle at the centre of a circle is double the angle at the circumference that stands on the same arc (Fig. 20.10).

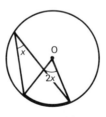

Fig. 20.10

The theorem is also true for the reflex angle at the centre (Fig. 20.11).

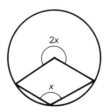

Fig. 20.11

Angles on the same arc are equal

Angles at the circumference that stand on
the same arc are equal.

Fig. 20.12

Angles on a diameter are 90°

Angles at the circumference that stand on
a diameter are right angles.

Fig. 20.13

Opposite angles of a cyclic quadrilateral make 180°

Opposite angles of a cyclic quadrilateral add
up to 180°.

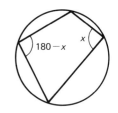

Fig. 20.14

The reverse of this also applies, i.e. any quadrilateral known to
have opposite angles that add up to 180° is cyclic.

It follows that the exterior angle of a cyclic
quadrilateral is equal to the interior opposite
angle.

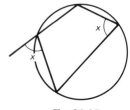

Fig. 20.15

Note: When finding angles in a circle, remember that any triangle with two sides equal to the radius is isosceles.

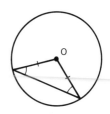

Fig. 20.16

Examples (*i*) A$\hat{\text{C}}$B = 30°, A$\hat{\text{B}}$D = 100° (see Fig. 20.17). Find
(a) A$\hat{\text{D}}$B   (b) D$\hat{\text{A}}$B.

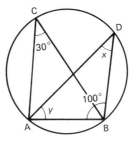

Fig. 20.17

(a) A$\hat{\text{D}}$B = A$\hat{\text{C}}$B = 30° (angles on the same arc, AB).

(b) In triangle ADB, A$\hat{\text{B}}$D = 100°, A$\hat{\text{D}}$B = 30°. But

D$\hat{\text{A}}$B + A$\hat{\text{B}}$D + A$\hat{\text{D}}$B = 180° (sum of angles in a triangle)

Therefore

D$\hat{\text{A}}$B = 180° − 100° − 30° = 50°

(*ii*) ABCD is a cyclic quadrilateral; O is the centre of the circle; A$\hat{\text{D}}$C = 140° (Fig. 20.18). Find
(a) A$\hat{\text{B}}$C   (b) A$\hat{\text{O}}$C   (c) O$\hat{\text{A}}$C.

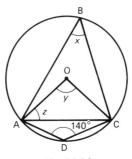

Fig. 20.18

(a) A$\hat{\text{D}}$C + A$\hat{\text{B}}$C = 180° (opposite angles of a cyclic quadrilateral). So

A$\hat{\text{B}}$C = 180° − A$\hat{\text{D}}$C = 180° − 140° = 40°

267

(b) $A\widehat{O}C = 2 \times A\widehat{B}C$ (angle at centre is twice that at circumference). Therefore

$$A\widehat{O}C = 2 \times 40° = 80°$$

(c) OA is a radius of the circle and so is OC. Thus OA = OC and triangle OAC is isosceles. Hence $O\widehat{A}C = O\widehat{C}A$. But, as $A\widehat{O}C = 80°$, $O\widehat{A}C + O\widehat{C}A = 100°$ (sum of angles in a triangle). Therefore

$$O\widehat{A}C = \tfrac{1}{2} \times 100° = 50°$$

EXERCISE 20b Find the angle x in each of the following and give a reason for your answer.

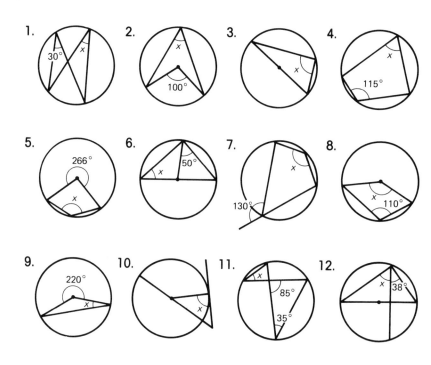

In Questions 13 to 24 find the angles indicated x, y and z. Give a reason for each step in your calculations.

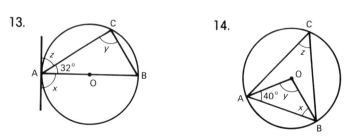

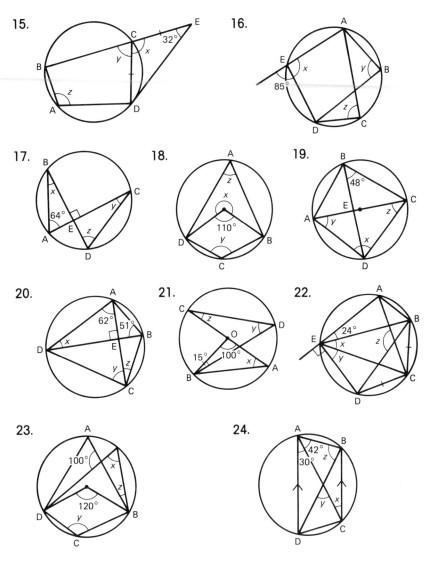

25. AC and BD are diameters of a circle. Show that the quadrilateral ABCD is a rectangle.

26.

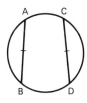

Fig. 20.19

AB and CD are two non-parallel chords of the same circle such that AB = CD (Fig. 20.19). Copy the diagram, adding lines, AC, BD, AD and BC. If the diagonals of the quadrilateral ABCD meet at X, prove that

269

(a) triangles ABX and CXD are congruent

(b) triangle AXC is isosceles

(c) AC∥BD, and hence that ABCD is an isosceles trapezium.

27.

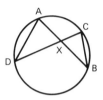

Fig. 20.20

Two chords of a circle, AB and CD, intersect at X (Fig. 20.20). Use angles on the same arc to prove that triangles AXC and DXB are similar. Hence show that AX×BX = CX×DX.

28.

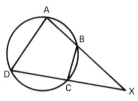

Fig. 20.21

ABCD is a cyclic quadrilateral. AB and CD are extended to a point X where they intersect (Fig. 20.21). Prove that triangles AXD and CXB are similar, and hence show that AX×BX = CX×DX.

ALTERNATE SEGMENT THEOREM

If a tangent and a chord meet on the circumference of a circle, then the angle between them is equal to the angle that stands on the chord in the alternate (opposite) segment (see Fig. 20.22).

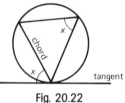

Fig. 20.22

Examples (*i*) Find the angles (a) $A\hat{B}T$, (b) $B\hat{T}S$ in Fig. 20.23.

(a) $A\hat{B}T = A\hat{T}U = 70°$ (alternate segment theorem).

(b) $B\hat{T}S = B\hat{A}T = 60°$ (alternate segment theorem).

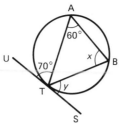

Fig. 20.23

(*ii*) A tangent touches a circle at T. A chord of the circle, AB, is parallel to the tangent (Fig. 20.24). Prove that the triangle TAB is isosceles.

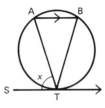

Fig. 20.24

Let the angle $S\widehat{T}A$ be x. Then $T\widehat{B}A = x$ (alternate segment theorem). But also $T\widehat{A}B = x$ (alternate angles). So in triangle TAB, $T\widehat{A}B = A\widehat{B}T$, and hence TAB is isosceles.

EXERCISE 20c Find the angle marked x in the following. Give a reason for each step in your calculation.

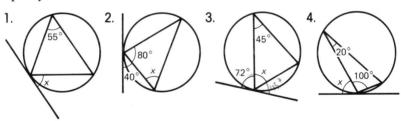

Find the angles marked x, y and z in Questions 5 to 13. Be sure to give a reason for every step in your calculations.

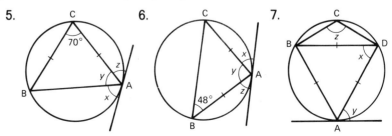

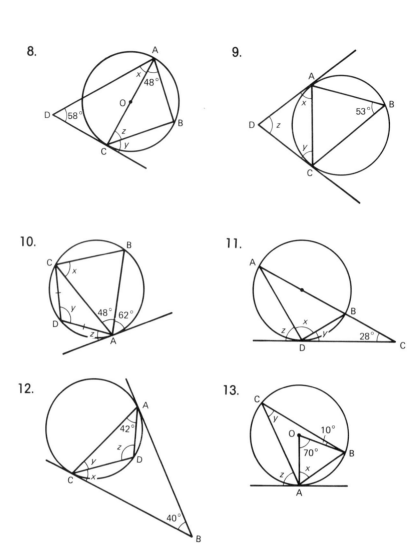

8.

9.

10.

11.

12.

13.

14. Two circles, one inside the other, as shown in Fig. 20.25, have a common tangent at their point of contact, E. Prove that AB‖CD.

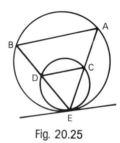

Fig. 20.25

15. A tangent is drawn from a point X to touch a circle, centre O, at T. P is any point on the circumference of the circle. Prove that angle TOP is twice angle XTP.

272

16.

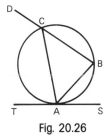

Fig. 20.26

In Fig. 20.26, TAS is a tangent to the circle. BCD is a chord, extended to D outside the circle, as shown. Prove that $D\hat{C}A = C\hat{A}S$.

INTERSECTING CHORDS THEOREM

If two chords, AB and CD, intersect at X then $AX \times BX = CX \times DX$.

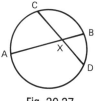

Fig. 20.27

The theorem also applies to

(*i*)   chords that intersect outside the circle (Fig. 20.28),

(*ii*)   a tangent and a chord (Fig. 20.29).

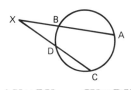

$$AX \times BX = CX \times DX$$

Fig. 20.28

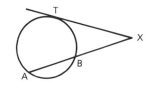

$$AX \times BX = TX^2$$

Fig. 20.29

Examples (*i*)   Find the length DX in Fig. 20.30.

$$AX \times BX = CX \times DX.$$

Thus

$$2 \times 6 = 3 \times DX$$

Hence

$$DX = \frac{12}{3} = 4 \text{ cm}$$

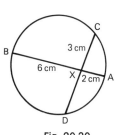

Fig. 20.30

(*ii*) Find the lengths *x* and *y* in Fig. 20.31.

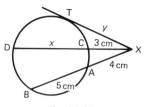

Fig. 20.31

First, find BX and DX:

$$BX = 5 + 4 = 9 \text{ cm}$$

$$DX = x + 3$$

Applying the intersecting chords theorem to chords AB and CD:

$$AX \times BX = CX \times DX$$

$$4 \times 9 = 3 \times (x + 3)$$

Hence

$$36 = 3x + 9$$

$$x = 9 \text{ cm}$$

Applying the theorem a second time, to the chord AB and the tangent:

$$AX \times BX = TX^2$$

$$4 \times 9 = y^2$$

Hence

$$y = \sqrt{36} = 6 \text{ cm}$$

EXERCISE 20d 1. Chords AB and CD intersect inside a circle, as shown in Fig. 20.32.

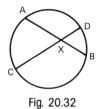

Fig. 20.32

(a) Find DX if AX = 3 cm, BX = 12 cm and CX = 9 cm.

(b) Find CX if AX = 15 cm, BX = 5 cm and DX = 6 cm.

(c) Find AB (i.e. the complete length of the chord) if AX = 4 cm, CX = 5 cm and DX = 8 cm.

(d) Find AB if AX = 12 cm, CX = 8 cm and CD = 17 cm.

2.

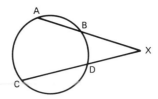

Fig. 20.33

Chords AB and CD intersect outside the circle (Fig. 20.33).

(a) Find DX if $AX = 18$ cm, $BX = 10$ cm and $CX = 15$ cm.

(b) Find CX if $AX = 20$ cm, $BX = 9$ cm and $DX = 6$ cm.

(c) Find AB if $AX = 24$ cm, $CX = 30$ cm and $DX = 6$ cm.

(d) Find CD if $CX = 18$ cm, $AX = 27$ cm and $BX = 10$ cm.

3.

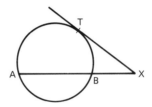

Fig. 20.34

A chord AB meets a tangent at a point X, outside the circle (Fig. 20.34).

(a) Find TX if $AX = 18$ cm and $BX = 8$ cm.

(b) Find AB if $TX = 8$ cm and $AX = 16$ cm.

In Questions 4 to 14, find the lengths indicated.

4.

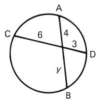

5.

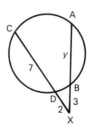

6.

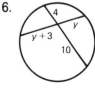

7.

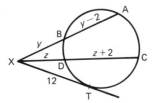

8.

275

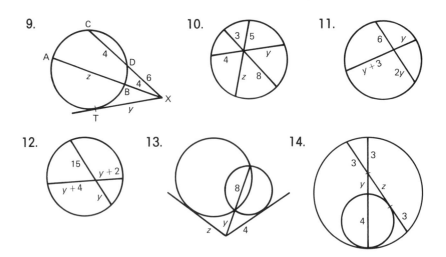

MISCELLANEOUS EXERCISE 20

1. In the diagram (Fig. 20.35), which is not drawn to scale, PT is a tangent to the circle, centre O, and the line PAB cuts the circle at A and B. Given that the radius of the circle is 8 cm, $PT = 15$ cm and $AB = 6$ cm, calculate

   (a) the length of OP,

   (b) the size of angle AOB.

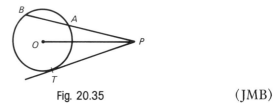

Fig. 20.35 (JMB)

2. In the sector OAB (Fig. 20.36), O is the centre of the circle and the angle $AOB = 45°$. The radius of the circle is 12 cm and C and D are both 4 cm from O.

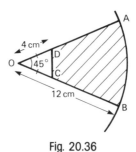

Fig. 20.36

Calculate the shaded area ABCD. Take π as 3.14 and give your answer to the nearest square centimetre.

3.

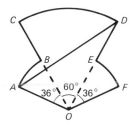

Fig. 20.37

The diagram (Fig. 20.37) represents a badge made from sectors of two circles with a common centre O.

The radius $OA = 5$ cm, and the radius $OC = 9$ cm.

$$A\hat{O}B = E\hat{O}F = 36° \quad \text{and} \quad C\hat{O}D = 60°.$$

Take π to be 3.142 and give all your answers correct to 3 significant figures.

(a) Find the length of the arc EF.

(b) Gold braid, of negligible width, is sewn round the perimeter $OABCDEFO$ of the badge. Calculate the length of gold braid used.

(c) Calculate the area of cloth used for the sector OCD.

(d) A thin straight silver wire runs from A to D. Calculate its length. (C)

4. (a) A satellite follows a circular path above the Earth's surface. It passes over the North and South poles and travels in a circle whose centre is the centre of the Earth and whose radius is 7000 km.
   (i)   If the satellite takes $1\frac{1}{2}$ hours to make one complete orbit of the Earth, calculate its speed in km/h, giving your answer correct to the nearest 100 km/h.
   (ii) At a certain time the satellite is passing over the South pole. Find the latitude of the position on the Earth vertically below the satellite 20 minutes later.

   (b) A second satellite also follows a circular path whose centre is the centre of the Earth. It travels at 30 000 km/h and completes an orbit in 2 hours. Calculate
   (i)   the radius of the circle in which it moves,
   (ii) its height above the Earth's surface, correct to the nearest 100 km.

   (Take π to be 3.142 and the Earth's radius to be 6371 km.)
   (C)

5.

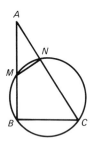

Fig. 20.38

In the diagram (Fig. 20.38), a circle, drawn through the vertices B and C of a triangle ABC, cuts AB at M and AC at N. Prove that the triangles ANM and ABC are similar.

Given that $BC = 15$ cm, $AC = 25$ cm, $AN = 4$ cm and $AM : AB = 1 : 4$,

(a) find the length of AM,

(b) show that angle ABC is a right angle,

(c) calculate the radius of the circle. (JMB)

6.

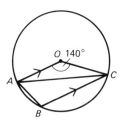

Fig. 20.39

In the diagram (Fig. 20.39), O is the centre of the circle, AO is parallel to BC and $A\hat{O}C = 140°$. Calculate the value of

(a) $A\hat{C}B$ (b) $A\hat{B}C$. (C)

7.

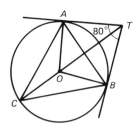

Fig. 20.40

In the diagram (Fig. 20.40), TA and TB are tangents to a circle, centre O. TOC is a straight line and $A\hat{T}B = 80°$. Calculate

(a) $A\hat{B}T$,   (b) $A\hat{O}B$,   (c) $A\hat{C}O$. (C)

8.

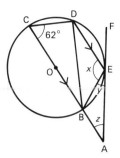

Fig. 20.41

In Fig. 20.41, FEA is a tangent to the circle. DE is parallel to the diameter COBA. Calculate the three angles

(a) DÊB   (b) BÊA   (c) EÂB.

9.

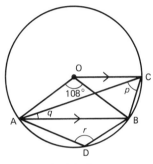

Fig. 20.42

In the diagram (Fig. 20.42), the points A, D, B and C are on the circumference of the circle, centre O. Given that OC is parallel to AB and that the angle AÔB = 108°, calculate

(a) p (b) q (c) r.   (AEB '81)

10.

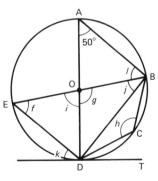

Fig. 20.43

ABCDE are points on a circle, centre O (Fig. 20.43). DT is the tangent to the circle at D. DÂB = 50°. Calculate, but do not prove, the value of the angles marked f, g, h, i, j, k, l.

(WJEC)

11.

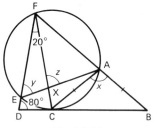

Fig. 20.44

In Fig. 20.44, A, C, E, F all lie on the circumference of a circle. ABC is an isosceles triangle, BCD is a tangent to the circle, and EA and FC meet at X. Calculate

(a) $\hat{CAB}$ (b) $\hat{FEA}$ (c) $\hat{FXA}$.

12.

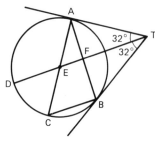

Fig. 20.45

TA and TB are tangents to a circle ABCD from an external point T. E is the centre of the circle, AC is a diameter and $\hat{ATB} = 64°$. DEFT is a straight line bisecting $\hat{ATB}$ (Fig. 20.45). Find (but do not prove) the size of angles $\hat{CAT}$, $\hat{ABC}$, $\hat{TAB}$, $\hat{CAB}$, $\hat{AFE}$, $\hat{AEF}$, $\hat{ADE}$ and $\hat{BCD}$.   (WJEC)

21 THREE-DIMENSIONAL FIGURES

VOLUMES

The volume, V, of the figures shown in Fig. 21.1, with *upright sides*, i.e. sides perpendicular to the ends, can be generalised by

$$V = \text{base area} \times \text{height}$$

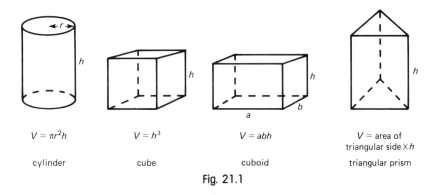

$V = \pi r^2 h$	$V = h^3$	$V = abh$	$V = \text{area of triangular side} \times h$
cylinder	cube	cuboid	triangular prism

Fig. 21.1

For figures with *sloping sides* (Fig. 21.2), the volume is given by

$$V = \tfrac{1}{3} \text{base area} \times \text{vertical height}$$

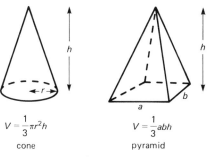

$V = \dfrac{1}{3}\pi r^2 h$	$V = \dfrac{1}{3}abh$
cone	pyramid

Fig. 21.2

The sphere is a special case:

$$V = \tfrac{4}{3}\pi r^3$$

where r is its radius (Fig. 21.3).

Fig. 21.3

SURFACE AREAS

For straight-sided figures, it is best to work out the area of the separate sides and add them together to find the total surface area of the shape.

The curved surface area of a cylinder is given by

$$A = \text{base circumference} \times \text{height} = 2\pi r h$$

The curved surface area of a cone is given by

$$A = \pi r l$$

where l is the *slant height* (Fig. 21.4).

Fig. 21.4

The circular tops and bottoms may also be required as part of the total surface area of the cylinder or cone, so check.

The curved surface area of a sphere is given by $4\pi r^2$.

Examples (*i*) Find the volume and the surface area of an open-topped cylindrical water tank 0.5 m in radius and 1 m high (see Fig. 21.5).

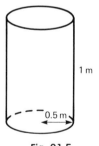

1 m

0.5 m

Fig. 21.5

The volume V is given by

$$V = \pi r^2 h$$
$$= \pi (0.5)^2 \times 1$$
$$= 3.142 \times 0.25 \times 1$$
$$= 0.786 \text{ m}^3 \quad (3 \text{ s.f.})$$

The area of the curved surface is given by

$$2\pi rb = 2 \times \pi \times 0.5 \times 1$$
$$= 3.142 \text{ m}^2$$

The area of the circular bottom is

$$\pi r^2 = 3.142 \times (0.5)^2$$
$$= 0.786 \text{ m}^2$$

Thus

the total surface area $= 3.142 + 0.786 = 3.928$
$$= 3.93 \text{ m}^2 \quad (3 \text{ s.f.})$$

(*ii*) Find the total surface area and the volume of a cone with *slant* height of 20 cm and sides inclined at $30°$ to the base.

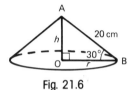

Fig. 21.6

First we need to find the radius of the cone and its vertical height, using trigonometry. In the triangle OAB (Fig. 21.6) (formed from half of the vertical cross-section of the cone)

$$\cos 30° = \frac{\text{adjacent}}{\text{hypotenuse}} = \frac{\text{radius}}{\text{slant height}}$$

Hence, the radius, r, is given by

$$r = \cos 30° \times \text{slant height} = 0.866 \, 03 \times 20 = 17.32 \text{ cm}$$

We know also that

$$\sin 30° = \frac{\text{opposite}}{\text{hypotenuse}} = \frac{\text{vertical height}}{\text{slant height}}$$

So the vertical height, b, is given by

$$b = \sin 30° \times \text{slant height} = 0.5 \times 20 = 10 \text{ cm}$$

The curved surface area of the cone is given by

$$\pi rl = 3.142 \times 17.32 \times 20$$
$$= 1088.4 \text{ cm}^2$$

The area of the circular base is given by

$$\pi r^2 = 3.142 \times (17.32)^2$$
$$= 942.5 \text{ cm}^2$$

So the total surface area of the cone is

1088.4 + 942.5 = 2031 cm² (to the nearest whole number)

The volume of the cone is given by

$$\tfrac{1}{3}\pi r^2 h = \tfrac{1}{3} \times 3.142 \times (17.32)^2 \times 10$$

$$= 3142 \text{ cm}^3 \text{ (to the nearest whole number)}$$

EXERCISE 21a *Throughout this exercise take π as 3.1416.*

1. Find the volume and curved surface area of a cylinder of radius 6 m and height 10 m.

2. Find the volume and total surface area of a cube of sides 2 m.

3. Find the volume of a cone of radius 4 cm and height 6 cm. What is the slant height of this cone? Find also its total surface area (including the base).

4. Find the volume of the pyramid shown in Fig. 21.7, given that it is 10 cm high and the base is square with sides of 5 cm.

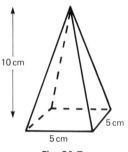

10 cm

5 cm

5 cm

Fig. 21.7

5. Find the volume and surface area of a sphere of radius 10 cm.

6. Find the volume and total surface area (including the top and base) of a cylinder of radius 8 cm and height 20 cm.

7. Find the volume and surface area of a closed rectangular-based water tank with sides 2 m, 1 m and height 1.5 m.

8.

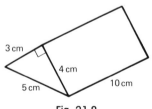

3 cm

4 cm

5 cm

10 cm

Fig. 21.8

Find the volume and surface area of a prism that is 10 cm long and has sides 3 cm, 4 cm and 5 cm as illustrated in Fig. 21.8.

9.

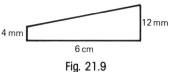

Fig. 21.9

A plastic door-wedge has a trapezium cross-section, as shown in Fig. 21.9. If the wedge is 3 cm wide, find the volume of plastic required to manufacture it, in cm^3.

10. Which has the greater volume, a sphere of radius 2 cm or a cube of side length 3 cm? Which has the greater surface area? Justify your answers.

11. Show that the surface area of a closed cylinder of radius 10 cm and height 20 cm is exactly equal to that of a cone of radius 15 cm and height 20 cm.

12. A wigwam has an irregular base covering 2.6 m^2 of ground. If it is 2 m high, what is its volume?

13. The luggage space of a popular modern motor car is found to be 1.6 m long. If the manufacturers claim the car's luggage capacity to be 2.4 m^3, what must the area of the cross-section be?

14.

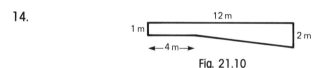

Fig. 21.10

Figure 2.10 shows the cross-section of a swimming pool. What is the area of this cross-section? If the pool is 6 m wide, what volume of water could it contain?

15.

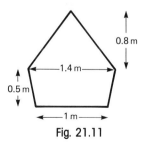

Fig. 21.11

Figure 21.11 shows the cross-section of a tent. What is the area of this cross-section? If the tent is 2 m long, what is its volume?

285

16.

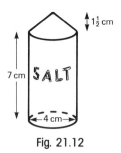

Fig. 21.12

A salt cellar consists of a cylindrical base, 7 cm high and 4 cm in diameter, and a conical cap $1\frac{1}{2}$ cm high (see Fig. 21.12). Find its volume.

17. Water flows through a 2 cm diameter pipe at 3 cm/s. What is the volume of a 3 cm length of pipe. Hence deduce the rate of flow of water, in cm³/s.

18. Oil gushes through a pipeline at 0.4 m/s. If the diameter of the pipe is 0.2 m find the volume of a 0.4 m length of pipe and so deduce the rate of oil flow in m³/s.

How long, to the nearest minute, would it take to fill a rectangular oil tank 4 m by 6 m by 2 m at this rate?

SIMILAR OBJECTS

A three-dimensional object is said to be similar to another if it is the same shape but different in size.

Suppose the height and other linear dimensions (such as radius) of the larger object are k times those of the smaller one. We say that k is the *linear scale factor* (see similar triangles, Chapter 16). The *area scale factor* is k^2 (*not* k) and the *volume scale factor* is k^3. This means that

surface area of larger object $= k^2 \times$ *surface area of smaller object*

volume of larger object $= k^3 \times$ *volume of smaller object*

Example A manufacturer of baked beans sells his product in various sizes of cylindrical tin. The small tin is 6 cm tall and has a radius of 3 cm; the 'jumbo' size is similar in shape to the small can but it is 12 cm tall and has a radius of 6 cm. Find the volume of the small can and the area of the label stuck on to its curved side. Find, too, the volume of the larger can and the area of its label. (Refer to Fig. 21.13.)

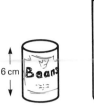

Fig. 21.13

The volume of the small can is

$$V = \pi r^2 h = 3.142 \times 3^2 \times 6$$
$$= 169.67 \text{ cm}^3$$

The area of the label is

$$A = 2\pi r h = 2 \times 3.142 \times 3 \times 6$$
$$= 113.1 \text{ cm}^2$$

To find the volume and curved surface area of the 'jumbo' can, we could repeat these calculations from scratch, but it is easier to use the similarity of the cans' shapes.

$$\text{linear scale factor} = \frac{\text{height of larger can}}{\text{height of smaller can}} = \frac{12}{6} = 2$$

The height and the radius of the larger can are twice the height and radius, respectively, of the smaller version, i.e. the linear scale factor is 2. Hence the area factor is $2^2 = 4$ and the volume factor is $2^3 = 8$.

Thus the area of the 'jumbo' label $= 4 \times$ area of small label

$$= 4 \times 113.1$$
$$= 452.4 \text{ cm}^2$$

the volume of the 'jumbo' can $= 8 \times$ volume of small can

$$= 8 \times 169.67$$
$$= 1357.4 \text{ cm}^3$$

EXERCISE 21b   1. Three cubes, A, B and C, have side lengths 1 cm, 2 cm and 3 cm. For each of the cubes find

(a) the surface areas   (b) the volume

Write down, in their lowest terms, the ratios

(c) area A : area B : area C

(d) volume A : volume B : volume C.

287

2. Three spheres, P, Q and R, have radii 1 cm, 2 cm and 3 cm. Find

   (a) the surface area   (b) the volume

   of the three spheres, leaving π in your answers.

   Write down, in lowest terms, the ratios

   (c) area P : area Q : area R

   (d) volume P : volume Q : volume R.

3. Three cones, X, Y and Z, are all similar. The first has radius 1 cm and height 2 cm, the second has radius 2 cm and height 4 cm and the third has radius 3 cm and height 6 cm. Find the volumes of the three cones leaving π in your answers. Write down, in lowest terms, the ratio

   $$\text{volume X} : \text{volume Y} : \text{volume Z}$$

4. A piece of metal is melted down and moulded into 24 model elephants. How many similar models of twice the height might have been made from the same piece of metal?

5. 1600 ball-bearings of radius 0.5 cm have the same volume as n larger ball-bearings with radius 2 cm. Find n.

6. Find the volume and surface area of a sphere of radius 3 cm. *Write down* the volume and surface area of a sphere of radius 30 cm. (Take π as 3.142.)

7. Find the volume of a 9 cm high pyramid with a square base of side length 5 cm. *Write down* the volume of a similar pyramid 36 cm high.

8. A small water tank in my house holds 5 litres. The man next door has a similar tank, made and installed by the same people, but its sides are twice as long and it is twice as high as mine. How much water does it hold?

9. A small sherry glass holds 80 ml. The large wine goblet in the same set is 1.4 times the height of the sherry glass. How much wine does it hold?

10.

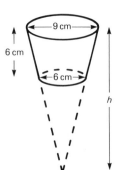

Fig. 21.14

An ice-cream tub consists of the top part of a cone (Fig. 21.14).
The diameter at the top of the tub is 9 cm; at the bottom the
diameter is 6 cm; it is 6 cm high. Find

(a) the height of the complete cone, h

(b) the volume of the complete cone, taking π as 3.142

(c) the volume of the tub, using similarity.

11.

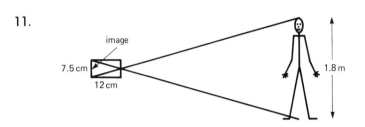

Fig. 21.15

A man is 1.8 m tall. Someone is to take his picture using an
old-fashioned pin-hole camera. If the camera is 7.5 cm tall and
12 cm deep (Fig. 21.15), how far from the camera must the
man stand if his head and feet are to be included in the
picture?

The man is holding a scroll, 30 cm by 21 cm. What are the
dimensions of the scroll's image on the back of the camera?

12.

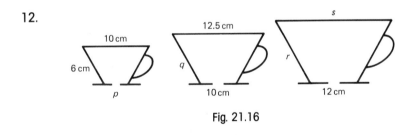

Fig. 21.16

Figure 21.16 shows the cross-sections of three similar coffee
filter cones.

(a) Calculate the lengths p, q, r and s.

(b) If the filter for the smallest size is made from 160 cm² of
paper, how much paper is needed to make the filter for
(i) the medium size   (ii) the large size?

(c) The largest size holds 756 cm³ of liquid. What is the
volume of
(i) the medium size   (ii) the small size?

1. $ABCD$ is the cross-section of a bar of metal with $AB = 6$ cm, $BC = 13$ cm, $AD = 12$ cm, and $D\hat{A}B = A\hat{D}E = D\hat{E}B = 90°$ (Fig. 21.17).

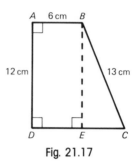

Fig. 21.17

If the bar is 1 m long calculate

(a) the length of EC and hence DC,

(b) the area of the cross-section,

(c) the volume of the bar of metal,

(d) the weight of the bar of metal, in kilograms, given that 1 cm^3 of metal weighs 2.3 grams. (WJEC)

2.

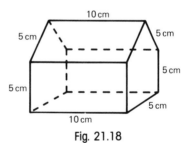

Fig. 21.18

The diagram (Fig. 21.18) shows a paper model house that can be made from a sheet of paper 20 cm square, by a certain method of folding, cutting, etc. There is no floor, but there are two vertical walls and two sloping roof-sections, all of which are rectangles 10 cm × 5 cm, and two end walls which are vertical pentagons. Write down the angle of slope of each roof-section, and calculate

(a) the area of each end wall,

(b) the total area of all the walls and roof-sections,

(c) the answer to (b) expressed as a percentage of the area of the sheet of paper from which the model was made,

(d) the volume of the model.

State what would be the effect of your answers to (b), (c) and (d) above, if the model were made from a sheet of paper 40 cm square, so that all the linear dimensions were doubled.   (LU)

3.

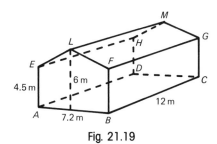

Fig. 21.19

The diagram (Fig. 21.19) shows a large greenhouse which has the following dimensions: length 12 m, width 7.2 m, height of sides 4.5 m and height to roof-ridge (which is parallel to, and half-way between, the long sides) 6 m.

Calculate

(a) the area of the end *ABFLE*,

(b) the volume of air contained in the greenhouse,

(c) the length of the slanting edge *EL*,

(d) the total area of glass, consisting of the four walls and the roof.   (O & C)

4.

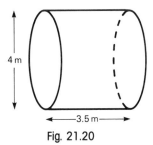

Fig. 21.20

A cylindrical oil tank, with its axis horizontal, is exactly half full of oil. The tank has a diameter of 4 m and a length of 3.5 m (Fig. 21.20).

Taking π to be $\frac{22}{7}$, calculate

(a) the area of the horizontal oil surface,

(b) the area of the tank in contact with the oil,

(c) the mass of oil in the tank if 1 m³ of oil has a mass of 900 kg.   (AEB '81)

5. A cylindrical wooden rod has a diameter of 2 cm and is 1 m long. Taking π to be 3.14 calculate

(a) the *total* surface area, in cm², of the rod,

(b) the mass of the rod if 1 cm³ of the wood has a mass of 0.8 g.

Another cylindrical rod, made of the same wood, has a diameter of 1 cm and is 1 m long.

(c) Write down the mass of this rod.   (AEB '82)

6. During a storm, the depth of the rainfall was 15.4 mm. The rain which fell on a horizontal roof measuring 7.5 m by 3.6 m was collected in a cylindrical tank of radius 35 cm which was empty before the storm began. Calculate

(a) the area, in cm², of the roof;

(b) the volume, in cm², of the rain which fell on the roof.

Taking π as $\frac{22}{7}$, find

(c) the area, in cm², of the cross section of the tank;

(d) the height, in cm, of the rain water in the tank.

Given that a watering can holds five litres, how many times could it be filled completely from the rain water?   (LU)

7.

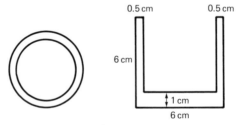

Fig. 21.21

A plan and elevation of a cylindrical glass container are shown in Fig. 21.21.

(a) Calculate the volume of glass in the container.

(b) Calculate the total surface area of the container.

(c) A number of identical containers are to be filled with liquid up to 0.5 cm below the brim. How many of these containers may be filled from a litre of liquid?   (Ox)

8.

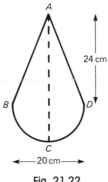

Fig. 21.22

A solid consists of a cone and a hemisphere which have a common base of diameter 20 cm. The perpendicular height of the cone is 24 cm. Fig. 21.22 represents a cross section $ABCD$ through the vertical axis AC of the solid.

Calculate

(a) the slant height of the cone,

(b) the area, correct to the nearest 1 cm², of the cross section $ABCD$,

(c) the total volume, correct to the nearest 10 cm³, of the solid,

(d) the total curved surface area, correct to the nearest 10 cm², of the solid. (AEB '82)

22 LATITUDE AND LONGITUDE

Any point on the Earth's surface can be pin-pointed by its *latitude*, i.e. degrees north or south of the equator, and its *longitude*, i.e. degrees east or west of Greenwich (in London).

A *great circle* is a circle whose radius is equal to that of the Earth (6370 km). The equator is a great circle; so are all circles, or *meridians*, of longitude passing through the North and South Poles.

A journey of 1852 m along the equator will change the traveller's longitude by 1 minute (1 minute $= \frac{1}{60}$ of a degree). This distance is called a *nautical mile*. A speed of 1 nautical mile per hour is 1 *knot*.

Circles of latitude or *parallels* (parallel to the equator) are *not* great circles; their radius depends upon their nearness to the poles: the nearer the parallel to the pole the smaller its radius. We can show by simple trigonometry that the radius, r, of a circle of latitude $\alpha°$ north or south of the equator is $r = R \cos \alpha$, where R is the radius of the Earth (see Fig. 22.1).

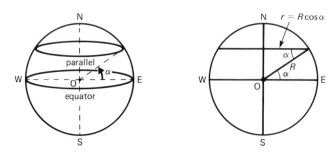

Fig. 22.1

Examples (*i*) Find the radius of the circle of latitude that passes through Madrid, Spain (41°N, 3°W) and New York, USA (41°N, 76°W). Find the distance between the two cities.

As the two cities are both located on the parallel 41° north of the equator, the radius of the circle will be

$$r = R \cos \alpha = 6370 \cos 41° = 4807.5 = 4810 \, \text{km} \quad (3 \, \text{s.f.})$$

To find the distance between Madrid and New York, the length of the arc of the circle formed by the angle of 73° (i.e. the difference in longitudes of the two cities) must be calculated (Fig. 22.2).

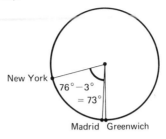

Fig. 22.2

$$\text{length of arc} = \frac{73}{360} \times 2\pi r$$

$$= \frac{73}{360} \times 2 \times 3.142 \times 4807.5 = 6125.9$$

$$= 6130 \,\text{km} \quad (3 \text{ s.f.})$$

(*ii*) Show that Phoenix, USA (34° N, 112° W) and Kabul, Afghanistan (34° N, 68° E) lie on the same meridian.
Find the distance between the two cities

(a) travelling over the North Pole,

(b) travelling along the 34th parallel.

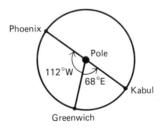

Fig. 22.3

As Pheonix is 112° west of Greenwich and Kabul is 68° east, we can see from Fig. 22.3 that the angle at the North Pole is 68° + 112° = 180°. i.e. the towns lie on the same great circle. (In general, a point $x°$ W lies on the same meridian as another point $y°$ E if $x + y = 180°$.)

(a) Travelling over the pole is to travel along an arc of $180 - (2 \times 34°) = 112°$ of the great circle (see Fig. 22.4). Thus the distance over the pole between the cities is

$$\frac{112}{360} \times 2 \times \pi \times 6370 = 12\,452 \text{ km}$$

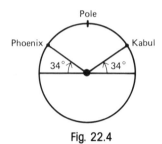

Fig. 22.4

(b) Travelling along the 34th parallel is to travel along a semi-circular arc of the small circle of radius $r = R \cos \alpha = 6370 \cos 34° = 5281$ km. Thus the distance between the cities along the 34th parallel is

$$\pi \times 5281 = 16\,591 \text{ km}$$

MISCELLANEOUS EXERCISE 22

Throughout this exercise take the Earth's radius as 6370 km and π as 3.1416.

1. Find the radius of these parallels of latitude:
   (a) $52°$N   (b) $34°$S   (c) $72°$N   (d) $63°$S.

2. Find the distance along the parallels of latitude between the points
   (a) A $(54°$N, $32°$E$)$ and B $(54°$N, $78°$W$)$,
   (b) P $(32°$S, $42°$W$)$ and Q $(32°$S, $24°$W$)$.

3. Find the distance in kilometres along meridians of longitude, between the points
   (a) A $(43°$N, $52°$E$)$ and B $(23°$S, $52°$E$)$,
   (b) P $(54°$N, $110°$E$)$ and Q $(23°$N, $110°$E$)$.

4. (a) How far is it from the North Pole to the South Pole (assuming the Earth is a perfect sphere)?
   (b) What is the circumference of the equator?

5. (a) Find the distance in nautical miles between the South American town of Macapa $(0°, 52°\,W)$ and Libreville $(0°, 9°\,E)$ in Africa. What is this distance in kilometres?

   (b) A ship can sail at a maximum of 30 knots. How long would it take to sail from Macapa to Libreville? What is the ship's speed in km/h?

6. Show that the points $P\,(23°\,N, 131°\,W)$ and $Q\,(23°\,N, 49°\,E)$ lie on the same meridian. How much further is it to travel from P to Q along the parallel of latitude than to travel over the North Pole?

7. Four positions on the Earth's surface are:

   $$P\,(25°\,N, 40°\,E); \quad Q\,(61°\,N, 40°\,E);$$
   $$R\,(44°\,N, 20°\,E); \quad S\,(44°\,N, 160°\,W).$$

   Calculate to the nearest 10 km

   (a) the distance from P to Q, along the circle of longitude $40°\,E$,

   (b) the distance from R to S, along the circle of latitude $44°\,N$.

8. A point X has latitude and longitude $(51°\,N, 160°\,E)$.

   (a) Write down the latitude and longitude of the point Y which is on the same circle of latitude as X and which is at the opposite end of the diameter through X.

   (b) Calculate the distance in kilometres from X to Y measured on the surface of the earth over the North Pole.

   Another point Z has latitude and longitude $(51°\,N, 60°\,W)$. Calculate the shortest distance in kilometres from X to Z round the circle of latitude. (Ox)

9. A and B are two points on the equator with longitudes $40°\,W$ and $25°\,E$ respectively. Taking the earth to be a sphere of radius 6370 km, calculate the shorter of the two distances, in kilometres, along the equator between A and B.

   Two points C and D are both in latitude $35°\,S$ and have the same longitudes as A and B respectively. Calculate the corresponding distance between C and D along their parallel of latitude.

   Calculate also the distance between A and C measured along their common meridian.

   (Take π as 3.142 and give your answers correct to the nearest 10 km.) (O & C)

23 MATRICES

A *row* matrix has only one row, e.g. (2   4   7).

A *column* matrix has only one column, e.g. $\begin{pmatrix} 2 \\ 4 \\ 7 \end{pmatrix}$.

A column matrix is sometimes called a *vector* or a *column vector*.

In general, a matrix has m rows and n columns and is described as an $m \times n$ matrix. For example:

(a) a 2×2 matrix $\begin{pmatrix} 10 & 9 \\ 8 & -7 \end{pmatrix}$ (b) a 3×2 matrix $\begin{pmatrix} 2 & 1 \\ 3 & 4 \\ 0 & 5 \end{pmatrix}$.

Note:

(*i*)   A matrix does not take a single value: it is a table of numbers.

(*ii*) Two matrices are equal only if they have the same number of rows and columns and the numbers in corresponding positions are equal.

Thus $\begin{pmatrix} 3 & 8 \\ 8 & 1 \end{pmatrix}$ equals $\begin{pmatrix} 3 & 8 \\ 8 & 1 \end{pmatrix}$ but *not* $\begin{pmatrix} 3 & 8 \\ 8 & 2 \end{pmatrix}$ nor $\begin{pmatrix} 8 & 3 \\ 1 & 8 \end{pmatrix}$.

And (5   4   3) is quite different from $\begin{pmatrix} 5 \\ 4 \\ 3 \end{pmatrix}$ since the arrangement of columns and rows is different.

ADDITION AND SUBTRACTION

If two matrices are to be added or subtracted, they must have the same number of rows and columns. Then it is simply a matter of adding (or subtracting) the numbers in equivalent positions.

Examples (*i*) $\begin{pmatrix} 10 & 9 \\ 8 & -7 \end{pmatrix} + \begin{pmatrix} 2 & 9 \\ 7 & 8 \end{pmatrix} = \begin{pmatrix} 10+2 & 9+9 \\ 8+7 & -7+8 \end{pmatrix} = \begin{pmatrix} 12 & 18 \\ 15 & 1 \end{pmatrix}$

(*ii*) $\begin{pmatrix} 3 & 7 \\ 6 & 3 \end{pmatrix} - \begin{pmatrix} 2 & 4 \\ 4 & 2 \end{pmatrix} = \begin{pmatrix} 3-2 & 7-4 \\ 6-4 & 3-2 \end{pmatrix} = \begin{pmatrix} 1 & 3 \\ 2 & 1 \end{pmatrix}$

MULTIPLICATION

Multiplication by numbers

Matrices may be multiplied by ordinary numbers by simply multiplying each number inside the matrix. For example

$$2 \times \begin{pmatrix} 3 & 7 \\ 6 & 3 \end{pmatrix} = \begin{pmatrix} 6 & 14 \\ 12 & 6 \end{pmatrix}$$

Multiplication by other matrices

Multiplication of two matrices is quite different from ordinary multiplication. It is only possible to multiply matrices A and B if the number of *columns* in A is the same as the number of *rows* in B.

Example

$$\begin{pmatrix} 2 & 8 \\ 5 & 7 \end{pmatrix} \times \begin{pmatrix} 1 & 3 \\ 4 & 0 \end{pmatrix}$$

$$A \qquad\quad B$$

Take the first row in A, i.e. $\begin{pmatrix} 2 & 8 \end{pmatrix}$ with the first column in B,

i.e. $\begin{pmatrix} 1 \\ 4 \end{pmatrix}$.

$$\begin{pmatrix} 2 & 8 \\ 5 & 7 \end{pmatrix} \begin{pmatrix} 1 & 3 \\ 4 & 0 \end{pmatrix}$$

Multiply the first numbers in each, i.e. 2×1. Then multiply the second numbers in each, i.e. 8×4. Finally, add the two results:

$$2 \times 1 + 8 \times 4 = 2 + 32 = 34$$

Put 34 in the first row, first column of the answer matrix.

$$\begin{pmatrix} 34 & - \\ - & - \end{pmatrix}$$

Repeat the process with the second column in B:

$$\begin{pmatrix} 2 & 8 \\ 5 & 7 \end{pmatrix} \begin{pmatrix} 1 & 3 \\ 4 & 0 \end{pmatrix} = \begin{pmatrix} 34 & 2 \times 3 + 8 \times 0 \\ - & - \end{pmatrix} = \begin{pmatrix} 34 & 6 + 0 \\ - & - \end{pmatrix}$$

$$= \begin{pmatrix} 34 & 6 \\ - & - \end{pmatrix}$$

Then, taking the *second* row of A with each column in B, repeat the process twice more:

$$\begin{pmatrix} 2 & 8 \\ 5 & 7 \end{pmatrix} \begin{pmatrix} 1 & 3 \\ 4 & 0 \end{pmatrix} = \begin{pmatrix} 34 & 6 \\ 5 \times 1 + 7 \times 4 & 5 \times 3 + 7 \times 0 \end{pmatrix}$$

$$= \begin{pmatrix} 34 & 6 \\ 33 & 15 \end{pmatrix}$$

Similarly

$$\begin{pmatrix} 2 & 3 & 4 \\ 1 & 0 & 2 \end{pmatrix} \begin{pmatrix} 1 \\ 2 \\ 3 \end{pmatrix} = \begin{pmatrix} 2 \times 1 + 3 \times 2 + 4 \times 3 \\ 1 \times 1 + 0 \times 2 + 2 \times 3 \end{pmatrix}$$

$$= \begin{pmatrix} 2 + 6 + 12 \\ 1 + 0 + 6 \end{pmatrix} = \begin{pmatrix} 20 \\ 7 \end{pmatrix}$$

Matrix multiplication is not commutative, that is $AB \neq BA$. For example, when A *pre*-multiplies B, it is placed *before* B and gives (as above):

$$\underset{A}{\begin{pmatrix} 2 & 8 \\ 5 & 7 \end{pmatrix}} \underset{B}{\begin{pmatrix} 1 & 3 \\ 4 & 0 \end{pmatrix}} = \underset{AB}{\begin{pmatrix} 34 & 6 \\ 33 & 15 \end{pmatrix}}$$

But if A *post*-multiplies B, it is placed *after* B and the result is different:

$$\underset{B}{\begin{pmatrix} 1 & 3 \\ 4 & 0 \end{pmatrix}} \underset{A}{\begin{pmatrix} 2 & 8 \\ 5 & 7 \end{pmatrix}} = \begin{pmatrix} 1 \times 2 + 3 \times 5 & 1 \times 8 + 3 \times 7 \\ 4 \times 2 + 0 \times 5 & 4 \times 8 + 0 \times 7 \end{pmatrix}$$

$$= \begin{pmatrix} 2 + 15 & 8 + 21 \\ 8 + 0 & 32 + 0 \end{pmatrix} = \underset{BA}{\begin{pmatrix} 17 & 29 \\ 8 & 32 \end{pmatrix}}$$

EXERCISE 23a   1. How many rows and columns are there in these matrices?

(a) $(1 \quad 3 \quad 2)$ (b) $\begin{pmatrix} 2 & 1 \\ 3 & 4 \end{pmatrix}$ (c) $(1 \quad 2)$

(d) $\begin{pmatrix} 1 \\ 2 \end{pmatrix}$ (e) $\begin{pmatrix} 2 & 1 \\ 3 & 4 \\ 5 & 6 \end{pmatrix}$.

2. Find

(a) $\begin{pmatrix} 2 & 3 \\ 1 & 2 \end{pmatrix} + \begin{pmatrix} 4 & 1 \\ 2 & 8 \end{pmatrix}$

(b) $\begin{pmatrix} 2 & 3 \\ 1 & 2 \end{pmatrix} - \begin{pmatrix} 4 & 1 \\ 2 & 8 \end{pmatrix}$

(c) $\begin{pmatrix} 2 & 3 \\ 1 & 2 \end{pmatrix} \times \begin{pmatrix} 4 & 1 \\ 2 & 8 \end{pmatrix}$.

3. Find *if possible*

(a) $\begin{pmatrix} 3 & 2 & 1 \\ 0 & 3 & 2 \end{pmatrix} + \begin{pmatrix} 1 \\ 2 \\ 3 \end{pmatrix}$

(b) $\begin{pmatrix} 3 & 2 & 1 \\ 0 & 3 & 2 \end{pmatrix} \times \begin{pmatrix} 1 \\ 2 \\ 3 \end{pmatrix}$

(c) $(1 \quad 4) \times \begin{pmatrix} 3 & 4 & 5 \\ 2 & 0 & -1 \end{pmatrix}$

(d) $\begin{pmatrix} 1 & 2 \\ 3 & 4 \end{pmatrix} \times \begin{pmatrix} 1 & 2 \\ 3 & 4 \end{pmatrix}$

(e) $\begin{pmatrix} 1 & 2 \\ 3 & 4 \end{pmatrix}^3$

(f) $\begin{pmatrix} 1 & 0 \\ 1 & 2 \end{pmatrix}^2$.

4. $A = \begin{pmatrix} 4 & 1 \\ 2 & 1 \end{pmatrix}$ and $B = \begin{pmatrix} 1 & 0 \\ 2 & 1 \end{pmatrix}$. Find

(a) $A + B$ (b) $A - B$ (c) $2A$ (d) $2A - B$

(e) $4A + 2B$ (f) $10A + 3B$ (g) $\frac{1}{2}A$ (h) $-2A$

(i) $\frac{1}{4}B$ (j) $\frac{3}{4}B$ (k) $\frac{1}{2}A + \frac{1}{4}B$ (l) $\frac{3}{4}B - 2A$

(m) AB (n) BA (o) A^2 (p) B^2

(q) B^4 (r) $(AB)^2$.

5. $A = \begin{pmatrix} 2 & 1 & 2 \\ 3 & 2 & 1 \end{pmatrix}$, $B = \begin{pmatrix} 1 & 0 \\ 2 & 1 \\ 1 & 2 \end{pmatrix}$, $C = \begin{pmatrix} 2 & 0 \\ 1 & 2 \end{pmatrix}$, $D = \begin{pmatrix} 3 \\ 4 \\ 5 \end{pmatrix}$,

$E = (1 \quad -2)$, $F = \begin{pmatrix} 1 \\ -2 \end{pmatrix}$. Find *where possible*

(a) $3B$ (b) $2A$ (c) $A - B$ (d) AB

(e) BA (f) $\frac{1}{2}C$ (g) C^2 (h) C^4

(i) BC (j) $2(AB)$ (k) $(2A)B$ (l) BD

(m) EC (n) EF (o) FE (p) BF

(q) EA (r) CF (s) $(3C)(2F)$ (t) $6CF$

(u) BC (v) CA.

6. $2\begin{pmatrix} a \\ b \end{pmatrix} + \begin{pmatrix} 3 \\ 1 \end{pmatrix} = \begin{pmatrix} 9 \\ 5 \end{pmatrix}$. Find a and b.

7. $2\begin{pmatrix} 3 & x \\ 4 & 2 \end{pmatrix} + 3\begin{pmatrix} 4 & -1 \\ 2 & y \end{pmatrix} = \begin{pmatrix} 18 & 3 \\ 14 & 1 \end{pmatrix}$. Find x and y.

8. $3\begin{pmatrix} 5 & a \\ b & 7 \end{pmatrix} + 2\begin{pmatrix} c & 1 \\ 2 & d \end{pmatrix} = \begin{pmatrix} 19 & 5 \\ 1 & 5 \end{pmatrix}$. Find a, b, c and d.

9. $\begin{pmatrix} a & 3 \\ b & 2 \end{pmatrix}\begin{pmatrix} -1 \\ 1 \end{pmatrix} = \begin{pmatrix} 2 \\ 4 \end{pmatrix}$. Find a and b.

10. $\begin{pmatrix} x & (x+1) \\ y & 2y \end{pmatrix}\begin{pmatrix} 1 \\ 2 \end{pmatrix} = \begin{pmatrix} 8 \\ 20 \end{pmatrix}$. Find x and y.

THE IDENTITY MATRIX, *I*

The *identity* matrix or *unit* matrix multiplies another matrix to leave this other matrix unchanged.

$$I \times A = A \times I = A$$

For a 2×2 matrix $I = \begin{pmatrix} 1 & 0 \\ 0 & 1 \end{pmatrix}$.

DETERMINANTS

If $A = \begin{pmatrix} a & b \\ c & d \end{pmatrix}$ then its determinant, written $\det A$ or $|A|$ or

$\begin{vmatrix} a & b \\ c & d \end{vmatrix}$, is a numerical value given by

$$\begin{vmatrix} a & b \\ c & d \end{vmatrix} = ad - bc$$

Example $\begin{vmatrix} 6 & 4 \\ 3 & 1 \end{vmatrix} = 6 \times 1 - 4 \times 3 = 6 - 12 = -6.$

INVERSES

The inverse of a matrix A is written as A^{-1}. The original matrix and its inverse multiply together to give the identity matrix, I. That is

$$A \times A^{-1} = A^{-1} \times A = I$$

Finding the inverse of a 2 × 2 matrix

(*i*) Swap the element on the top left with that on the bottom right.

(ii) Change the signs of the other two elements.

(iii) Divide by the value of the determinant.

Example Find the inverse of $\begin{pmatrix} 6 & 4 \\ 3 & 1 \end{pmatrix}$.

First, swap the 6 with the 1. Secondly, change the signs of the 4 and the 3. Then find the determinant (which is -6, see previous) and divide by it. Thus

$$\begin{pmatrix} 6 & 4 \\ 3 & 1 \end{pmatrix}^{-1} = \begin{pmatrix} 1 & -4 \\ -3 & 6 \end{pmatrix} \div -6 = \begin{pmatrix} -\frac{1}{6} & \frac{2}{3} \\ \frac{1}{2} & -1 \end{pmatrix}$$

Check $\begin{pmatrix} -\frac{1}{6} & \frac{2}{3} \\ \frac{1}{2} & -1 \end{pmatrix}\begin{pmatrix} 6 & 4 \\ 3 & 1 \end{pmatrix} = \begin{pmatrix} 1 & 0 \\ 0 & 1 \end{pmatrix}$.

SINGULAR MATRICES

Some matrices do not have an inverse; they are called *singular* matrices. The determinant of a singular matrix is zero.

Example $\begin{pmatrix} 8 & 4 \\ 2 & 1 \end{pmatrix}$ is a singular matrix, as its determinant is zero:

$$\begin{vmatrix} 8 & 4 \\ 2 & 1 \end{vmatrix} = 8 \times 1 - 4 \times 2 = 0$$

So the inverse of $\begin{pmatrix} 8 & 4 \\ 2 & 1 \end{pmatrix}$ does not exist.

EXERCISE 23b

1. Multiply $\begin{pmatrix} 1 & 4 \\ 2 & 7 \end{pmatrix}\begin{pmatrix} -7 & 4 \\ 2 & -1 \end{pmatrix}$. What is the inverse of $\begin{pmatrix} 1 & 4 \\ 2 & 7 \end{pmatrix}$?

2. Multiply $\begin{pmatrix} 3 & 1 \\ 2 & 2 \end{pmatrix}\begin{pmatrix} \frac{1}{2} & -\frac{1}{4} \\ -\frac{1}{2} & \frac{3}{4} \end{pmatrix}$. What is the inverse of $\begin{pmatrix} 3 & 1 \\ 2 & 2 \end{pmatrix}$?

3. Find (i) the determinant, (ii) the inverse of the following. In each case, check that the inverse multiplies the original matrix to give $\begin{pmatrix} 1 & 0 \\ 0 & 1 \end{pmatrix}$.

(a) $\begin{pmatrix} 1 & 2 \\ 3 & 7 \end{pmatrix}$ (b) $\begin{pmatrix} 4 & 1 \\ 11 & 3 \end{pmatrix}$ (c) $\begin{pmatrix} 3 & 2 \\ 5 & 3 \end{pmatrix}$ (d) $\begin{pmatrix} 6 & 5 \\ 3 & 3 \end{pmatrix}$

(e) $\begin{pmatrix} 4 & 2 \\ 3 & 2 \end{pmatrix}$ (f) $\begin{pmatrix} 4 & 2 \\ 9 & 5 \end{pmatrix}$ (g) $\begin{pmatrix} 9 & 0 \\ 1 & 1 \end{pmatrix}$ (h) $\begin{pmatrix} 5 & 6 \\ 3 & 4 \end{pmatrix}$

(i) $\begin{pmatrix} 4 & 2 \\ 1 & 2 \end{pmatrix}$ (j) $\begin{pmatrix} 4 & 6 \\ 3 & 4 \end{pmatrix}$ (k) $\begin{pmatrix} 6 & 4 \\ 4 & 3 \end{pmatrix}$ (l) $\begin{pmatrix} 4 & 3 \\ 6 & 4 \end{pmatrix}$.

4. $P = \begin{pmatrix} 1 & 3 \\ 2 & 5 \end{pmatrix}$, $Q = \begin{pmatrix} 2 & 8 \\ -1 & 5 \end{pmatrix}$. Find

    (a) $|P|$ (b) $\det Q$ (c) P^{-1} (d) Q^{-1}.

5. Find

    (a) $\begin{vmatrix} 3 & 4 \\ 2 & 1 \end{vmatrix}$ (b) $\begin{pmatrix} 5 & 6 \\ 2 & 3 \end{pmatrix}^{-1}$ (c) $\begin{vmatrix} 2 & 1 \\ 4 & 5 \end{vmatrix}$

    (d) $\det \begin{pmatrix} 3 & 1 \\ 2 & 2 \end{pmatrix}$ (e) $\begin{pmatrix} 3 & 1 \\ 2 & 2 \end{pmatrix}^{-1}$.

6. If $X = \begin{pmatrix} 3 & 2 \\ 1 & 1 \end{pmatrix}$, $Y = \begin{pmatrix} 2 & 2 \\ 1 & 3 \end{pmatrix}$, find

    (a) X^{-1} (b) Y^{-1} (c) XY (d) $(XY)^{-1}$

    (e) YX (f) $(YX)^{-1}$ (g) $X^{-1}Y^{-1}$ (h) $Y^{-1}X^{-1}$.

    Hence show that $(XY)^{-1} = Y^{-1}X^{-1}$ and $(YX)^{-1} = X^{-1}Y^{-1}$.

7. What is the value of the determinant of a singular matrix, i.e. one that has no inverse? Which of these are singular matrices?

    (a) $\begin{pmatrix} 2 & 3 \\ 4 & 6 \end{pmatrix}$ (b) $\begin{pmatrix} 4 & -5 \\ 2 & -2\frac{1}{2} \end{pmatrix}$ (c) $\begin{pmatrix} 6 & 9 \\ 2 & 3 \end{pmatrix}$

    (d) $\begin{pmatrix} 2 & 3 \\ -8 & -12 \end{pmatrix}$.

8. Solve these equations:

    (a) $\det \begin{pmatrix} x & 4 \\ x & 5 \end{pmatrix} = 2$ (b) $\begin{vmatrix} x & 5 \\ 2 & x \end{vmatrix} = 6$

    (c) $\begin{vmatrix} 2y & 3 \\ 2 & y \end{vmatrix} = 12$ (d) $\begin{vmatrix} (x+1) & 3 \\ x & 2 \end{vmatrix} = -4$

    (e) $\begin{vmatrix} (x-1) & (x-2) \\ 2 & 3 \end{vmatrix} = 5$ (f) $\det \begin{pmatrix} z & 2 \\ (z+1) & 3 \end{pmatrix} = 12$

    (g) $\begin{vmatrix} a & (a+2) \\ (a+1) & (a-1) \end{vmatrix} = 18$.

USING MATRICES TO SOLVE SIMULTANEOUS EQUATIONS

Example Solve $2x - 3y = 2$

              $x + 2y = 8$.

Rewrite the equation in matrix form:

$$\begin{pmatrix} 2 & -3 \\ 1 & 2 \end{pmatrix}\begin{pmatrix} x \\ y \end{pmatrix} = \begin{pmatrix} 2 \\ 8 \end{pmatrix}$$

Note that this multiplies out to give $\begin{pmatrix} 2x - 3y \\ x + 2y \end{pmatrix} = \begin{pmatrix} 2 \\ 8 \end{pmatrix}$.

Find the inverse of $\begin{pmatrix} 2 & -3 \\ 1 & 2 \end{pmatrix}$:

$$\begin{pmatrix} 2 & -3 \\ 1 & 2 \end{pmatrix}^{-1} = \begin{pmatrix} 2 & 3 \\ -1 & 2 \end{pmatrix} \div 7 = \begin{pmatrix} \frac{2}{7} & \frac{3}{7} \\ -\frac{1}{7} & \frac{2}{7} \end{pmatrix}$$

Pre-multiply both sides of the matrix equation by this inverse:

$$\begin{pmatrix} \frac{2}{7} & \frac{3}{7} \\ -\frac{1}{7} & \frac{2}{7} \end{pmatrix}\begin{pmatrix} 2 & -3 \\ 1 & 3 \end{pmatrix}\begin{pmatrix} x \\ y \end{pmatrix} = \begin{pmatrix} \frac{2}{7} & \frac{3}{7} \\ -\frac{1}{7} & \frac{2}{7} \end{pmatrix}\begin{pmatrix} 2 \\ 8 \end{pmatrix}$$

Remembering that any matrix multiplied by its own inverse gives the identity matrix, we get:

$$\begin{pmatrix} 1 & 0 \\ 0 & 1 \end{pmatrix}\begin{pmatrix} x \\ y \end{pmatrix} = \begin{pmatrix} 4 \\ 2 \end{pmatrix}$$

Hence

$$\begin{pmatrix} x \\ y \end{pmatrix} = \begin{pmatrix} 4 \\ 2 \end{pmatrix}$$

which means that $x = 4$ and $y = 2$.

EXERCISE 23c

1. (a) Multiply out the matrices $\begin{pmatrix} 3 & 7 \\ 2 & 5 \end{pmatrix}\begin{pmatrix} x \\ y \end{pmatrix}$. Hence show that the matrix equation

$$\begin{pmatrix} 3 & 7 \\ 2 & 5 \end{pmatrix}\begin{pmatrix} x \\ y \end{pmatrix} = \begin{pmatrix} 11 \\ 7 \end{pmatrix}$$

is equivalent to the two simultaneous equations

$$3x + 7y = 11$$
$$2x + 5y = 7$$

(b) Show that the inverse of $\begin{pmatrix} 3 & 7 \\ 2 & 5 \end{pmatrix}$ is $\begin{pmatrix} 5 & -7 \\ -2 & 3 \end{pmatrix}$.

(c) Now simplify the two sides of the equation.

$$\begin{pmatrix} 5 & -7 \\ -2 & 3 \end{pmatrix}\begin{pmatrix} 3 & 7 \\ 2 & 5 \end{pmatrix}\begin{pmatrix} x \\ y \end{pmatrix} = \begin{pmatrix} 5 & -7 \\ -2 & 3 \end{pmatrix}\begin{pmatrix} 11 \\ 7 \end{pmatrix}$$

and so solve the simultaneous equations.

2. A pair of simultaneous equations
$$3x + 5y = 22$$
$$x + 2y = 8$$
are to be solved by a matrix method. Complete the matrices below, which show the equations in matrix form.

$$\begin{pmatrix} 3 & \cdots \\ \cdots & \cdots \end{pmatrix} \begin{pmatrix} x \\ y \end{pmatrix} = \begin{pmatrix} \cdots \\ \cdots \end{pmatrix}$$

Show that the inverse of $\begin{pmatrix} 3 & 5 \\ 1 & 2 \end{pmatrix}$ is $\begin{pmatrix} 2 & -5 \\ -1 & 3 \end{pmatrix}$.

Pre-multiply each side of this matrix equation by $\begin{pmatrix} 2 & -5 \\ -1 & 3 \end{pmatrix}$ and so solve the equations.

3. The simultaneous equations
$$2x + 3y = 7$$
$$x + y = 3$$
are to be solved using matrices. Write down a 2×2 matrix, M, such that $M \begin{pmatrix} x \\ y \end{pmatrix} = \begin{pmatrix} 7 \\ 3 \end{pmatrix}$.

Find the inverse of M. Hence solve the equations.

4. Find the inverse of $\begin{pmatrix} 5 & 3 \\ 3 & 2 \end{pmatrix}$. Use it to solve the matrix equations

(a) $\begin{pmatrix} 5 & 3 \\ 3 & 2 \end{pmatrix} \begin{pmatrix} x \\ y \end{pmatrix} = \begin{pmatrix} 9 \\ 5 \end{pmatrix}$
(b) $\begin{pmatrix} 5 & 3 \\ 3 & 2 \end{pmatrix} \begin{pmatrix} a & 2 \\ 1 & b \end{pmatrix} = \begin{pmatrix} -2 & 19 \\ -1 & 12 \end{pmatrix}$

Use matrices to solve the following simultaneous equations:

5. $2x + 3y = 4$
   $4x + 7y = 10$

6. $3x + 2y = 16$
   $5x + 4y = 22$

7. $8x + 2y = 15$
   $x + y = 3$

8. $x - 2y = -7$
   $3x + 4y = 29$

9. $2a + 4b = 3$
   $2a + 3b = 5$

10. $4p - 2q = 13$
    $3p + q = 15$

11. $3x - 2y = 5$
    $2y + 3x = 7$

12. $5x - 3y = 4$
    $7y + x = 16$

13. $3y = -7$
    $2x + y = 11$

14. $5y + 2x = 8$
    $2x - 3y = 4$

15. $2y - 3x = 12$
    $3y - 2x = 6$

16. $10x - 2y - 3 = 0$
    $5x - 2y + 6 = 2.$

MATRIX ARITHMETIC

Matrices are just tables of numbers. Cumbersome problems of arithmetic can often be set out in matrix form. This must be done with some care, so that when the various matrices are combined by the rules of matrix addition, subtraction and multiplication they give meaningful results. The amount of work involved is not reduced by setting out the problem in this way — but the systematic presentation is a considerable advantage.

Example Laurie and Diana buy flowers for Mother's Day. Laurie buys 2 bunches of daffodils, costing 25p per bunch, a bunch of violets at 20p and two tulip blooms at 22p each. Diana buys 3 bunches of violets, no daffodils but 4 tulip blooms.

We might begin a problem of this sort by setting out the information given as a table, showing the purchases of each child. Obviously we must be careful to get the right numbers under each heading.

daffodils	violets	tulips	
2	1	2	Laurie
0	3	4	Diana

In effect, we have written the information as a 2×3 matrix. We shall call this matrix F:

$$F = \begin{matrix} & d & v & t & \\ & \begin{pmatrix} 2 & 1 & 2 \\ 0 & 3 & 4 \end{pmatrix} & & & \begin{matrix} L \\ D \end{matrix} \end{matrix}$$

In the same way we could write the cost of the flowers as a 3×1 matrix, C

$$C = \begin{matrix} & \text{Cost (pence)} & \\ \begin{pmatrix} 25 \\ 20 \\ 22 \end{pmatrix} & \begin{matrix} d \\ v \\ t \end{matrix} \end{matrix}$$

Multiplying F and C together will create a further matrix, FC.

$$FC = \begin{pmatrix} 2 & 1 & 2 \\ 0 & 3 & 4 \end{pmatrix} \begin{pmatrix} 25 \\ 20 \\ 22 \end{pmatrix} = \begin{pmatrix} 2 \times 25 + 1 \times 20 + 2 \times 22 \\ 0 \times 25 + 3 \times 20 + 4 \times 22 \end{pmatrix} = \begin{pmatrix} 114 \\ 148 \end{pmatrix}$$

Now consider Laurie's spending. He spends 2×25 p on daffodils, 1×20 p on violets and 2×22 p on tulips, making a total of $2 \times 25 + 1 \times 20 + 2 \times 22 = 114$ p. But this is *exactly* the calculation made when the matrices were multiplied together: the top row of FC therefore shows how much Laurie has spent. Similarly, the bottom row of FC shows how much Diana spent.

We could find the total spent by both children by pre-multiplying FC by $(1 \quad 1)$:

$$(1 \quad 1) \begin{pmatrix} 114 \\ 148 \end{pmatrix} = 1 \times 114 + 1 \times 148 = (262)$$

That is, the children spent a total of 262 p or £2.62.

When laying out a problem in this way remember that the order in which matrices are multiplied and the arrangement of rows and columns are *crucial* if the final values are to have sensible meaning.

EXERCISE 23d
1. Three local football teams, City, Rovers and United, should have each played 10 games in the league but United are still to play their tenth match. City have won 6, drawn 2 and lost 2; Rovers have won 4, drawn 4 and lost 2; United have won only 3 matches, drawn 1 and lost 5. This information can be written as a matrix, R, part of which is shown:

$$\begin{matrix} & \text{Won} & \text{Drawn} & \text{Lost} \\ \text{City} & \\ \text{Rovers} & \\ \text{United} & \end{matrix} \begin{pmatrix} 6 & 2 & 2 \\ \cdot & \cdot & \cdot \\ \cdot & \cdot & \cdot \end{pmatrix} = R$$

(a) Copy and complete the matrix.

(b) The matrix G is $\begin{pmatrix} 1 \\ 1 \\ 1 \end{pmatrix}$. Find RG. What do the numbers in RG mean?

(c) If a win earns 2 points, a draw 1 point and a loss 0 points, write a 3×1 matrix, P, so that RP gives the points won by each team. Find RP.

2. Bill and Ben go shopping. Their purchases are shown in the table.

	New flowerpots	Packets of fertiliser	Packets of weed killer
Bill	2	1	2
Ben	3	2	1

(a) Write this information as a 2×3 matrix, P.

(b) Flowerpots cost 30p each, fertiliser costs 70p a packet and weed killer costs 80p. Write this information as a 3×1 matrix, C, so that PC shows the total spent by Bill and Ben. Work out PC.

(c) Use (1 1) to pre-multiply PC. What does this tell you?

3. The local telephone manager at Sometown Exchange, in Nowhereland, monitors for a day the telephone calls through the exchange. Calls are either local or trunk and may be made at peak, standard or cheap rates according to the time of day. The results are shown in the table:

	Peak	Standard	Cheap
Local	800	900	500
Trunk	1000	1200	200

(a) Show this information as a 2×3 matrix, T.

(b) Trunk calls use five 'call-units' and local calls use only one. Work out the matrix $U = (1 \quad 5)T$ and explain its meaning.

(c) If peak-time call-units cost 50p, standard units cost 30p and cheap-period units cost only 10p, write down a 3×1 matrix, C, so that UC gives the total cost *in pounds* of the calls made through the Sometown Exchange on that day.

(d) Find UC.

4. In one week a newsagent sells 3000 newspapers, 420 comics, 1320 magazines and 150 paperbacks. In the following week he sells 3100 newspapers, 425 comics, 1320 magazines and 140 paperbacks. The price of a newspaper is 24p, of a comic 40p, of a magazine £1 and of a paperback £2.

Set out this information as two matrices and use them to work out the receipts of the newsagent for each week. Find another matrix that will multiply your previous answer to give the receipts over the fortnight.

MISCELLANEOUS EXERCISE 23

1. Solve the following equations:

   (a) $\begin{vmatrix} x & -4 \\ x & 2 \end{vmatrix} = 18$

   (b) $\begin{vmatrix} x & -4 \\ 2 & x \end{vmatrix} = 12$

   (c) $\begin{vmatrix} x & 4 \\ x & x \end{vmatrix} = -4.$

2. Find a and b in the matrix $\begin{pmatrix} a & 1 \\ b & 0 \end{pmatrix}$ if $\begin{pmatrix} a & 1 \\ b & 0 \end{pmatrix}\begin{pmatrix} 2 \\ 5 \end{pmatrix} = \begin{pmatrix} 7 \\ 8 \end{pmatrix}.$

3. $A = \begin{pmatrix} 2 & 1 \\ 3 & 2 \end{pmatrix}$ and $B = \begin{pmatrix} -1 & 2 \\ -2 & 0 \end{pmatrix}.$

   (a) Determine AB, BA, A^2, A^{-1}.

   (b) Calculate m and n, where m and n are real numbers such that $A^2 = mA + nI$ and I is the unit matrix.

   (c) Find the matrix C if $BC = A$.   (SUJB)

4. (a) If $A = \begin{pmatrix} a & b \\ 6 & -3 \end{pmatrix}$ and $A^2 = A$, determine the elements a and b.

   (b) If $B = \begin{pmatrix} 2 & 3 \\ 2 & 4 \end{pmatrix}$ and $BC = \begin{pmatrix} 1 & 0 \\ 3 & 2 \end{pmatrix}$ find B^{-1} and hence, or otherwise, find C (where C is a 2×2 matrix).

   (c) If $D = \begin{pmatrix} 2 \\ 5 \end{pmatrix}$ and $E = (-3 \quad 1)$ determine DE and ED.
   (SUJB)

5. (a) Find the inverse of $\begin{pmatrix} 5 & 6 \\ 4 & 5 \end{pmatrix}.$

   (b) Use it to solve the equation $\begin{pmatrix} 5 & 6 \\ 4 & 5 \end{pmatrix}\begin{pmatrix} x \\ y \end{pmatrix} = \begin{pmatrix} 17 \\ 13 \end{pmatrix}.$

   (c) Use it again to find a, b, c and d if

   $$\begin{pmatrix} 5 & 6 \\ 4 & 5 \end{pmatrix}\begin{pmatrix} a & b \\ c & d \end{pmatrix} = \begin{pmatrix} -5 & 2 \\ -4 & 2 \end{pmatrix}$$

6. Matrices P and Q are defined: $P = \begin{pmatrix} 0 & 1 \\ -1 & 2 \end{pmatrix}$, $Q = \begin{pmatrix} 0 & 2 \\ -1 & 2 \end{pmatrix}.$

   (a) Write down the inverses, P^{-1} and Q^{-1}, of P and Q, and hence evaluate the product $P^{-1}Q^{-1}$.

   (b) Evaluate the products PQ and QP.

   (c) Write down the inverses, $(PQ)^{-1}$ and $(QP)^{-1}$, of PQ and QP.
   (Ox)

7. Find, in its simplest form, the determinant of each of the following matrices.

(a) $\begin{pmatrix} x & 3 \\ 3 & 2 \end{pmatrix}$ (b) $\begin{pmatrix} 3x+2 & 2x-3 \\ x-2 & x-1 \end{pmatrix}$.

In each case, obtain the value(s) of x for which it is impossible to form an inverse matrix. Give your answers correct to two places of decimals where appropriate.   (JMB)

8. During September an apple costs 3 p, an orange 5 p and a pear 4 p. This information can be written as a 3×1 cost matrix

$$M = \begin{pmatrix} 3 \\ 5 \\ 4 \end{pmatrix}$$

(a) In the first week a boy buys 2 apples, 4 oranges and 1 pear, and in the next week 3 apples, 1 orange and 2 pears. Write this information as a matrix **F** in such a way that **FM** can be evaluated.

(b) Evaluate **FM** and say what information is contained in this product.

(c) When the product **FM** is pre-multiplied by a certain matrix **K**, **KFM** gives the total in pence that the boy spent on fruit during the fortnight. Write down the matrix **K**.   (O & C)

9. The matrix below records how many 1 p, 2 p, 5 p, 10 p and 50 p coins each of three children Alan, Bob and Carol have:

$$\begin{array}{c} \\ \text{Alan} \\ \text{Bob} \\ \text{Carol} \end{array} \begin{array}{ccccc} 1\text{p} & 2\text{p} & 5\text{p} & 10\text{p} & 50\text{p} \\ \left(\begin{array}{ccccc} 3 & 0 & 0 & 1 & 1 \\ 1 & 0 & 1 & 2 & 0 \\ 0 & 1 & 1 & 0 & 1 \end{array}\right) \end{array}.$$

(a) Denoting the above matrix by **Q**, calculate $Q \begin{pmatrix} 1 \\ 2 \\ 5 \\ 10 \\ 50 \end{pmatrix}$. What do the numbers in your answer tell you?

(b) The answer to the matrix multiplication **QX** is the number of coins which each child has. Write down the matrix **X**.

(c) Evaluate $(1 \quad 1 \quad 1)Q$. What do the numbers in your answer represent?

(d) Write down, but do not work out, a product of three matrices which would give the total sum of money which these children have altogether.   (O & C)

311

10. Given that $S = \{A, B, C, D\}$ where

$$A = \begin{pmatrix} 1 & 0 \\ 0 & -1 \end{pmatrix}, \quad B = \begin{pmatrix} -1 & 0 \\ 0 & 1 \end{pmatrix}, \quad C = \begin{pmatrix} -1 & 0 \\ 0 & -1 \end{pmatrix},$$

$$D = \begin{pmatrix} 1 & 0 \\ 0 & 1 \end{pmatrix},$$

copy and complete the following table in which the operation * is matrix multiplication.

*	A	B	C	D
A	.	C	.	.
B	.	.	.	.
C	.	.	D	.
D	.	.	.	.

For this operation write down

(a) the identity element in S,

(b) the inverse of B in S,

(c) the element of S which is equal to
    (i) A^4 (ii) B^{10} (ii) the inverse of C^{11}.   (O & C)

24 TRANSFORMATIONS

A point on a graph, $P(x, y)$, can be mapped to another point, the *image*, $P'(x', y')$, by various *transformations* — such as translation, rotation, reflection, etc.

TRANSLATION

Suppose, for example, three points, A, B, C, are mapped to their images, A', B', C', by adding two units to their x-coordinates and subtracting one unit from their y-coordinates:

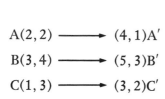

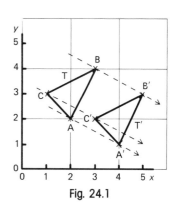

Fig. 24.1

If the three points are plotted on a graph (Fig. 24.1) and joined to make a triangle, T, then the three image points are the corners of another triangle, T', which looks exactly like T except that it has moved a short distance in a rightward and downward direction. This type of transformation is called a *translation*.

In general terms, the point $P(x, y)$ maps on to the point $P'(x + 2, y - 1)$. If the point (x, y) is written as the column matrix, or *vector*, $\begin{pmatrix} x \\ y \end{pmatrix}$ then

$$\begin{pmatrix} x \\ y \end{pmatrix} \longrightarrow \begin{pmatrix} x + 2 \\ y - 1 \end{pmatrix}$$

This is equivalent to addition of a vector $\begin{pmatrix} 2 \\ -1 \end{pmatrix}$:

$$\begin{pmatrix} x \\ y \end{pmatrix} + \begin{pmatrix} 2 \\ -1 \end{pmatrix} = \begin{pmatrix} x + 2 \\ y - 1 \end{pmatrix}$$

313

The reverse of any transformation is called its *inverse*. In this example, the reverse of the translation $\begin{pmatrix} 2 \\ -1 \end{pmatrix}$ is another translation: $\begin{pmatrix} -2 \\ 1 \end{pmatrix}$.

$$\begin{pmatrix} x+2 \\ y-1 \end{pmatrix} + \begin{pmatrix} -2 \\ 1 \end{pmatrix} = \begin{pmatrix} x \\ y \end{pmatrix}$$

In general, any translation may be represented by the addition of the vector $\begin{pmatrix} a \\ b \end{pmatrix}$ and be reversed by the translation $\begin{pmatrix} -a \\ -b \end{pmatrix}$.

EXERCISE 24a

1. Find the images of A(2, 2), B(3, 4) and C(1, 3) under the translation $\begin{pmatrix} 3 \\ 2 \end{pmatrix}$.

   Draw the triangle ABC and its image A′B′C′ on a graph. What transformation is the inverse of this translation?

2. What translation would map the following points to their given images:

   (a) (4, 6) to (7, 3)   (b) (6, 5) to (9, 5)

   (c) (4, 3) to (3, 4)   (d) (5, 6) to (2, 6)

   (e) (7, 9) to (2, 3)   (f) (5, 9) to (19, −8).

3. What single translation is equivalent to a translation $\begin{pmatrix} 2 \\ 3 \end{pmatrix}$

   followed by another translation $\begin{pmatrix} 1 \\ 2 \end{pmatrix}$?

4. A translation transforms the point (3, 7) to (7, 3). Write down the column matrix equivalent of this translation. Where would the point (2, 3) be moved to under this translation?

5. What are the inverses of the following translations (give your answers as column matrices):

   (a) $\begin{pmatrix} 2 \\ 1 \end{pmatrix}$ (b) $\begin{pmatrix} -1 \\ 2 \end{pmatrix}$ (c) $\begin{pmatrix} 3 \\ -1 \end{pmatrix}$ (d) $\begin{pmatrix} 5 \\ 3 \end{pmatrix}$ (e) $\begin{pmatrix} 4 \\ -2 \end{pmatrix}$.

6.

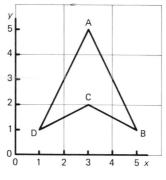

Fig. 24.2

The arrow-head shape ABCD shown in Fig. 24.2 is moved to A'B'C'D' by the translation $\begin{pmatrix} -2 \\ 2 \end{pmatrix}$.

Show ABCD and its image on a diagram of your own.

Show also A"B"C"D", the image of A'B'C'D' under this same translation. What single translation would map A"B"C"D" on to the original ABCD?

7. Plot the points P(1, 7), Q(4, 3), R(4, 5) and S(1, 1) on a grid marked from -3 to $+11$ on both axes. Join them up to make the shape PQRS. Show on the same graph the images of PQRS after translation by

(a) $\begin{pmatrix} 4 \\ 0 \end{pmatrix}$ (b) $\begin{pmatrix} 0 \\ 4 \end{pmatrix}$ (c) $\begin{pmatrix} 4 \\ 4 \end{pmatrix}$ (d) $\begin{pmatrix} -4 \\ -4 \end{pmatrix}$.

REFLECTION IN THE y-AXIS, M$_y$

Consider the point $(2, 1)$. Its distance from the y-axis is given by its x-coordinate. It is two units in front, and so, under reflection in the y-axis, will be reflected to a point two units behind, i.e. to $(-2, 1)$ (Fig. 24.3).

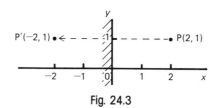

Fig. 24.3

In general, the point (x, y) maps to $(-x, y)$ when reflected in the y-axis.

If three points, A, B, C, are the corners of a triangle, T, then their images, A', B', C', are the three corners of another triangle, T' (see Fig. 24.4).

A(2, 2) ⟶ (−2, 2) A'

B(3, 4) ⟶ (−3, 4) B'

C(1, 3) ⟶ (−1, 3) C'

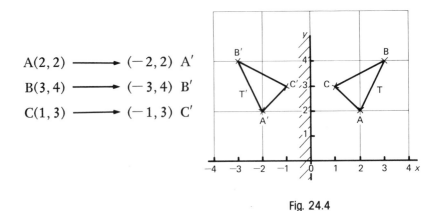

Fig. 24.4

Matrix equivalent

Note that the transformation of triangle T in Fig. 24.4 corresponds to the matrix multiplication

$$\begin{matrix} & A & B & C \\ \end{matrix}$$
$$\begin{pmatrix} -1 & 0 \\ 0 & 1 \end{pmatrix} \begin{pmatrix} 2 & 3 & 1 \\ 2 & 4 & 3 \end{pmatrix} = \begin{pmatrix} -2 & -3 & -1 \\ 2 & 4 & 3 \end{pmatrix}$$

Under reflection in the y-axis, $P(x, y) \longrightarrow P'(-x, y)$. Writing the points as column vectors:

$$\begin{pmatrix} x \\ y \end{pmatrix} \longrightarrow \begin{pmatrix} -x \\ y \end{pmatrix}$$

Now,
$$\begin{pmatrix} -1 & 0 \\ 0 & 1 \end{pmatrix} \begin{pmatrix} x \\ y \end{pmatrix} = \begin{pmatrix} -x \\ y \end{pmatrix}$$

Thus pre-multiplication by the matrix $\begin{pmatrix} -1 & 0 \\ 0 & 1 \end{pmatrix}$ is equivalent to reflection in the y-axis.

Note that

$$\begin{pmatrix} -1 & 0 \\ 0 & 1 \end{pmatrix}^{-1} = \begin{pmatrix} -1 & 0 \\ 0 & 1 \end{pmatrix}$$

i.e. the matrix is its own inverse, just as reflection in the y-axis is its own inverse.

OTHER REFLECTIONS

Reflection in the x-axis, M_x

Reflections in other lines follow the same principles as reflection in the y-axis. If a point is reflected in the x-axis, for example, then it is moved to a point as far below the axis as the original point is above (see Fig. 24.5). In general

$$(x, y) \longrightarrow (x, -y)$$

which is equivalent to the matrix $\begin{pmatrix} 1 & 0 \\ 0 & -1 \end{pmatrix}$ pre-multiplying $\begin{pmatrix} x \\ y \end{pmatrix}$.

$$\text{P}(2, 1) \longrightarrow (2, -1) \ \text{P}'$$

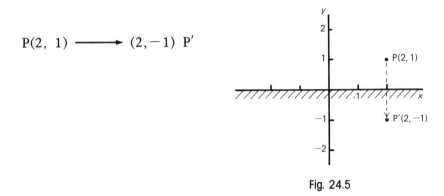

Fig. 24.5

Reflection in the line $y = x$

In general, a reflection in the line $y = x$ maps $(x, y) \longrightarrow (y, x)$ (see Fig. 24.6), which is equivalent to the matrix $\begin{pmatrix} 0 & 1 \\ 1 & 0 \end{pmatrix}$ pre-multiplying $\begin{pmatrix} x \\ y \end{pmatrix}$.

$$\text{P}(3, 1) \longrightarrow (1, 3) \ \text{P}'$$
$$\text{Q}(3, 5) \longrightarrow (5, 3) \ \text{Q}'$$

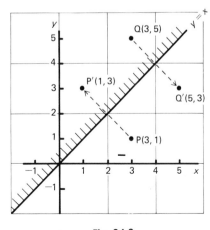

Fig. 24.6

317

Reflection in the line $y = -x$

In general, a reflection in $y = -x$ maps $(x, y) \longrightarrow (-y, -x)$ (Fig. 24.7), which is equivalent to the matrix $\begin{pmatrix} 0 & -1 \\ -1 & 0 \end{pmatrix}$ premultiplying $\begin{pmatrix} x \\ y \end{pmatrix}$.

$$P(3, 2) \longrightarrow (-2, -3)\, P'$$
$$Q(-4, 2) \longrightarrow (-2, 4)\, Q'$$

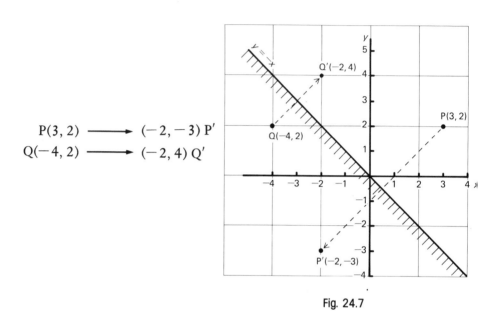

Fig. 24.7

Properties of reflection

(*i*)   The mirror line is the same distance from a point and its image, and is an *axis of symmetry*.

(*ii*) Points actually on the mirror line do not move. (The mirror line is said to be *invariant*.)

(*iii*) The shape of a reflected figure is unaltered.

(*iv*) Reflection is its own inverse.

Finding the line of reflection

To find an unknown line of reflection given a point P and its image P', join P to P' and construct the mirror line as the perpendicular bisector of PP'.

EXERCISE 24b   1. Show the letters J, S and F reflected in:

(a) the x-axis

(b) the y-axis

(c) $y = x$

(d) $y = -x$.

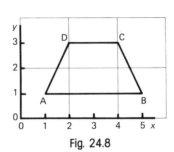

2.

Fig. 24.8

The trapezium ABCD with vertices at A(1,1), B(5,1), C(4,3) and D(2,3), as shown in Fig. 24.8, is reflected in the x-axis. Draw ABCD and its image A′B′C′D′ on a graph of your own. List the coordinates of A′, B′, C′ and D′ and show that they could have been found using the matrix multiplication:

$$\begin{pmatrix} 1 & 0 \\ 0 & -1 \end{pmatrix}\begin{pmatrix} 1 & 5 & 4 & 2 \\ 1 & 1 & 3 & 3 \end{pmatrix} = \begin{pmatrix} \cdots & \cdots & \cdots & \cdots \\ \cdots & \cdots & \cdots & \cdots \end{pmatrix}$$

         A B C D   A′ B′ C′ D′

3. The trapezium in Question 2 undergoes another transformation to a different image A″(−1,−1), B″(−1,−5), C″(−3,−4) and D″(−3,−2). Show A″B″C″D″ on your graph. What is this second transformation? What matrix multiplication is equivalent to this?

4. The trapezium in Question 2 is reflected again so that A → B, B → A, C → D and D → C. What is the equation of the mirror-line?

319

5.

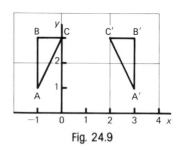

Fig. 24.9

The triangle ABC, shown in Fig. 24.9, is reflected in a line (not the x- or y-axis) to A'B'C', as indicated. What is the equation of the mirror line?

6. For each of the reflections illustrated in Fig. 24.10, copy the diagram and mark in the line of reflection.

(a) (b)

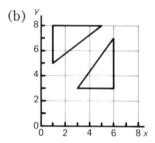

(c)

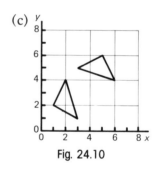

Fig. 24.10

7. The point $(3, 7)$ is mapped on to the point $(7, 3)$ by a reflection. Write down the equation of the mirror line. Where would the point $(2, 3)$ be moved under this reflection?

8. The triangle ABC with vertices at A(1, 1), B(5, 1) and C(5, 5) is first reflected in the y-axis and then translated by the vector $\begin{pmatrix} 0 \\ -2 \end{pmatrix}$. (Such a combined reflection and translation is called a *glide*.) Show ABC and its final image on a graph.

9. Points A(3,5), B(5,1), C(3,2) and D(1,1) are joined to form an arrow-head shape ABCD (see Fig. 24.2, page 315). Draw graphs showing ABCD and its images after reflection in the following lines:

(a) the y-axis   (b) $x = -1$ (c) $y = -x$ (d) $y = x$.

10. Illustrate on a grid, the shape PQRS with vertices P(1,7), Q(4,3), R(4,5) and S(1,1). Show also its images P'Q'R'S' and P"Q"R"S" under transformations represented by

$$A = \begin{pmatrix} 0 & 1 \\ 1 & 0 \end{pmatrix} \text{ and } B = \begin{pmatrix} 0 & -1 \\ -1 & 0 \end{pmatrix}$$ respectively. Describe the

transformations A and B.

ROTATION, R

A point that has been moved through an arc of a circle is said to have been *rotated*. The *centre* of this rotation O is the centre of the circular path (Fig. 24.11). The centre is often (but *not* always) the origin.

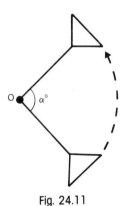

Fig. 24.11

Properties of rotation

(*i*)   Anticlockwise rotation is considered positive; clockwise is negative.

(*ii*)   Only the centre of the rotation, O, does not move (remains *invariant*).

(*iii*)   Every point (except O) moves through the same angle; thus rotation does not alter the shape or size of the rotated object.

Locating the centre of rotation

Example Figure 24.12 shows a triangle ABC and its image A'B'C' after rotation about an unknown centre.

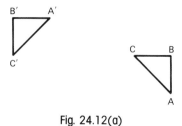

Fig. 24.12(a)

Join two corresponding corners of the triangles, say C and its image C'. Construct the perpendicular bisector of this line.

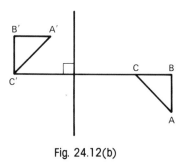

Fig. 24.12(b)

Repeat the process for another pair of corresponding points, say B and B'

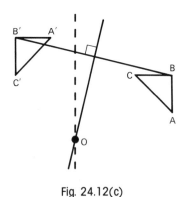

Fig. 24.12(c)

The centre of rotation, O, is the point where the second perpendicular bisector meets the first.

ROTATION ABOUT THE ORIGIN

Only rotations centred on the origin have 2×2 matrix equivalents.

90° Rotation, $R_{90°}$

$$(x, y) \longrightarrow (-y, x)$$

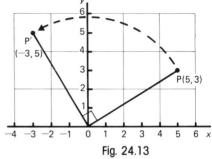

$$P(5, 3) \longrightarrow (-3, 5)\ P'$$

Fig. 24.13

which is equivalent to the matrix $\begin{pmatrix} 0 & -1 \\ 1 & 0 \end{pmatrix}$ pre-multiplying $\begin{pmatrix} x \\ y \end{pmatrix}$.

180° Rotation, $R_{180°}$

$$(x, y) \longrightarrow (-x, -y)$$

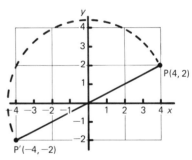

$$P(4, 2) \longrightarrow (-4, -2)\ P'$$

Fig. 24.14

equivalent to the matrix $\begin{pmatrix} -1 & 0 \\ 0 & -1 \end{pmatrix}$ pre-multiplying $\begin{pmatrix} x \\ y \end{pmatrix}$.

Alternatively, rotation about the origin by 180° could be viewed as two successive rotations of 90°; this would be represented by

$$\begin{array}{ccc} R_{90°} & R_{90°} & = & R_{180°} \end{array}$$

$$\begin{pmatrix} 0 & -1 \\ 1 & 0 \end{pmatrix}\begin{pmatrix} 0 & -1 \\ 1 & 0 \end{pmatrix} = \begin{pmatrix} -1 & 0 \\ 0 & -1 \end{pmatrix}$$

which is consistent with the results above.

Rotation by $180°$ can also be shown to be the equivalent of reflection in the y-axis together with reflection in the x-axis, since

$$\begin{matrix} \mathbf{M}_x & \mathbf{M}_y & = & \mathbf{R}_{180°} \\ \begin{pmatrix} 1 & 0 \\ 0 & -1 \end{pmatrix} & \begin{pmatrix} -1 & 0 \\ 0 & 1 \end{pmatrix} & = & \begin{pmatrix} -1 & 0 \\ 0 & -1 \end{pmatrix} \end{matrix}$$

Check this graphically for yourself.

$270°$ Rotation, $\mathbf{R}_{270°}$

This can be viewed either as a turn of $180°$ followed by a turn of $90°$, or as a turn of $-90°$.

$\mathbf{R}_{270°}$ is equivalent to the matrix $\begin{pmatrix} 0 & 1 \\ -1 & 0 \end{pmatrix}$ pre-multiplying $\begin{pmatrix} x \\ y \end{pmatrix}$.

$360°$ Rotation, $\mathbf{R}_{360°}$

A full turn restores the point to its original position, and the co-ordinates of P and P' are the same. So a rotation of $360°$ is represented by the identity matrix.

EXERCISE 24c

1. Copy Fig. 24.15 on to squared paper and show on your graph the images after
   (a) rotation by $90°$ about A
   (b) rotation by $180°$ about B
   (c) rotation by $270°$ about C
   (d) rotation by $-90°$ about D.

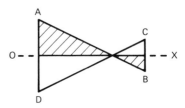

Fig. 24.15

2. The trapezium ABCD with vertices at $A(1,1)$, $B(5,1)$, $C(4,3)$ and $D(2,3)$ is rotated through $90°$ anticlockwise about the origin. Draw ABCD and its image $A'B'C'D'$ on a graph. List the coordinates of A', B', C' and D', and show that they could have been found using the equivalent matrix multiplication:

$$\begin{pmatrix} 0 & -1 \\ 1 & 0 \end{pmatrix} \begin{pmatrix} 1 & 5 & 4 & 2 \\ 1 & 1 & 3 & 3 \end{pmatrix} = \begin{pmatrix} \cdots & \cdots & \cdots & \cdots \\ \cdots & \cdots & \cdots & \cdots \end{pmatrix}$$

$$\begin{matrix} \;\; A \;\; B \;\; C \;\; D \;\;\;\;\;\;\; A' \;\; B' \;\; C' \;\; D' \end{matrix}$$

3. The trapezium in Question 2 is subjected to another transformation, giving images A″(−1,−1), B″(−5,−1), C″(−4,−3) and D″(−2,−3). Draw A″B″C″D″ on your graph. What is this second transformation? What matrix multiplication is equivalent to this?

4. The trapezium in Question 2 is rotated again, but *not* about the origin. If A → (6,6), B → (6,2), C → (9,3) and D → (9,5), show the effect of this transformation on a graph and write down the centre and angle of rotation.

5. Find the centre of the 90° rotations illustrated in Fig. 24.16.

(a)
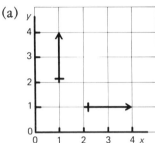

(b)
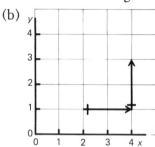

Fig. 24.16

6. The point (3,7) is mapped on to the point (7,3) by a rotation centred on (7,7). What is the angle of turn?

7. The point (3,7) is mapped on to the point (7,3) by a rotation of 180°. Where is the centre of this rotation?

8. The triangle ABC with vertices at A(1,1), B(5,1) and C(5,5) is first reflected in the y-axis and then reflected in the x-axis. Show ABC and the final image on a graph. What single transformation is equivalent to these two reflections?

9. Points A(3,5), B(5,1), C(3,2) and D(1,1) are joined to form an arrow-head shape ABCD (see Fig. 24.2, page 315). Draw graphs showing ABCD and its images after rotations of:
   (a) 90° centred on the origin
   (b) 180° centred on (3,2)
   (c) 90° centred on the origin followed by another of 180° centred on (3,2)
   (d) 180° centred on (3,2) followed by another of 90° centred on the origin.

10. Illustrate, on a grid, the shape PQRS with vertices at P(1,7), Q(4,3), R(4,5) and S(1,1). Show also its images P′Q′R′S′ and P″Q″R″S″ under transformations represented by
$$A = \begin{pmatrix} 0 & -1 \\ 1 & 0 \end{pmatrix} \text{ and } B = \begin{pmatrix} 0 & 1 \\ -1 & 0 \end{pmatrix} \text{ respectively.}$$

Work out the matrices

(a) **AB** (b) **B**$^{-1}$ (c) **A**^{2}.

What is the effect of the transformations they represent?

ENLARGEMENT, E

Enlargement is rather like projecting a slide on to a screen. The *centre of enlargement* is often (but not always) the origin. If the point P moves to P' under an enlargement, then the distance of P' from O is k times the distance of P from O, i.e. OP' = kOP (Fig. 24.17). k is called the *linear scale factor* of the enlargement.

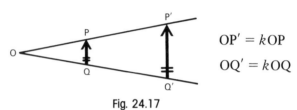

$$OP' = k\,OP$$
$$OQ' = k\,OQ$$

Fig. 24.17

Consider, for example, an enlargement with $(0,0)$ as centre and a scale factor of 3, acting on the three corners of the triangle T in Fig. 24.18. A$(2,2)$, B$(3,4)$ and C$(1,3)$.

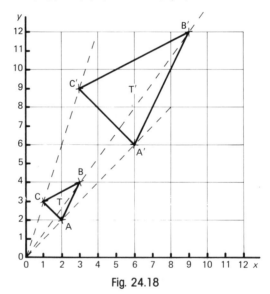

Fig. 24.18

From the definition of enlargement:

$$OA' = 3OA$$
$$OB' = 3OB$$
$$OC' = 3OC$$

Also, from the diagram:

$$A\,(2,2) \longrightarrow (6,6)\ A'$$
$$B\,(3,4) \longrightarrow (9,12)\ B'$$
$$C\,(1,3) \longrightarrow (3,9)\ C'$$

If the centre of the enlargement is the origin, then we may generalise and say

$$(x,y) \longrightarrow (kx,\,ky)$$

which is equivalent to the matrix $\begin{pmatrix} k & 0 \\ 0 & k \end{pmatrix}$ pre-multiplying $\begin{pmatrix} x \\ y \end{pmatrix}$.

If the centre of the enlargement is not *the origin* then no simple matrix equivalent exists, and questions will depend upon a drawing technique.

Example A triangle ABC has corners $(1,4)$, $(2,3)$ and $(3,5)$ respectively. It is enlarged under a transformation E, to $A'B'C'$ at $(1,8)$, $(4,5)$, and $(7,11)$ respectively. Find the centre and the scale factor of this enlargement.

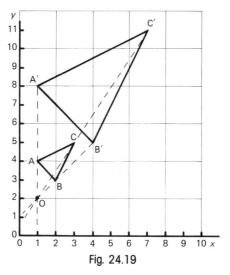

Fig. 24.19

By drawing the lines $A'A$, $B'B$, $C'C$ and extending them until they meet (Fig. 24.19), we can see that the point where they intersect $(1,2)$ is the centre of the enlargement, O. Moreover, by measuring, we find

$$OA' = 3OA$$
$$OB' = 3OB$$
$$OC' = 3OC$$

so the scale factor is 3.

Properties of enlargement

(*i*) The shape of the original figure is unaltered but its size is changed.

(*ii*) Side lengths in the enlarged figure are k times the corresponding length in the original figure.

(*iii*) The area of the enlarged figure is k^2 times the area of the original, i.e.

$$\frac{\text{area of image}}{\text{area of original}} = k^2$$

Notice that this is equal to the determinant of the matrix $\begin{pmatrix} k & 0 \\ 0 & k \end{pmatrix}$. This is an important general result for any transformation matrix, M:

$$\frac{\text{area of image}}{\text{area of original}} = \det M$$

(*iv*) If the scale factor is negative, then the image lies on the opposite side of the enlargement centre and is turned upside down (Fig. 24.20). None the less, $OP' = kOP$ and $OQ' = kOQ$ as before.

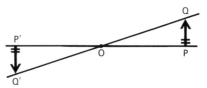

Fig. 24.20

(*v*) If the scale factor is less than 1, then the image will be smaller than the original figure and closer to O (though the transformation is still called an enlargement!).

EXERCISE 24d

1. (a) Figure 24.21 shows the first steps of an enlargement centred on the point $(2, 1)$ but is incomplete. Copy the diagram and use it to show how you would enlarge △ABC by scale factors of

(i) 2   (ii) $\frac{1}{2}$.

(b) How should the diagram be modified for *negative* enlargements?

Show, on a second copy of the figure and using the same centre $(2, 1)$, how you would enlarge △ABC by

(i) -2 (ii) $-\frac{1}{2}$.

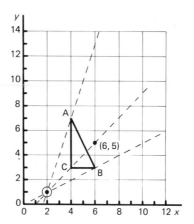

Fig. 24.21

2. Copy the figure in Fig. 24.22 and enlarge it by scale factor of 2 centred on the points

(a) P(2, 9)   (b) Q(5, 6)   (c) R(−1, 4).

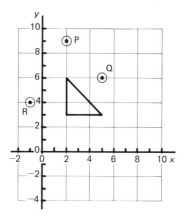

Fig. 24.22

3. A square ABCD has vertices at A(1, 1), B(1, 3), C(3, 3) and D(3, 1). This can be summarised by matrix M where

$$\begin{array}{cccc} A & B & C & D \end{array}$$
$$M = \begin{pmatrix} 1 & 1 & 3 & 3 \\ 1 & 3 & 3 & 1 \end{pmatrix}$$

Use this matrix to find the images of ABCD after the following enlargements:

(a) $\begin{pmatrix} 2 & 0 \\ 0 & 2 \end{pmatrix}$ (b) $\begin{pmatrix} 3 & 0 \\ 0 & 3 \end{pmatrix}$ (c) $\begin{pmatrix} -2 & 0 \\ 0 & -2 \end{pmatrix}$ (d) $\begin{pmatrix} \frac{1}{2} & 0 \\ 0 & \frac{1}{2} \end{pmatrix}$

Show ABCD and its four images on a graph.

4. A trapezium ABCD, with vertices at A(1, 1), B(5, 1), C(4, 3) and D(2, 3), is subjected to an enlargement, centred on the origin, of scale factor 2.

(a) Draw ABCD and its image A′B′C′D′ on a graph. List the coordinates of A′B′C′D′ and show that they could have been found using the equivalent matrix multiplication:

$$\begin{pmatrix} 2 & 0 \\ 0 & 2 \end{pmatrix} \begin{pmatrix} 1 & 5 & 4 & 2 \\ 1 & 1 & 3 & 3 \end{pmatrix} = \begin{pmatrix} \ldots & \ldots & \ldots & \ldots \\ \ldots & \ldots & \ldots & \ldots \end{pmatrix}$$
$$ \text{A} \text{B} \text{C} \text{D} \text{A}′ \text{B}′ \text{C}′ \text{D}′$$

(b) The area of ABCD is 6 square units. What is the area of A′B′C′D′?

5. The same trapezium in Question 4 is subjected to another transformation represented by $\begin{pmatrix} \frac{1}{2} & 0 \\ 0 & \frac{1}{2} \end{pmatrix}$. Show the image A″B″C″D″ on your graph and state its area.

6. The trapezium in Question 4 is enlarged so that $A \rightarrow (-1\frac{1}{2}, -1\frac{1}{2})$, $B \rightarrow (-7\frac{1}{2}, -1\frac{1}{2})$, $C \rightarrow (-6, -4\frac{1}{2})$ and $D \rightarrow (-3, -4\frac{1}{2})$. Show this image on your graph.

(a) What is the scale factor and where is the centre of this enlargement?

(b) What matrix multiplication is equivalent to this transformation?

(c) What is the area of the enlarged trapezium?

(d) What is the ratio $\dfrac{\text{area of enlarged trapezium}}{\text{area of original trapezium}}$.
How is this related to the scale factor?

7. (a) Draw a grid with the x-axis ranging from 0 to +10 and the y-axis ranging from −5 to +10. On it show the triangle ABC with vertices at A(1, 1), B(3, 1) and C(3, 3).

(b) Show the triangle A′B′C′, the image of ABC after enlargement by $\begin{pmatrix} 3 & 0 \\ 0 & 3 \end{pmatrix}$.

(c) Write down the ratio $\dfrac{\text{area A′B′C′}}{\text{area ABC}}$.

(d) A′B′C′ is subjected to the translation T where $T = \begin{pmatrix} -2 \\ -8 \end{pmatrix}$. Show this second image A″B″C″ on your diagram.

(e) A further enlargement, *not* centred on the origin, will transform A″B″C″ back on to the original triangle ABC. Find the scale factor and the centre of this enlargement.

8. (a) Draw a grid ranging from -2 to $+3$ on the x-axis and from 0 to $+6$ on the y-axis. On it show the arrow shape ABCD with vertices at A(2,1), B(3,3), C(2,2) and D(1,3).

   (b) Show the image of ABCD after an enlargement of scale factor 2, centred on (4,0). Label this image A′B′C′D′.

   (c) Write down the ratio $\dfrac{\text{area } A'B'C'D'}{\text{area } ABCD}$.

   (d) Show the image of A′B′C′D′ after translation by $\begin{pmatrix} 2 \\ 0 \end{pmatrix}$. Label this A″B″C″D″.

   (e) Find the centre and scale factor of the enlargement that will map A″B″C″D″ back on to the original shape ABCD.

9. (a) On a grid ranging from -3 to $+5$ on both axes, draw the arrow-head shape ABCD with vertices at A(3,5), B(5,1), C(3,2) and D(1,1).

   (b) Show on the same diagram A′B′C′D′, the image of ABCD after enlargement by scale factor $-\frac{1}{2}$ about the centre (1,3).

   (c) Show also A″B″C″D″, the image of A′B′C′D′ after translation by $\begin{pmatrix} 3 \\ -4\frac{1}{2} \end{pmatrix}$.

   (d) Find the centre and scale factor of the enlargement that will map A″B″C″D″ on to ABCD.

STRETCH

A figure is stretched if it is 'enlarged' in one direction only. Clearly this will distort the shape (see Fig. 24.23).

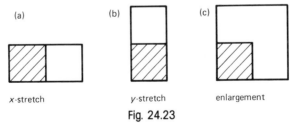

(a)   (b)   (c)

x-stretch   y-stretch   enlargement

Fig. 24.23

x-stretch

Only the x-coordinates are altered: $(x, y) \rightarrow (kx, y)$.

This is equivalent to the matrix $\begin{pmatrix} k & 0 \\ 0 & 1 \end{pmatrix}$ pre-multiplying $\begin{pmatrix} x \\ y \end{pmatrix}$.

y-stretch

Only the y-coordinates are altered: $(x, y) \to (x, ky)$.

This is equivalent to the matrix $\begin{pmatrix} 1 & 0 \\ 0 & k \end{pmatrix}$ pre-multiplying $\begin{pmatrix} x \\ y \end{pmatrix}$.

In both cases, $\dfrac{\text{area of the image}}{\text{area of original}} = k$. Again, notice that the

determinants of $\begin{pmatrix} k & 0 \\ 0 & 1 \end{pmatrix}$ and $\begin{pmatrix} 1 & 0 \\ 0 & k \end{pmatrix}$ are equal to this area ratio.

Example The stretch $\begin{pmatrix} 3 & 0 \\ 0 & 1 \end{pmatrix}$ acts on triangle ABC with vertices at A(2, 2), B(3, 4) and C(1, 3) as follows:

$$
\begin{matrix}
 & A & B & C \\
\end{matrix}
\qquad
\begin{matrix}
A' & B' & C' \\
\end{matrix}
$$

$$
\begin{pmatrix} 3 & 0 \\ 0 & 1 \end{pmatrix}
\begin{pmatrix} 2 & 3 & 1 \\ 2 & 4 & 3 \end{pmatrix}
\qquad
\begin{pmatrix} 6 & 9 & 3 \\ 2 & 4 & 3 \end{pmatrix}
$$

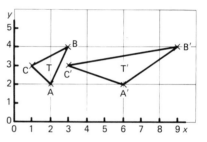

Fig. 24.24

Clearly, this transformation changes the shape of the figure (see Fig. 24.24). Corresponding angles are not equal, and the sides of the triangles are not in proportion.

The area of the image A'B'C' is three times the area of ABC.

SHEAR

A figure is sheared if it is 'pushed over' in one direction (Fig. 24.25). Clearly this distorts the shape. However, the *area* of a figure is unchanged by shear.

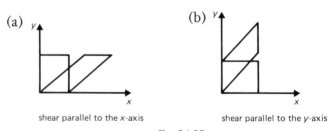

(a) shear parallel to the x-axis

(b) shear parallel to the y-axis

Fig. 24.25

Shear parallel to the *x*-axis

$(x, y) \rightarrow (x + ay, y)$, which is equivalent to the matrix $\begin{pmatrix} 1 & a \\ 0 & 1 \end{pmatrix}$ pre-multiplying $\begin{pmatrix} x \\ y \end{pmatrix}$.

Shear parallel to the *y*-axis

$(x, y) \rightarrow (x, y + bx)$, which is equivalent to the matrix $\begin{pmatrix} 1 & 0 \\ b & 1 \end{pmatrix}$ pre-multiplying $\begin{pmatrix} x \\ y \end{pmatrix}$.

Example The shear $\begin{pmatrix} 1 & 2 \\ 0 & 1 \end{pmatrix}$ acts on the triangle ABC with vertices A(2,2), B(3,4) and C(1,3) as follows:

$$\begin{pmatrix} 1 & 2 \\ 0 & 1 \end{pmatrix} \overset{\text{A B C}}{\begin{pmatrix} 2 & 3 & 1 \\ 2 & 4 & 3 \end{pmatrix}} \longrightarrow \overset{\text{A' B' C'}}{\begin{pmatrix} 6 & 11 & 7 \\ 2 & 4 & 3 \end{pmatrix}}$$

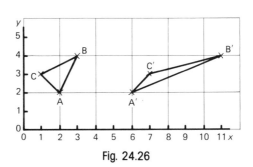

Fig. 24.26

INVERSE TRANSFORMATIONS

The inverse of a stretch or shear is another stretch or shear, represented by the inverse of the matrix equivalent. For example, the inverse of the shear in the example above is $\begin{pmatrix} 1 & 2 \\ 0 & 1 \end{pmatrix}^{-1} = \begin{pmatrix} 1 & -2 \\ 0 & 1 \end{pmatrix}$.

This inverse matrix will map A'B'C' back to the original triangle ABC.

SUCCESSIVE TRANSFORMATIONS

Two or more transformations can be combined into a single matrix equivalent.

Example A figure is sheared by $S = \begin{pmatrix} 1 & 2 \\ 0 & 1 \end{pmatrix}$ and then enlarged by $E = \begin{pmatrix} 2 & 0 \\ 0 & 2 \end{pmatrix}$.

The process 'enlargement following shear' is represented by the matrix product ES (notice the order: this compares with the order rules for composite functions, see page 126). So the equivalent matrix is

$$\underset{E}{\begin{pmatrix} 2 & 0 \\ 0 & 2 \end{pmatrix}} \underset{S}{\begin{pmatrix} 1 & 2 \\ 0 & 1 \end{pmatrix}} = \underset{ES}{\begin{pmatrix} 2 & 4 \\ 0 & 2 \end{pmatrix}}$$

The ratio $\dfrac{\text{area of image}}{\text{area of original}}$ is found from the determinant of ES:

$$\det ES = \begin{vmatrix} 2 & 4 \\ 0 & 2 \end{vmatrix} = 2 \times 2 - 4 \times 0 = 4$$

So the area of the image is four times the area of the original shape.

EXERCISE 24e

1. The unit square OABC with vertices at $O(0,0)$, $A(1,0)$, $B(1,1)$ and $C(0,1)$ is subjected to a series of different stretches. On separate graphs, show OABC and its images under

   (a) $\begin{pmatrix} 1 & 0 \\ 0 & 2 \end{pmatrix}$ (b) $\begin{pmatrix} 1 & 0 \\ 0 & 3 \end{pmatrix}$ (c) $\begin{pmatrix} 2 & 0 \\ 0 & 1 \end{pmatrix}$ (d) $\begin{pmatrix} 3 & 0 \\ 0 & 1 \end{pmatrix}$

   (e) $\begin{pmatrix} \frac{1}{2} & 0 \\ 0 & 1 \end{pmatrix}$.

   In each case write down the ratio $\dfrac{\text{area of image}}{\text{area of OABC}}$.

2. The trapezium ABCD has vertices at $A(1,1)$, $B(5,1)$, $C(4,3)$ and $D(2,3)$. Plot ABCD on a grid, allowing for both x and y to vary from 0 to 10.

   (a) ABCD is mapped on to $A'B'C'D'$ by a stretch represented by $X = \begin{pmatrix} 2 & 0 \\ 0 & 1 \end{pmatrix}$. Find the coordinates of A', B', C' and D' and plot them on your graph.

(b) Find the inverse matrix X^{-1}. Plot on your diagram the image of ABCD after transformation by X^{-1}. Describe the transformation represented by X^{-1}.

(c) What is the image of $A'B'C'D'$ under the transformation X^{-1}?

3. The trapezium in Question 2 is to be stretched again. Draw a second diagram, again allowing for x and y to vary from 0 to 10, and plot ABCD.

(a) Plot $A'B'C'D'$, the image of ABCD under $X = \begin{pmatrix} 2 & 0 \\ 0 & 1 \end{pmatrix}$.

(b) Plot $A''B''C''D''$, the image of ABCD under $Y = \begin{pmatrix} 1 & 0 \\ 0 & 2 \end{pmatrix}$.

Describe the transformation Y.

(c) Plot $A'''B'''C'''D'''$, the image of $A'B'C'D'$ under Y. Describe the effect of the combined transformation YX and write down its matrix equivalent.

4. The unit square OABC with vertices at $0(0,0)$, $A(1,0)$, $B(1,1)$ and $C(0,1)$ is subjected to a series of shears. On separate graphs, show OABC and its images under

(a) $\begin{pmatrix} 1 & 1 \\ 0 & 1 \end{pmatrix}$ (b) $\begin{pmatrix} 1 & 0 \\ 1 & 1 \end{pmatrix}$ (c) $\begin{pmatrix} 1 & 2 \\ 0 & 1 \end{pmatrix}$ (d) $\begin{pmatrix} 1 & 0 \\ 2 & 1 \end{pmatrix}$.

In each case, the image is a parallelogram; use the formula

area of parallelogram = *base length* $\times$ *perpendicular height*

to show that the areas of OABC and its image after shearing are the same.

5. Plot the trapezium ABCD with vertices at $A(1,1)$, $B(5,1)$, $C(4,3)$ and $D(2,3)$ allowing room for x to vary from -4 to $+10$, and y from 0 to 4.

(a) Plot $A'B'C'D'$, the image of the trapezium after shearing by $M = \begin{pmatrix} 1 & -2 \\ 0 & 1 \end{pmatrix}$.

(b) Find the inverse matrix M^{-1}. Show the image of ABCD after transformation by M^{-1}. Describe the transformation represented by M^{-1}.

(c) What is the image of $A'B'C'D'$ under the transformation M^{-1}?

6. Plot the points $A(3,5)$, $B(5,1)$, $C(3,2)$ and $D(1,1)$ and join them to form an arrowhead shape. Allow for values up to 20 on your y-scale.

M is the stretch $\begin{pmatrix} 1 & 0 \\ 0 & 2 \end{pmatrix}$ N is the shear $\begin{pmatrix} 1 & 2 \\ 0 & 1 \end{pmatrix}$

Show the images of ABCD after transformations represented by the matrices

(a) M (b) M^2 (c) M^{-1} (d) N

(e) N^2 (f) N^{-1} (g) MN (h) NM.

Is the effect of 'stretch following shear', MN, the same as 'shear following stretch', NM?

7. The unit square OABC with vertices at O(0, 0), A(1, 0), B(1, 1) and C(0, 1) is subjected to two shears: $X = \begin{pmatrix} 1 & 3 \\ 0 & 1 \end{pmatrix}$ and $Y = \begin{pmatrix} 1 & 0 \\ 3 & 1 \end{pmatrix}$.

(a) Find a single matrix equivalent to
    (i) XY (ii) YX.

(b) On separate diagrams, show the effects of XY and YX on OABC.

(c) The area of the original square is 1 unit. Find the areas of the images after the square has been transformed by
    (i) X alone   (ii) XY together.

MISCELLANEOUS EXERCISE 24

1. On squared paper, allowing space for x to vary from 0 to 8 and y to vary from -3 to 6, draw triangle ABC where A is point (1, 1) B is (1, 2) C is (4, 3).

   Transformation M is determined by matrix $\begin{pmatrix} 1 & 0 \\ 0 & -1 \end{pmatrix}$ and transformation E is determined by matrix $\begin{pmatrix} 2 & 0 \\ 0 & 2 \end{pmatrix}$.

   Triangle ABC is mapped onto $A_1 B_1 C_1$ by M. Draw this triangle on your diagram and describe transformation M.

   Triangle ABC is mapped onto $A_2 B_2 C_2$ by E. Draw this triangle on your diagram and describe transformation E.   (WJEC)

2. On squared paper, draw the usual rectangular axes, placing the origin near the centre of the page. On your diagram, plot and draw the triangle T whose vertices are (1, 1), (1, 3), (2, 3).

   (a) P is the image of T under an anticlockwise rotation of $90°$ about the point (1, 1). Draw and label P on your diagram.

(b) Q is the image of P under an anticlockwise rotation of 90° about the point $(-2, 0)$. Draw and label Q on your diagram.

(c) State the angle and centre of the rotation which maps T to Q.

(d) A is the image of T under reflection in the line $y = x$. Draw and label A on your diagram.

(e) B is the image of A under the translation $\begin{pmatrix} 2 \\ -2 \end{pmatrix}$. Draw and label B on your diagram.

(f) Draw and label clearly on your diagram the line m which is the axis of the reflection which maps T to B.   (O & C)

3. Lines l, m and n, intersecting at O, are fixed in the plane, and $ABCDEF$ is a regular hexagon, centre O, whose original position is as shown (Fig. 24.27). The following transformations of the hexagon are defined:

  R is an anticlockwise rotation of 60° about O;

  L is a reflection in line l;

  M is a reflection in line m;

  N is a reflection in line n.

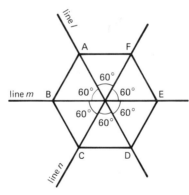

Fig. 24.27

(a) What single rotations are equivalent to R^2, R^6, R^{-1}?

(b) Show that LM and ML are equivalent to rotations, and express each of them in the form R^p where p is a positive whole number.

(c) Express LMN and LML as single reflections.   (Ox)

337

4.

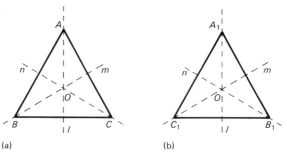

Fig. 24.28

Triangle ABC is equilateral, and is symmetrical about the lines l, m and n, which are fixed and intersect at O (Fig. 24.28(a)). The triangle is reflected in l so that $A \to A_1$, $B \to B_1$ and $C \to C_1$, as shown in the second diagram (Fig. 24.28(b)).

(a) Under reflection in m, $A_1 \to A_2$, $B_1 \to B_2$ and $C_1 \to C_2$.
  (i) Draw a diagram to show l, m, n and the positions of A_2, B_2, C_2.
  (ii) Describe the single transformation which is equivalent to reflection in l followed by reflection in m.

(b) The triangle $A_2B_2C_2$ is now reflected in n so that $A_2 \to A_3$, $B_2 \to B_3$ and $C_2 \to C_3$.
  (i) On another diagram, show l, m, n and the positions of A_3, B_3, C_3.
  (ii) What transformation would map $A_3 \to A$, $B_3 \to B$, $C_3 \to C$? (O & C)

5. The following transformations in a plane are defined:

  P is an enlargement, centre $(0,0)$, scale factor 2;
  Q is a reflection in the line $x = -1$;
  R is an enlargement, centre $(-4,0)$, scale factor $\frac{1}{2}$.

The square S has vertices, $O(0,0)$, $A(1,0)$, $B(1,1)$ and $C(0,1)$. Show on a single sheet of graph paper, labelling each image carefully,

(a) S,   (b) $P(S)$,   (c) $QP(S)$,   (d) $RQP(S)$.

State fully what single transformation produces the same effect as RQP. (Ox)

6. (a) Taking values of x from -8 to 12 and values of y from -6 to 14, draw and label the triangle X, with vertices $(2,4)$, $(4,4)$ and $(4,1)$.

(b) The single transformation U maps the triangle X onto the triangle $U(X)$ which has vertices $(6,12)$, $(12,12)$ and $(12,3)$. Draw and label the triangle $U(X)$ and describe fully the transformation U.

338

(c) The transformation R is a clockwise rotation of $90°$ about the origin. Draw and label the triangle $R(X)$.

(d) The transformation T is the translation $\begin{pmatrix} -8 \\ 4 \end{pmatrix}$. Draw and label the triangle $T(X)$ and the triangle $RT(X)$.

(e) The single transformation V is represented by the matrix $\begin{pmatrix} 0 & -1 \\ -1 & 0 \end{pmatrix}$. Draw and label the triangle $V(X)$ and describe fully the transformation V. (C)

7. Placing the origin near the centre of the graph paper, draw $\triangle ABC$, where A is $(3,3)$, B is $(5,3)$ and C is $(3,4)$. Draw also $\triangle PQR$ where P is $(-1,5)$, Q is $(-1,7)$ and R is $(-2,5)$.

By construction, find the centre M of the rotation which can be used to rotate $\triangle ABC$ on to $\triangle PQR$.

Mark on your diagram an angle of rotation. Measure it and write down its value.

The triangle PQR is to be enlarged by a scale factor of 2 with centre $(1,4)$. Construct the image triangle, and write down the coordinates of its vertices. (LU)

8. The points $A(1,1)$, $B(5,1)$ and $C(3,2)$ are joined to form $\triangle ABC$.

(a) On graph paper, putting the origin in the lower left corner of the paper, draw $\triangle ABC$.

(b) Calculate the coordinates of the vertices of $\triangle A'B'C'$, which is formed by transforming $\triangle ABC$ using the matrix
$$\begin{pmatrix} 1 & -1 \\ 1 & 2 \end{pmatrix}$$

(c) Draw $\triangle A'B'C'$ on the same graph.

(d) Calculate the coordinates of the vertices of $\triangle A''B''C''$, which is formed by transforming $\triangle A'B'C'$ using the matrix
$$\begin{pmatrix} 2 & 1 \\ -1 & 1 \end{pmatrix}$$

(e) Draw $\triangle A''B''C''$ on the same graph and state the scale factor of the enlargement from $\triangle ABC$ to $\triangle A''B''C''$.

(f) State the ratios of the areas of the three triangles. (LU)

25 VECTORS

Time, energy, heat and mass are all *scalar* quantities; that is they are fully described by their size or *magnitude. Vector* quantities need a direction as well as a magnitude if they are to be fully described. For example, a force of 100 newtons acting vertically has an effect (squashing) different from another force of 100 newtons acting horizontally (which would push along). So describing a force simply as '100 newtons' is incomplete. Other vector quantities that similarly require a direction to be specified are position, velocity and acceleration.

REPRESENTING VECTORS

Vectors may be represented by accurately scaled lines, since these show both a magnitude and a direction.

If a line AB represents a vector, then the vector is written $\overrightarrow{AB}$ (notice the top arrow) or **AB** (i.e. in heavy type).

Frequently, vectors are given as 'x units along and y units up', as if they were lines drawn on a grid. Vectors given in this component form are written as *column* matrices, e.g.

$$v_1 = \begin{pmatrix} 2 \\ 3 \end{pmatrix} \quad \text{and} \quad v_2 = \begin{pmatrix} 3 \\ -1 \end{pmatrix}$$

(see Fig. 25.1). [This convention distinguishes vectors from points, which are always written as row matrices, e.g. $(2, 3)$ or $(3, -1)$.]

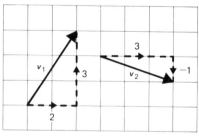

Fig. 25.1

Alternatively, but on exactly the same basis, we may write:

$$v_1 = 2i + 3j \quad \text{and} \quad v_2 = 3i - j$$

where i and j are *unit vectors* (i.e. vectors of magnitude one unit) parallel to the x- and y-axis respectively.

MAGNITUDE AND DIRECTION

If a vector is given as $\begin{pmatrix} x \\ y \end{pmatrix}$ or in the form $xi + yj$ we may find its magnitude and direction from Pythagoras' theorem and elementary trigonometry (Fig. 25.2).

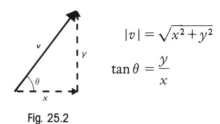

$$|v| = \sqrt{x^2 + y^2}$$

$$\tan \theta = \frac{y}{x}$$

Fig. 25.2

The magnitude of a vector v is sometimes called its *modulus*, and is written $|v|$. Its direction is usually denoted by the Greek letter theta, θ.

Examples (*i*) $v_1 = 2i + 3j$

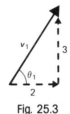

Fig. 25.3

$$|v_1| = \sqrt{2^2 + 3^2} = \sqrt{13} = 3.61$$
$$\tan \theta_1 = \tfrac{3}{2}$$
$$\theta_1 = 56.3°$$

(*ii*) $v_2 = \begin{pmatrix} 3 \\ -1 \end{pmatrix}$

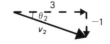

Fig. 25.4

$$|v_2| = \sqrt{3^2 + (-1)^2} = \sqrt{10} = 3.16$$

$$\tan \theta_2 = \frac{-1}{+3} = -\frac{1}{3}$$

$$\theta_2 = -18.4°$$

Note that the negative angle $-18.4°$ is measured clockwise, below the x-axis. As always, positive angles are measured anti-clockwise. This angle of $-18.4°$ could equally well have been given as $360-18.4 = +341.6°$. Be sure to sketch a vector when finding θ, for you may mistake the direction for its precise reverse, especially if you use a calculator.

(iii) $v_3 = \begin{pmatrix} -3 \\ 1 \end{pmatrix}$.

$$|v_3| = \sqrt{(-3)^2 + 1^2} = \sqrt{10} = 3.16$$

$$\tan \theta_3 = \frac{+1}{-3} = -\frac{1}{3}$$

Now, using the inverse tan key, most calculators will give $\theta = -18.4°$, suggesting that v_3 has the same direction as v_2 in Example (ii). This is incorrect, for v_3 acts in precisely the reverse direction. A quick sketch of the vector representing three steps back and one step up makes this obvious

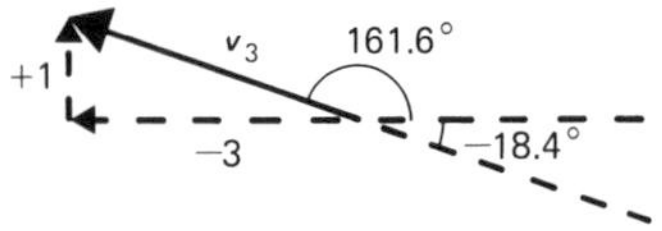

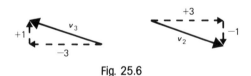

Fig. 25.5

In fact,

$$\theta_3 = 180° + (-18.4°) = 161.6°$$

Notice that the *magnitudes* of v_2 and v_3 are the same. v_3 is the reverse of v_2, i.e. $v_3 = -v_2$ (Fig. 25.6).

Fig. 25.6

In general, any vector $-v$, is of equal magnitude to $+v$ but acts in the opposite direction. If $v = \overrightarrow{AB}$ then $-v = \overrightarrow{BA}$.

Fig. 25.7

EXERCISE 25a   1. Represent these vectors by scaled lines:

   (a) 4 newtons acting vertically upwards

   (b) 5 km due east

   (c) 3 m s^1 at an angle of 70° with the horizontal

   (d) 10 m s^{-2} at an angle of $-90°$

   (e) 7.2 newtons at 135°.

2. The lines shown in Fig. 25.8 represent vectors. Write each one in the equivalent component form $\begin{pmatrix} x \\ y \end{pmatrix}$.

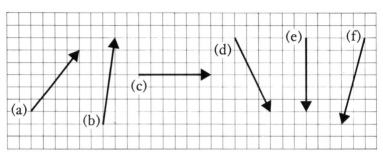

Fig. 25.8

3. Show the following vectors as lines drawn on graph paper:

   (a) $\begin{pmatrix} 2 \\ 2 \end{pmatrix}$ (b) $4i + 3j$ (c) $4i - 3j$ (d) $\begin{pmatrix} 5 \\ -3 \end{pmatrix}$

   (e) $\begin{pmatrix} -7 \\ 1 \end{pmatrix}$ (f) $-3i - 5j$.

4. Find (i) by measurement (ii) by calculation the magnitude and the direction of the vectors in Question 3.

5. Find the magnitude and direction of the following:

   (a) $\begin{pmatrix} 5 \\ 12 \end{pmatrix}$ (b) $\begin{pmatrix} -5 \\ 12 \end{pmatrix}$ (c) $\begin{pmatrix} -5 \\ -12 \end{pmatrix}$ (d) $\begin{pmatrix} 5 \\ -12 \end{pmatrix}$

   (e) $\begin{pmatrix} 12 \\ 5 \end{pmatrix}$ (f) $\begin{pmatrix} -12 \\ -5 \end{pmatrix}$.

6. If $\overrightarrow{PQ} = \begin{pmatrix} 3 \\ 2 \end{pmatrix}$, find

   (a) $\overrightarrow{QP}$ (b) $|\overrightarrow{PQ}|$ (c) $|\overrightarrow{QP}|$.

7. Find the magnitude and direction of

   (a) $\begin{pmatrix} -4 \\ 5 \end{pmatrix}$ (b) $\begin{pmatrix} -8 \\ 10 \end{pmatrix}$ (c) $\begin{pmatrix} -10 \\ 12\frac{1}{2} \end{pmatrix}$.

   What can you say about these vectors?

8. Which of these vectors are parallel?

$$a = \begin{pmatrix} 2 \\ 5 \end{pmatrix} \quad b = \begin{pmatrix} 5 \\ 2 \end{pmatrix} \quad c = \begin{pmatrix} 3 \\ 1 \end{pmatrix} \quad d = \begin{pmatrix} 2 \\ 0 \end{pmatrix}$$

$$e = \begin{pmatrix} 6 \\ 2 \end{pmatrix} \quad f = \begin{pmatrix} -5 \\ 2 \end{pmatrix}.$$

ADDING VECTORS

Adding (or subtracting) vectors written in component form is simply a matter of adding (or subtracting) the horizontal components and then, separately, adding (or subtracting) the vertical components.

Example $\begin{pmatrix} 2 \\ 3 \end{pmatrix} + \begin{pmatrix} 3 \\ -1 \end{pmatrix} = \begin{pmatrix} 2+3 \\ 3+(-1) \end{pmatrix} = \begin{pmatrix} 5 \\ 2 \end{pmatrix}.$

The same vectors written in i, j form are treated in exactly the same way:

$$(2i + 3j) + (3i - j) = (2+3)i + (3-1)j$$
$$= 5i + 2j$$

Vectors can be added graphically by arranging them 'nose to tail'. The vector $v_1 + v_2$ completes the triangle and is called the *resultant* (Fig. 25.9).

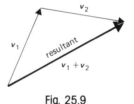

Fig. 25.9

This *triangle law* is equivalent to adding together the separate components of vectors represented algebraically (Fig. 25.10).

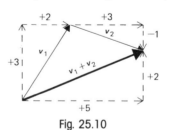

Fig. 25.10

$$\begin{pmatrix} 2 \\ 3 \end{pmatrix} + \begin{pmatrix} 3 \\ -1 \end{pmatrix} = \begin{pmatrix} 5 \\ 2 \end{pmatrix}$$

Any number of vectors can be added in this way. The resultant vector joins the 'tail' of the first vector to the 'nose' of the last (Fig. 25.11):

$$\overrightarrow{OA} + \overrightarrow{AB} + \overrightarrow{BC} + \overrightarrow{CD} = \overrightarrow{OD}$$

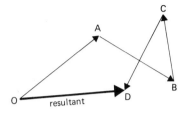

Fig. 25.11

SUBTRACTION

As $-\overrightarrow{CD} = +\overrightarrow{DC}$ we can treat $\overrightarrow{AB} - \overrightarrow{CD}$ as $\overrightarrow{AB} + \overrightarrow{DC}$.

Example $a = \begin{pmatrix} 2 \\ 3 \end{pmatrix}$ and $b = \begin{pmatrix} 3 \\ -1 \end{pmatrix}$ (Fig. 25.12).

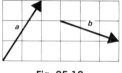

Fig. 25.12

Using column matrices:

$$a - b = \begin{pmatrix} 2 \\ 3 \end{pmatrix} - \begin{pmatrix} 3 \\ -1 \end{pmatrix} = \begin{pmatrix} -1 \\ 4 \end{pmatrix}$$

By first reversing the direction of b (to get $-b$) and repositioning $-b$ so that it follows on 'nose to tail' with a, we can show the same result on a graph (Fig. 25.13).

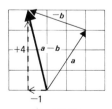

Fig. 25.13

345

MULTIPLICATION

Vectors may be multiplied by ordinary numbers. For example if $v = \begin{pmatrix} 3 \\ 2 \end{pmatrix}$ then $2v = \begin{pmatrix} 6 \\ 4 \end{pmatrix}$, $3v = \begin{pmatrix} 9 \\ 6 \end{pmatrix}$, and so on. The vector $2v$ is twice the magnitude of v but acts in the same direction; likewise $3v$ is three times and $\frac{1}{2}v$ is half the magnitude of v and parallel to it (Fig. 25.14).

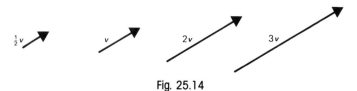

Fig. 25.14

EXERCISE 25b

1. Draw the vector $\begin{pmatrix} 4 \\ 5 \end{pmatrix}$ on graph paper. Draw a second vector $\begin{pmatrix} 3 \\ 2 \end{pmatrix}$ 'nose to tail' with the first. Hence show that

$$\begin{pmatrix} 4 \\ 5 \end{pmatrix} + \begin{pmatrix} 3 \\ 2 \end{pmatrix} = \begin{pmatrix} 7 \\ 7 \end{pmatrix}$$

2. Draw the vector $\begin{pmatrix} 4 \\ 5 \end{pmatrix}$, again, and the vector $-\begin{pmatrix} 3 \\ 2 \end{pmatrix}$ 'nose to tail' with it. Hence show that $\begin{pmatrix} 4 \\ 5 \end{pmatrix} - \begin{pmatrix} 3 \\ 2 \end{pmatrix} = \begin{pmatrix} 1 \\ 3 \end{pmatrix}$.

3. Draw the vectors $\begin{pmatrix} 8 \\ 10 \end{pmatrix}$, $\begin{pmatrix} 12 \\ 15 \end{pmatrix}$, $\begin{pmatrix} 2 \\ 2\frac{1}{2} \end{pmatrix}$ and $\begin{pmatrix} 10 \\ 12\frac{1}{2} \end{pmatrix}$ on graph paper. Hence show that these vectors are all parallel to $\begin{pmatrix} 4 \\ 5 \end{pmatrix}$, but of different magnitudes. Find the magnitude of each vector by measuring it.

In Questions 4 to 15 $a = \begin{pmatrix} 1 \\ 4 \end{pmatrix}$, $b = \begin{pmatrix} 3 \\ -1 \end{pmatrix}$, $c = \begin{pmatrix} -2 \\ -1 \end{pmatrix}$.

Find (without drawing)

4. $a + b$

5. $a - b$

6. $2a$

7. $2a - c$

8. $2a + 3c$

9. $a + 2b + c$

10. $b + \frac{1}{2}(a + c)$

11. $c - a - 2b$

12. $3b - 2a + 7c$

13. $a + 2b + 1\frac{1}{2}c$

14. $5b - 3c$

15. $2a - 3b + c$.

Find k in the following equations:

16. $2\begin{pmatrix}3\\1\end{pmatrix} + k\begin{pmatrix}3\\0\end{pmatrix} = \begin{pmatrix}9\\2\end{pmatrix}$

17. $3\begin{pmatrix}2\\1\end{pmatrix} + 2k\begin{pmatrix}2\\1\end{pmatrix} = k\begin{pmatrix}6\\3\end{pmatrix}$

18. $-k\begin{pmatrix}3\\2\end{pmatrix} + 2k\begin{pmatrix}1\frac{1}{2}\\k\end{pmatrix} = \begin{pmatrix}0\\12\end{pmatrix}$

19. $k\begin{pmatrix}3\\-1\end{pmatrix} + \begin{pmatrix}-2\\-1\end{pmatrix} = \begin{pmatrix}k^2\\1-k^2\end{pmatrix}$.

20. Find m and n in the equation $2\begin{pmatrix}3\\m\end{pmatrix} + n\begin{pmatrix}1\\2\end{pmatrix} = \begin{pmatrix}8\\4\end{pmatrix}$.

21. Find p and q in the equation $p\begin{pmatrix}1\\3\end{pmatrix} + q\begin{pmatrix}2\\-2\end{pmatrix} = \begin{pmatrix}2\\4\end{pmatrix}$.

22. Find r and s in the equation $2\begin{pmatrix}r\\s\end{pmatrix} + \begin{pmatrix}2s\\-r\end{pmatrix} = \begin{pmatrix}4\\4\end{pmatrix}$.

23. Find c in the equation $c\begin{pmatrix}c\\1\end{pmatrix} + 2c\begin{pmatrix}3\\c\end{pmatrix} + 2\begin{pmatrix}4\\-3\end{pmatrix} = \begin{pmatrix}0\\0\end{pmatrix}$.

24. Find x in the equation $x\begin{pmatrix}x-2\\x\end{pmatrix} - 2\begin{pmatrix}x\\x+1\end{pmatrix} = \begin{pmatrix}5\\13\end{pmatrix}$.

VECTOR GEOMETRY

Many geometrical results can be established using vectors. Remember the following points:

(*i*) The reverse of a vector is negative:

(*ii*) Vectors represented by parallel lines are multiples of each other:

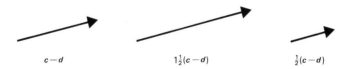

Conversely, lines representing multiples of the same vector are parallel.

(*iii*) Vectors arranged nose to tail have a single equivalent: $\overrightarrow{OA} + \overrightarrow{AB} + \overrightarrow{BC} = \overrightarrow{OC}$. This works in reverse, too. So a single vector can be broken up into a series of consecutive steps: $\overrightarrow{OC} = \overrightarrow{OA} + \overrightarrow{AB} + \overrightarrow{BC}$. You might like to think of this as a journey from O to C made in a very roundabout way: 'O to A, A to B, then B to C'.

Examples (*i*) ABCDEF is a regular hexagon (Fig. 25.15). If $\overrightarrow{AB} = a$ and $\overrightarrow{BC} = b$, write in terms of *a* and *b* the vectors

(a) $\overrightarrow{ED}$ (b) $\overrightarrow{EF}$ (c) $\overrightarrow{AD}$ (d) $\overrightarrow{CD}$ (e) $\overrightarrow{EA}$.

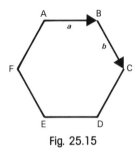

Fig. 25.15

(a) The opposite sides of a regular hexagon are equal in length and parallel, i.e. ED = AB and ED ∥ AB. So the vectors $\overrightarrow{ED}$ and $\overrightarrow{AB}$ are equal:

$$\overrightarrow{ED} = \overrightarrow{AB} = a$$

(b) Similarly, the sides EF and BC are equal and parallel: EF = BC and EF ∥ BC. However, the vector $\overrightarrow{EF}$ acts upwards and to the left; vector $\overrightarrow{BC}$ acts downwards and to the right. So

$$\overrightarrow{EF} = -\overrightarrow{BC} = -b$$

(c) The diagonal, AD, of the regular hexagon is parallel to the side BC but twice its length: AD = 2BC and AD ∥ BC. So

$$\overrightarrow{AD} = 2\overrightarrow{BC} = 2b$$

(d) To find $\overrightarrow{CD}$ we must choose an indirect route from C to D using vectors that we already know. We can go from C to B, B to A and then A to D. That is

$$\overrightarrow{CD} = \overrightarrow{CB} + \overrightarrow{BA} + \overrightarrow{AD}$$
$$= -\overrightarrow{BC} + (-\overrightarrow{AB}) + \overrightarrow{AD}$$
$$= -b - a + 2b$$
$$= b - a$$

(e) To find $\overrightarrow{EA}$ we again choose a route using known vectors:

$$\overrightarrow{EA} = \overrightarrow{ED} + \overrightarrow{DC} + \overrightarrow{CB} + \overrightarrow{BA}$$
$$= \overrightarrow{ED} - \overrightarrow{CD} - \overrightarrow{BC} - \overrightarrow{AB}$$

$$= a - (b - a) - b - a$$
$$= a - 2b$$

(As an alternative method we could have established that $\overrightarrow{FA} = \overrightarrow{DC}$ and then used $\overrightarrow{EA} = \overrightarrow{EF} + \overrightarrow{FA}$: the result would have been the same.)

(*ii*) ABCD is a parallelogram. K, L, M and N are the mid-points of the sides (Fig. 25.16). If $\overrightarrow{AB} = a$ and $\overrightarrow{BC} = b$, find in terms of a and b

(a) $\overrightarrow{KB}$ (b) $\overrightarrow{KL}$ (c) $\overrightarrow{ND}$ (d) $\overrightarrow{NM}$.

Use your results to prove that KLMN is also a parallelogram.

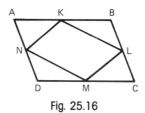

Fig. 25.16

(a) KB = $\frac{1}{2}$AB and has the same direction as AB since it is part of the same line. So
$$\overrightarrow{KB} = \tfrac{1}{2}\overrightarrow{AB} = \tfrac{1}{2}a$$

(b) Similarly, $\overrightarrow{BL} = \frac{1}{2}\overrightarrow{BC} = \frac{1}{2}b$. So
$$\overrightarrow{KL} = \overrightarrow{KB} + \overrightarrow{BL} = \tfrac{1}{2}a + \tfrac{1}{2}b$$

(c) AD ∥ BC and AD = BC (opposite sides of parallelogram ABCD). Thus
$$\overrightarrow{AD} = \overrightarrow{BC} = b$$
Hence $\qquad \overrightarrow{ND} = \tfrac{1}{2}\overrightarrow{AD} = \tfrac{1}{2}b$

(d) Similarly, $\qquad \overrightarrow{DC} = \overrightarrow{AB} = a$

and $\qquad\qquad \overrightarrow{DM} = \tfrac{1}{2}\overrightarrow{DC} = \tfrac{1}{2}a$

Therefore $\qquad \overrightarrow{NM} = \overrightarrow{ND} + \overrightarrow{DM}$
$$= \tfrac{1}{2}b + \tfrac{1}{2}a$$

As both $\overrightarrow{KL}$ and $\overrightarrow{NM}$ are represented by $\frac{1}{2}a + \frac{1}{2}b$ they are the same vector: equal in magnitude and direction. That is KL = MN and KL ∥ NM. So the quadrilateral KLMN is a parallelogram as opposite sides are equal and parallel.

EXERCISE 25c   1. In Fig. 25.17, $\overrightarrow{OA} = a$, $\overrightarrow{OB} = b$ and $\overrightarrow{BC} = 2a$. Find

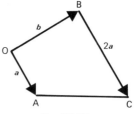

Fig. 25.17

(a) $\overrightarrow{AO}$ (b) $\overrightarrow{AB}$ (c) $\overrightarrow{BA}$ (d) $\overrightarrow{OC}$.

2.

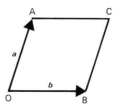

Fig. 25.18

OACB is a parallelogram; $\overrightarrow{OA} = a$ and $\overrightarrow{OB} = b$ (see Fig. 25.18). Find, in terms of a and b, the vectors

(a) $\overrightarrow{AC}$ (b) $\overrightarrow{BC}$ (c) $\overrightarrow{OC}$ (d) $\overrightarrow{AB}$

(e) $\overrightarrow{CA}$ (f) $\overrightarrow{CB}$ (g) $\overrightarrow{CO}$ (h) $\overrightarrow{BA}$.

3.

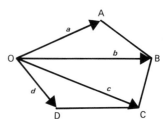

Fig. 25.19

Given the pentagon OABCD, in which $\overrightarrow{OA} = a$, $\overrightarrow{OB} = b$, $\overrightarrow{OC} = c$ and $\overrightarrow{OD} = d$ (Fig. 25.19), find in terms of a, b, c and d the vectors

(a) $\overrightarrow{AB}$ (b) $\overrightarrow{BD}$ (c) $\overrightarrow{BC}$ (d) $\overrightarrow{AD}$ (e) $\overrightarrow{DA}$

(f) $\overrightarrow{DB}$ (g) $\overrightarrow{DC}$ (h) $\overrightarrow{DO}$.

4.

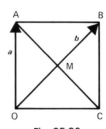

Fig. 25.20

OABC is a square; the diagonals OB and AC intersect at M (Fig. 25.20). If $\overrightarrow{OA} = a$ and $\overrightarrow{OB} = b$ find in terms of a and b the vectors

(a) $\overrightarrow{AB}$ (b) $\overrightarrow{OC}$ (c) $\overrightarrow{BC}$ (d) $\overrightarrow{OM}$ (e) $\overrightarrow{BM}$

(f) $\overrightarrow{MC}$ (g) $\overrightarrow{MA}$.

5.

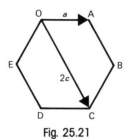

Fig. 25.21

OABCDE is a regular hexagon. Given that $\overrightarrow{OA} = a$ and $\overrightarrow{OC} = 2c$ (Fig. 25.21) find in terms of a and c the vectors

(a) $\overrightarrow{AB}$ (b) $\overrightarrow{OB}$ (c) $\overrightarrow{BC}$ (d) $\overrightarrow{CD}$ (e) $\overrightarrow{DE}$

(f) $\overrightarrow{EO}$ (g) $\overrightarrow{DA}$ (h) $\overrightarrow{DB}$ (i) $\overrightarrow{DO}$ (j) $\overrightarrow{EC}$.

6.

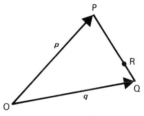

Fig. 25.22

In the triangle OPQ, $\overrightarrow{OP} = p$ and $\overrightarrow{OQ} = q$ (Fig. 25.22). If R is a point on PQ such that $PR = \frac{3}{4}PQ$ find, in terms of p and q, the vectors

(a) $\overrightarrow{PQ}$ (b) $\overrightarrow{PR}$ (c) $\overrightarrow{OR}$.

7.

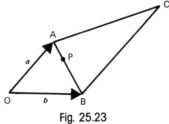

Fig. 25.23

In the trapezium OACB, OA ∥ BC and $\overrightarrow{OA} = \frac{1}{2}\overrightarrow{BC}$ (Fig. 25.23). If $\overrightarrow{OA} = a$ and $\overrightarrow{OB} = b$, find in terms of a and b the vectors

(a) $\overrightarrow{BC}$ (b) $\overrightarrow{OC}$ (c) $\overrightarrow{AB}$ (d) $\overrightarrow{AC}$.

If the point P lies on the diagonal AB such that $AP = \frac{1}{2}PB$ show that $\overrightarrow{AP} = \frac{1}{3}(b - a)$. Find the vector $\overrightarrow{OP}$ and hence show that P also lies on the diagonal OC. Write down the ratio OP : PC.

8.

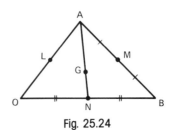

Fig. 25.24

In the triangle OAB, M and N are the mid-points of the sides AB and OB respectively. G is a point on AN such that $AG = \frac{2}{3}AN$ (Fig. 25.24). $\overrightarrow{OA} = 2a$ and $\overrightarrow{OB} = 2b$. Find in terms of a and b the vectors

(a) $\overrightarrow{ON}$ (b) $\overrightarrow{AN}$ (c) $\overrightarrow{AG}$ (d) $\overrightarrow{OG}$ (e) $\overrightarrow{AB}$

(f) $\overrightarrow{AM}$ (g) $\overrightarrow{OM}$.

Use your answers to prove that G also lies on the line OM. Write down the ratio OG : GM.

If L is the mid-point of OA, find the vectors $\overrightarrow{OL}, \overrightarrow{BL}, \overrightarrow{BA}$ and $\overrightarrow{BG}$. Show that G also lies on BL.

9.

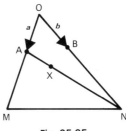

Fig. 25.25

In the triangle OMN shown in Fig. 25.25, $\overrightarrow{OA} = a$, $\overrightarrow{OM} = 3a$, $\overrightarrow{OB} = b$ and $\overrightarrow{ON} = 3b$. Find vectors $\overrightarrow{AB}$ and $\overrightarrow{MN}$ in terms of a and b. Hence prove that AB ∥ MN. X is a point on AN such that $AN = 4AX$. Find the vectors $\overrightarrow{AX}, \overrightarrow{BX}$ and $\overrightarrow{BM}$ in terms of a and b, and hence prove that X also lies on BM.

10. OVWXYZ is a regular hexagon. If $\overrightarrow{OV} = v$ and $\overrightarrow{OZ} = z$, write down in terms of v and z the vectors

(a) $\overrightarrow{ZW}$ (b) $\overrightarrow{OW}$ (c) $\overrightarrow{VZ}$.

If P is a point on VZ such that $VP = \frac{1}{3}VZ$, find the vectors

(d) $\overrightarrow{VP}$ (e) $\overrightarrow{OP}$.

Hence show that P lies on OW and that $OP = \frac{1}{3}OW$.

11. If OABC is a rhombus and $\overrightarrow{OA} = a$ and $\overrightarrow{OB} = b$, show that

(a) $|a| = |b|$ (b) $a - b$ is perpendicular to $a + b$.

12. (a) Three points, P, Q, R, have position vectors given by $\overrightarrow{OP} = a + 3b$, $\overrightarrow{OQ} = 2a + 5b$ and $\overrightarrow{OR} = 7a + 15b$. Find the vectors $\overrightarrow{PQ}$ and $\overrightarrow{PR}$, and hence show that P, Q and R lie on the same line.

(b) X, Y and Z are three other points such that $\overrightarrow{OX} = a - b$, $\overrightarrow{OY} = 4a + 5b$ and $\overrightarrow{OZ} = -3b$. Show that X, Y and Z also lie on one line.

(c) Write down two facts relating the lines PR and XZ.

NAVIGATION

The position of one place relative to another is a vector quantity. For example, if we say 'Brighton is 54 miles due south of London', we are quoting a magnitude (54 miles) and a direction (due south). Similarly, the motion of an aircraft or boat is a vector quantity, for it will have magnitude (say 200 m.p.h.) in a certain direction (perhaps due south again). The motion of a car, bicycle or pedestrian along a road is more difficult to analyse, since the speed and direction are continually changing; but none the less the main aspects of travel – the destination and the motion – are vector quantities and obey vector laws.

Example A boat sails due north at 20 km/h but is driven off-course by a current of 10 km/h from the west. Find the actual course of the boat.

As we know both the piloted course and the speed of the boat as well as the speed and direction of the current, it is fairly easy to construct the appropriate vector triangle. The piloted course is accurately plotted and the current vector arranged 'nose to tail', as shown in Fig. 25.26. The vector representing the *actual* course of the boat completes the triangle. By measuring the angle and the length of this line, it is clear that the boat travels at $22\frac{1}{2}$ km/h on a bearing of 027°. (The triangle could also be solved using trigonometry rather than accurate drawing.)

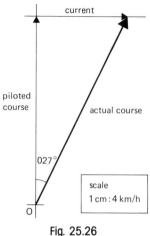

current

piloted course

actual course

027°

scale
1 cm : 4 km/h

O

Fig. 25.26

Plotting a route to take account of countervailing winds or currents is more tricky.

Example The course of the boat in the example above is to be corrected so that it travels directly to its destination which lies 34 km due north. What course should the Master of the boat set in order to offset the current, and how long will the journey take?

In this case we know only the current vector and the *speed* of the boat *in the water*; we do not know its piloted course or the actual headway it makes towards its destination. Since the boat must travel *against* the current (at least in part) it follows that it will be travelling northwards more slowly than could have been the case if the current were not flowing.

Procedure

(*i*) Mark the *direction* of the final course – due north (Fig. 25.27). Do *not* attempt to place the destination on the diagram, since this is to be a triangle of *velocities*.

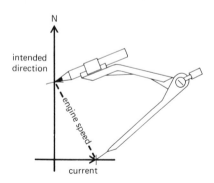

N

intended direction

engine speed

current

Fig. 25.27

(ii)   Draw the current vector, according to the scale you choose.

(iii) Take a pair of compasses and set them accurately to the radius that represents the engine speed of the boat. Put the point to the 'nose' of the current vector (Fig. 25.27), and mark where the arc cuts the line representing the intended direction (due north). Complete the triangle; this line represents the piloted course.

(iv)   Measure the direction in which the boat should head from this third line and measure the speed at which it travels from the actual course.

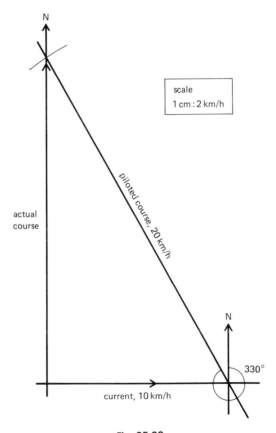

Fig. 25.28

The scale drawing is shown in Fig. 25.28. From the figure, we see that the boat should steer on a bearing of 330° and will actually travel at 17 km/h in a northerly direction.

$$\text{journey time} = \frac{\text{distance travelled}}{\text{speed}} = \frac{34}{17} = 2\,\text{h}$$

1. An aircraft heads due north at 200 km/h but is blown off-course by a 50 km/h wind blowing *from* the east. Find, by drawing, the actual course of the aircraft.

2. A boat heads out of the harbour on a bearing of 070° at 15 knots but encounters a current of 8 knots flowing due south. Find, by drawing, the actual course of the boat.

3. A boy swims in a river at 5 km/h. He tries to swim directly across but the river is flowing at 4 km/h. Find by drawing or by calculation
   (a) the boy's actual course in the river
   (b) the time it would take him to cross the river if it is 500 m wide
   (c) the distance he will have drifted downstream when he reaches the other bank.

4. A girl on a raft can paddle at a maximum of 3 km/h. She tries to paddle directly across a river that is 100 m wide and which is flowing at 2 km/h. Find
   (a) the girl's actual course on the river
   (b) the time it takes her to cross the river
   (c) the distance she drifts downstream before reaching the other bank.

5.

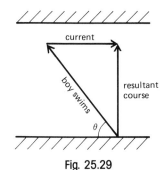

Fig. 25.29

If the boy in Question 3 wants to ensure that his *resultant* travel is directly across the river by swimming at an angle, θ, to the bank (see Fig. 25.29), find, by scale drawing, the course he should set and his actual speed across the river. How long does he take to get across?

6. If the girl in Question 4 wants to ensure that her *resultant* travel is directly across the river, find, by scale drawing, the course she should set and the time it takes her to cross the river.

7. A trainee pilot intends to fly his aircraft due north. He flies for 2 h at 120 km/h. There is a wind of 50 km/h blowing from the east.

    (a) If the pilot sets a course due north, what will be the actual speed and direction of the aircraft?

    (b) What course should the pilot set if his actual course is to be due north? What headway will the aircraft make?

8. A boat heads out of harbour on a bearing of 045° at 16 knots but encounters a current of 8 knots flowing from the south. Find

    (a) the actual course and speed of the boat

    (b) the bearing that the Master of the boat should set in order to travel on a course of 045°.

9. Another boat heads out of the same harbour at 040° at 18 knots and encounters the same current of 8 knots flowing from the south. Find

    (a) the actual course and speed of the boat

    (b) the course that should be set to travel on a bearing of 040°.

10. A helicopter pilot intends to fly to a rendezvous 150 km at a bearing of 135° from his present position. If there is a wind of 30 km/h blowing *from* the north, and his helicopter's maximum airspeed is 80 km/h, what course should he set in order to fly directly to his destination? How long will the journey take him?

What course should the pilot set for the return flight? How long will that flight take?

MISCELLANEOUS EXERCISE 25

1. If $a = \begin{pmatrix} 3 \\ 4 \end{pmatrix}$, $b = \begin{pmatrix} -4 \\ 3 \end{pmatrix}$, $c = \begin{pmatrix} 2 \\ 1 \end{pmatrix}$. Find

    (a) $|a|$ (b) $|b|$ (c) $|a-b|$.

    Does $|a-b| = |a| - |b|$?

    Find also

    (d) $|\tfrac{1}{2}(a-b)|$ (e) $|3c-2a|$ (f) $|a+2b-3c|$.

2. (a) The vectors a and b are given by $a = \begin{pmatrix} 2 \\ -3 \end{pmatrix}$ and $b = \begin{pmatrix} -4 \\ 2 \end{pmatrix}$.

      (i) Find the vector y such that $y = 2a - 3b$.

(ii) Find the vector x such that $2x + 3a = b$.

(iii) Find numbers h and k such that $ha + kb = \begin{pmatrix} 6 \\ -17 \end{pmatrix}$.

(b) The origin is O and $\overrightarrow{OP} = p$, $\overrightarrow{OQ} = q$. The mid-point of PQ is M. Express $\overrightarrow{PQ}$ and $\overrightarrow{OM}$ in terms of p and q.   (C)

3.

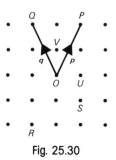

Fig. 25.30

(a) On the grid of squares shown (Fig. 25.30), **OP** = p and **OQ** = q. Express in terms of either p or q or both:
(i) **OR**;   (ii) **RQ**;   (iii) **QP**.
Hence express both **OU** and **OV** in terms of p and q.

(b) Denoting **OU** by u and **OV** by v, express **OS** in terms of u and v, and hence in terms of p and q. Simplify your answer.

(c) Use the diagram to express p and q in terms of u and v. Hence express the vector **OA** in terms of u and v, where **OA** = $\frac{5}{4}$p $-\frac{3}{4}$q. Draw a sketch of the grid, and mark the points O and A on it.   (O & C)

4.

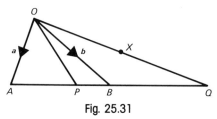

Fig. 25.31

In the diagram (Fig. 25.31), the point P is such that **AP** = 3**PB** and the point Q is such that **AB** = **BQ**.

(a) Given that **OA** = a and **OB** = b, express as simply as possible, in terms of a and b, the vectors
(i) **AB**,   (ii) **AP**,   (iii) **OP**,   (iv) **AQ**.

The point X is on QO and is such that **QX** = $\frac{1}{2}$a $-$ b. Use vectors to prove that **BX** is parallel to **AO**.

(b) Given also that $A\hat{O}Q = 90°$, $O\hat{Q}A = 20°$ and $|a| = 5$, calculate
(i) $A\hat{B}O$,   (ii) $|BX|$.   (C)

358

5.

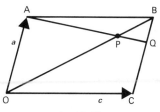

Fig. 25.32

In the parallelogram OABC, $OP = \frac{3}{4}OB$ and APQ is a straight line. $OA = a$ and $OC = c$ (Fig. 25.32).

(a) Find **OB**, **OP** and **AP** in terms of a and c.

(b) By writing **OQ** as $OA + xAP$ express **OQ** in terms of a, c and x.

(c) By writing **OQ** as $OC + yCB$ express **OQ** in terms of a, c and y.

(d) Find the value of x which makes the terms in c equal in the two expressions for **OQ**. Hence find the value of y.

(e) Use the value of y to find $\dfrac{CQ}{QB}$. 　　　　　　　(O & C)

6.

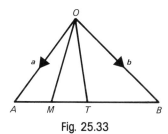

Fig. 25.33

(a) In the diagram (Fig. 25.33), T is the mid-point of AB and M is the mid-point of AT. Given that $OA = a$ and $OB = b$, express as simply as possible in terms of a and b,
(i) **AB**,　(ii) **AM**,　(iii) **OM**.

(b) Two points P and Q have position vectors p and q respectively, relative to the origin O. Given that $p = \begin{pmatrix} 5 \\ 3 \end{pmatrix}$ and $PQ = \begin{pmatrix} -2 \\ 1 \end{pmatrix}$, find

(i) q,　(ii) $|PQ|$,

(iii) the coordinates of the point R, which is such that $OR = QP$.

Given also that $s = \begin{pmatrix} 1 \\ 1 \end{pmatrix}$, $t = \begin{pmatrix} 8 \\ 2 \end{pmatrix}$ and $lp + ms = t$, write down two simultaneous equations in l and m, and solve them. 　　　　　　　(C)

7. *ABCD* is a square. *P, Q, R, S* are points on *AB, BC, CD, DA* one third the length of each side from *A, B, C, D* respectively. If $\overrightarrow{DA}$ = p and $\overrightarrow{AB}$ = q find $\overrightarrow{SA}, \overrightarrow{AP}, \overrightarrow{SP}, \overrightarrow{PQ}, \overrightarrow{QS}, \overrightarrow{PR}$, and hence show that $\overrightarrow{PR} - \overrightarrow{QS} = 2\overrightarrow{PQ}$.

If $p = \begin{pmatrix} 0 \\ 2 \end{pmatrix}$ and $q = \begin{pmatrix} 2 \\ 0 \end{pmatrix}$ calculate the magnitude and direction of the displacement $\overrightarrow{PR} - \overrightarrow{QS}$. (SUJB)

8.

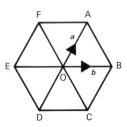

Fig. 25.34

The figure (Fig. 25.34) shows a regular hexagon *ABCDEF* whose diagonals *AD, BE, CF* meet at *O*.

$$\overrightarrow{OA} = a \quad \text{and} \quad \overrightarrow{OB} = b.$$

In terms of a and b write down

(a) $\overrightarrow{EF}$,   (b) $\overrightarrow{OF}$,   (c) $\overrightarrow{CA}$.

Explain why the position vector, relative to *O*, of any point on the line *CA* may be expressed as

$$a + p(2a - b)$$

where *p* is a number. Write down an expression for the position vector of any point on the line *EF*. Hence, or otherwise, find the position vector, in terms of a and b, of the point where the line *CA* meets the line *EF*. (Ox)

9. On squared paper, draw the usual *x*- and *y*-axes; place the origin near the centre of the left-hand edge of the paper and label each axis, using a scale of 2 cm to represent 10 units.

(a) A powerboat leaves a buoy *O* and heads south at 40 km/h. However, a current running *from* due west at 10 km/h carries the boat off course. Represent these velocities as vectors on your diagram and, by drawing and measurement, find the bearing on which the powerboat actually travels.

(b) A helicopter which travels through the air at 50 km/h leaves the buoy *O* at the same time as the powerboat. The pilot wishes to travel due east, but he has to allow for a wind blowing *from* the north at 14 km/h, so he heads the helicopter slightly north of east just sufficiently to ensure that he actually travels due east. Represent these velocities on your diagram and find by measurement the speed at which the helicopter travels eastwards.

(c) Find by measurement and suitable calculation how far apart the powerboat and helicopter are after three hours.

(O & C)

10. (a) A boat has a speed relative to the water of 5 m/s. It is sailing in the sea where there is a steady current of 2 m/s in a direction 090° (i.e. due east). Taking north up the page find, either by means of a scale drawing or by a sketch and calculation, the direction in which the boat should head so that it sails due north. Find also its speed (relative to a fixed buoy) in this direction. Give your answers correct to the nearest degree and to two significant figures.

(b) Under the same conditions as in (a) the boat now has to sail around a square course, starting by sailing 400 m due north, and then turning due east, keeping at the same steady speed of 5 m/s relative to the water. State the direction in which the boat should head, and the speed of of the boat relative to the fixed buoy, for each of the four sides of this square. Find also the total time taken to complete the course. Give your answers correct to the nearest degree or to two significant figures. (O & C)

26 PROBABILITY

If all possible outcomes are equally likely, then the chance or *probability* that an event X occurs is given by

$$p(X) = \frac{\text{number of ways that X can happen}}{\text{number of all possible outcomes}}$$

Thus if an ordinary coin is spun, the probability of it showing 'heads' is

$$p(H) = \frac{\text{number of ways that coin can show heads}}{\text{number of all possible ways the coin can land}}$$

$$= \frac{1}{2}$$

If a card is drawn from a well-shuffled pack, then the probability that it is, say, an ace is

$$p(\text{ace}) = \frac{\text{number of ways of drawing an ace}}{\text{number of all possible ways of drawing a card}}$$

$$= \frac{4}{52} = \frac{1}{13}$$

A *certain* outcome will happen every time and an *impossible* outcome will never happen, so

$$p(\text{certainty}) = 1; \qquad p(\text{impossibility}) = 0$$

It follows that all other probabilities must lie between 0 and 1. It also follows that

$$p(\text{event happens}) + p(\text{event does } not \text{ happen}) = 1$$

(since the number of ways an event can happen and the number of ways it does not happen make up the total of all possible outcomes).

EXERCISE 26a

1. If I throw a die, what is the chance I score
   (a) 6   (b) 2   (c) an even number?

2. In general, I am late for work one morning a week in a five day working week. What is the chance that I shall be late tomorrow?

3. If I take a card from a pack at random, what is the chance that it is

    (a) the ace of spades   (b) any queen

    (c) any diamond?

4. In a raffle, 2455 tickets are sold. I bought 5 of them. What is my chance of winning the first prize?

5. Asked the chance of a coin showing tails after he has spun it, a boy answers '$\frac{1}{2}$'. Is he right? Asked the chance of spinning three heads in a row, the boy answers '3 times $\frac{1}{2}$ or $1\frac{1}{2}$'. Why *must* he be wrong?

6. What is the probability that it will get dark tonight?

7. What is the probability that the Sun will still be shining at midnight tonight?

8. Three chestnuts in a bag of 20 are bad. What is my chance of picking a good one?

9. The chance of my being late for work is 0.1. What is the chance I am on time?

10. A boy has 0.8 chance of success in a maths test. What is the chance he fails.

11. A rifleman has 0.95 chance of hitting a target. What is his chance of missing it?

12. In a raffle, I have 1/100 chance of winning the first prize. What is my chance of not winning?

EITHER ONE OR ANOTHER

Provided the two events A and B cannot both happen together, the probability that *either A or B happens* is given by:

$$p(A \ or \ B) \ = \ p(A) + p(B)$$

Examples (*i*) A card is drawn from a well-shuffled pack. What is the chance of it being either a diamond or a heart?

$$p(\text{a diamond or a heart}) \ = \ p(\text{a diamond}) + p(\text{a heart})$$

$$= \ \frac{13}{52} + \frac{13}{52} = \frac{26}{52} = \frac{1}{2}$$

(This would seem a reasonable answer, as half the pack is is red.)

(*ii*) What is the chance of scoring 1 or 6 on a normal die?

$$p(1 \text{ or } 6) = p(1) + p(6) = \frac{1}{6} + \frac{1}{6} = \frac{2}{6} = \frac{1}{3}$$

EXERCISE 26b

1. If I draw a card from an ordinary pack what is the chance it is
   (a) either a heart or a club   (b) either a 4 or a 5.

2. If I throw an ordinary die, what is the chance I score
   (a) either 1 or 2   (b) 1, 2 or 3.

3. A bag contains 12 marbles, of which 5 are green, 3 are yellow, 2 are blue and 2 are red. What is the chance that the marble I pick is
   (a) either green or red   (b) either green or blue
   (c) either yellow, green or blue.

4. I am generally late for work one day in five, but never twice in one week. What is the chance that I am late on either Thursday or Friday of next week?

5. In my collection of 100 records, 11 are by the Beatles and 5 are by the Rolling Stones. If I select a record at random, what is the chance it will be by one or the other of these two groups?

6. In a bag of 100 Scrabble tiles, there are 12 tiles marked E, 8 marked O and 9 marked I. If I take a tile at random, what is the chance it is
   (a) either an E or an O   (b) an E, an O or an I.

7. When I turn on my television set the probability that it is tuned to any one of four stations is $\frac{1}{4}$. What is the chance that it is tuned to BBC1 or BBC2 when I turn it on tonight?

8. The chance that I pick a banana at random from a basket of mixed fruit is $\frac{1}{3}$; the chance that I pick an apple is $\frac{1}{4}$. What is the chance I pick an apple or a banana?

9. The chance that I pick a red jelly-baby out of a packet is $\frac{1}{7}$; the chance that I pick a black one is $\frac{1}{5}$. What is the chance I pick either a red or a black jelly-baby out of the packet? What is the chance that the one I pick is *neither* red *nor* black?

10. Late for a date, I grab a rose from a large vase to present to my girlfriend by way of apology. In my haste I fail to notice the colour (she likes red or pink). If the chance of picking a red rose is $\frac{1}{8}$ and the chance of a pink one is $\frac{1}{6}$, what is the chance that the rose I have is neither of these colours?

EVENTS FOLLOWING ON

The probability that two events, A and B, *both happen* and happen *in that order*, i.e. A followed by B, is

$$p(A \text{ then } B) = p(A) \times p(B)$$

where $p(B)$ has been worked out assuming that A has already happened.

Similarly, the probability of three events A, B and C happening *in that order* is

$$p(A \text{ then } B \text{ then } C) = p(A) \times p(B) \times p(C)$$

and so on.

Order *must* be taken into account, even when the events happen simultaneously or when order is not specified. Thus

$$p(A \text{ and } B \text{ in any order}) = p(A \text{ then } B) + p(B \text{ then } A)$$

Examples (*i*) Two cards are drawn, one by one and without replacing them, from a pack of 52. What is the chance that they are an ace and a king (a) in that order, (b) in any order.

(a) Since there are 52 cards in the pack, of which 4 are aces

$$p(\text{ace on first draw}) = \frac{4}{52}$$

Once an ace has been removed, there are only 51 cards in the pack, of which 4 are kings. Hence

$$p(\text{king on second draw}) = \frac{4}{51}$$

The sequence ace then king will happen with chance

$$p(\text{ace then king}) = \frac{4}{52} \times \frac{4}{51} = \frac{16}{2652} = \frac{4}{663}$$

(b) We can show also that

$$p(\text{king then ace}) = \frac{4}{52} \times \frac{4}{51} = \frac{4}{663}$$

So

$$p(\text{ace and king in any order}) = p(\text{ace then king})$$
$$+ p(\text{king then ace})$$
$$= \frac{4}{663} + \frac{4}{663} = \frac{8}{663}$$

(*ii*) Two dice are thrown together. What is the chance of the combined score on the dice being (a) 12, (b) 11.

(a) To score a total of 12 requires a 6 on both dice:

$$p(6 \text{ then } 6) = p(6 \text{ on first die}) \times p(6 \text{ on second die})$$
$$= \frac{1}{6} \times \frac{1}{6} = \frac{1}{36}$$

(b) To score 11 requires a 6 on one die and a 5 on the other, *in either order*:

$$p(11) = p(6 \text{ then } 5) + p(5 \text{ then } 6)$$
$$= \frac{1}{36} + \frac{1}{36} = \frac{1}{18}$$

EXERCISE 26c　1. I throw two dice, one red, one blue. What is the chance
(a) the red die shows a 3 and the blue die a 4
(b) the dice show a 3 and a 4.

2. I take two cards out of a pack of 52. What is the chance that I draw
(a) a queen and then a king
(b) a queen and a king in any order.

3. I spin a coin three times. What is the probability that it will show
(a) heads, then tails then heads
(b) two heads and a tail in any order.

4. The chance that an egg produced on a particular farm is brown is $\frac{1}{3}$. If I select six eggs at random what is the chance I select three white eggs and then three brown eggs (in that order).

5. The probability that a darts player hits the target area he is aiming at with any one dart is $\frac{1}{4}$. What is the chance that, with three darts, he

    (a) hits the target, misses it and then hits it again

    (b) hits the target twice and misses once, in any order.

6. If I throw two dice, what is the chance that my total score is

    (a) 11   (b) 10   (c) 9   (d) more than 8.

7. I throw a die three times. What is the chance of scoring

    (a) three 6s   (b) two 6s and then a 5

    (c) two 6s and then something else

    (d) two 6s and a 5 (in any order)

    (e) two 6s and something else (in any order).

8. A bag contains 10 marbles: 5 are red, 3 are orange and 2 are yellow. If I take two marbles out of the bag, one after the other without replacing the first, what is the chance that

    (a) both are red

    (b) the first is red then the second orange

    (c) one is red and the other orange.

9. How are your answers to Question 8 altered if the first marble *is replaced* before the second is taken out?

10. A large bag of 100 draw tickets contains 40 red tickets, 30 blue and 30 white. What is the chance, if three tickets are taken out, of drawing

    (a) a red, a blue and then a white ticket

    (b) a red, a blue and a white ticket in any order.

AT LEAST ONCE

The chance that, in a long chain of events, something happens *at least once* should be worked out using:

p(event happens at least once) $= 1 - p$(event does not happen at all)

Examples (*i*) I throw a die three times. What is the chance that I score at least one 6?

$$p(\text{at least one 6}) = 1 - p(\text{no 6s})$$

Now any one throw, the chance of *not* scoring 6 is $\frac{5}{6}$.

So on three successive throws

$$p(\text{no } 6) = \left(\frac{5}{6}\right) \times \left(\frac{5}{6}\right) \times \left(\frac{5}{6}\right) = \frac{125}{216}$$

Hence $\quad p(\text{at least one } 6) = 1 - \frac{125}{216} = \frac{91}{216}$

(*ii*) I take three markers out of a box containing 10 white and 10 black markers. What is the chance of at least one white marker among the three?

$$p(\text{at least one white}) = 1 - p(\text{all black})$$

Now

$$p(\text{1st black}) = \frac{10}{20}$$

$$p(\text{2nd black}) = \frac{9}{19} \quad \text{(as one black marker has been removed)}$$

$$p(\text{3rd black}) = \frac{8}{18} \quad \text{(as two black markers have been removed)}$$

Hence

$$p(\text{three black markers}) = \left(\frac{10}{20}\right) \times \left(\frac{9}{19}\right) \times \left(\frac{8}{18}\right) = \frac{2}{19}$$

$$p(\text{at least one white}) = 1 - \frac{2}{19} = \frac{17}{19}$$

EXERCISE 26d   1. I throw a die twice. What is the chance that I throw
(a) two 6s   (b) one 6 exactly
(c) no 6 at all   (d) at least one 6?

2. I throw two dice together. What is the chance that I throw
(a) no odd numbers
(b) one odd number and one even number
(c) at least one odd number.

3. If I spin three coins, what is the chance that they land showing
(a) no heads   (b) at least one head.

4. I cut a pack of cards twice. Prove that the chance of showing an ace at least once is $\frac{25}{169}$. What is the chance of finding at least one club?

5. The chance that I am late for work is 0.2. What is the chance of my not being late for a whole week (5 days). What is the chance that I am late at least once? $[(0.8)^5 = 0.328.]$

6. A rather naughty boy is in trouble in one-third of his lessons. If he has six lessons in one day, what is the chance that he stays out of trouble all day? What is the chance of him being in trouble at least once in the day?

7. A girl falls off her horse, on average, once every ten rides. What is the chance she will fall off *at least once* in her next ten rides? $[(0.9)^{10} = 0.35.]$

8. A bag contains ten beads: three are yellow, two are red and the rest are green. If I take a bead out at random, what is the chance that it is green? If I take out two beads together, what is the chance that exactly one of them is green. What is the chance of at least one being green?

9. In a box of 32 chess pieces, half are white and the rest are black. If I take out three pieces at random, what is the chance that at least one is white?

   There are 8 white pawns and 8 black pawns in the box. If I take out three pieces, what is the chance that I have

   (a) at least one pawn   (b) at least one white pawn.

10. I withdraw three cards from a normal pack, one after the other without replacing them. Find the probability that the cards include

    (a) at least one picture card   (b) at least one red card

    (c) at least one diamond.

PROBABILITY TREES

Complicated sequences can be 'mapped out' by means of a *probability tree*. Each *branch* or *path* of the tree illustrates one possible chain of events. The probabilities of each stage are written on the tree; these probabilities are multiplied together to find the chance of the whole sequence.

Example A rat in a maze must choose between left and right at the next junction. If he turns left, he is free; if he turns right he will meet another junction at which he must choose between left, right and straight on. Both left and right turns lead to dead ends; only if he goes straight on will he be free. Assuming the rat chooses between paths at random, what is the chance the rat will escape the maze without turning back?

The possibilities can be plotted on a probability tree (Fig. 26.1).

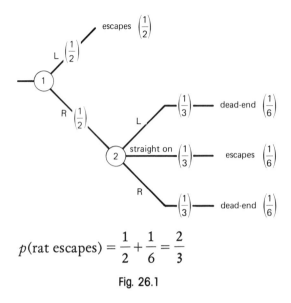

$$p(\text{rat escapes}) = \frac{1}{2} + \frac{1}{6} = \frac{2}{3}$$

Fig. 26.1

At junction 1, the rat has two choices – to turn left or to turn right. He makes his choice at random, i.e.

$$p(\text{turns left}) = p(\text{turns right}) = \tfrac{1}{2}$$

At junction 2, he has three choices. He is as likely to go straight on as he is to turn left or right, i.e.

$$p(\text{straight on}) = p(\text{turns left}) = p(\text{turns right}) = \tfrac{1}{3}$$

He escapes the maze either by turning left at junction 1 or by carrying on to junction 2 and then going straight on. The probability tree makes this clear. The chance that he escapes is therefore

$$p(\text{left at junction 1}) + p(\text{right at junction 1, then straight on})$$

$$= \frac{1}{2} + \left(\frac{1}{2} \times \frac{1}{3}\right) = \frac{1}{2} + \frac{1}{6} = \frac{2}{3}$$

EXERCISE 26e 1. A bag contains five marbles: two are red, two blue, and one green. I take out two marbles. Complete the probability tree (Fig. 26.2), and use it to find the chance that

(a) one marble is blue and one is red

(b) the two marbles are of different colour.

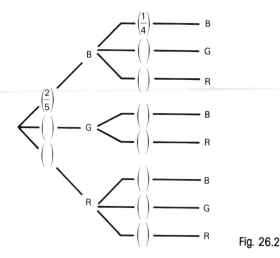

Fig. 26.2

2. In a fairground draw, I win a prize for 'finding the lady', i.e. drawing the one queen in a pack of 12 cards. If I draw one of the four kings, the card is replaced and I can have another go. Otherwise I lose. If I draw a second king, then I can have a third go, after which the game finishes.

Copy and complete the probability tree in Fig. 26.3 and find my chance of winning.

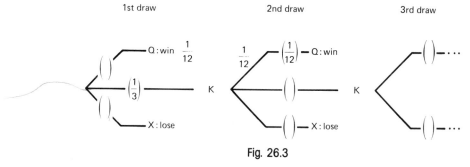

Fig. 26.3

3. A ferret in a rabbit warren turns left or right at junction A at random. Having turned left or right once, he is twice as likely

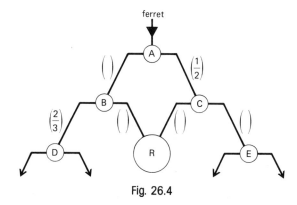

Fig. 26.4

371

to repeat himself at the next junction (B or C) as he is to turn the other way. Copy the probability tree in Fig. 26.4 and mark on the appropriate probabilities. Find the chance that the ferret finds the rabbits hiding at R.

4. A bag contains ten marbles: seven red, two orange and one yellow. I play a game in which I try to find the yellow marble, taking marbles unseen out of the bag. If I draw a red one at any stage, I lose. If I draw an orange one, I keep it out and have another go. How many marbles, at most, could I take out of the bag? Draw a probability tree to show all the possibilities. What is my chance of winning?

5. A young girl picks chocolates out of a box at random. Though she loves chocolate and would not normally stop until she had eaten all six of the sweets that remain, unfortunately she cannot bear the taste of coffee. If she picks one of the two coffee-creams at any point, she is certain to put it back and stop immediately.

   Show, with a probability tree, all the possibilities. What is the chance she will stop, leaving

   (a) five sweets

   (b) at least four sweets in the box?

MISCELLANEOUS EXERCISE 26

You are advised to work in fractions throughout this exercise.

1. Calculate the probabilities that, when two ordinary dice are thrown,

   (a) both dice show 5,

   (b) at least one of the two dice shows 5,

   (c) the total score of the two dice is 5.

   Given that one die is thrown four times, calculate the probability that

   (d) the die will show 5 on each of the four throws,

   (e) the die will show 5 on at least three of the four throws.

   (JMB)

2. I throw two ordinary fair dice, one of which is red and the other is white. Calculate, giving your answer in each case as a fraction in its lowest terms, the probability that

   (a) the total shown on the dice is eight;

(b) the score on the red die is exactly three more than the score on the white die;

(c) the score on one die is exactly three more than the score on the other die. (Ox)

3. The probabilities that each of three marksmen, Tom, Dick and Harry, will hit a target at a single attempt are $\frac{1}{3}, \frac{1}{4}, \frac{1}{5}$ respectively.

(a) If they all fire simultaneously at the target, find the probabilities that:
   (i)   Harry misses it;
   (ii) all three men hit it;
   (iii) all three men miss it;
   (iv) at least one man hits it.

(b) They now each prepare to fire once at the target in the order Tom, Dick and Harry. In this case once the target has been hit no more shots are fired. Copy and complete the tree diagram (Fig. 26.5) by inserting all the outcomes and one-stage probabilities in the correct places on it.

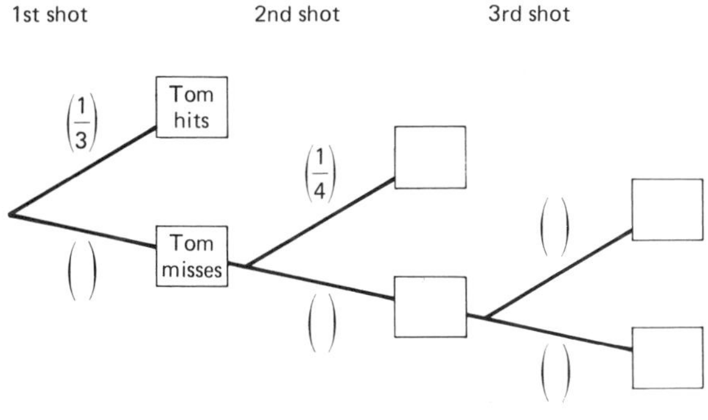

Fig. 26.5

Find the probabilities that
   (i)   the target is hit by Dick;
   (ii) the target is hit by either Tom or Dick;
   (iii) the target is hit by Harry;
   (iv) the target is hit. (O & C)

4. A bag contains 6 green and 9 red counters. The counters are drawn at random, one at a time, and are not replaced. Calculate the probability that:

(a) the first counter is green;

(b) the first two counters are green;

(c) at least one of the first two counters is red;

(d) if three counters are drawn, then just one of them is green.

Another bag also contains 6 green and 9 red counters. Three counters are drawn in succession, each one being replaced before the next one is drawn. What is the probability that at least one of the three counters is red? (Ox)

5. The probability that there are one or more misprints on any one page of the *Wessex Mercury* is $\frac{1}{3}$. The sports section of this newspaper always contains two pages.

State the probability that a page contains no misprints and calculate the probability that in the sports section

(a) there are no misprints,

(b) at least one of the pages contains one or more misprints.

In the *New Herald*, some of the pages are completely filled with full-page advertisements. On such pages, the probability that there are one or more misprints is $\frac{1}{10}$; on all other pages it is $\frac{1}{3}$.

Given that on any particular day the probability that page three contains a full-page advertisement is $\frac{1}{4}$, calculate the probability that

(c) page three contains a full-page advertisement and one or more misprints,

(d) page three contains one or more misprints.

Last year the *New Herald* appeared 280 times. Estimate the number of times that page three had no misprints. (AEB '82)

6. A student is supposed to attend a course of six lectures. He is sure to attend the first lecture, and the probability that he will attend the second one is $\frac{3}{4}$. If he ever misses a lecture, he is sure to attend the next one, and the probability that he will attend the one after that is $\frac{3}{4}$. If he has attended two or more lectures in succession, the probability that he will attend the next one is $\frac{1}{2}$. Find the probability that he will attend

(a) the first three lectures

(b) the first and third, but not the second

(c) the third lecture, whether or not he attends the second

(d) all six lectures.

Find

(e) the smallest number of lectures he can attend, and the probability that he will attend this smallest number. (LU)

7. A bag contains 100 discs which are identical except for colour. Of these discs, x are red, y are yellow and the rest are green.

   (a) A disc is selected at random from the bag. Given that the probability that it is red is $\frac{9}{50}$, find x.

   (b) A disc is selected at random from the 100 discs, is not replaced, and a second disc is then selected at random. Given that the probability that the first disc is red and the second is yellow is $\frac{2}{25}$, find y.

   (c) Two discs are selected at random from the 100 discs. Find, as a fraction, the probability that one is red and the other is yellow. (C)

8. (a) There are 30 blue balls and x red balls in a bag. A ball is drawn at random from the bag.

   (i) Write down, in terms of x, an expression for the probability that the ball drawn is red.

   (ii) Given that this probability is $\frac{7}{13}$, find x.

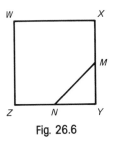

Fig. 26.6

   (b) M and N are the midpoints of adjacent sides of the square $WXYZ$ (Fig. 26.6).

   A point is selected at random in the square. Calculate the probability that it lies in triangle MYN. (C)

27 AVERAGES

MEAN

The *mean* is the proper name for the common idea of average (strictly it should be called the 'arithmetic mean').

$$\text{mean} = \frac{\text{total of all the numbers}}{\text{number of numbers}}$$

For example, the set of seven numbers $\{2, 3, 4, 7, 8, 8, 9\}$ has a mean average given by

$$\text{mean} = \frac{2+3+4+7+8+8+9}{7} = \frac{41}{7} = 5.86$$

It follows that the total of a set of numbers can be found from the mean:

$$\text{total} = \text{number of numbers} \times \text{mean}$$

This is important for solving problems.

Example A batsman has a mean average of 23 runs over his last five innings. How many must he score in his next innings if he is to increase his average to 25?

The batsman's total number of runs in five innings $= 5 \times 23 = 115$. If the mean is to rise to 25 in six innings, his total must rise:

$$\text{new total for six innings} = 6 \times 25 = 150$$

Therefore he must score $150 - 115 = 35$ runs during his sixth innings.

MODE

The *mode* is the number that occurs most frequently in the set. For example, the mode of $\{2, 3, 4, 7, 8, 8, 9\}$ is 8, since there are two 8s in the set but only one each of the other numbers.

Sometimes, there is no mode; sometimes there is more than one. For example, the set $\{2, 3, 4, 5, 6, 7\}$ has no mode, as no number is repeated. But the set $\{2, 2, 2, 3, 4, 5, 5, 5, 7, 7\}$ has *two* modes, 2 and 5, since both numbers are repeated three times. (7 is repeated too, but not as often as 2 or 5.)

MEDIAN

The *median* value in a set of numbers is the one in the middle *when they are arranged in order*. For example, the median value of {2, 3, 4, 7, 8, 8, 9} is 7 since it lies exactly in the middle.

If *two* numbers lie in the centre of the set (which is always the case when the set contains an even number of numbers) the median is the mean of the two numbers. There can *never* be two medians.

Example Find the median of the set of six numbers {6, 1, 3, 5, 4, 2}.

Rearranging the numbers into order gives {1, 2, 3, 4, 5, 6}.

Now *two* numbers, 3 and 4, lie in the middle, so the median is

$$\frac{3+4}{2} = 3\tfrac{1}{2}$$

EXERCISE 27a Calculate (i) the mean (ii) the mode(s) (iii) the median for the following:

1. 2, 4, 5, 8, 3, 4, 7, 2, 1.

2. 3, 4, 9, 2, 8, 4, 6, 7, 3, 6, 7, 3, 3.

3. 11, 3, 9, 3, 9, 8, 12, 9.

4. −3, −1, 0, 7, 6, 4, 1.

5. 56.5, 52.1, 53.2, 53.1, 51.1.

6. 103, 104, 105, 106, 104, 108.

7. Charlotte scores 63% in maths, 43% in English, 57% in French and 67% in Science. What is her mean score?

8. The wages paid in a small local factory are (per week) £90, £90, £90, £90, £90, £90 and £390 (for the boss). The workers claim the average wage is £90. The boss says it is £140 per week. Both are right − explain.

9. Five numbers have a mean of 6. If a sixth number is added to the set, the mean rises to 7. What is the extra number?

10. A set of ten numbers have a mean of 6.5. An eleventh number raises the mean to 6.6. What is the number?

11. A set of four odd numbers have a mode of 3, a median of 4 and a mean of $4\tfrac{1}{2}$. What are the numbers?

12. If the set $\{2, 7, x, 4, 3\}$ has a mean of 4.4 what is the value of x?

13. If the set $\{2, 7, y, 4, 3\}$ has a mode of 3 what is the value of y?

14. In a class of 18 boys and 12 girls, the boys' mean score in a maths test was $7\frac{1}{2}$ out of 10. How many marks did the 18 boys gain altogether?

    The girls scored an average of 8 out of 10. How many marks did the 12 girls gain altogether?

    What was the mean for the whole class of 30?

15. The same class of 18 boys and 12 girls also took a French test. The boys' mean score was 11 out of 20 and the girls' was only 9. Find the mean score for the whole class.

16. Over 20 games of golf, I have a mean score of 60 strokes per round. If my average over the first 12 games was 64 strokes, what has been my mean score in the last 8?

17. In a class of 15 girls and 12 boys, the girls' mean score in a test was 21 marks and the boys' mean score was 18. What was the mean score for the whole class?

18. Jack and Jill bring back, on average, 8.8 litres of water whenever they are asked to fetch it. If they fall down and spill it all on one journey in five, what must be their (mean) average for the *successful* journeys?

19. The mean of five numbers is 39. Two of the numbers are 103 and 35 and each of the other three is equal to x. Find the numerical value of

    (a) the total of the five numbers,　　(b) x　　　　　　　　(C)

20. Wanderers have a mean goal average of 2.25 after eight matches. What was their score in the ninth match if, afterwards, the average fell to exactly 2?

21. The average age of a group of 6 fifth-formers is 16 years and 5 months. Another student joins the group and the average age rises to 16 years 7 months. How old is the newcomer?

FREQUENCY DISTRIBUTIONS

A large set of numbers can be summarised by a table, called a *frequency distribution*, showing the number of times (or *frequency*) each number occurs. Such a table reduces the amount of work involved in finding the mean, mode and median.

Example The following set of thirty-five numbers

$$\{8, 2, 1, 5, 2, 5, 2, 6, 7, 2, 8, 5, 6, 9, 2, 3, 7, 1, 6, 7, 4, 3, 6, 7, 7, 2, 4,$$
$$7, 9, 3, 4, 6, 7, 9, 7\}$$

has been checked and contains the numbers 1 to 9 as follows:

Number, x	1	2	3	4	5	6	7	8	9
Frequency, f	2	6	3	3	3	5	8	2	3

Thus in the set of thirty-five numbers, there are two 1s, six 2s, three 3s, three 4s, and so on. You should check the set for yourself to make sure you understand where the numbers in the table have come from.

The mode — the one that occurs most often — is easy to find. Look at the frequencies of the numbers: there are eight 7s, but only six 2s, five 6s, and so on. There are more 7s than any other number, and hence the mode is 7.

We can find *the median* — the one in the middle — using the *cumulative frequency*, shown in Column (*iii*) of the table below:

(*i*) Number x	(*ii*) Frequency f	(*iii*) Cumulative frequency cf	(*iv*) $f \times x$
1	2	2	$1 \times 2 = 2$
2	6	$2 + 6 = 8$	$2 \times 6 = 12$
3	3	$8 + 3 = 11$	$3 \times 3 = 9$
4	3	$11 + 4 = 14$	$4 \times 3 = 12$
5	3	$14 + 3 = 17$	$5 \times 3 = 15$
6	5	$17 + 5 = 22$	$6 \times 5 = 30$
7	8	$22 + 8 = 30$	$7 \times 8 = 56$
8	2	$30 + 2 = 32$	$8 \times 2 = 16$
9	3	$32 + 3 = 35$	$9 \times 3 = 27$
	Total 35		179

The cumulative frequency builds up stage by stage, as we count through the thirty-five numbers in the set. So, when we have counted the 2s, there are eight numbers marked off (six 2s and two 1s); when we have marked off the three 3s then eleven numbers have been counted, and so on, until all thirty-five have been checked off. As there are thirty-five numbers, the eighteenth lies exactly in the centre and is the median value. The cumulative frequency shows that when all the 5s have been marked off we will have counted *seventeen* numbers, i.e. one short of the eighteenth. So the eighteenth must be a 6: the median value is 6.

Column (*iv*) in the table on the previous page shows the calculations necessary to find *the mean*. The two 1s contribute 2 (i.e. 2×1) to the final total of all the numbers; the six 2s contribute 12 (i.e. 6×2) to the total; the three 3s contribute 9 (i.e. 3×3); the three 4s contribute 12 (i.e. 3×4), and so on. In each case the number is multiplied by its frequency. The results are then added to find the total of all thirty-five numbers. In this example, the total is 179: thus the mean is 179 ÷ 35 = 5.11.

GROUPED DATA

Sometimes it is not convenient to show all the numbers individually in a frequency distribution and instead the data is grouped together in *classes* such as '0-9', '10-19' etc. It is not possible to calculate the *exact* value of the mean in such cases (since we do not have the exact value of the individual numbers); but it is possible to *estimate* it, if we assume that all the numbers in a class are represented by the mid-value of that class. So the class '0-9' is taken to be the value $4\frac{1}{2}$ $= \left(\dfrac{0+9}{2}\right)$; the class '10-19' is taken to be $14\frac{1}{2}$ $= \left(\dfrac{10+19}{2}\right)$, and so on. Otherwise the procedure is the same as above.

Example Estimate the mean of the following frequency distribution:

	Mid-point, x	Frequency, f	f×x
5-9	7	3	7×3 = 21
10-14	12	5	12×5 = 60
15-19	17	4	17×4 = 68
20-24	22	3	22×3 = 66
	Total	15	215

$$\text{estimated mean} = \frac{\text{total of all the numbers}}{\text{number of numbers}} = \frac{215}{15} = 14\frac{1}{3}$$

EXERCISE 27b In Questions 1, 2 and 3 find (a) the mean (b) the mode and (c) the median of the following distributions.

1.

Number	1	2	3	4	5	6
Frequency	2	3	6	3	4	2

2.

Number	2	3	4	5	6	7
Frequency	1	3	5	10	8	3

3.

Number	0	1	2	3	4
Frequency	10	8	6	4	2

4. A survey of 50 families showed the number of children per family distributed as follows:

Number of children	1	2	3	4	5
Frequency	19	18	9	3	1

(a) Write down the modal number of children per family.

(b) Find the median number of children per family.

(c) Calculate the mean number of children per family.

(AEB '81)

5. The hours of sunshine per day were recorded at a seaside resort over a period of 50 days. The results were as follows:

Hours of sunshine per day	5	6	7	8	9	10	11
Frequency of days	6	11	9	8	7	5	4

(a) Write down the modal hours of sunshine per day.

(b) Find the median number of hours of sunshine per day.

(c) Calculate the mean hours of sunshine per day. (AEB '82)

6. In a football season a team played 54 matches, the number of goals they scored in each match was recorded and the following results obtained:

3, 2, 2, 0, 0, 1, 0, 5, 1, 3, 2, 2, 1, 3, 4, 0, 0, 2,
4, 1, 2, 3, 3, 0, 1, 0, 0, 0, 5, 2, 2, 0, 1, 2, 3, 1,
3, 2, 1, 1, 0, 1, 0, 2, 2, 4, 3, 3, 1, 1, 0, 0, 1, 2.

Construct a frequency distribution table for the number of goals scored and state the mode. (JMB)

7. A die was thrown 40 times and the frequency of each score was as follows:

Score	1	2	3	4	5	6
Frequency	5	4	9	8	8	6

(a) Write down the modal score.

(b) Find the median score.

(c) Calculate the mean of these scores.

The die was then thrown another 20 times. The mean of these 20 throws was 3.4.

(d) Calculate the overall mean for all 60 throws.　　(AEB '81)

8. A shopkeeper examines 100 records and lists the number of faults on each record. The result is shown below:

Number of faults per record	0	1	2	3	4	5
Number of records	13	13	36	23	9	6

Calculate the mean number of faults per record.

He has a further 200 records in stock and the mean number of faults on these is m. Given that the mean number of faults on his total stock is 2, calculate the value of m.　　(JMB)

9. What is the mid-point of the class '1 to 5'?

Copy and complete the following table and hence estimate the mean of the distribution.

Score	Mid-value x	Frequency f	Frequency × mid-value fx
1–5	. . .	11	. . .
6–10	8	12	. . .
11–15	. . .	15	. . .
16–20	. . .	9	. . .
21–25	. . .	3	. . .
Total		50	. . .

10. The following are marks scored by 31 students in a maths test:

1, 12, 13, 12, 10, 9, 8, 13, 7, 11, 13, 9, 12, 6, 17, 11, 17, 6, 5, 12, 3, 13, 12, 5, 7, 6, 12, 13, 12, 10, 13

(a) Find the mean, mode and median of the marks.

(b) Group the data into five classes, 1–4 marks, 5–8 marks, etc. Estimate the mean mark from this frequency distribution.

Calculate an estimate of the mean from the following frequency distributions:

11.

Length (cm)	$0 \leqslant x < 4$	$4 \leqslant x < 8$	$8 \leqslant x < 12$
Frequency	5	8	17

Length (cm)	$12 \leqslant x < 16$	$16 \leqslant x < 20$
Frequency	13	7

12.

Weight (kg)	$0 \leqslant x < 10$	$10 \leqslant x < 20$	$20 \leqslant x < 30$
Frequency	22	12	8

Weight (kg)	$30 \leqslant x < 40$	$40 \leqslant x < 50$
Frequency	4	4

13.

Score	0–4	5–9	10–14	15–19	20–24
Frequency	3	9	15	10	3

14.

Mark	0–4	5–7	8–9	10	11	12
Frequency	3	5	7	4	6	8

Mark	13–15	16–20
Frequency	4	3

28 STATISTICAL GRAPHS

PIE CHARTS

The pie chart is an excellent way of showing how a total is broken up into its constituent parts.

Example An A-level statistics group of 20 students have the following number of passes at O-level:

Number of O-levels	2–4	5	6	7	8–12
Number of students	3	3	6	5	3

As 3 out of 20 people have 2–4 O-level passes, they are $\frac{3}{20}$ of the statistics class. We can convert this fraction to a percentage:

$$\frac{3}{20} \times 100\% = 15\%$$

and into an angle in a similar fashion:

$$\frac{3}{20} \times 360° = 54°$$

So $\frac{3}{20}$ of the class with 2–4 O-levels should be shown as 15% of the total or a portion of a pie chart of angle 54°.

Show the *percentages* (*not* the angles) on the pie-chart portions and label them fully or show what they represent by a colour key.

For this example:

Number of O-level passes	Frequency	%	Angle
2–4	3	$\frac{3}{20} \times 100 = 15\%$	$\frac{3}{20} \times 360° = 54°$
5	3	$\frac{3}{20} \times 100 = 15\%$	$\frac{3}{20} \times 360° = 54°$
6	6	$\frac{6}{20} \times 100 = 30\%$	$\frac{6}{20} \times 360° = 108°$
7	5	$\frac{5}{20} \times 100 = 25\%$	$\frac{5}{20} \times 360° = 90°$
8–12	3	$\frac{3}{20} \times 100 = 15\%$	$\frac{3}{20} \times 360° = 54°$
Total	20	100%	360°

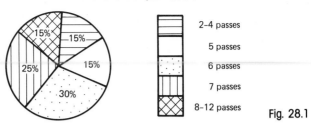

students' O-level qualifications

2–4 passes
5 passes
6 passes
7 passes
8–12 passes

Fig. 28.1

SIMPLE BAR CHARTS

Pie charts are excellent for showing parts of a total, but not a way of comparing *different* totals; a bar chart is used instead.

Example All the fifth-formers in a school took maths, English, history and French at O-level. The totals passing in each subject are illustrated in Fig. 28.2. Even a quick glance at the chart is enough to see the relative success of the four departments.

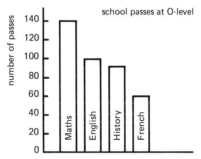

Fig. 28.2

EXERCISE 28a 1. From the bar chart in Fig. 28.3, find

(a) the mode

(b) the median number of goals scored by Village Rangers.

(c) How many games have the Rangers played? How many goals have they scored? What is their mean number of goals scored per match?

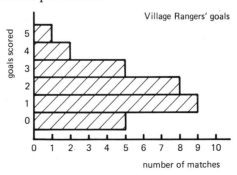

Fig. 28.3

385

2. The candidates in an examination are awarded grades A, B, C or F. Two classes take the same exam and their results are as listed:

Class 1 (20 students) A, B, A, B, C, F, C, B, A, B, C, F, B, B, B, C, B, A, F, B

Class 2 (25 students) A, B, C, C, C, C, F, F, C, F, B, A, B, B, C, C, C, B, C, C, A, C, C, B, C

(a) Draw two pie charts, one for each class, to show the proportion of students awarded each grade.

(b) Draw *one* bar chart to compare the performances of the two classes.

3. The pie chart in Fig. 28.4 shows how Whereonearth County divide their education budget between primary, secondary and further education. Find

(a) the *percentage* spent on secondary schools

(b) the *angle* on the chart representing primary school expenditure.

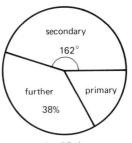

Fig. 28.4

4. The pie chart in Fig. 28.5 shows the allocation of hourly air time between pop music, D.J.'s chat, news and advertisements for a local radio station.

If $P\hat{O}Q = 120°$ and $Q\hat{O}R = 54°$ find the number of minutes of pop music broadcast per hour given that the hourly news bulletin lasts 3 minutes and the headlines (on the half-hour) last another 1 minute.

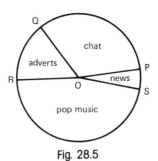

Fig. 28.5

5. The table shows how the assets of an International Commercial Bank were distributed in 1975 and 1980.

	Percentage of total assets			
	Europe	Africa	America	The East
1975	34	41	5	20
1980	24	28	24	24

(a) Draw circular diagrams, each of radius 5 cm, to compare the data for these two years.

(b) The total value of the Bank's assets in 1980 was £13 000 million. Calculate the value of the assets in Africa for that year. (JMB)

6. Georgina is taking four of her school subjects to O-level and four more to CSE. The numbers of lessons per week she has for each subject are shown:

O-level subject	Number of lessons	CSE subject	Number of lessons
Maths	5	French	4
English	5	Physics	4
Biology	4	Home Economics	6
History	4	Geography	4

She also has three lessons a week of PE and one lesson a week of RE. Show, using a pie chart, how Georgina's week of 40 lessons is divided. Your chart should illustrate not only the various subjects, but the proportion of time spent in O-level, CSE and general lessons.

7. In a recent by-election 25% of those voting voted for the Liberal/S.D.P. Alliance, 35% voted for Labour and 40% voted for the Conservative Party. 20% of those entitled to vote did not do so.

(a) Find the percentage of those entitled to vote who voted
(i) Alliance (ii) Labour (iii) Conservative.

(b) Use a pie chart to show how the electorate behaved in this election.

HISTOGRAMS

A *histogram* is a special kind of bar chart, drawn with pin-point accuracy on graph paper, with uses beyond simply illustrating data. The features of a histogram are:

(*i*) the blocks of the chart meet each other

(*ii*) the widths of the blocks of the chart may vary (as well as the height) according to the widths of the classes

(*iii*) the heights of the blocks represent the *frequency density* (*not* frequency) of each class:

$$\text{frequency density} = \frac{\text{frequency of class}}{\text{class width}}$$

(The *frequency density* indicates how tightly packed a class is; *frequency* measures how many items there are in it. A wide class might have a high frequency but a low frequency density.)

(*iv*) the frequency of a class is represented by the *area* of the corresponding block.

Use

A histogram can be used to estimate the mode. First, find the tallest block representing the most densely packed class (the *modal class*). Draw the 'diagonals' to the neighbouring classes (Fig. 28.6), and read off the mode from the point where the diagonals cross.

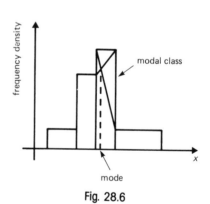

Fig. 28.6

Examples (*i*) A survey finds the heights of 150 adult males to be as follows:

Height (cm)	$160 \leqslant x < 165$	$165 \leqslant x < 168$	$168 \leqslant x < 172$
Frequency	15	27	30

Height (cm)	$172 \leqslant x < 175$	$175 \leqslant x < 180$	$180 \leqslant x < 190$
Frequency	21	25	32

Draw a histogram from this data and estimate the mode.

Setting out the calculation of frequency density:

Height x cm	Frequency f	Class width w	Frequency density f ÷ w
$160 \leqslant x < 165$	15	5	$15 \div 5 = 3$
$165 \leqslant x < 168$	27	3	$27 \div 3 = 9$
$168 \leqslant x < 172$	30	4	$30 \div 4 = 7.5$
$172 \leqslant x < 175$	21	3	$21 \div 3 = 7$
$175 \leqslant x < 180$	25	5	$25 \div 5 = 5$
$180 \leqslant x < 190$	32	10	$32 \div 10 = 3.2$

The histogram can be plotted, as shown in Fig. 28.7. From the graph, the (estimated) mode is 167.2 cm.

men's heights (taken from a sample of 150)

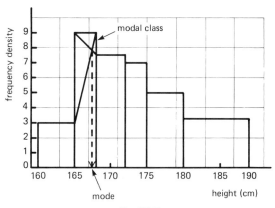

Fig. 28.7

Notice that the class with the highest *frequency* (i.e. 180–190 cm with a frequency of 32) is the widest class. But, because of the width, it has a relatively low frequency density.

(*ii*) Returning to the A-level statistics group's O-level passes (page 384);

Number of O-levels	Frequency f	Class width w	Frequency density f ÷ w
2–4	3	3*	$3 \div 3 = 1$
5	3	1	$3 \div 1 = 3$
6	6	1	$6 \div 1 = 6$
7	5	1	$5 \div 1 = 5$
8–12	3	5*	$3 \div 5 = 0.6$

*Notice that the class 2–4 is *three* units wide, as it includes people with 2 passes, 3 passes and 4 passes at O-level; similarly the 8–12 class is *five* units wide. (This problem did not arise in Example (*i*) because the classes were defined differently.)

As the classes in this table do not meet (e.g. the 2–4 class does not meet the next class 5) the histogram blocks are extended by one-half in each direction. So the 2–4 class is drawn from $1\frac{1}{2}$ to $4\frac{1}{2}$, the 5 class is drawn from $4\frac{1}{2}$ to $5\frac{1}{2}$, the 6 class is drawn from $5\frac{1}{2}$ to $6\frac{1}{2}$, and so on (see Fig. 28.8). Notice, however, that the block $1\frac{1}{2}$ to $4\frac{1}{2}$ is still *three* units wide – just as it should be since the class 2–4 is three units wide.

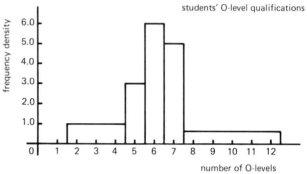

Fig. 28.8

EXERCISE 28b

1. Copy the histograms in Fig. 28.9. For each find
   (a) the frequency densities of each class
   (b) the frequencies of each class
   (c) the modal class.

   Estimate, from your drawing, the value of the mode.

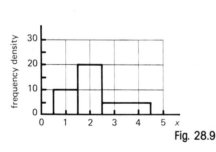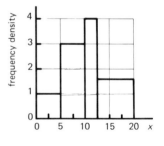

Fig. 28.9

Draw a histogram for each of the following distributions. Remember to divide the frequency of each class by its width to find the frequency density. In each case (a) state the modal class (b) estimate the mode.

2.

Length (x cm)	$0 \leqslant x < 10$	$10 \leqslant x < 15$	$15 \leqslant x < 17.5$
Frequency	8	12	10

Length (x cm)	$17.5 \leqslant x < 20$	$20 \leqslant x < 25$
Frequency	15	15

3.

Weight (x kg)	$2 \leqslant x < 8$	$8 \leqslant x < 12$	$12 \leqslant x < 14$
Frequency	12	16	8

Weight (x kg)	$14 \leqslant x < 15$	$15 \leqslant x < 20$
Frequency	9	10

4.

Volume (x cm^3)	$100 \leqslant x < 110$	$110 \leqslant x < 115$
Frequency	10	10

Volume (x cm^3)	$115 \leqslant x < 117.5$	$117.5 \leqslant x < 125$
Frequency	10	10

5.

Time (x s)	$0 \leqslant x < 5$	$5 \leqslant x < 10$
Frequency	25	42

Time (x s)	$10 \leqslant x < 12$	$12 \leqslant x < 15$
Frequency	18	12

Draw a histogram for each of the following distributions. Remember to adjust the blocks so that they meet each other. In each case (a) state the modal class (b) estimate the mode.

6.

Marks	0–4	5–9	10–14	15–19	20–25
Frequency	5	8	11	4	2

7.

Score	0–3	4	5	6–8	9–12
Frequency	9	5	7	12	8

8.

Points	0–9	10–19	20–39	40–59	60–99
Frequency	25	38	52	32	40

9. The ages of 150 cars were tabulated as follows:

Age x years	$0 < x \leqslant 1$	$1 < x \leqslant 2$	$2 < x \leqslant 3$
Frequency	17	24	26

Age x years	$3 < x \leqslant 4$	$4 < x \leqslant 5$	$5 < x \leqslant 6$
Frequency	15	13	14

Age x years	$6 < x \leqslant 7$	$7 < x \leqslant 8$	$8 < x \leqslant 14$
Frequency	13	10	18

(a) Draw a histogram to illustrate these results.

(b) Calculate an estimate of the mean age of these cars.

(c) The mean age of one hundred other cars is 4.70 years. Calculate an estimate of the mean age of the 250 cars.

(Ox)

CUMULATIVE FREQUENCY CURVES

The graph of the cumulative frequency is called the *cumulative frequency curve*. It is usually drawn as an S-shaped, smooth curve. (A graph drawn with straight lines is called the *cumulative frequency polygon*.)

The cumulative frequency curve is used to estimate the *median* (the middle item), the *lower* and *upper quartiles* (the values of the items one-quarter and three-quarters through the data), and various *percentiles* (items at given percentage points through the distribution).

Note the *interquartile range* = upper quartile − lower quartile and the *semi-interquartile range* = interquartile range ÷ 2.

Example 200 students take an exam and their marks are as shown:

Mark (%)	20–29	30–39	40–49	50–59	60–69	70–79	80–89
Frequency	11	24	48	58	39	13	7

Draw up a cumulative frequency table, draw the cumulative frequency curve and use it to find (a) the median (b) the upper and lower quartiles and hence the interquartile range (c) the 85th percentile (d) the number of students to score less than 35%.

The cumulative frequency table is as follows:

Mark	Cumulative frequency c.f.
less than 30	11
less than 40	35 (= 11 + 24)
less than 50	83 (= 35 + 48)
less than 60	141 (= 83 + 58)
less than 70	180 (= 141 + 39)
less than 80	193 (= 180 + 13)
less than 90	200 (= 193 + 7)

Plotting the points $(30, 11)$, $(40, 35)$, $(50, 83)$, and so on, gives the graph shown in Fig. 28.10.

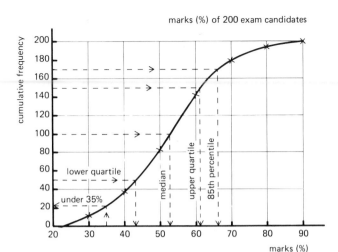

Fig. 28.10

(a) There are 200 students; thus the hundredth student is in the middle and his score is the median mark. Reading across the graph, at cumulative frequency 100, and down to the horizontal axis, we see this mark is $52\frac{1}{2}$%.

(b) The lower quartile is the mark of the student 50th from bottom. Similarly, as there are 200 students, the three-quarters position is 150th from bottom. Reading across the graph from cumulative frequencies of 50 and 150 down to the horizontal axis, we see that the lower and upper quartiles are 43% and 62% respectively. So the interquartile range is $62 - 43 = 19$%.

(c) The 85th percentile is the mark gained by the student who is $\frac{85}{100} \times 200 = 170$th. From the graph, his mark is 66%.

(d) To find the number of students who scored less than 35%, read the graph *up* from the horizontal axis at 35% and across to the cumulative frequency axis. We find about 22 students out of the 200 scored less than 35%.

EXERCISE 28c In Questions 1–3 on page 394:

(a) Draw up a cumulative frequency table from the frequencies given.

(b) Draw the cumulative frequency curve on graph paper.

(c) From your graph, estimate (i) the median (ii) the lower quartile (iii) the upper quartile (iv) the 35th percentile.

(d) Write down the interquartile range.

1.

Men's heights (x cm)	$160 \leqslant x < 165$	$165 \leqslant x < 170$	$170 \leqslant x < 175$
Frequency	8	10	22

Men's heights (x cm)	$175 \leqslant x < 176$	$176 \leqslant x < 178$	$178 \leqslant x < 188$
Frequency	20	28	42

2.

Price (£)	0–9.99	10–19.99	20–24.99
Frequency	10	15	24

Price (£)	25–29.99	30–39.99
Frequency	22	11

3.

Exam score (marks out of 20)	0–4	5–8	9–10	11	12	13–20
Number of students	4	3	8	7	6	8

4. 1000 candidates sit a mathematics examination and the results are distributed as follows:

Percentage mark	0–10	11–20	21–30	31–40
Number of candidates	10	40	90	140

Percentage mark	41–50	51–60	61–70	71–80
Number of candidates	240	180	120	100

Percentage mark	81–90	91–100
Number of candidates	60	20

(a) Draw a cumulative frequency curve to represent these data.

(b) From your curve estimate the median mark.

(c) The top 60% of candidates are to be awarded a 'pass' grade. Estimate the minimum mark required to pass the examination.

(d) The top 30% of candidates are to be awarded a 'merit' grade. Calculate an estimate of the mean mark of those candidates who achieve 'merit' in the examination. (Ox)

5. A sample number of married people were questioned concerning the age at which they were first married. From the answers received the frequency distribution of the ages, in complete years, is given in the following table.

Age in complete years	17–21	22–26	27–31	32–36	37–41	42–56
Number of people	42	69	24	19	15	11

Using squared paper, draw a cumulative frequency polygon to illustrate this distribution.

Use your diagram to estimate

(a) the median,

(b) the semi-interquartile range,

(c) the percentage of this sample of people who first married at age 23 to 30 inclusive. (AEB '82)

6. (a) On a particular weekend the mean attendance at the 34 football league matches played on the Saturday was 25 500 and the mean attendance at the 12 matches played on the Sunday was 16 750. Calculate the mean attendance for that weekend, giving your answers to three significant figures.

(b) A manufacturer gives a 'two year' guarantee with a car battery. The lengths of life, in days, of 500 batteries sold by this manufacturer are summarised in the frequency table.

Length of life (x days)	Frequency
$690 \leqslant x < 720$	40
$720 \leqslant x < 750$	120
$750 \leqslant x < 780$	140
$780 \leqslant x < 810$	110
$810 \leqslant x < 840$	70
$840 \leqslant x < 870$	20

Draw up a table of cumulative frequencies and draw the cumulative frequency diagram for this distribution.

Use your cumulative frequency diagram to estimate
(i) the median,
(ii) the interquartile range,
(iii) the probability that a battery chosen at random from this group fails before the guarantee expires. (Take 2 years = 730 days.) (JMB)

ANSWERS

Exercise 1a

1. $7, -2$
2. all of them
3. (a) no   (b) yes   (c) yes   (d) yes
4. $\sqrt{2}, \pi$
5. $20; 75; 10$
6. (a) 9   (b) -3 (c) 14   (d) 6
   (e) 12   (f) -16 (g) -9 (h) -48
   (i) -2 (j) 21   (k) 2   (l) -6

Exercise 1b

1. $1, 2, 3, 4, 6, 9, 12, 18, 36$
2. $1, 2, 3, 4, 6, 9, 12, 18, 27, 36, 54, 108$
3. 36
4. (a) $1, 2, 4, 8, 16$
   (b) $1, 2, 3, 4, 6, 8, 12, 24$
5. 8
6. (a) $1, 13$ (b) $1, 17$; prime numbers
7. $2, 3, 5, 7, 11$
8. yes, 2 is a prime number
9. $5, 10, 15, 20, 25, 30, 35, 40, 45, 50$
10. (a) $6, 12, 18, 24, 30, 36$
    (b) $15, 30, 45, 60, 75, 90$
11. (a) 30   (b) 30
12. (a) 12   (b) 24   (c) 12
13. $LCM = 15$; $HCF = 1$
14. $LCM = 300$; $HCF = 5$
15. (a) $T = \{3, 6, 9, 12, 15, 18, 21, 24, 27, 30,$
    $33, 36, 39\}$
    (b) $F = \{4, 8, 12, 16, 20, 24, 28, 32, 36,$
    $40\}$

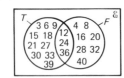

(c) $12, 24, 36$ (d) 12
16. (a) $S = \{1, 2, 3, 4, 6, 8, 9, 12, 18, 24, 36,$
    $72\}$
    $F = \{1, 2, 3, 6, 9, 18, 27, 54\}$

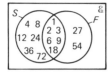

(b) $1, 2, 3, 6, 9, 18$ (c) 18

Exercise 1c

1. (a) 230   (b) 2300   (c) 230 000
   (d) 230
2. (a) 230   (b) 23   (c) 2.3
   (d) 0.0023
3. (a) 34.5   (b) 345   (c) 34 500
   (d) 3 450 000
4. (a) 34.5   (b) 3.45   (c) 0.0345
   (d) 0.000 345
5. (a) 7.89×10^1 (b) 5.421×10^2
   (c) 3.2×10^4 (d) 3.2×10^7
6. (a) 1.34×10^{-2} (b) 5.1×10^{-4}
   (c) 1×10^{-2} (d) 1.1×10^{-5}
7. (a) 3.456×10^3 (b) 3.456×10^{-1}
   (c) 3.456×10^{-4} (d) 3.456×10^{-8}
8. (a) 5.2×10^3 (b) 5×10^2
   (c) 2.781×10^8 (d) 3.0547×10^{10}

Exercise 1d

1. (a) 5.8   (b) 0.73   (c) 2.109
   (d) 2.091
2. (a) 0.046   (b) 0.000 46   (c) 2700
   (d) 27
3. (a) 1.079   (b) 102.1002
   (c) 0.1331   (d) 110 000
4. (a) 0.0012   (b) 4000   (c) 1200
   (d) 30 000
5. (a) 0.000 009   (b) 0.0001
   (c) 1.17   (d) 10 020.01
6. (a) 0.02   (b) 2100   (c) 14
7. (a) 0.09   (b) 1.1   (c) 1000
8. (a) 0.1   (b) 0.2   (c) 0.02
9. (a) 0.005   (b) 4.5   (c) 1
10. (a) 2.5   (b) 2   (c) 0.09

Exercise 1e

1. (a) 7.77   (b) 9.79   (c) 10.01
   (d) 10.00   (e) 6.67
2. (a) 5.05   (b) 12.1   (c) 122
   (d) 10.1   (e) 10.0
3. (a) (i) 0.123 (ii) 0.001 (iii) 123.457
   (b) (i) 0.123 (ii) 0.001 23 (iii) 123
4. (a) 3   (b) 4   (c) 3 or 4   (d) 4
   (e) 5   (f) 3   (g) 3   (h) 1
   (i) 4   (j) 1
5. (a) 40 000   (b) 6000   (c) 1 000 000
   (d) 3000   (e) 0.01   (f) 30
   (g) 0.1

6. (a) 13325.02   (b) 269.533
    (c) 150.321   (d) 13 890.0
7. 2.6458; 2.65 (3 s.f.)
8. 0.707 11; 0.577 35
    (a) 0.837   (b) -0.448
9. (a) 1.114; 1.105   (b) 1.244; 1.235
    (c) 1.424; 1.415   (d) 1.544; 1.535
    (e) 1.554; 1.545   (f) 1.004; 0.995
10. (a) 1.235; 1.244   (b) 1.2395; 1.2404

Exercise 1f

1. $1000; \frac{1}{1000}$
2. 100; 3000
3. 2 534 000
4. (a) $30\,\text{m}^3$ (b) $3 \times 10^7\,\text{cm}^3$
    (c) 3×10^4 litres
5. 60 cm
6. 12.1 m : 1210 cm : 533 mm
7. $1.76 \times 10^4\,\text{kg}$
8. $8.77 \times 10^{-5}\,\text{g/cm}^3 : 3.5\,\text{g}$
9. 1.166 litres; 1.2 litres; 336 ml less
10. 15 m/s : 45 ms
11. 86.4 km

Exercise 1g

1. (a) 150   (b) 105
2. (a) 10   (b) 15   (c) 40   (d) 60
3. (a) 7   (b) 10   (c) 12   (d) 15
4. (a) 6   (b) 12   (c) 18   (d) 73
5. (a) 33_4 (b) 21_7 (c) 120_3
6. (a) 132_5 (b) 60_7 (c) 101010_2
7. (a) 10000_2 (b) 110000_2
8. (a) 1110_2 (b) 11001_2
9. (a) 10110_2 (b) 101100_2
    (c) 1011000_2
10. (a) 110_3 (b) 1100_3 (c) 11000_3
11. (a) 5   (b) 13   (c) 36   (d) 15
12. (a) 111_2 (b) 1100_2 (c) 11001_2
    (d) 100101_2
13. (a) 2102_3 (b) 230_5
14. (a) 92   (b) 128
15. (a) 10100_2 (b) 100010_2
    (c) 111_2
16. (a) 11011_2
    (b) $1000000_2; 11011000000_2$
17. (a) 101001_2 (b) 51_8 (c) 29_{16}
18.

	Base 10	Base 8	Base 6	Base 4	Base 3	Base 2
a	111	157	303	1233	11010	1101111
b	73	111	201	1021	2201	1001001
c	43	53	111	223	1121	101011
d	21	25	33	111	210	10101
e	13	15	21	31	111	1101
f	7	7	11	13	21	111

19. (a) 200_4 (b) 132_4 (c) 2013_4
20. (a) 4   (b) 7   (c) 11

Miscellaneous Exercise 1

1. (a) all   (b) 1, 11, 101
    (c) $-101, 0, 1, 11, 101$
    (d) all except $\sqrt{11}$
2. (a)

    (b) (i) P (ii) Q (iii) Q, I, N (iv) Q, I
3. (a) 0.0018   (b) 0.2
    (c) 7.2×10^{-3}
4. (a) 256 580 240
    (b) 0.000 256 580 24
5. (a) 3.15   (b) 233.1   (c) 0.0074
6. (a) 4460.592   (b) 293.1
    (c) 6650.594
7. (a) 5.4   (b) 5.40   (c) 5
8. (a) 0.0505   (b) 0.05051
    (c) 0.1   (d) 0.05
9. (a) $7.3 \times 10^9; 2.352 \times 10^{13};$
     5.88×10^{12}
    (b) 4   (c) 2×10^{10}
10. (a) 2.99×10^{-23} (b) 6×10^{-26}
    (c) 3.3×10^{22} (d) 89%
11. (a) 70147
    (b) 101010_2; (i) 10101_2
      (ii) 1010100_2
12. (a) 333_4 (b) 101_2 (c) 144_8
13. (a) (i) 1202_3 (ii) 2121_3 (iii) 2101_3
    (b) (i) 10100_2 (ii) 101001_2
      (iii) 110001_2
14. (a) 111001_2 (b) 2010_3
    (c) 321_4 (d) 71_8 (e) 49_{12}
15. $7m + n; n$
16. (a) 27   (b) 35   (c) 130
    (d) 11_{12} (e) 100_{12} (f) $E1_{12}$
    (g) 4_{12} (h) 16_{12} (i) TT_{12}
    (j) TE_{12}

Exercise 2a

1. (a) $\frac{7}{12}$ (b) $\frac{9}{20}$ (c) $1\frac{5}{12}$ (d) $1\frac{7}{20}$
2. (a) $\frac{3}{10}$ (b) $\frac{4}{15}$ (c) $\frac{13}{28}$ (d) $\frac{1}{8}$
3. (a) $\frac{1}{14}$ (b) $\frac{3}{5}$ (c) $1\frac{3}{17}$ (d) 15
4. (a) $1\frac{1}{4}$ (b) $2\frac{2}{3}$ (c) $\frac{1}{5}$ (d) $2\frac{2}{7}$
5. (a) $1\frac{3}{4}$ (b) $1\frac{4}{7}$ (c) $\frac{4}{5}$ (d) $-1\frac{7}{12}$
6. (a) $3\frac{7}{8}$ (b) $\frac{3}{8}$ (c) $3\frac{23}{32}$ (d) $1\frac{3}{14}$
7. (a) $4\frac{5}{9}$ (b) $1\frac{8}{9}$ (c) $4\frac{8}{27}$ (d) $2\frac{5}{12}$

8. (a) 0.67   (b) 0.35   (c) 0.63   (d) 0.56
   (e) 0.29

9. (a) $\frac{1}{5}$ (b) $\frac{3}{4}$ (c) $1\frac{3}{5}$ (d) $\frac{4}{25}$
   (e) $\frac{11}{20}$ (f) $\frac{1}{20}$ (g) $\frac{12}{25}$ (h) $\frac{1}{8}$
   (i) $\frac{3}{8}$ (j) $\frac{1}{125}$

10. (a) $0.\dot{1}$ (b) $0.\dot{3}\dot{6}$ (c) $0.8\dot{1}$
    (d) $0.\dot{5}7142\dot{8}$ (e) $3.\dot{1}4285\dot{7}$
    (f) $0.0\dot{9}$

Exercise 2b

1. (a) 31%   (b) 5%   (c) 150%
   (d) $\frac{1}{2}$%   (e) $\frac{1}{10}$%

2. (a) 60%   (b) $66\frac{2}{3}$%   (c) 4%
   (d) $37\frac{1}{2}$%   (e) $10\frac{1}{2}$%

3. (a) 175%   (b) $166\frac{2}{3}$ (c) 280%
   (d) $362\frac{1}{2}$%   (e) $218\frac{1}{2}$%

4. (a) 0.32   (b) 0.89   (c) 1.02
   (d) 0.675   (e) 0.885

5. (a) $\frac{3}{4}$ (b) $\frac{3}{5}$ (c) $\frac{8}{25}$ (d) $\frac{13}{10}$
   (e) $\frac{3}{200}$ (f) $\frac{31}{200}$ (g) $\frac{1}{8}$ (h) $\frac{1}{30}$
   (i) $\frac{21}{400}$ (j) $\frac{1}{6}$

6. (a) 8.5   (b) £9   (c) 75   (d) £1.30
   (e) £7.80   (f) £3

7. 60%; 70%; English

8. 70%   (a) 4%   (b) $13\frac{1}{3}$%

9. 42 m.p.g.; $2\frac{1}{2}$%

10. 2100; 26%

Exercise 2c

1. (a) 75 p   (b) £$1.27\frac{1}{2}$ (c) £$1.54\frac{1}{2}$
   (d) £2.08

2. £30

3. £25.20

4. £6000

5. (a) £144   (b) £192   (c) £300
   (d) £222

6. (a) £504   (b) £1008   (c) £2520

7. £8125

8. 4 years

9. £35.24; 80%

10. 56 p; 25%

11. £5

12. £2.88

13. (a) £5.20   (b) £150

14. £30 000; £4500

15. £400

Miscellaneous Exercise 2

1. (a) $\frac{5}{18}$ (b) $2\frac{1}{2}$ (c) $\frac{1}{5}$ (d) $3\frac{1}{2}$
   (e) $\frac{1}{5}$ (f) $\frac{5}{7}$ (g) $3\frac{3}{4}$ (h) 2

2. (a) £125   (b) £54   (c) £594
   (d) £306   (e) £108   (f) £13.13

3. £320

4. 55%; English 55%; French 55.6%

5. 45 m

6. £150; 8%

7. 75 p; 90 p; 60 p; 80%

10. (a) (i) £40.25   (ii) £6.30   (iii) £33.01
    (b) £1970

11. £72; 27.8%; £80; (i) £103.50   (ii) $12\frac{1}{2}$%

12. 20%; $62\frac{1}{2}$ p

13. (a) £233; 7.77%   (b) £5400; £1098

14. (b) (i) $\frac{1}{2}$ (ii) $\frac{1}{4}$
    (d) C eats $\frac{3}{8}$, B eats $\frac{9}{40}$, A eats $\frac{3}{20}$, $\frac{1}{4}$ left

Exercise 3a

1. (a) 1:2   (b) 1:3   (c) 3:2
   (d) 1:2:4   (e) 3:5:6   (f) 2:3:4:6

2. (a) 1:100   (b) 1:1000   (c) 1:100 000
   (d) 1:400 000

3. 1:400; 12 m; 5 cm

4. 1:25 000; $8\frac{1}{2}$ km

5. (a) 4:8   (b) 2:4:6   (c) 1:4:7

6. (a) 27:18:9   (b) 18:18:12:6
   (c) 9:15:12:18

7. (a) 63:45   (b) 24:36:48
   (c) 18:27:27:36

8. £14

9. 4:1:2; 324:81:162

10. 5 cm; 7 cm

11. 40°, 40°, 100°

12. 20:28:21

13. 18:30:35

14. 10:15:12

15. 64:40:15

16. 8:1

17. 4:63

18. 21:2

19. (a) $4\frac{1}{2}$ km
    (b) 100 m × 250 m; 25 000 m²
    (c) 1:30 000

20. (a) $\frac{1}{2}$ km   (b) 48 cm   (c) 5 km²

Exercise 3b

1. (a) 6   (b) 40

2. (a) 12   (b) 8

3. (a) 3   (b) 12

4. (a) 9   (b) 12

5. (a) $40\frac{1}{2}$ (b) 6

6. (a) 6   (b) 16

7. $13\frac{1}{2}$ cm

8. 6

9. 12

10. (a) 16 min   (b) 10 min   (c) $7\frac{1}{2}$ min

11. 90 N/m^2

12. £32; £260

13. $12\frac{1}{2}$ days

14. $x = 4.5$; $y = 7.2$; $z = 7.5$

Exercise 4a

1. (a) 2^3 (b) 3^4 (c) 4^3 (d) 7^6
2. (a) 16   (b) 27   (c) 49   (d) 4
      (e) 81   (f) 64   (g) 32   (h) 216
3. (a) 2^8 (b) 3^6 (c) 2^2 (d) 3^2
      (e) 2^{15} (f) 3^8
4. (a) (i) 4   (ii) 16   (iii) 64   (iv) 256
      (b) yes   (c) (i) $\frac{256}{64} = 4 (= 2^2)$
        (ii) $16 \times 16 = 256 (= 2^8)$
5. (a) 10^2 (b) 10^3 (c) 10^6
6. (a) 10^5 (b) 10^8 (c) 10^9 (d) 10^{12}

Exercise 4b

1. (a) 1   (b) 1   (c) 1   (d) 1
2. (a) $\frac{1}{2}$ (b) $\frac{1}{9}$ (c) $\frac{1}{100}$ (d) $\frac{1}{10\,000}$
3. (a) 3   (b) $\frac{1}{3}$ (c) 3   (d) 27
4. (a) 27   (b) $\frac{1}{27}$ (c) 100   (d) $\frac{1}{100}$
5. (a) 2^1 or 2   (b) 2^1 or 2   (c) 2^{-2} or $\frac{1}{4}$
      (d) 2^3 or 8   (e) 2^{-6} or $\frac{1}{64}$
      (f) 2^{-4} or $\frac{1}{16}$ (g) 2^2 or 4   (h) 2^{-1} or $\frac{1}{2}$
6. (a) $\frac{1}{3}$ (b) 3^5 (c) 4^6 (d) 1
7. (a) 3   (b) 4   (c) $\frac{1}{3}$ (d) $\frac{1}{11}$
8. (a) 2   (b) 8   (c) $\frac{1}{8}$ (d) 32
9. (a) 0   (b) -5 (c) $+25$ (d) -125
10. (a) 4   (b) 0   (c) $\frac{1}{5}$ (d) 3

Exercise 4c

1. 6×10^9
2. 1.25×10^{-4}
3. 9.24×10^1
4. 3×10^5
5. 2×10^{-9}
6. 9.5×10^8
7. 1×10^4
8. 2.52×10^3
9. 2.08×10^3
10. 3.74×10^4

11. 3.66×10^{-2}

12. 5.0113×10^{-2}

13. 4×10^{-7}

14. 5.25×10^{-2}

15. 3.67×10^{-3}

16. 3×10^{12}

Exercise 4d

1. (a) p^5 (b) p^6 (c) p^6 (d) p^{-6}
2. (a) q^{-4} (b) q^{-3} (c) q^2 (d) 1
3. (a) x^5y (b) x^4y^2 (c) xy^2 (d) y^{-1}
4. (a) yz (b) $y^{-1}z$ (c) $x^{-1}y^3z^{-1}$
      (d) y^4
5. (a) a (b) $a^{\frac{1}{2}}$ (c) ab (d) $a^{-\frac{1}{4}}$
6. (a) a^8 (b) a^7 (c) $a^{-\frac{11}{3}}$ (d) $a^{\frac{5}{4}}$
7. (a) y^2 (b) p^4q^4r (c) m^4n (d) m^2n^4
8. (a) p^{-4} (b) y^6 (c) q^{-4} (d) x^{-1}
9. (a) a^{-1} (b) $p^{\frac{1}{2}}q^r$ (c) $p^{-1}q^2$ (d) $t^{\frac{1}{2}}$
10. (a) abc (b) $x^9y^{-4}z^{-1}$
11. (a) $2pqr^{-1}$ (b) $3p^{-3}$
12. $\dfrac{bc^2}{m^4d^3}$

Exercise 5a

1. (a) set A contains set B
      (b) 2 is an element of C
      (c) C is not a subset of D
      (d) C has 10 elements
2. (a) $X \supset Y$ (b) $S \neq \emptyset$ or $n(S) \neq 0$
      (c) $\frac{1}{2} \notin Z$ (d) $n(Z) = 5$ (e) $A \notin B$
      (f) $\mathcal{E} = \{1 \leqslant x \leqslant 30\}$
3. (a), (b) and (d) are true; (c) is false
4. (a), (c), (d) and (g) are true; (b), (e) and
   (f) are false
5. (a) $\{5.2\}$ (b) $\{2, 4, 5, 6\}$
      (c) $\{3, 4, 6\}$ (d) $\{1\}$
      (e) $\{3\}$
6. (a) {London, Edinburgh}
      (b) {Bristol, Manchester, London,
          Liverpool, Edinburgh, Paris, Bonn,
          Rome}
      (c) {Bristol, Manchester, Liverpool}
      (d) {Paris, Bonn, Rome}
7. (a) $\{5\}$ (b) $\{2, 3, 4, 5, 6, 7, 8\}$
      (c) $\{1, 6, 7, 8, 9\}$ (d) $\{1, 9\}$

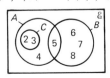

8. $A = \{3, 6, 9, 12, 15\}$ $B = \{1, 2, 3, 4, 6, 12\}$

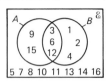

(a) $\{3, 6, 12\}$
(b) $\{1, 2, 4, 5, 7, 8, 10, 11, 13, 14, 16\}$
(c) $\{1, 2, 3, 4, 6, 9, 12, 15\}$
(d) $\{1, 2, 4\}$

9.

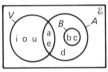

(a), (c), (f), (g) and (h) are true; (b), (d) and (e) are false; consonants

10.

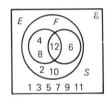

(a) $\{12\}$ (b) $\{2, 10\}$ (c) $\emptyset$
(d) no odd number is a multiple of 6
(e) some even numbers are not multiples of 6
(f) all multiples of 4 are even numbers

11. (a) Terraced and semi-detached houses are not the only type in my road
(b) detached   (c) $T \cap B = \emptyset$
(d) $B \cap S \neq \emptyset$

12. (a) no   (b) yes   (c) no   (d) yes

Exercise 5b

1. (a) (b)

(c) (d)

(e)

2.

3.

4. (a) (b)

(c)

5. (a) $(X \cup Y)'$ or $X' \cap Y'$
(b) $Y \cap X'$ (c) $(X \cup Y)' \cup (X \cap Y$

6. (a) 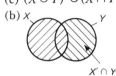 (b)

$X \cap Y'$ $X \cap Y$ $X' \cap Y$

7. (a) 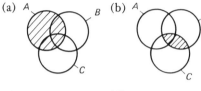 (b)

(c) (d)

(e) (f)

8.

Exercise 5c

1. (a) 5   (b) 17   (c) 13   (d) 25
(e) 5   (f) 13

2. $(54 - x) + x + (47 - x) + 12 = 88$; $x = 25$

3.

$52 - x$; $(52 - x) + (20 - x) + x + 28 = 88$; $x = 12$

4. 30
5. 15
6. 4
7. 13

8.

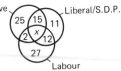
Conservative — Liberal/S.D.P.
25, 15, 11, 2, x, 12, 27
Labour

$x = 8$

Miscellaneous Exercise 5

1. (a) $2 \in E \cap O'$ (b) $2 \in P \cap E$
   (c) $O \cap E = \emptyset$

2. (a) pupils who bring a packed lunch and come to school by car
   (b) pupils who either come to school by car or who are in the sixth form or both
   (c) pupils who do not come to school by car and who have a school lunch
   (d) pupils who are neither in the sixth form nor have a school lunch;
   $x \in P \cap C'$

3. (a)

   (b)

   (c) (d)

4. (a) (b)

   (c)

5. (c), (e), (g) and (h) are true; (a), (b), (d), (f) and (i) are false

6. (a) 9   (b) true   (c) true
   (d) 12   (e) 10

7. 28; 3; 19

8. (a) 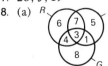 (b) (i) 1 (ii) 4 (iii) 8

9. (a) $\{5, 6, 7, 8, 9, 10, 11, 12\}$
   (b) $\{2, 3, 5, 7, 11, 13, 17, 19\}$
   (c) $\{2, 4, 5, 10, 20\}$

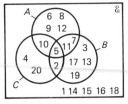

(d) $\{2, 3, 13, 17, 19\}$
(e) $\{1, 4, 14, 15, 16, 18, 20\}$
(f) $\{1, 6, 8, 9, 12, 14, 15, 16, 18\}$
(g) $\{10, 5, 2\}$

10. (a) 24 trains stop at Aton;
    (b) all trains stopping at Ceton also stop at Beton;
    (c) $A \cap B \cap C \neq \emptyset$ or $n(A \cap B \cap C) \neq 0$
    (d) $n(B) = 30$

   14; 9

Exercise 6a

1. 20
2. -45
3. 12.8
4. $17\frac{1}{2}$
5. $\frac{13}{16}$
6. 1
7. -1
8. 5.292
9. 13
10. $21\frac{1}{4}$
11. (a) 616   (b) 6.16
12. (a) 113.1   (b) 0.1131
13. 40.5
14. 7
15. 4.4
16. 4.4
17. 0.06
18. $4\frac{4}{9}$
19. $1\frac{1}{2}$
20. $3\frac{3}{7}$

Exercise 6b

1. $3a$
2. $7b$
3. $5a$
4. a^4
5. $8a + 4b$
6. $6x^2$
7. $2mn$
8. $2m + 2p$

9. $3ab + a + b$

10. $5x + 7y$

11. $5x^3 - 3y$

12. $6 + x - xy$

13. $12p^3q$

14. $30d^3ef$

15. $8p + pq^2 + 3p^2q$

16. $9m^2$

17. $3mn$

18. $5st$

19. $3jsf$

20. 21, 22. no simplification is possible

Exercise 6c

1. $11 + 2x$

2. $5x + x^2$

3. $4ab - 3a$

4. $4xy - 3x - 3y$

5. $pq - pq^2$

6. $2a + 3b - ab$

7. $8c - 8d$

8. $mn + 2n^2$

9. $7p - qp - 12q$

10. $8r - 7s - 1$

11. $u^2 + 8u + 12$

12. $v^2 + 2v - 15$

13. $np - 2n + p^2 - 2p$

14. $4mn - 4n^2 - m^2$

15. $5c^2 - 28cd + 15d^2$

16. $12e^2 - 25ef + 12f^2$

17. $a^2 + 2ab + b^2$

18. $a^2 + 4ab + 4b^2$

19. $a^2 - 2ab + b^2$

20. $9e^2 - 6ef + f^2$

21. $4e^2 + 12ef + 9f^2$

22. $25g^2 - 20gh + 4h^2$

23. $15 + 4a + 3b$

24. $15 + 8a + a^2 + ab + 3b$

25. $c^2 + 3c + 3d - d^2$

26. $2e - 2f - e^2 + f^2$

27. $c + 3d + dc - d^2$

28. $e - 2f + fe + f^2$

Exercise 6d

1. $\dfrac{8a}{15}$

2. $\dfrac{5b}{6}$

3. $\dfrac{7c + 6d}{21}$

4. $\dfrac{3e^2 - 2f}{4}$

5. $\dfrac{g^3}{12}$

6. $\dfrac{3g - 4g^2}{12}$

7. $\dfrac{3}{4g}$

8. $\dfrac{b - 2}{6}$

9. $\dfrac{11b + 6}{6}$

10. $\dfrac{7j + 4}{6}$

11. $\dfrac{17k - 8}{12}$

12. $\dfrac{19k - 3}{6}$

13. $\dfrac{5m + 7}{6}$

14. $\dfrac{7n + 11}{12}$

15. $\dfrac{p - 8}{4}$

16. $\dfrac{5q - r}{6}$

17. $\dfrac{5s - 9t - 4u}{20}$

18. $\dfrac{k + j}{jk}$

19. $\dfrac{2m - 3l}{lm}$

20. $\dfrac{4nq + 5p^2}{pq}$

21. $\dfrac{18q^2 - 2r^2}{3qr^2}$

22. $\dfrac{5q^2 - 2r^2s}{rq}$

23. $\dfrac{4}{r}$

24. $\dfrac{11us - 9s}{3ut}$

25. $\dfrac{11u}{9}$

26. $\dfrac{r^2 + 2s^2}{2sr}$

27. $\dfrac{1}{2}$

28. $\dfrac{p^3 m}{q}$

29. $pm^3 q$

30. $\dfrac{p^2 m^3 q + p}{mq}$

31. $\dfrac{2u + v^2}{6v}$

32. $\dfrac{x + xy}{y^2}$

33. $\dfrac{4u + v^2}{6vw}$

34. $\dfrac{x + xy}{y^2 z}$

35. $\dfrac{a^2 - 9c}{12bc^2}$

36. $\dfrac{16e - 15d}{20d^2 e^2}$

37. $\dfrac{4u}{v^2}$

38. $\dfrac{1}{y}$

39. $\dfrac{a^2}{9c}$

40. $\dfrac{16e}{15d}$

41. $\dfrac{b^3 d}{ac}$

42. $\dfrac{3m^4 p^4}{q^2}$

Exercise 6e

1. $2(3 + m)$
2. $3(1 + 4e)$
3. $3(5 + 12p)$
4. $5f(1 - 3g)$
5. $8q(2 - r)$
6. $7x(1 - 3x)$
7. $q(5 - q)$
8. $11x(1 - 11y)$
9. $7mn(3m + 4)$
10. $lmn(m - 1)$
11. $yz(y + z)$
12. $2a^2(b + 3)$
13. $3m(p + 2q - r^2)$
14. $(m + 1)(n + 2)$

15. $(q + 1)(p + 2)$
16. $(3 + k)(5 + l)$
17. $(4 - i)(j + 2)$
18. $(3 + d)(2 - c)$
19. $(f + g)(h + i)$
20. $(a + b)(c + d)$
21. $(t + u)(v + 2w)$
22. $(e + f)(2g + h)$
23. $(r - s)(u + t)$
24. $(j + k)(2l - m)$
25. $(2w - 3y)(x + z)$
26. $(3n - p)(q + r)$
27. $(2a^3 - b)(y - z)$
28. $(s^2 + t)(u - v)$
29. $(3m^2 - 2n)(3p - 2q)$
30. $(w^2 + x)(2y - z)$
31. $(3t + 2u)(3w + 2v)$
32. $(2a + 3b)(4c + d)$
33. $(3x^2 - 2y)(3x + 2z)$
34. $(5e + 6f)(2e - h)$
35. $b(a + c + d)$
36. $3a^2(a + 2b + c^2)$
37. $(p + q)(2 + m + n^2)$
38. $(d + e)(3 + f^2 + g)$
39. $(x - y)(y + z + 2)$
40. $(h - i)(j + k - 4)$

Exercise 6f

1. $(x + 4)(x + 2)$
2. $(x + 8)(x + 2)$
3. $(x + 9)(x + 3)$
4. $(x + 5)(x + 3)$
5. $(x + 5)(x + 2)$
6. $(x + 6)(x - 3)$
7. $(x + 5)(x - 2)$
8. $(x - 7)(x - 4)$
9. $(x + 3)(x + 1)$
10. $(x - 5)(x - 1)$
11. $(3 + x)(8 + x)$
12. $(5 + x)(4 + x)$
13. $(y + 2)(y + 17)$
14. $(y + 5)(y + 13)$
15. $(z + 4)(z - 11)$
16. $(x - 5)(x + 6)$
17. $(n + 9)(n - 4)$
18. $(p - 11q)(p + 6q)$
19. $(x - 9y)(x - 2y)$
20. $(xy - 3)(xy - 8)$
21. $(2x + 3)(x + 2)$
22. $(2x + 1)(3x + 5)$
23. $(2x + 1)(x + 7)$
24. $(3x + 1)(x + 2)$
25. $(2x + 5)(x + 3)$

26. $(3x-2)(x+8)$
27. $(4x-1)(x+5)$
28. $(5x-1)(x-4)$
29. $(7x-2)(x-1)$
30. $(12v-1)(v-12)$
31. $(2c+3)(3c+2)$
32. $(3r-5)(7r+1)$
33. $(2t+1)(5t-7)$
34. $(l-2)(3l-2)$
35. $(5p+3)(2p-7)$
36. $(4s+3)(s+8)$
37. $(2f-9)(f-6)$
38. $(m+5)(3m-2)$
39. $(8e-5)(e+6)$
40. $(d+2)(6d-11)$
41. $(2x+1)(1-3x)$
42. $(2x+3)(2-3x)$
43. $(5x+2)(1-2x)$
44. $(3x+5)(1-4x)$
45. $(2x+1)(1-x)$
46. $(2x+3)(2-x)$
47. $(3x+4)(3-x)$
48. $(5x+1)(7-x)$
49. $(4x-1)(8-x)$
50. $(x-3)(2-11x)$
51. $(3x-7)(2-x)$
52. $(4x-13)(1-x)$
53. $(7g+3)(7-g)$
54. $(5+b)(3-2b)$
55. $(11+3k)(5+2k)$
56. $(5+l)(3-4l)$
57. $(4-9m)(1+4m)$
58. $(m+12n)(m-2n)$
59. $(p-8q)(p+3q)$
60. $(6p+7q)(2p-7q)$

Exercise 6g

1. $(3-y)(3+y)$
2. $(p-q)(p+q)$
3. $(r-s)(r+s)$
4. $(p-3q)(p+3q)$
5. $(mn-p)(mn+p)$
6. $(uv-3)(uv+3)$
7. $(5-y)(5+y)$
8. $(11-w)(11+w)$
9. $(9-r)(9+r)$
10. $(12-5x)(12+5x)$
11. $(9s-t)(9s+t)$
12. $(6y-x)(6y+x)$
13. $(3t-2u)(3t+2u)$
14. $(11f-7j)(11f+7j)$
15. $(8s-7t)(8s+7t)$
16. $2(3r-s)(3r+s)$

17. $2(2d-e)(2d+e)$
18. $20(a-2b)(a+2b)$
19. $12(d-2e)(d+2e)$
20. $2(5c-7)(5c+7)$
21. $8(5-2z)(5+2z)$
22. 9400
23. 6200
24. 14 600
25. 5900
26. 320
27. 0.000 08
28. 1 028 000
29. 996 000
30. 1 018 000

Exercise 7a

1. 4
2. 3
3. 1
4. 2
5. 1
6. 3
7. 2
8. ± 3
9. 2
10. 3
11. 16
12. 25
13. 6
14. 8
15. 2.4
16. 5
17. 1
18. -3
19. $-3\frac{1}{2}$
20. $\frac{1}{2}$
21. 4
22. 2
23. 9
24. 7
25. $1\frac{1}{2}$
26. 1
27. 4
28. 0
29. 2.4
30. -1
31. 3
32. 2
33. 10
34. 8
35. 1
36. -4

37. 2
38. 3
39. 3
40. 16
41. 11
42. 3
43. 0.2
44. $11\frac{2}{3}$
45. 2
46. 3
47. 2
48. 3
49. 3
50. 0

Exercise 7b

1. $\dfrac{P}{4}$

2. (a) $\dfrac{V}{r}$ (b) $\dfrac{V}{i}$

3. $\dfrac{F}{a}$

4. $\dfrac{A}{2r}$

5. $\dfrac{E}{mg}$

6. $\dfrac{100I}{Pt}$

7. $\dfrac{2A}{a}$

8. $\dfrac{3V}{ab}$

9. $1-p$

10. (a) bs (b) $\dfrac{o}{s}$

11. (a) $v-at$ (b) $\dfrac{v-u}{t}$

12. (a) $\dfrac{v^2-u^2}{2s}$ (b) $\sqrt{v^2-2as}$

13. $\dfrac{S-2\pi r}{2\pi}$ or $\dfrac{S}{2\pi}-r$

14. (a) $\dfrac{2E}{m}$ (b) $\sqrt{\dfrac{2E}{m}}$

15. $\sqrt{\dfrac{A}{\pi}}$

16. (a) $y-mx$ (b) $\dfrac{y-c}{m}$

17. $\sqrt[3]{\dfrac{3V}{4\pi}}$

18. (a) r^2-x^2 (b) $\sqrt{r^2-x^2}$

19. (a) $\dfrac{mv^2}{P}$ (b) $\sqrt{\dfrac{rP}{m}}$

20. (a) $\dfrac{s-\frac{1}{2}at^2}{t}$ (b) $\dfrac{2(s-ut)}{t^2}$

21. (a) $\dfrac{2A}{a+b}$ (b) $\dfrac{2A}{b}-b$

22. $\dfrac{s^2}{p(1-p)}$

23. (a) $g\left(\dfrac{T}{2\pi}\right)^2$ (b) $l\left(\dfrac{2\pi}{T}\right)^2$

24. (a) $\dfrac{1}{f}-\dfrac{1}{v}$ (b) $\dfrac{vf}{v-f}$

Exercise 7c

1. (a) 7   (b) 31
2. 5
3. -2
4. 13, 14, 15
5. $n+6$; 10, 12, 14, 16
6. 2 cm; 12 cm
7. 192 cm^2
8. 7 cm
9. $20l$; 81 cm^2
10. 20
11. 6, 12
12. $9q+28$; 31 p/kg
13. 21p
14. $ts+TS$
15. (a) $m+2q$ (b) $m+5q$ (c) $m+xq$
16. (a) $5+m+5q$ (b) $5+m+8q$
    (c) $5+m+(3+x)q$

Exercise 7d

1. $x=4, y=1$
2. $x=3, y=6$
3. $x=4, y=3$
4. $x=1\frac{1}{2}, y=2\frac{1}{2}$
5. $a=5, b=2$
6. $p=3, q=1$
7. $y=2, z=3$
8. $p=19, q=2$
9. $x=5, y=3$
10. $m=3, n=-2$
11. $p=7, q=0$
12. $c=-1, d=5$

13. $x = 3, y = 2$
14. $x = 1, y = \frac{1}{2}$
15. $x = 1, y = 4$
16. $y = \frac{1}{2}, z = -2$
17. $g = -\frac{1}{2}, b = -1$
18. $e = 1, f = \frac{1}{3}$
19. $m = -\frac{2}{3}, n = \frac{1}{10}$
20. $p = 8\frac{1}{2}, q = 20\frac{1}{2}$

Exercise 7e

1. $9, 6$
2. $18, 6$
3. $10\,p; 16\,p$
4. peas $18\,p$; beans $21\,p$
5. child's £1.50; adults £3.00
6. 10
7. $x = 14; y = 6$
8. $x = £3; y = £5$
9. $16\,p; 80\,p$
10. (a) $m = 5; c = 3$ (b) $n = 2; d = -3$
    (c) $y = 6x - 1$
11. $a = 5; d = 4$
12. $a = 4; d = 5$

Exercise 7f

1. $x = 2$ or 3
2. $x = -4$ or 3
3. $p = -3$ or -2
4. $x = 0$ or 2
5. $x = 0$ or $y = 0$
6. $x = 0, 1$ or 2
7. $x = -3$ or 0
8. $x = 0$ or 2
9. $z = 0$ or 4
10. $z = 0$ or 5
11. $p = 0$ or 1
12. $x = 0$ or $\frac{1}{2}$
13. $r = 0$ or 5
14. $s = 0$ or 3
15. $r = -3$ or 0
16. $r = -1$ or 0
17. $x = -2$ or -4
18. $a = -8$ or 2
19. $b = -3$ or 5
20. $x = 2$ or 5
21. $x = \frac{1}{2}$ or -3
22. $c = \frac{1}{2}$ or $2\frac{1}{2}$
23. $c = \frac{3}{11}$ or -1
24. $x = -\frac{3}{4}$ or $-\frac{1}{3}$
25. $x = -\frac{2}{5}$ or 1

26. $d = -\frac{7}{5}$ or 1
27. $x = \frac{9}{4}$ or $-\frac{1}{3}$
28. $q = \dfrac{-6}{7}$ or $\dfrac{-7}{2}$
29. $x = -9$ or 3
30. $x = 1$ or -2
31. $x = \dfrac{1}{2}$ or $\dfrac{-2}{3}$
32. $x = -5$ or $\frac{1}{3}$
33. $a = 7$ or 4
34. $x = -4\frac{1}{2}$ or -2
35. $x = \frac{1}{2}$ or -2
36. $x = \frac{1}{5}$ or $1\frac{1}{2}$
37. $x = -5$ or $\dfrac{-3}{4}$
38. $x = 3$ or $\frac{1}{2}$
39. $b = \dfrac{-2}{7}$ or $\dfrac{4}{3}$
40. $x = \dfrac{-1}{3}$ or $\dfrac{5}{2}$
41. $w = \dfrac{-7}{4}$ or $\dfrac{4}{5}$
42. $x = 3$ or 8
43. $y = -1\frac{1}{2}$ or -2
44. $q = -3$ or $\frac{1}{5}$
45. $a = 1$ or -2
46. $x = -1$ or 3
47. $b = -1$ or 6
48. $y = -\frac{1}{2}$ or 1
49. $c = 1\frac{1}{2}$ or -5
50. $z = \dfrac{2}{5}$ or $\dfrac{-2}{3}$

Exercise 7g

1. $x = -2$ or -1
2. $x = -0.5$ or -2
3. $x = -\frac{1}{3}$ or -2
4. $x = 0.82$ or -1.82
5. $x = 1.79$ or -2.79
6. $x = 7.32$ or 0.68
7. $x = 5.45$ or 0.55
8. $x = 4.83$ or -0.83
9. $x = 3.56$ or -0.56
10. $x = 1.90$ or -1.23
11. $y = -2.85$ or 0.35
12. $y = 1.45$ or -3.45
13. $z = -4.37$ or 1.37
14. $p = -1.30$ or 2.30
15. $a = 1.30$ or -2.30

16. $a = -0.73$ or 2.73

17. $m = 1$ or -3

18. $z = -0.37$ or 1.37

19. $b = -0.22$ or -2.28

20. $a = -1.77$ or -0.57

21. $y = 0.26$ or -1.26

22. $x = -0.36$ or -4.14

23. $y = 3.41$ or 0.59

24. $y = 0.78$ or -1.28

Exercise 7h

1. $-7, 6$

2. $4, -4\frac{1}{2}; -4\frac{1}{2}$

3. $-8, 5; 5$

4. 6 cm

5. 3 cm

6. 2 m

7. 16 ft wide, 19 ft long

8. $1\frac{1}{2}$ m wide, 3 m long

9. 20 cm

10. 13 cm

11. 9 cm, 12 cm, 15 cm

12. $\dfrac{7}{(x-1)}; \dfrac{18}{x} + \dfrac{7}{x-1} = 6; x = 4\frac{1}{2}$ km/h

13. 2 km/h

14. 120 km/h

15. 15 m/min

Exercise 7i

2. no

3. $(x+1)$

4. $(x-1), (x+1)$

6. 24

7. $-\frac{3}{4}$

8. 9

9. $(x+1)(x-2)(x-3)$

10. $12; (x-1), (x-3)$

11. $0; 0;$ (a) 2 (b) $2, \pm\frac{1}{2}$

12. $(x-\frac{1}{3})(x+1)(x-3)$

13. $p = -10, q = 8$

14. $a = -2\frac{1}{2}, b = -\frac{1}{2}$

15. $a = 2$

16. 6

17. $p = 3, q = 4$

18. $p = 5, q = 4; (x-1)(x+2)$

Miscellaneous Exercise 7

1. (a) (i) 14 (ii) 8 (b) (i) 470 (ii) 3

2. (a) (i) $6p^2 - pq - 15q^2$ (ii) $\dfrac{a-1}{6}$

   (b) (i) $5ab(3ab - a + 5)$ (ii) $(4-y)(x-y)$
   (iii) $3ab(b-2a)$ (iv) $(x-5)(x-1)$

3. (a) $x = 1, y = 5$ (b) $x = 2, y = 3$
   (c) $x = 4, y = -3$

4. (a) $2x(3y+1)$ (b) $x^2(3 + 2xy)$
   (c) $4xy(3xy+1)$ (d) $(m+p)(n+2m)$
   (e) $(2r-s)(t-v^2)$ (f) $(x+7)(x-2)$
   (g) $(2x+7)(x-3)$

5. (a) $x = -4$ or -5 (b) $x = 3$ or -2
   (c) $x = -\frac{2}{3}$ or 1
   (d) $x = 1.47$ or -1.14
   (e) $x = 1.71$ or -3.21
   (f) $x = 3.79$ or -0.791

6. (a) $x = 2\frac{1}{2}$ (b) $x = 2, y = -1$
   (c) $x = 1\frac{1}{2}$ or -5

7. (a) $x = 2, y = -\frac{1}{3}$
   (b) (i) $-7\frac{1}{2}$ (ii) -3 or $\frac{1}{2}$ (iii) -5

8. (a) (i) $x^2 - 8x - 9$ (ii) $(x-8)(x+1)$

   (b) (i) $\dfrac{yx}{x}$ (ii) $\dfrac{y-c}{x}$

   (c) $x = -2, y = -1$

9. (a) &   (b) $\{2\}$ (c) $\emptyset$
   (d) $\{0, 8\}; -4$

10. (a) (i) 7 (ii) $\frac{1}{3}$ (b) $\dfrac{1-x}{2}$

    (d) $p = 0.57$ or -0.73

11. (a) $55°F$ (b) 100 chirps per minute
    (c) $40°F$ (d) $C = \dfrac{40}{9} + \dfrac{5N}{36}$

12. (a) nx (b) $\dfrac{nx}{y}$

13. (a) (i) 68 p (ii) $8y + 12$ (iii) $6x + 12$
    (iv) $8a + bx + 12$

    (b) $\dfrac{y-12}{8}$

14. (a) $\dfrac{ny}{x}$ grams;   (b) $£\dfrac{xz}{n}$

15. $x = 2, y = 1$

16. $b = £2.50, c = £3.50$

17. (a) 3 p   (b) $x = 7.54$ or 1.46

18. (a) $(x+1)(x-2)$ cm^2
    (b) 18 cm   (d) 13 cm by 16 cm

19. (a) $(x-1)$ cm   (b) $\dfrac{x}{1}; \dfrac{1}{x-1}$

    (c) 1.62 cm

20. $\dfrac{75}{V}$ h; $\dfrac{75}{V+20}$ h; $2\frac{1}{2}$ h; $37\frac{1}{2}$ km/h

Exercise 8a

1. (a) 5 (b) 8 (c) 5 (d) 9
   (e) 15 (f) -5
2. (a) 4 (b) 24 (c) 15 (d) 16
   (e) 25 (f) 6
3. (a) 1 (b) $1\frac{1}{2}$ (c) $1\frac{1}{2}$ (d) $3\frac{1}{2}$
   (e) $3\frac{1}{2}$
4. (a) 6 (b) 21 (c) 5 (d) 0
   (e) 0 (f) 1 (g) $x = 5$
   (h) $y = 5$ (i) $z = 7$
5. (a) $x = 2$ (b) $x = 5$ (c) $x = 0$
   (d) $x = -6$
6. (a) $x = 3$ (b) $x = 5$ (c) $x = 2$
   (d) $x = 2$
7. (a) 7 (b) 8 (c) $x = 9$
   (d) $x = 3$
8. (a) 9 (b) 11 (c) -9
   (d) $x = 8$ (e) $x = -8$ (f) $x = 5$
9. (a) 1 (b) 8 (c) 11
   (d) $x = 1$ (e) $x = 5$ (f) $x = 6$
10. (a) 7 (b) 21 (c) $x = 1$
    (d) $x = 12$ (e) 0 (f) 0
11. (a) 23 (b) 3 (c) -17
    (d) $x = 4$ (e) $y = 1\frac{3}{4}$ (f) $z = -\frac{3}{4}$
12. (a) -7 (b) 7 (c) 0
    (d) $0; a = \pm 5$

Exercise 8b

1. (a) 10 (b) 12 (c) 18 (d) 20; no
2. (a) 3 (b) 3 (c) 4 (d) 4; yes
3. (a) 5 (b) 5 (c) 13 (d) 13; yes
4. (a) 20 (b) 18; no
6. (a) 2 (b) $2\frac{1}{4}$; no
7. (a) 48 (b) 80 (c) 960
   (d) 960; yes; yes
8. (a) 9 (b) 7 (c) 14 (d) 14; yes
9. (a) 2 (b) 4 (c) 2 (d) 2; yes
10. (a) 0 (b) -2; no
11. (a) 13 (b) 13; yes

Exercise 8c

1. (a) (i) 4 (ii) 6 (iii) 7 (iv) $\frac{1}{2}$ (v) -1
   (vi) x
   (b) 3 (c) 3, 1 (d) 2
   (e) -2
2. (a) 5 (b) 7 (c) $-1; 2$
   (d) 0 (e) 3 (f) $-5; 0, 3, -5$
3. (a) $2\frac{1}{2}$ (b) 5 (c) 10 (d) 2
   (e) $\frac{2}{3}; \frac{2}{3}$ (f) $\frac{1}{2}, \frac{1}{2}$

4. -4
5. 11
6. (c) $\frac{1}{80}$
7. (a) 4 (b) 8 (c) 6 (d) 5
   (e) -2
8. (a) 3 (b) 1 (c) $2\frac{1}{2}$ (d) $2\frac{1}{3}$
   (e) $2\frac{1}{4}$
9. no
11. $0;$ (a) $-\frac{1}{2}$ (b) $-\frac{4}{5}$; no
12. (a) $\begin{pmatrix} 3 & 4 \\ 4 & 5 \end{pmatrix}$ (b) $\begin{pmatrix} 1 & 0 \\ 0 & 1 \end{pmatrix}$

Exercise 8d

1.

$\times$ mod. 6	1	2	3	4	5
1	1	2	3	4	5
2	2	4	0	2	4
3	3	0	3	0	3
4	4	2	0	4	2
5	5	4	3	2	1

(a) no
(b) 1; (i) 5 (ii) 1 (iii) 3 has no inverse
(c) 1 or 4

2.

$+$ mod. 9	0	3	6
0	0	3	6
3	3	6	0
6	6	0	3

(a) 0
(b) $0^{-1} = 0; 3^{-1} = 6; 6^{-1} = 3$
(c) yes

3.

$+$ mod. 9	0	3	6	7
0	0	3	6	7
3	3	6	0	1
6	6	0	3	4
7	7	1	4	5

(a) 0
(b) $0^{-1} = 0; 3^{-1} = 6; 6^{-1} = 3;$
    $7^{-1} (= 2)$ not in set (c)
(c) No

408

4.

× mod. 7	1	2	3	4	5	6
1	1	2	3	4	5	6
2	2	4	6	1	3	5
3	3	6	2	5	1	4
4	4	1	5	2	6	3
5	5	3	1	6	4	2
6	6	5	4	3	2	1

yes; 1; (a) 4 (b) 5 (c) 3
(d) $x = 3$ (e) $y = 6$

5.

× mod. 4	1	2	3
1	1	2	3
2	2	0	2
3	3	2	1

1; (a) 1
(b) 3; the set is not closed because
$2 \times 2 = 0$, $0 \notin \{1, 2, 3\}$; $2 * x = 1$ has no solution

Miscellaneous Exercise 8

1. (a) 24 (b) $2b^2 + ba$
   (c) $x = -6$

2. (a) 12 (b) $2b^2 - 3a$
   (c) $a = 0$ or 2

3. (a) $\frac{3}{4}$ (b) $1\frac{1}{5}$ (c) $x = 3$
   (d) $y = 8$ (e) $2\frac{3}{14}$
   (f) $1\frac{2}{3}$; the operation is not associative

4. (a) 5 (b) 125 (c) 46
   (d) 23 (e) 2 (f) 28
   (g) $x = 4$ (h) $y = 4$ (i) $z = 1$

5. (a) 57 (b) 9 (c) 2
   (d) 3 (e) 50 (f) 0
   (g) $x = 4$ (h) $y = 0$ or -2
   (i) $z = -3$ or 1

6. (a) (i) $1\frac{1}{5}$ (ii) $1\frac{13}{47}$ (iii) $\frac{1}{6}$
   (b) (i) $\frac{x}{2}$ (ii) $\frac{x}{4}$ (c) $x = 2\frac{4}{5}$

7. (a) -1 (c) 2; $1\frac{1}{2}$; $1\frac{1}{3}$;
   (d) $y = \frac{z - x}{1 - x}$ (e) $\frac{x}{x - 1}$

8. (a)

×	2	4	8	6
2	4	8	6	2
4	8	6	2	4
8	6	2	4	8
6	2	4	8	6

(b) (i) 6 (ii) 8

9. (a) the operation is commutative

(b)

*	1	2	3	4	0
1	2	0	0	2	1
2	0	3	3	0	4
3	0	3	3	0	4
4	2	0	0	2	1
0	1	4	4	1	0

(c) (i) $\{0\}$ (ii) $\{2, 3\}$ (iii) $\emptyset$

10. $Q = \begin{pmatrix} -1 & 0 \\ 0 & -1 \end{pmatrix}$ $R = \begin{pmatrix} -1 & -2 \\ 1 & 1 \end{pmatrix}$

(a)

×	I	P	Q	R
I	I	P	Q	R
P	P	Q	R	I
Q	Q	R	I	P
R	R	I	P	Q

(b)

×	1	3	9	7
1	1	3	9	7
3	3	9	7	1
9	9	7	1	3
7	7	1	3	9

Exercise 9a

1. (a) 2 (b) 6 (c) 8 (d) $\frac{2}{3}$
   (e) 0 (f) -10 (g) $-\frac{1}{2}$

2. (a) 3 (b) 19 (c) -5 (d) 5
   (e) 1 (f) 6 (g) 0

3. (a)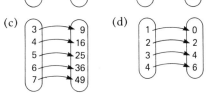

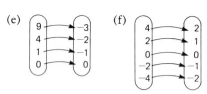

(e)

(f)

(c) $fh: x \to \frac{1}{4}x^2$

(d) $hf: x \to \frac{1}{2}x^2$

(e) $gh: x \to \frac{1}{2}x - 3$

(f) $hg: x \to \frac{1}{2}x - 1\frac{1}{2}$

9. (a) $fg: x \to x^{12}$ (b) $gf: x \to x^{12}$

Exercise 9c

1. $f^{-1}: x \to \dfrac{x-4}{2}$

2. (a) $f^{-1}: x \to 3(x+1)$

  (b) $g^{-1}: x \to \dfrac{4x-2}{3}$

3. $f^{-1}: x \to \frac{1}{2}x;$ (a) 8   (b) 4

4. $f^{-1}: x \to \frac{1}{4}x;$ (a) 16   (b) 4

5. $f^{-1}: x \to \dfrac{x-6}{5};$ (a) 26   (b) 4

6. $f^{-1}: x \to \dfrac{x-5}{3};$ (a) 17   (b) 4

7. $f^{-1}: x \to \dfrac{x+2}{6};$ (a) 22   (b) 4

8. $f^{-1}: x \to 2(x-1);$ (a) 3   (b) 4

9. $f^{-1}: x \to 4(x+2);$ (a) -1 (b) 4

10. $f^{-1}: x \to 3x-2;$ (a) 2   (b) 4

11. $f^{-1}: x \to 2x+5;$ (a) $-\frac{1}{2}$ (b) 4

12. $f^{-1}: x \to 8x+4;$ (a) 0   (b) 4

13. $f^{-1}: x \to \dfrac{1}{x};$ (a) $\frac{1}{4}$ (b) 4

14. $f^{-1}: x \to \dfrac{4}{x};$ (a) 1   (b) 4

15. $f^{-1}: x \to -x$ (a) -4 (b) 4

16. $f^{-1}: x \to \sqrt{x+1};$ (a) 15   (b) 4

17. $f^{-1}: x \to \sqrt{\dfrac{x-1}{2}};$ (a) 33   (b) 4

18. $f^{-1}: x \to \sqrt{\dfrac{x-2}{3}};$ (a) 50   (b) 4

19. $f^{-1}: x \to \sqrt{x}+1;$ (a) 9   (b) 4

20. $f^{-1}: x \to \dfrac{x^2-1}{2};$ (a) 3   (b) 4

21. (a) $g^{-1}: x \to \dfrac{x-1}{3}$ (b) 7   (c) 2

22. (a) $h^{-1}: x \to \dfrac{5-x}{2}$ (b) 7   (c) -1

23. (a) $j^{-1}: x \to 3-3x$ (b) -1 (c) 6

24. (a) $s^{-1}: x \to 1-2x$ (b) $\frac{1}{2}$ (c) $\frac{1}{4}$

25. (a) $f^{-1}: x \to 2-8x$ (b) 3   (c) $-\frac{1}{8}$

4. (a)

(b)

(c)

(d)

5. (a) $\frac{1}{2}$ (b) $\frac{1}{3}$ (c) 1   (d) $-\frac{1}{2}$

  (e) -1 (f) 2   (g) 3   (h) 4

6. (a) 6   (b) 12   (c) 6   (d) 12

  (e) 22   (f) $4\frac{1}{2}$

7. (a) 2   (b) 5   (c) -1 (d) $\frac{1}{3}$

  (e) $\frac{1}{2}$

8. (a) 0   (b) $-\frac{3}{2}$ (c) -4 (d) $-\frac{5}{2}$

  (e) 14   (f) 26   (g) -1 (h) $-\frac{1}{4}$

  (i) $-1\frac{3}{4}$

9. (a) 4   (b) $\frac{1}{2}$ (c) 0   (d) $-1\frac{1}{2}$

  (e) 5   (f) 3   (g) -2 (h) -3

10. (a) $2\frac{1}{2}$ (b) $1\frac{2}{3}$ (c) $2\frac{1}{3}$ (d) 1

11. (a) $-\frac{1}{2}$ (b) ± 1.73

12. (a) $-2, 4$ (b) $\frac{1}{4}, 1$ (c) $0, \frac{2}{3}$

Exercise 9b

1. (a) 5   (b) 3   (c) 10   (d) 5

  (e) 11   (f) 15   (g) 21   (h) 25

2. (a) $\frac{1}{2}$ (b) 4   (c) $\frac{1}{3}$ (d) 9

  (e) $\frac{1}{4}$ (f) $\frac{1}{9}$ (g) $\frac{1}{4}$ (h) $\frac{1}{9}$

3. (a) 9   (b) 2   (c) 6   (d) 8

  (e) 8   (f) $6; fg(x) = 3x - 3$

4. (a) 4   (b) 3   (c) 12

  (d) $6; jh(x) = 4x + 2$

5. (a) -2 (b) -2 (c) 10   (d) 6

  (e) -5 (f) 3

6. (a) 0   (b) 2   (c) 16   (d) 4

  (e) x (f) $(x-2)^2$

7. (a) 2   (b) 4

8. (a) $fg: x \to (x-3)^2$

  (b) $gf: x \to x^2 - 3$

Miscellaneous Exercise 9

1. (a) {negative odd numbers}
   (b) {positive even numbers}
   (c) {positive even numbers}
2. (a) {positive integers}
   (b) {positive integers}
   (c) {positive rational numbers}
3. (a) $\{\frac{1}{4}\}$ (b) $\{-2\frac{1}{2}\}$ (c) {0}
   (d) $\emptyset$ (e) {2} (f) {0, 1}
   (g) {0, 2} (h) {−1, 2}
4. (a) $1\frac{1}{3}$ or $2\frac{1}{3}$
   (b) $(x-2)(x-7)$; 2 or 7
   (c) 5.24 or 0.76
5. (a) 14 (b) 20 (c) 13
6. (a) 4 (b) 9 (c) 11 (d) 12
   (e) $\emptyset$ (f) 18
7. (a) 10; 5; 6 (b) 14; 16 or 7
   (c) {even numbers}; {odd numbers}
   (d) *ff* must halve
   (e) prints 2, 1, 2, 1, . . .
8. $g: x \to 2x$; $h: x \to x + 1$
9. (a) 0; 4 (b) *i*
   (c) $h: x \to 4 - x$; $i: x \to x^2$
   (d) *ih*
10. (b) $g^{-1}: x \to \dfrac{x}{3}$

   (c) (i) $f^{-1}g^{-1}: x \to \dfrac{x+3}{6}$

   (ii) $gf: x \to 3(2x - 1)$

   (iii) $(gf)^{-1}: x \to \dfrac{x+3}{6}$

Exercise 10a

1. Points are all on the line $y = 2x + 1$;
   yes; no
2. (4, 4)
3. no; three points
4. (a)

x	y
0	5
5	0
1	4

(b)

x	y
0	3
−3	0
1	4

(c)

x	y
0	−1
1	0
2	1

(a) and (b) intersect at (1, 4); (b) and (c)
are parallel − they do not intersect

5. all except (e) and (f)
6. (a)

x	y
0	7
$3\frac{1}{2}$	0
1	5

(b)

x	y
0	−1
$\frac{1}{2}$	0
1	1

(a) and (b) intersect at (2, 3); $x = 2$,
$y = 3$ is the solution to the equations of
the lines solved simultaneously

7. (a) $x = 4, y = 1$ (b) $x = 3, y = 6$
   (c) $x = 4, y = 3$ (d) $x = 1\frac{1}{2}, y = 2\frac{1}{2}$
   (e) $x = 1, y = 4$ (f) $x = 3, y = 2$

Exercise 10b

1. (a) (i) 4 (ii) 3 (b) (i) −1 (ii) 2
   (c) (i) −4 (ii) 5 (d) (i) 5 (ii) 4
   (e) (i) 1 (ii) 3 (f) (i) $-\frac{2}{3}$ (ii) $\frac{4}{3}$

2. $y = \dfrac{-5x + 3}{4}$; $\dfrac{-5}{4}$; $\dfrac{3}{4}$

3. $y = \dfrac{2x - 5}{6}$; $\dfrac{1}{3}$; $\dfrac{-5}{6}$

4. (a) (i) $-\frac{7}{2}$ (ii) $\frac{5}{2}$ (b) (i) $-\frac{1}{3}$ (ii) $\frac{5}{9}$
   (c) (i) $-\frac{5}{9}$ (ii) $\frac{8}{9}$ (d) (i) $\frac{3}{2}$ (ii) 1
   (e) (i) 1 (ii) 0 (f) (i) −2 (ii) $\frac{5}{2}$
5. (a), (c) and (e)
6. (d), (f), (g) and (i) are true
7. (a) $y = \dfrac{x}{3} + 1$ (b) $y = \dfrac{3x}{4}$

   (c) $y = \dfrac{x}{6} + 3$ (d) $y = -x + 5$

   (e) $y = \dfrac{x}{6}$ (f) $y = \dfrac{7x}{2} + \dfrac{1}{2}$

   (g) $y = -x + 6$ (h) $y = \dfrac{3x}{2} + \dfrac{1}{2}$

   (i) $y = 3$ (j) $y = \dfrac{2x}{3} + \dfrac{4}{3}$

   (k) $y = -5x + 16$ (l) $y = \dfrac{3x}{4} + \dfrac{1}{2}$

8. (a) 1 (b) 1 (c) −1 (d) $\frac{3}{5}$
   (e) −1 (f) $1\frac{1}{2}$ (g) 0 (h) −1
9. (a) $y = x + 1$ (b) $y = -\dfrac{x}{2} + 7$
   (c) $y = -x + 9$ (d) $y = -x + 5$
   (e) $y = \frac{2}{3}x$ (f) $y = 7$
   (g) $y = -\frac{5}{2}x + \frac{1}{2}$ (h) $y = 2x - 7$

10. (i) (d) (ii) (a) (iii) (e) (iv) (f) (v) (c)
    (vi) (b)

11. 18 square units

Miscellaneous Exercise 10

1.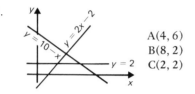

   A(4, 6)
   B(8, 2)
   C(2, 2)

   Area of $\triangle ABC = 12$ square units

2. (a) 1   (b) $-1\frac{1}{2}$ (c) 0   (d) 2
   (e) -2 (f) $\frac{1}{5}$ (g) $-\frac{1}{5}$ (h) -5

3. P(2, 4); R(8, 6); S(6, 2)
   $y = -\frac{1}{2}x + 10; y = 2x - 10$

4. (a) $A(0, 3); D(0, 12); AD = 9$ units
   (b) $F(4, 6)$
   (c) 18 square units; 30 square units

5.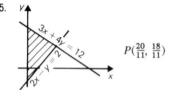

   $P(\frac{20}{11}, \frac{18}{11})$

6. $\{2, 5\}$

7. $y = x + 1; y = \frac{1}{2}x + 2\frac{1}{2}$
   $D(2, 1); \frac{1}{2}; 1$

8. (a) $4.4°C$ (b) $15.6°C$ (c) $59°F$
   (d) $89.6°F$
   $1.8; 32; y = 1.8x + 32$

9. gradient 2; intercept 3; $y = 2x + 3$

5.
   $\begin{array}{c}\leftarrow\!\!\!+\!\!\!-\!\!\!\circ\!\!\!-\!\!\!+\!\!\!-\!\!\!+\!\!\!-\!\!\!+\!\!\!\bullet\!\!\!-\!\!\!+\!\!\!\rightarrow \\ -2\ -1\quad 0\quad 1\quad 2\quad 3\end{array}$

6. $x < 5$
7. $x \geqslant 2$
8. $x \geqslant 1\frac{2}{3}$
9. $x < 24$
10. $x > \frac{1}{2}$
11. $x < -\frac{10}{3}$
12. $x \leqslant -3$
13. $x \geqslant 16$
14. $x < 7$
15. $x > 8$
16. $x < -\frac{5}{2}$
17. $x > 0$
18. $x < 15$
19. $x > 5$
20. $x > 23$
21. $x \leqslant 1$
22. $x \leqslant -13$
23. $x < 0$
24. $x < -\frac{3}{2}$
25. $x \leqslant \frac{2}{7}$
26. $x > \frac{3}{4}$
27. $x \leqslant -\frac{3}{2}$
28. $x > 2, x < -2$
29. $-5 < x < 5$
30. $x \leqslant -1.5, x \geqslant 1.5$
31. $x < -4, x > 4$
32. $x < 3$
33. (a) $\{3\}$ (b) $\{1, 2\}$ (c) $\{1, 2$
34. $\{1, 2\}$
35. $\{x \geqslant 2\}$
36. (a) $\{1, 2, 7, 8\}$ (b) $\emptyset$ (c) $\{1, 2$

Exercise 11a

1. (a) $1 \leqslant x \leqslant 5$ (b) $-2 \leqslant x < 2$
   (c) $-2 < x < 2$

2. (a) $\begin{array}{c}\leftarrow\!\!\!+\!\!\!\bullet\!\!\!-\!\!\!+\!\!\!-\!\!\!+\!\!\!-\!\!\!+\!\!\!\bullet\!\!\!-\!\!\!+\!\!\!\rightarrow \\ -4\ -3\ -2\ -1\ \ 0\ \ 1\ \ 2\end{array}$

   (b) $\begin{array}{c}\leftarrow\!\!\!+\!\!\!-\!\!\!+\!\!\!-\!\!\!+\!\!\!-\!\!\!+\!\!\!-\!\!\!\circ\!\!\!-\!\!\!\circ\!\!\!\rightarrow \\ 0\ \ 1\ \ 2\ \ 3\ \ 4\ \ 5\ \ 6\end{array}$

   (c) $\begin{array}{c}\leftarrow\!\!\!+\!\!\!-\!\!\!+\!\!\!-\!\!\!+\!\!\!-\!\!\!\circ\!\!\!-\!\!\!\bullet\!\!\!-\!\!\!+\!\!\!\rightarrow \\ 0\ \ 1\ \ 2\ \ 3\ \ 4\ \ 5\ \ 6\end{array}$

   (d) $\begin{array}{c}\leftarrow\!\!\!+\!\!\!-\!\!\!+\!\!\!-\!\!\!+\!\!\!-\!\!\!+\!\!\!-\!\!\!+\!\!\!-\!\!\!+\!\!\!\rightarrow \\ 0\ \ 1\ \ 2\ \ 3\ \ 4\ \ 5\ \ 6\ \ 7\end{array}$

3. (a) $\{0 \leqslant x \leqslant 2\}$ (b) $\{-3 \leqslant x < 4\}$
   (c) $\{x < -3, x > 2\}$ (d) $\{2 < x < 4\}$

4. (a) $\begin{array}{c}\leftarrow\!\!\!+\!\!\!-\!\!\!\circ\!\!\!-\!\!\!+\!\!\!-\!\!\!\bullet\!\!\!-\!\!\!+\!\!\!-\!\!\!+\!\!\!\rightarrow \\ 0\ \ 1\ \ 2\ \ 3\ \ 4\ \ 5\end{array}$

   (b) $\begin{array}{c}\circ\!\!\!-\!\!\!+\!\!\!-\!\!\!+\!\!\!-\!\!\!+\!\!\!-\!\!\!+\!\!\!-\!\!\!+\!\!\!-\!\!\!+\!\!\!\circ \\ -2\ -1\ \ 0\ \ 1\ \ 2\ \ 3\ \ 4\ \ 5\end{array}$

Exercise 11b

1. (a) $x \leqslant 2$ (b) $y < 4$
   (c) $x + y \leqslant 6$ (d) $y < 3x$

2. (a) (b)

   (c) 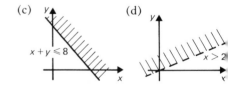 (d)

3. C
4. A
5. C

6.
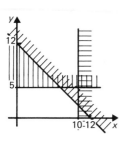

7.
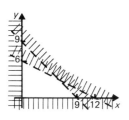

8.
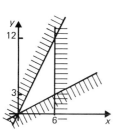

9.
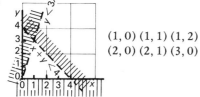

(1, 0) (1, 1) (1, 2)
(2, 0) (2, 1) (3, 0)

10.
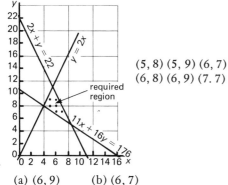

(5, 8) (5, 9) (6, 7)
(6, 8) (6, 9) (7. 7)

(a) (6, 9)   (b) (6, 7)

11.
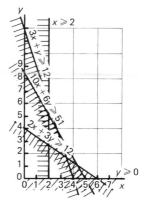

(a) $5\frac{1}{2}$ at $(4\frac{1}{2}, 1)$; $9\frac{1}{3}$ at $(2\frac{2}{3}, 4)$

(b) 6 at (6, 0), (5, 1) and (4, 2);
    10 at (3, 4) and (4, 2)

12. (a)
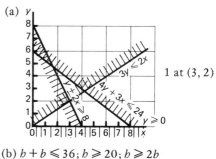

1 at (3, 2)

(b) $b + b \leqslant 36$; $b \geqslant 20$; $b \geqslant 2b$

Exercise 11c

1. (c) $3x + 2y \leqslant 42$; $4x + y \leqslant 36$
   (e) $P = 50x + 30y$
   (f) 6 whichits, 12 whatsits; £660

2. (a) $x + 2y$ hours
   (b) $x + 2y \leqslant 10$
   (c) $x + y \leqslant 9$
   (f) 8 batches of cakes, 1 batch of pies;
       profit £114

3. $b \geqslant 15$; $p > 25$; $45 \leqslant b + p < 60$;
   25 hardback, 30 paperback

4. (a) $x > y$ (b) $x < 3y$
   (c) $x + 2y < 120$
   (d) 39
   (e) 95 (71 children and 24 adults)

5. (a) $x > 2$; $y \geqslant 1$ (c) more small jars
   (f) 37

6. $x + y \geqslant 800$; $3y + 5y \leqslant 3600$; max.
   660 bottles Plonko; max profit is £420
   with 200 bottles of Plonko and 600
   Sofistiko

413

Miscellaneous Exercise 12

1.

x	-4	-3	-2	-1	0	1	2	3	4
x^2	16	9	4	1	0	1	4	9	16
-4	-4	-4	-4	-4	-4	-4	-4	-4	-4
y	12	5	0	-3	-4	-3	0	5	12

(a) -2 and 2   (b) -4
(c) (i) ± 2.8 (ii) ± 3.2
(d) $x = 4, x = -1$
(e) $y = 2x - 1$ intersects at $x = -1$ and 3
(f) 4

2.

x	-4	-3	-2	-1	0	1	2	3	4	5
x^2	$+16$	$+9$	$+4$	$+1$	0	1	4	9	16	25
$-x$	$+4$	$+3$	$+2$	$+1$	0	-1	-2	-3	-4	-5
-6	-6	-6	-6	-6	-6	-6	-6	-6	-6	-6
y	14	6	0	-4	-6	-6	-4	0	6	14

(a) -2 and 3
(b) (i) -3.4 (ii) -5.8 (iii) -2.6
(c) (i) 4.5 or -3.5 (ii) -0.64 or 1.64
    (iii) -3.3 or 4.3
(d) (i) $-2 < x < 3$ (ii) $-3.3 \leqslant x \leqslant 4.3$
(e) (i) $x < -3.4; x > 4.4$
    (ii) $x < -1.6; x > 2.6$
(f) $-3; +3$
(g) $y = 3 - x$ intersects at $x = \pm 3$
(h) $y = 2x - 2$ intersects at $x = 4$ and -1

3.

x	-5	-4	-3	-2	-1	0	1	2	3	4	5
y	-16	-7	0	5	8	9	8	5	0	-7	-16

(a) -3 and 3
(b) (i) 1.2 (ii) -4.7
(c) (i) ± 2.7 (ii) ± 2.2
(d) $-3 < x < 3$
(e) (i) $x < -2.4; x > 2.4$
    (ii) $x < -3.2; x > 3.2$
(f) $2; -4$
(g) $y = 5$ intersects at $x = \pm 2$
(h) $y = 2x + 1$ intersects at $x = -4$ and 2
    $x = 1.85$ or -4.85

4.

x	-3	-2.5	-2	-1.5	-1	-0.5
y	6	-1.875	-6	-7.125	-6	-3.375

x	0	0.5	1	1.5	2	2.5	3
y	0	3.375	6	7.125	6	1.875	-6

$0.6 < x < 2.3; y = x$ intersects at $x = 0$
and ± 2.45

5.

x	-1	-0.5	0	0.5	1	1.5	2	2.5
y	21	5.125	0	4.875	19	41.625	72	109.575

(a) $-0.49, 0.51$ (b) $-0.98, 1.03$
(c) 0

6. (b) $0.27; 3.73$
(c) $\dfrac{1}{x} = 4 - x; x^2 - 4x + 1 = 0$

7. (a)

x	1	1.5	2	3	4	5	6
y	6	3.17	2	1.33	1.5	2	2.67

(c) $1.75 < x < 5.75$
(e) 2.3

8. (a)

x	0	1	2	3	4	5	6
y	1	2	4	8	16	32	64

(c) 4.3   (d) $7\frac{1}{2}$ (e) 10

Exercise 13a

1. $2x$
2. $4x$
3. $3x^2$
4. $9x^2$
5. $6x$
6. 1
7. 5
8. 0
9. 0
10. $-x^{-2}$
11. $-4x^{-5}$
12. $-6x^{-3}$
13. $+15x^{-4}$
14. $\frac{1}{3}x^{-2/3}$
15. $\frac{2}{5}x^{-3/5}$
16. $-\frac{1}{2}x^{-3/2}$
17. $3x^{-1/4}$
18. $-\frac{3}{2}x^{-1/2}$
19. $\dfrac{-1}{x^2}$
20. $\dfrac{-9}{x^4}$
21. $\dfrac{-32}{x^5}$
22. $\dfrac{1}{x^6}$
23. $\frac{1}{2}x^{-1/2}$
24. $-2x^{-3/2}$
25. $\frac{3}{2}x^{1/2}$

414

26. 3

27. 5

28. -1

29. -2

30. $6x$

31. $6x - 2$

32. $10x + 6$

33. $12x^2 - 2$

34. $\frac{5}{2}x^{-1/2} + x^{-2}$

35. $\frac{14}{5}x^{-3/5} + \frac{1}{3}x^{-4/3}$

36. $2x - 1$

37. $18x^2 + 6x$

38. $2x$

39. $8x - 12$

40. $18x - 6$

41. $\dfrac{dy}{dx} = 2x$;

   (a) 2   (b) 4   (c) -6 (d) 0

42. $\dfrac{dy}{dx} = 6x - 2$;

   (a) 4   (b) 10   (c) -2 (d) -8

43. $\dfrac{dy}{dx} = 3x^2$;

   (a) 12   (b) 3   (c) 0   (d) 3

   (e) 12

44. $\dfrac{dy}{dx} = 12x^2 + 2$;

   (a) 14   (b) 14   (c) 2

45. $\dfrac{dy}{dx} = 12x^3 - 4x$;

   (a) 8   (b) 88   (c) -88

46. $\dfrac{dy}{dx} = \frac{1}{2}x^{-1/2}$;

   (a) $\frac{1}{2}$ (b) $\frac{1}{6}$ (c) 1

47. $\dfrac{dy}{dx} = -2x^{-3}$;

   (a) -2 (b) $+2$ (c) -16 (d) $-\frac{1}{4}$

48. $\dfrac{dy}{dx} = -\frac{1}{2}x^{-3/2}$;

   (a) $-\frac{1}{2}$ (b) -4 (c) -0.177

Exercise 13b

1. $\dfrac{dy}{dx} = 8x - 12$; $x = 2$; $y = -13$

2. $\dfrac{dy}{dx} = 6x - 12$; $x = 3$; $y = 6$

3. $\dfrac{dy}{dx} = 4x + 1$; $x = 1$; $y = 10$

4. (a) $(1, 2)$ (b) $(\frac{1}{2}, 2\frac{1}{4})$

   (c) $(1\frac{1}{2}, 3\frac{1}{4})$

5. (a) $(1, -5\frac{1}{2})$ (b) $(-1, -5\frac{1}{2})$

   (c) $(\frac{1}{2}, -5\frac{31}{32})$ (d) $(-\frac{1}{2}, -5\frac{31}{32})$

   (e) $(0, -6)$

6. $(1, 7)$; $(-1, 7)$

7. (a) $(4, 10)$ (b) $(4, 17)$

   (c) $(-\frac{3}{2}, -\frac{9}{4})$

   (d) $(-1, 15)$, $(3, -17)$

   (e) $(\frac{2}{3}, \frac{16}{9})$, $(-\frac{2}{3}, -\frac{16}{9})$

   (f) $(\frac{1}{2}, 2\frac{1}{4})$, $(1, 2)$

8. $\dfrac{dy}{dx} = 24x^2 - 6$; max. $(-\frac{1}{2}, 7)$;

   min. $(\frac{1}{2}, 3)$

9. max. $(1, 7)$; min $(3, 3)$

10. max. $(-2, 37)$; min. $(2, -27)$

11. $P(0, 23)$; $Q(1, 0)$; $R(2, -5)$; $S(3, -4)$

12. $A(0, -1)$; $B(0.4, -1.01)$; $C(1, 0)$

Exercise 13c

1. $50\,\text{m}^2$

2. $\dfrac{400}{x}$; $\dfrac{dP}{dx} = 2 - 800x^{-2}$

3. $\dfrac{dA}{dx} = 4x - \dfrac{256}{x^2}$; $96\,\text{m}^2$

4. 256

5. 12.65

6. (a) $\dfrac{200}{x}\,\text{h}$ (b) $\dfrac{3200}{x} + \dfrac{x}{2}$

   (c) 80 km/h

7. $y = 24 - 8x$; 2; $A_{max} = 144\,\text{cm}^2$

8. $2x^2 + 6xh$; $\dfrac{dV}{dx} = 200 - 2x^2$;

   $x = 10$ cm; $V = 1333\frac{1}{3}\,\text{cm}^3$

9. (a) $18 - 2x$

   (b) $4x^2 - 72x + 324$

   (c) $4x^3 - 72x^2 + 324x$

Exercise 13d

1. $\dfrac{x^3}{3} + C$

2. $x^3 + C$

3. $\dfrac{x^4}{4} + C$

4. $x^4 + C$

5. $6x + C$

6. $2x + C$

7. C

8. $x^6 + C$

9. $\dfrac{5x^7}{7} + C$

10. $-x^{-1} + C$

11. $-\dfrac{x^{-3}}{3} + C$

12. $-3x^{-1} + C$

13. $\frac{5}{2}x^{-2} + C$

14. $\frac{3}{4}x^{4/3} + C$

15. $\frac{5}{7}x^{7/5} + C$

16. $\frac{3}{2}x^{2/3} + C$

17. $\frac{16}{7}x^{7/4} + C$

18. $-2x^{3/2} + C$

19. $-3x^{-1} + C$

20. $2x^{-2} + C$

21. $3x^{-4} + C$

22. $x^{-3} + C$

23. $\frac{2}{3}x^{3/2} + C$

24. $8x^{1/2} + C$

25. $\frac{2}{5}x^{5/2} + C$

26. $\frac{3}{2}x^2 - x + C$

27. $\frac{5}{2}x^2 + 2x + C$

28. $3x - \dfrac{x^2}{2} + C$

29. $5x - x^2 + C$

30. $x^3 - 2x + C$

31. $x^3 - x^2 + x + C$

32. $\frac{5}{3}x^3 + 3x^2 - 2x + C$

33. $x^4 - x^2 + x + C$

34. $4x^{3/2} - 2x^{1/2} + C$

35. $5x^{7/5} - \frac{3}{2}x^{2/3} + C$

36. $\dfrac{x^3}{3} - \dfrac{x^2}{2} + C$

37. $x^4 + \frac{2}{3}x^3 + C$

38. $\dfrac{x^3}{3} - x + C$

39. $\frac{4}{3}x^3 - 6x^2 + 9x + C$

40. $3x^3 - 3x^2 + x + C$

Exercise 13e

1. 25

2. 25

3. -1

4. -5

5. $\frac{3}{4}$

6. $y = 9x - 3x^2 + \frac{1}{3}x^3 - 9$

7. $k = 3 \,; \, y = x^3 - 3$

8. $k = 4 \,; \, y = x^4 - x^2 - \frac{1}{2}$

Exercise 13f

1. 1

2. $\frac{1}{2}$

3. $4\frac{1}{2}$

4. 6

5. 6

6. $\frac{1}{2}$

7. $\frac{7}{24}$

8. $\frac{2}{3}$

9. $-1\frac{7}{8}$

10. $12\frac{2}{3}$

11. $11\frac{1}{4}$

12. 1016

13. 2

14. 624

15. 4

16. 56

17. $2\frac{2}{3}$

18. $333\frac{1}{3}$

19. 8

20. $9\frac{1}{3}$

21. -48

22. 24

23. $\frac{2}{5}$

24. $21\frac{1}{3}$

25. 20

26. $12\frac{2}{3}$

27. $\frac{5}{6}$

28. $4\frac{1}{2}$

29. $1\frac{1}{3}$

30. $1\frac{1}{3}$

31. $\frac{1}{6}$

32. $1\frac{1}{3}$

33. $(-1, 9), (5, 9); 36$

34. (a) $(1, 6), (-3, 6); 10\frac{2}{3}$
    (b) $(1, 4), (5, 4); 10\frac{2}{3}$
    (c) $(2, 5), (5, 5); 4\frac{1}{2}$
    (d) $(3, 1), (6, 4); 4\frac{1}{2}$
    (e) $(-1, 4), (4, 9); 20\frac{5}{6}$

35. $(3, 2), (2, 2); \frac{1}{3}$

36. (a) $(2, 0), (5, 9); 9$
    (b) $(4, 3), (2, 1); 2\frac{2}{3}$
    (c) $(0, 4), (1\frac{1}{2}, 1\frac{3}{4}); 1\frac{1}{8}$

Exercise 14a

1. 40 km
2. 105 min
3. 9.40 a.m.
4. 10.17 a.m.; 48 km from Ayton
5. (a) 3 km/h   (b) $5\frac{1}{2}$km/h; 11 km
   (c) 3 km/h
6. (a) 16 km/h   (b) 14.4 km/h
   (c) 18 km/h; 11.43 a.m. and 12.15 p.m.
7. (c) (i) 3.40 p.m. (ii) 30 m.p.h.
   (iii) 40 m.p.h. (iv) 3.15 p.m.
8. (a) (ii) 12.46 p.m.
   (b) (ii) 2.06 p.m. (iii) 1.26 p.m.;
       67 miles from A

Exercise 14b

1. (a) 15 m/s   (b) 4 m/s^2
   (c) 124.5 m   (d) 8.9 m/s
2. (a) 18 m/s   (b) 3.5 m/s^2
   (c) 4.5 m/s^2 (d) 260 m
   (e) 10.8 m/s
3. $10v$ m; 20 m/s
4. 50 m; 30 m/s
5. (a) 90 m   (b) 720 m
   (c) 22.5 m/s
6. 10 m/s; 325 m
7. 830 m
8. (a) 15.6 m/s   (b) 1.6 s   (c) 1.11 m/s^2
   (d) 160 m
9. -2; 40;
   (a) 0.65 s or 3.85 s
   (b) 2.25 s   (c) 15 m/s^2

Exercise 14c

1. (a) $v = 2t + 4$ (b) $a = 2$
   (c) 33 m; 10 m/s; 2 m/s^2
2. (a) $v = 3t^2 - 6t$ (b) $a = 6t - 6$
   (c) 0 m/s; 9 m/s; 12 m/s^2
3. (a) $v = 8t - 3$ (b) $a = 8$
   (c) 33 m; 21 m/s; 8 m/s^2
4. (a) $v = 6t^2 + 6t + 4$
   (b) $a = 12t + 6$
   (c) 92 m; 76 m/s; 42 m/s^2
5. (a) $v = -2t$ (b) $a = -2$
   (c) 91 m; -6 m/s; -2 m/s^2
6. (a) $v = 5$ (b) $a = 0$
   (c) 21 m; 5 m/s; 0 m/s^2
7. (a) $v = -4 + t$ (b) $a = 1$
   (c) -7.5 m; -1 m/s; 1 m/s^2
8. (a) $v = 2t^{-1/2}$ (b) $a = -t^{-3/2}$
   (c) 6.93 m; 1.15 m/s; -0.19 m/s^2

9. (a) $v = -25$ m/s   (b) $v = 75$ m/s
   (c) $a = 0$ m/s^2 (d) $a = 20$ m/s^2; 5 s
10. $v = 6t^2 - 18t + 12$; 5 m, -6 m/s^2
    4 m, 6 m/s^2
11. (a) $12t^2 - 6t - 6$ (b) 1 s
    (c) $a = 24t - 6$ (d) $\frac{1}{4}$ s
12. (a) 2 m   (b) never
    (c) -3 m/s   (d) 1 s or 3 s
13. (a) 8 m   (b) 3 m/s
    (c) 0.3 s; 8.45 m   (d) 1.6 s; -13 m/s
14. (a) 24 m   (b) 37 m/s
    (c) 3.7 s; 92.45 m   (d) 8 s; -43 m/s

Exercise 14d

1. (a) $v = 2t^2 + 2$ (b) $s = \frac{2}{3}t^3 + 2t$
   (c) 12 m/s^2; 20 m/s; 24 m
2. (a) $v = \dfrac{3t^2}{2} + 3$ (b) $s = \dfrac{t^3}{2} + 3t$
   (c) 9 m/s^2; 16.5 m/s; 22.5 m
3. (a) $v = -\dfrac{t^2}{4} + 6$ (b) $s = -\dfrac{t^3}{12} + 6t$
   (c) $-1\frac{1}{2}$ m/s^2; $3\frac{3}{4}$ m/s; $15\frac{3}{4}$ m
4. (a) $v = 6t - \frac{1}{3}t^2 + 2$ (b) $s = 3t^2 - \dfrac{t^4}{12} + 2t$
   (c) -3 m/s^2; 11 m/s; $26\frac{1}{4}$ m
5. (a) $v = 4t + 7$ (b) $s = 2t^2 + 7t$
   (c) 4 m/s^2; 19 m/s; 39 m
6. (a) $v = -t + 3$ (b) $s = -\frac{1}{2}t^2 + 3t$
   (c) -1 m/s^2; 0 m/s; 4.5 m
7. (a) $v = 100t - \frac{1}{3}t^3 + 5$
   (b) $s = 50t^2 - \dfrac{t^4}{12} + 5t$
   (c) 91 m/s^2; 296 m/s; $458\frac{1}{4}$ m
8. (a) $v = \frac{8}{3}t^{3/2} + 4$ (b) $\frac{16}{15}t^{5/2} + 4t$
   (c) 6.9 m/s^2; 17.9 m/s; 28.6 m
9. (a) $v = -\frac{2}{5}t^{5/2} + 6$ (b) $s = -\frac{4}{35}t^{7/2} + 6t$
   (c) -5.2 m/s^2; -0.24 m/s; 12.7 m
10. (a) $v = 4t^{1/2} + 2$ (b) $s = \frac{8}{3}t^{3/2} + 2t$
    (c) 1.15 m/s^2; 8.93 m/s; 19.86 m
11. $\frac{7}{30}$ m
12. (a) -8 m/s^2 (b) 303.3 m

Exercise 15a

1. (a) right angle   (b) acute angle
   (c) reflex angle   (d) obtuse angle
2. (a) opposite   (b) alternate
   (c) corresponding   (d) alternate
   (e) corresponding

3. (a) $70°$ (b) $40°$ (c) $120°$
    (d) $70°$ (e) $100°$ (f) $45°$
5. $a = b = e = g = 32°$;
    $c = d = f = 148°$
6. $x = 25°$
7. $a = 55°$; $b = 55°$; $c = 45°$; $d = 80°$
8. $a = c = 75°$; $b = d = e = 105°$
9. $a = 100°$; $b = 80°$; $c = 100°$;
    $d = 60°$; $e = 120°$; $f = 60°$
10. $a = 55°$; $b = 70°$; $c = 110°$; $d = 55°$
11. $x = 20°$
12. $x = 63°$
13. $x = 85°$; $y = 113°$
14. $p = 82°$; $q = 56°$; $r = 42°$; $s = 82°$;
    $t = 56°$
15. $x = 30°$; $y = 40°$; $z = 110°$
16. $x = 70°$; $y = 35°$; $z = 35°$
17. $a = 30°$; $b = 50°$; $c = 100°$; $d = 80°$
18. $a = 130°$; $b = 50°$; $c = 80°$; $d = 100°$

Exercise 15c

1. (a) $026°$ (b) $018°$ (c) $351°$
    (d) $255°$ (e) $168°$ (f) $107°$
2. (a) $40°$ (b) $5°$ (c) $325°$
    (d) $264°$ (e) $228°$ (f) $117°$
3. (a) $035°$ (b) $325°$ (c) $145°$
    (d) $215°$
4. (a) $180°$ (b) $135°$ (c) $225°$
    (d) $315°$
5. $138°$
6. $327°$
7. $229°$
8. $054°$
9. $219°$
10. $135°$
11. (a) $108°$ (b) $173°$
12. 23 km; $245°$
13. 161 km; $056°$
14. $242°$; 1.4 km; $8\frac{1}{2}$ min
15. $300°$; 64 km; 19 h

Exercise 16a

1. (a) $x = 70°$ (b) $x = 60°$, $y = 60°$
    (c) $x = 140°$ (d) $x = 35°$, $y = 55°$
    (e) $x = 30°$ (f) $x = 60°$, $y = 40°$
    (g) $x = 75°$, $y = 30°$
    (h) $x = 100°$, $y = 40°$
2. 10 cm^2
3. 12 cm
4. 8 cm
5. AP $= 12$ cm; AC $= 18$ cm
6. 10 cm
7. 8 cm

Exercise 16b

1. $\frac{3}{2}$; $x = 4\frac{1}{2}$, $y = 2\frac{2}{3}$
2. $\frac{2}{1}$; $x = 1.8$, $y = 1.5$
3. $\frac{3}{2}$; $x = 6$, $y = 4\frac{1}{2}$
4. $\frac{2}{1}$; $x = 13$, $y = 24$
5. $\frac{5}{4}$; $x = 7\frac{1}{2}$, $y = 8\frac{3}{4}$
6. $\frac{4}{3}$; $x = 4\frac{1}{2}$, $y = 4$
7. $\frac{2}{3}$; $x = 9.45$, $y = 6.3$
8. $\frac{2.1}{1}$; $x = 3.36$, $y = 3.78$
9. $\frac{5}{7}$; $x = 7.5$, $y = 5.6$
10. $\frac{3}{5}$; $x = 5.4$, $y = 4.5$
11. $\frac{3}{2}$; $x = 15$, $y = 22\frac{1}{2}$
12. $\frac{5}{4}$; $x = 2\frac{1}{2}$, $y = 3\frac{1}{8}$
13. $1 : 9$
14. $4 : 3$
15. LN $= 6$, ST $= 6\frac{2}{3}$; 32 square units
16. 2 cm; 5.5 cm; $24\frac{3}{4} \text{ cm}^2$
17. AXD and BXC are similar; 2 cm; $2\frac{1}{2}$ cm; 5 cm
18. 9 cm; 18 cm; 40 cm^2; 130 cm^2

Exercise 16c

1. (a) RHS   (b) SAS   (c) ASA
    (d) SSS   (e) SAS   (f) ASA

Miscellaneous Exercise 16

1. $u = 70°$; $v = 35°$; $w = 35°$; $x = 35°$;
    $y = 75°$
2. $A\widehat{B}F = 120°$; $B\widehat{C}F = 30°$;
    $C\widehat{F}G = 30°$; $B\widehat{F}C = 90°$
3. $u = 62°$; $v = 72°$; $w = 53°$; $x = 55°$;
    $y = 9°$; $z = 63°$
4. (a) $16 : 12 : 15$ (b) $256 : 144 : 225$
5. AD $= 18$ cm; DC $= 32$ cm
10. (a) $\frac{4}{9}$ (b) $\frac{2}{5}$ (c) $\frac{21}{25}$ (d) $\frac{2}{5}$
11. (c) $\frac{1}{2}$ (d) $\frac{1}{4}$
12. (b) 2400 cm^2, $20\frac{1}{4}$ cm

Exercise 17a

1. $x = 35°$; $y = 145°$
2. $x = 106°$; $y = 74°$
3. $x = 110°$; $y = 70°$
4. $x = 150°$; $y = 90°$
5. $x = 90°$; $y = 63°$
6. $x = 30°$; $y = 80°$
7. $x = 45°$; $y = 70°$
8. $x = 40°$; $y = 140°$
9. $x = 90°$; $y = 40°$

418

10.
| parallelogram |
| rectangle |
| rhombus |
| square |

11. (a) 21 cm^2 (b) 15 cm^2
   (c) 1.86 cm^2 (d) 24 cm^2
12. 3 cm; no
13. kite; 18 square units
14. 84.5 m^2
21. (a) rectangle
   (b) kite or isosceles trapezium
   (c) kite or trapezium

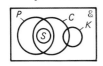

Exercise 17b

1. 180°; 540°
2. 4; 720°
3. 900°; 128.6°
4. 1080°; 135°
5. a square
6. (a) 4   (b) 5
7. 60°, 80°, 100°, 140°, 160°
8. (a) 144°, 108°, 72°, 144°, 108°, 144°
   (b) 1 : 2 : 3 : 1 : 2 : 1
9. 13
10. 15

Miscellaneous Exercise 18

1. (a)   (b)

  (c)   (d)

  (e)   (f)

  (g)   (h)

  (i)   (j)

(k)   (l)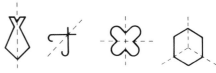

2. c, 4; d, 6; f, 3; g, 2; h, 2; i, 2; l, 2
3. c, d, g, h, i and l
4. kite, isosceles trapezium
5. rectangle, rhombus
6. parallelogram
7. rectangle
8.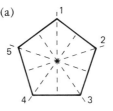

9. (i) (a)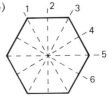

   (b)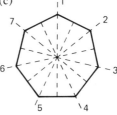

   (c)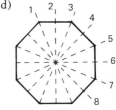

   (d)

   (ii) 5, 5, 5   6, 6, 6   7, 7, 7   8, 8, 8
   (iii) (b) and (d)
10. (a) (i) X, A, T   (ii) EXC   (iii) X
   (b)

419

11. (a) rectangle
    (b) square, isosceles trapezium or kite
    (c) parallelogram
    (d) rectangle or square
    (e) rectangle
12. 9; 3; infinite number

Exercise 19a

1. (a) 10   (b) 25   (c) 61   (d) 15
   (e) 84   (f) 3.9   (g) 12.0   (h) 5.0
   (i) 1.6   (j) 14.5   (k) 22   (l) 51.3
   (m) 18.0   (n) 5.39   (o) 6.2
2. 10.5 cm
3. 7.07 cm
4. 6 cm
5. 7.75 cm; 15.5 cm^2
6. 13 cm^2
7. 112 cm
8. 116.6 cm
9. 25
10. 13
12. $x = 33.5$ cm; $y = 36.7$ cm; $z = 39.7$ cm

Exercise 19b

1. (a) 14.1 cm   (b) 10 cm
   (c) 11.5 cm   (d) 1.09 cm
   (e) 8.72 cm   (f) 8.07 cm
   (g) 4.02 cm   (h) 15.4 cm
2. (a) 45° (b) 30° (c) 23.6°
   (d) 55.8° (e) 65.4° (f) 51.1°
   (g) 38.7° (h) 31.8°
3. (a) $x = 4.10$ cm, $y = 2.87$ cm
   (b) $x = 9.00$ cm, $y = 13.5$ cm
   (c) $x = 23.2$ cm, $y = 24.6$ cm
   (d) $x = 67.4^\circ$, $y = 26$ cm
   (e) $x = 51.3^\circ$, $y = 38.7^\circ$, $z = 6.24$ cm
   (f) $x = 56.9^\circ$, $y = 33.1^\circ$, $z = 9.22$ cm
4. 13.1 cm, 11.0 cm
5. (a) 9.14 cm   (b) 33.2°
6. $b = 11.3$ cm, 56.6 cm^2
7. 29.4 cm^2
8. 3.02 cm, 16.9 cm^2
9. 18.2 m
10. 46.3 m
11. 76.1°; 4.85 m

Exercise 19c

1. (a) 14.0 m   (b) 0 948 cm
   (c) 4.11 mm
   (d) $x = 4.26$ cm, $y = 4.61$ cm
   (e) $x = 19.5$ cm, $y = 21.9$ cm
   (f) $x = 4.63$ m, $y = 3.18$ m
   (g) 8.28 mm   (h) 8.01 cm

2. 10.9 cm; 49.0 cm^2
3. 2.76 m; 1.46 m^2
4. 13.7 m^2
5. 2.97 cm; 8.92 cm^2

Exercise 19d

1. 39 cm; 40.8 cm; 17.1°
2. 1.41 m; 4.24 m; 70.5°
3. (a) 4.24 m   (b) 45°
   (c) 35.3° (d) 70.5°
4. 51.3°; 77.4°
5. (a) 87.5 m   (b) 306°
   (c) 1.72 km   (d) 2.91°
6. (a) 7.07 cm   (b) 11.2 cm; 70.5°

Exercise 19e

1. (a) 38.7° (b) 51.7° (c) 28.3°
   (d) 6.39 cm   (e) 3.05 cm   (f) 65.8°
2. (a) 28.6 mm   (b) 41.8 cm
   (c) 37.3 cm   (d) 7.70 cm
   (e) 10.0 cm
3. (a) 79.5°, 56.1°, 44.4°
   (b) 41.4°, 55.8°, 82.8°
   (c) 125.0°, 42.1°, 12.9°
   (d) 110.5°, 41.3°, 28.1°
4. (a) $\widehat{A} = 64.9^\circ$; $\widehat{B} = 50.1^\circ$; $CB = 13.0$ cm
   (b) $\widehat{B} = 73.0^\circ$; $\widehat{C} = 59.0^\circ$; $AC = 16.7$ cm
   (c) $\widehat{X} = 33.9^\circ$; $\widehat{Z} = 43.1^\circ$; $XZ = 17.1$ cm
   (d) $\widehat{P} = 48.1^\circ$; $\widehat{R} = 21.9^\circ$; $PR = 42.9$ mm
   (e) $\widehat{R} = 56.1^\circ$; $\widehat{S} = 87.4^\circ$; $\widehat{T} = 36.5^\circ$
   (f) $\widehat{M} = 47.9^\circ$; $\widehat{N} = 96.4^\circ$; $\widehat{O} = 35.7^\circ$

Miscellaneous Exercise 19

1. (a) 0.6   (b) 0.8   (c) 4.8 cm
   (d) 6.4 cm   (e) 39.36 cm^2
2. (a) 40 cm; 24 cm
   (b) (i) $B\widehat{A}C$ (ii) 20 cm (iii) 30 cm
3. (a) 10 cm   (b) 34.6 cm   (c) 73.9°
4. (a) 68.0° (b) 1.35 cm   (c) 2.91 cm
5. (b) (i) 40 m (ii) 28 m (iii) 35°
6. (a) 54.0° (b) 35.0 m   (c) 35.2 m
   (d) 431 m^2 (e) 22.6°
7. (a) 13 cm; 13.34 cm; 17 cm
   (b) 50.7° (c) 85.5 cm^2
8. (a) 1.7 cm
   (b) (i) 170 cm^2 (ii) 150 cm^2; 2%
9. (a) 6 cm   (b) 13 cm   (c) $\frac{5}{12}$
10. 12.5°; 5.53 m^2; 43.95°; 4.03 m; 29.8°

11. (a) 15 m   (b) 17 m   (c) 33.7°
    (d) 28.1°
12. 3608 m; 028.4°; 1948 m; 18 s

Exercise 20a

1. 9.14 cm²; 12.3 cm
2. 14.1 cm²; 21.4 cm
3. 8.05 cm²; 14.1 cm
4. 2.86 cm²; 12.3 cm
5. 21.5 cm²
6. 62.8 cm²
7. 6.28 cm²
8. 75.4 cm²
9. (a) 6.28 cm; 15.7 cm²
   (b) 18.8 cm; 75.4 cm²
   (c) 40.8 cm; 306 cm²
10. (a) 2.5 cm   (b) 27 cm   (c) 12.5 cm
    (d) 5.95 cm
11. (a) 5 cm   (b) 15 cm   (c) 200 cm
    (d) 3.16 cm
12. 201 m; 497
13. 21 cm
14. 491 cm²
15. (a) 50 cm²   (b) 78.5 cm²
    (c) 28.5 cm²
16. (a) 9.06 cm²   (b) 6.72 cm²
17. 74.8 cm²

Exercise 20b

1. 30°
2. 50°
3. 90°
4. 65°
5. 133°
6. 40°
7. 130°
8. 140°
9. 20°
10. 90°
11. 35°
12. 52°
13. $x = 90°; y = 90°; z = 58°$
14. $x = 40°; y = 100°; z = 50°$
15. $x = 116°; y = 64°; z = 116°$
16. $x = 95°; y = 85°; z = 85°$
17. $x = 26°; y = 26°; z = 64°$
18. $x = 250°; y = 125°; z = 55°$
19. $x = 90°; y = 48°; z = 42°$
20. $x = 28°; y = 51°; z = 28°$
21. $x = 40°; y = 40°; z = 25°$
22. $x = 33°; y = 33°; z = 123°$

23. $x = 60°; y = 120°; z = 20°$
24. $x = 30°; y = 60°; z = 78°$

Exercise 20c

1. 55°
2. 60°
3. 63°
4. 60°
5. $x = 70°; y = 55°; z = 55°$
6. $x = 48°; y = 84°; z = 48°$
7. $x = 60°; y = 60°; z = 120°$
8. $x = 32°; y = 48°; z = 42°$
9. $x = 53°; y = 53°; z = 74°$
10. $x = 62°; y = 110°; z = 35°$
11. $x = 90°; y = 31°; z = 59°$
12. $x = 42°; y = 28°; z = 110°$
13. $x = 55°; y = 35°; z = 65°$

Exercise 20d

1. (a) 4 cm   (b) $12\frac{1}{2}$ cm   (c) 14 cm
   (d) 18 cm
2. (a) 12 cm   (b) 30 cm   (c) $16\frac{1}{2}$ cm
   (d) 3 cm
3. (a) 12 cm   (b) 12 cm
4. $y = 4\frac{1}{2}$
5. $y = 3$
6. $y = 5$
7. $y = 9; z = 8$
8. $y = 8$
9. $y = 7.75; z = 11$
10. $y = 6; z = 4.8$
11. $y = 9$
12. $y = 1$ or 8
13. $y = 1.66; z = 4$
14. $y = \frac{1}{2}; z = 1\frac{1}{2}$

Miscellaneous Exercise 20

1. (a) 17 cm   (b) 44°
2. 51 cm²
3. (a) 3.14 cm   (b) 33.7 cm   (c) 42.4 cm²
   (d) 10.7 cm
4. (a) (i) 29 300 km/h   (ii) 10°S
   (b) (i) 9548 km   (ii) 3200 km
5. (a) 5 cm   (c) 10.6 cm
6. (a) 20°   (b) 110°
7. (a) 50°   (b) 100°   (c) 25°
8. (a) 118°   (b) 28°   (c) 34°
9. (a) 54°   (b) 18°   (c) 126°
10. $f = 50°; g = 100°; h = 130°; i = 80°;$
    $j = 40°; k = 40°; l = 50°$
11. (a) 100°   (b) 60°   (c) 80°
12. 90°; 90°; 58°; 32°; 90°; 58°; 29°; 119°

Exercise 21a

1. 1131 m^3; 377 m^2
2. 8 m^3; 24 m^2
3. 101 cm^3; 7.21 cm; 141 cm^2
4. 83.3 cm^3
5. 4189 cm^3; 1257 cm^2
6. 4021 cm^3; 1407 cm^2
7. 3 m^3; 13 m^2
8. 60 cm^3; 132 cm^2
9. 14.4 cm^3
10. sphere ($33.5 \text{ cm}^3 > 27 \text{ cm}^3$)
    cube ($54 \text{ cm}^2 > 50.3 \text{ cm}^2$)
12. 1.73 m^3
13. 1.5 m^2
14. 16 m^2; 96 m^3
15. 1.16 m^2; 2.32 m^3
16. 94.2 cm^3
17. 9.43 cm^3; $9.43 \text{ cm}^3/\text{s}$
18. $0.0126 \text{ m}^3/\text{s}$; 64 min

Exercise 21b

1. (a) 6 cm^2, 24 cm^2, 54 cm^2
   (b) 1 cm^3, 8 cm^3, 27 cm^3
   (c) $1:4:9$ (d) $1:8:27$

2. (a) $4\pi \text{ cm}^2$, $16\pi \text{ cm}^2$, $36\pi \text{ cm}^2$
   (b) $\dfrac{4\pi}{3} \text{ cm}^3$, $\dfrac{32\pi}{3} \text{ cm}^3$, $36\pi \text{ cm}^3$
   (c) $1:4:9$ (d) $1:8:27$

3. $\dfrac{2\pi}{3} \text{ cm}^3$, $\dfrac{16\pi}{3} \text{ cm}^3$, $18\pi \text{ cm}^3$; $1:8:27$

4. 3
5. 25
6. 113.1 cm^3; 113.1 cm^2; $113\,100 \text{ cm}^3$; $11\,310 \text{ cm}^2$
7. 75 cm^3; 4800 cm^3
8. 40 litres
9. 220 ml
10. (a) 18 cm   (b) 382 cm^3
    (c) 269 cm^3
11. 2.88 m; $1.25 \text{ cm} \times 0.875 \text{ cm}$
12. (a) $p = 8 \text{ cm}$, $q = 7\frac{1}{2} \text{ cm}$, $r = 9 \text{ cm}$,
    $s = 15 \text{ cm}$
    (b) (i) 250 cm^2, (ii) 360 cm^2
    (c) (i) 437.5 cm^3 (ii) 224 cm^3

Miscellaneous Exercise 21

1. (a) 5 cm; 11 cm   (b) 102 cm^2
   (c) $10\,200 \text{ cm}^3$ (d) 23.5 kg

2. $60°$; (a) 35.8 cm^2 (b) 272 cm^2 (c) 67.9%
   (d) 358 cm^3;
   (b) $\times 4$; (c) no change; (d) $\times 8$
3. (a) 37.8 m^2 (b) 454 m^3
   (c) 3.9 m   (d) 277 m^2
4. (a) 14 m^2 (b) 34.6 m^2
   (c) 19 800 kg
5. (a) 634.28 cm^2 (b) 251.2 g
   (c) 62.8 g
6. (a) $270\,000 \text{ cm}^2$ (b) $415\,800 \text{ cm}^3$
   (c) 3850 cm^2
   (d) 108 cm; 83 times
7. (a) 71.5 cm^3 (b) 248 cm^2
   (c) 11
8. (a) 26 cm   (b) 397 cm^2
   (c) 4610 cm^3 (d) 1450 cm^2

Miscellaneous Exercise 22

1. (a) 3922 km   (b) 5281 km
   (c) 1968 km   (d) 2892 km
2. (a) 7188 km   (b) 1697 km
3. (a) 7338 km   (b) 3447 km
4. (a) 20 012 km   (b) 40 024 km
5. (a) 3660 nautical miles; 6778 km
   (b) 122 h; 55.6 km/h
6. 3523 km
7. (a) 4002 km   (b) 14 400 km
8. (a) $(51°\text{N}, 20°\text{W})$
   (b) 8672 km; 9795 km
9. 7227 km; 5920 km; 3890 km

Exercise 23a

1. (a) 1×3 (b) 2×2 (c) 1×2
   (d) 2×1
   (e) 3×2; (a) and (c) are row matrices,
   (d) is a column matrix

2. (a) $\begin{pmatrix} 6 & 4 \\ 3 & 10 \end{pmatrix}$ (b) $\begin{pmatrix} -2 & 2 \\ -1 & -6 \end{pmatrix}$
   (c) $\begin{pmatrix} 14 & 26 \\ 8 & 17 \end{pmatrix}$

3. (a) not possible   (b) $\begin{pmatrix} 10 \\ 12 \end{pmatrix}$
   (c) $(11 \ \ 4 \ \ 1)$
   (d) $\begin{pmatrix} 7 & 10 \\ 15 & 22 \end{pmatrix}$ (e) $\begin{pmatrix} 37 & 54 \\ 81 & 118 \end{pmatrix}$
   (f) $\begin{pmatrix} 1 & 0 \\ 3 & 4 \end{pmatrix}$

4. (a) $\begin{pmatrix} 5 & 1 \\ 4 & 2 \end{pmatrix}$ (b) $\begin{pmatrix} 3 & 1 \\ 0 & 0 \end{pmatrix}$ (c) $\begin{pmatrix} 8 & 2 \\ 4 & 2 \end{pmatrix}$

(d) $\begin{pmatrix} 7 & 2 \\ 2 & 1 \end{pmatrix}$ (e) $\begin{pmatrix} 18 & 4 \\ 12 & 6 \end{pmatrix}$ (f) $\begin{pmatrix} 43 & 10 \\ 26 & 13 \end{pmatrix}$

(g) $\begin{pmatrix} 2 & \frac{1}{2} \\ 1 & \frac{1}{2} \end{pmatrix}$ (h) $\begin{pmatrix} -8 & -2 \\ -4 & -2 \end{pmatrix}$

(i) $\begin{pmatrix} \frac{1}{4} & 0 \\ \frac{1}{2} & \frac{1}{4} \end{pmatrix}$ (j) $\begin{pmatrix} \frac{3}{4} & 0 \\ 1\frac{1}{2} & \frac{3}{4} \end{pmatrix}$ (k) $\begin{pmatrix} 2\frac{1}{4} & \frac{1}{2} \\ 1\frac{1}{2} & \frac{3}{4} \end{pmatrix}$

(l) $\begin{pmatrix} -7\frac{1}{4} & -2 \\ -2\frac{1}{2} & -1\frac{1}{4} \end{pmatrix}$

(m) $\begin{pmatrix} 6 & 1 \\ 4 & 1 \end{pmatrix}$ (n) $\begin{pmatrix} 4 & 1 \\ 10 & 3 \end{pmatrix}$ (o) $\begin{pmatrix} 18 & 5 \\ 10 & 3 \end{pmatrix}$

(p) $\begin{pmatrix} 1 & 0 \\ 4 & 1 \end{pmatrix}$ (q) $\begin{pmatrix} 1 & 0 \\ 8 & 1 \end{pmatrix}$ (r) $\begin{pmatrix} 40 & 7 \\ 28 & 5 \end{pmatrix}$

5. (a) $\begin{pmatrix} 3 & 0 \\ 6 & 3 \\ 3 & 6 \end{pmatrix}$ (b) $\begin{pmatrix} 4 & 2 & 4 \\ 6 & 4 & 2 \end{pmatrix}$

(c) not possible

(d) $\begin{pmatrix} 6 & 5 \\ 8 & 4 \end{pmatrix}$ (e) $\begin{pmatrix} 2 & 1 & 2 \\ 7 & 4 & 5 \\ 8 & 5 & 4 \end{pmatrix}$

(f) $\begin{pmatrix} 1 & 0 \\ \frac{1}{2} & 1 \end{pmatrix}$ (g) $\begin{pmatrix} 4 & 0 \\ 4 & 4 \end{pmatrix}$ (h) $\begin{pmatrix} 16 & 0 \\ 32 & 16 \end{pmatrix}$

(i) $\begin{pmatrix} 2 & 0 \\ 5 & 2 \\ 4 & 4 \end{pmatrix}$ (j) $\begin{pmatrix} 12 & 10 \\ 16 & 8 \end{pmatrix}$

(k) $\begin{pmatrix} 12 & 10 \\ 16 & 8 \end{pmatrix}$ (l) not possible

(m) $(0 \ -4)$ (n) (5)

(o) $\begin{pmatrix} 1 & -2 \\ -2 & 4 \end{pmatrix}$

(p) $\begin{pmatrix} 1 \\ 0 \\ -3 \end{pmatrix}$ (q) $(-4 \ -3 \ 0)$

(r) $\begin{pmatrix} 2 \\ -3 \end{pmatrix}$ (s) $\begin{pmatrix} 12 \\ -18 \end{pmatrix}$ (t) $\begin{pmatrix} 12 \\ -18 \end{pmatrix}$

(u) $\begin{pmatrix} 2 & 0 \\ 5 & 2 \\ 4 & 4 \end{pmatrix}$ (v) $\begin{pmatrix} 4 & 2 & 4 \\ 8 & 5 & 4 \end{pmatrix}$

6. $a = 3$, $b = 2$
7. $x = 3$, $y = -1$
8. $a = 1$, $b = -1$, $c = 2$, $d = -8$
9. $a = 1$, $b = -2$
10. $x = 2$, $y = 4$

Exercise 23b

1. $\begin{pmatrix} 1 & 0 \\ 0 & 1 \end{pmatrix}$; $\begin{pmatrix} -7 & 4 \\ 2 & -1 \end{pmatrix}$

2. $\begin{pmatrix} 1 & 0 \\ 0 & 1 \end{pmatrix}$; $\begin{pmatrix} \frac{1}{2} & -\frac{1}{4} \\ -\frac{1}{2} & \frac{3}{4} \end{pmatrix}$

3. (a) (i) 1 (ii) $\begin{pmatrix} 7 & -2 \\ -3 & 1 \end{pmatrix}$

(b) (i) 1 (ii) $\begin{pmatrix} 3 & -1 \\ -11 & 4 \end{pmatrix}$

(c) (i) -1 (ii) $\begin{pmatrix} -3 & 2 \\ 5 & -3 \end{pmatrix}$

(d) (i) 3 (ii) $\frac{1}{3}\begin{pmatrix} 3 & -5 \\ -3 & 6 \end{pmatrix}$

(e) (i) 2 (ii) $\frac{1}{2}\begin{pmatrix} 2 & -2 \\ -3 & 4 \end{pmatrix}$

(f) (i) 2 (ii) $\frac{1}{2}\begin{pmatrix} 5 & -2 \\ -9 & 4 \end{pmatrix}$

(g) (i) 9 (ii) $\frac{1}{9}\begin{pmatrix} 1 & 0 \\ -1 & 9 \end{pmatrix}$

(h) (i) 2 (ii) $\frac{1}{2}\begin{pmatrix} 4 & -6 \\ -3 & 5 \end{pmatrix}$

(i) (i) 6 (ii) $\frac{1}{6}\begin{pmatrix} 2 & -2 \\ -1 & 4 \end{pmatrix}$

(j) (i) -2 (ii) $\frac{1}{2}\begin{pmatrix} -4 & 6 \\ 3 & -4 \end{pmatrix}$

(k) (i) 2 (ii) $\frac{1}{2}\begin{pmatrix} 3 & -4 \\ -4 & 6 \end{pmatrix}$

(l) (i) -2 (ii) $\frac{1}{2}\begin{pmatrix} -4 & 3 \\ 6 & -4 \end{pmatrix}$

4. (a) -1 (b) 18 (c) $\begin{pmatrix} -5 & 3 \\ 2 & -1 \end{pmatrix}$

(d) $\frac{1}{18}\begin{pmatrix} 5 & -8 \\ 1 & 2 \end{pmatrix}$

5. (a) -5 (b) $\frac{1}{3}\begin{pmatrix} 3 & -6 \\ -2 & 5 \end{pmatrix}$

(c) 6 (d) 4 (e) $\frac{1}{4}\begin{pmatrix} 2 & -1 \\ -2 & 3 \end{pmatrix}$

6. (a) $\begin{pmatrix} 1 & -2 \\ -1 & 3 \end{pmatrix}$ (b) $\frac{1}{4}\begin{pmatrix} 3 & -2 \\ -1 & 2 \end{pmatrix}$

(c) $\begin{pmatrix} 8 & 12 \\ 3 & 5 \end{pmatrix}$ (d) $\frac{1}{4}\begin{pmatrix} 5 & -12 \\ -3 & 8 \end{pmatrix}$

(e) $\begin{pmatrix} 8 & 6 \\ 6 & 5 \end{pmatrix}$ (f) $\frac{1}{4}\begin{pmatrix} 5 & -6 \\ -6 & 8 \end{pmatrix}$

(g) $\frac{1}{4}\begin{pmatrix} 5 & -6 \\ -6 & 8 \end{pmatrix}$ (h) $\frac{1}{4}\begin{pmatrix} 5 & -12 \\ -3 & 8 \end{pmatrix}$

7. 0; all of them
8. (a) $x = 2$ (b) $x = \pm4$ (c) $y = \pm3$
   (d) $x = 6$ (e) $x = 4$ (f) $z = 14$
   (g) $a = -5$

Exercise 23c

1. $x = 6, y = -1$
2. $x = 4, y = 2$
3. $M = \begin{pmatrix} 2 & 3 \\ 1 & 1 \end{pmatrix}$; $M^{-1} = \begin{pmatrix} -1 & 3 \\ 1 & -2 \end{pmatrix}$;

   $x = 2, y = 1$
4. $\begin{pmatrix} 2 & -3 \\ -3 & 5 \end{pmatrix}$;

   (a) $x = 3, y = -2$ (b) $a = -1, b = 3$
5. $x = -1, y = 2$
6. $x = 10, y = -7$
7. $x = 1\frac{1}{2}, y = 1\frac{1}{2}$
8. $x = 3, y = 5$
9. $a = 5\frac{1}{2}, b = -2$
10. $p = 4.3, q = 2.1$
11. $x = 2, y = \frac{1}{2}$
12. $x = 2, y = 2$
13. $x = 6\frac{2}{3}, y = -2\frac{1}{3}$
14. $x = 2\frac{3}{4}, y = \frac{1}{2}$
15. $x = -4.8, y = -1.2$
16. $x = 1.4, y = 5.5$

Exercise 23d

1. (a) $\begin{pmatrix} 6 & 2 & 2 \\ 4 & 4 & 2 \\ 3 & 1 & 5 \end{pmatrix}$

(b) $\begin{pmatrix} 10 \\ 10 \\ 9 \end{pmatrix}$ = games played

(c) $\begin{pmatrix} 2 \\ 1 \\ 0 \end{pmatrix}$ (d) $\begin{pmatrix} 14 \\ 12 \\ 7 \end{pmatrix}$

2. (a) $\begin{pmatrix} 2 & 1 & 2 \\ 3 & 2 & 1 \end{pmatrix}$ (b) $\begin{pmatrix} 30 \\ 70 \\ 80 \end{pmatrix}$; $\begin{pmatrix} 290 \\ 310 \end{pmatrix}$

(c) (600) = total spent

3. (a) $\begin{pmatrix} 800 & 900 & 500 \\ 1000 & 1200 & 200 \end{pmatrix}$

(b) $(5800 \quad 6900 \quad 1500)$ = units used

(c) $\begin{pmatrix} 0.5 \\ 0.3 \\ 0.1 \end{pmatrix}$ (d) (5120)

4. $\begin{pmatrix} 3000 & 420 & 1320 & 150 \\ 3100 & 425 & 1320 & 140 \end{pmatrix}\begin{pmatrix} 0.24 \\ 0.40 \\ 1.00 \\ 2.00 \end{pmatrix}$;

$\begin{pmatrix} 2508 \\ 2514 \end{pmatrix}$; $(1 \quad 1)$; (5022)

Miscellaneous Exercise 23

1. (a) $x = 3$ (b) $x = \pm2$ (c) $x = 2$
2. $a = 1, b = 4$
3. (a) $\begin{pmatrix} -4 & 4 \\ -7 & 6 \end{pmatrix}$; $\begin{pmatrix} 4 & 3 \\ -4 & -2 \end{pmatrix}$; $\begin{pmatrix} 7 & 4 \\ 12 & 7 \end{pmatrix}$;

   $\begin{pmatrix} 2 & -1 \\ -3 & 2 \end{pmatrix}$

   (b) $m = 4, n = -1$ (c) $\begin{pmatrix} -1\frac{1}{2} & -1 \\ \frac{1}{4} & 0 \end{pmatrix}$

4. (a) $a = 4, b = -2$

   (b) $\begin{pmatrix} 2 & -1\frac{1}{2} \\ -1 & 1 \end{pmatrix}$; $\begin{pmatrix} -2\frac{1}{2} & -3 \\ 2 & 2 \end{pmatrix}$

   (c) $\begin{pmatrix} -6 & 2 \\ -15 & 5 \end{pmatrix}$

5. (a) $\begin{pmatrix} 5 & -6 \\ -4 & 5 \end{pmatrix}$ (b) $\begin{pmatrix} 7 \\ -3 \end{pmatrix}$

   (c) $\begin{pmatrix} -1 & -2 \\ 0 & 2 \end{pmatrix}$

6. (a) $\begin{pmatrix} 2 & -1 \\ 1 & 0 \end{pmatrix}$; $\begin{pmatrix} 1 & -1 \\ \frac{1}{2} & 0 \end{pmatrix}$; $\begin{pmatrix} 1\frac{1}{2} & -2 \\ 1 & -1 \end{pmatrix}$

   (b) $\begin{pmatrix} -1 & 2 \\ -2 & 2 \end{pmatrix}$; $\begin{pmatrix} -2 & 4 \\ -2 & 3 \end{pmatrix}$

   (c) $\begin{pmatrix} 1 & -1 \\ 1 & -\frac{1}{2} \end{pmatrix}$; $\begin{pmatrix} 1\frac{1}{2} & -2 \\ 1 & -1 \end{pmatrix}$

7. (a) $2x - 9$; 4.5
   (b) $x^2 + 6x - 8$; -7.12, 1.12

8. (a) $\begin{pmatrix} 2 & 4 & 1 \\ 3 & 1 & 2 \end{pmatrix}$

   (b) $\begin{pmatrix} 30 \\ 22 \end{pmatrix}$ = weekly spending

   (c) (1 1)

9. (a) $\begin{pmatrix} 63 \\ 26 \\ 57 \end{pmatrix}$ = each child's money

   (b) $\begin{pmatrix} 1 \\ 1 \\ 1 \\ 1 \\ 1 \end{pmatrix}$

   (c) (4 1 2 3 2) = number of coins of each value

   (d) (1 1 1) $\mathbf{Q}$ $\begin{pmatrix} 1 \\ 2 \\ 5 \\ 10 \\ 50 \end{pmatrix}$

10.

*	A	B	C	D
A	D	C	B	A
B	C	D	A	B
C	B	A	D	C
D	A	B	C	D

   (a) **D**   (b) **B**
   (c) (i) **D** (ii) **D** (iii) **C**

Exercise 24a

1. $(5, 4), (6, 6), (4, 5)$; $\begin{pmatrix} -3 \\ -2 \end{pmatrix}$

2. (a) $\begin{pmatrix} 3 \\ -3 \end{pmatrix}$ (b) $\begin{pmatrix} 3 \\ 0 \end{pmatrix}$ (c) $\begin{pmatrix} -1 \\ 1 \end{pmatrix}$

   (d) $\begin{pmatrix} -3 \\ 0 \end{pmatrix}$ (e) $\begin{pmatrix} -5 \\ -6 \end{pmatrix}$ (f) $\begin{pmatrix} 14 \\ -17 \end{pmatrix}$

3. $\begin{pmatrix} 3 \\ 5 \end{pmatrix}$

4. $\begin{pmatrix} 4 \\ -4 \end{pmatrix}$; $(6, -1)$

5. (a) $\begin{pmatrix} -2 \\ -1 \end{pmatrix}$ (b) $\begin{pmatrix} 1 \\ -2 \end{pmatrix}$ (c) $\begin{pmatrix} -3 \\ 1 \end{pmatrix}$

   (d) $\begin{pmatrix} -5 \\ -3 \end{pmatrix}$ (e) $\begin{pmatrix} -4 \\ 2 \end{pmatrix}$

6. $\begin{pmatrix} 4 \\ -4 \end{pmatrix}$

Exercise 24b

1. (a)   (b)

   (c)   (d)

2. $A'(1, -1)$; $B'(5, -1)$; $C'(4, -3)$; $D'(2, -3)$
3. reflection in $y = -x$ equivalent to
$$\begin{pmatrix} 0 & -1 \\ -1 & 0 \end{pmatrix}$$
4. $x = 3$
5. $x = 1$
7. $y = x$; $(3, 2)$
8. another glide: reflection in y-axis and

   translation of $\begin{pmatrix} 0 \\ 2 \end{pmatrix}$

10. reflections in $y = x$ and $y = -x$

Exercise 24c

1. (a)   (b)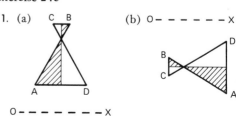

(c)

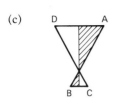

O – – – – – – – – X

(d) O – – – – – – – – X

2. $A'(-1, 1); B'(-1, 5); C'(-3, 4); D'(-3, 2)$

3. rotation by $180°$; $\begin{pmatrix} -1 & 0 \\ 0 & -1 \end{pmatrix}$

4. $(6, 1); 270°$
5. (a) $(1, 1)$ (b) $(3, 2)$
6. $90°$
7. $(5, 5)$
8. rotation by $180°$
10. (a) identity   (b) rotation by $90°$
    (c) rotation by $180°$

Exercise 24d

4. (a) $A'(2, 2); B'(10, 2); C'(8, 6); D'(4, 6)$
   (b) 24 square units
5. $1\frac{1}{2}$ square units
6. (a) $-1\frac{1}{2}; (0, 0)$ (b) $\begin{pmatrix} -1\frac{1}{2} & 0 \\ 0 & -1\frac{1}{2} \end{pmatrix}$

   (c) $13\frac{1}{2}$ square units
   (d) $2\frac{1}{4} = (-1\frac{1}{2})^2$
7. (c) $9:1$ (e) $\frac{1}{3}; (1, 4)$
8. (c) 4 (e) $(2, 0); \frac{1}{2}$
9. (d) $(3, 0); -2$

Exercise 24e

1. (a) $\frac{2}{1}$ (b) $\frac{3}{1}$ (c) $\frac{2}{1}$ (d) $\frac{3}{1}$ (e) $\frac{1}{2}$
2. (a) $A'(2, 1); B'(10, 1); C'(8, 3); D'(4, 3)$

   (b) $\begin{pmatrix} \frac{1}{2} & 0 \\ 0 & 1 \end{pmatrix}$; x-stretch

   (c) ABCD
3. (b) y-stretch

   (c) enlargement $\begin{pmatrix} 2 & 0 \\ 0 & 2 \end{pmatrix}$

426

5. (b) $M^{-1}\begin{pmatrix} 1 & 2 \\ 0 & 1 \end{pmatrix}$; another shear

   (c) ABCD

7. (a) (i) $\begin{pmatrix} 10 & 3 \\ 3 & 1 \end{pmatrix}$ (ii) $\begin{pmatrix} 1 & 3 \\ 3 & 10 \end{pmatrix}$

   (c) (i) 1 unit (ii) 1 unit

Miscellaneous Exercise 24

1. **M** is a reflection in x-axis;
   E is an enlargement, scale factor 2, centred on origin
2. (c) rotation of $180°$, centre $(-1, 2)$
   (f) $y = x - 2$
3. (a) rotation about the origin of $120°$, $360°, 300°$
   (b) $LM = R^2; ML = R^4$
   (c) LMN is a reflection in m; LML is a reflection in n
4. (a) (ii) rotation of $240°$
   (b) (ii) reflection in m
5. reflection in $x = -1\frac{1}{2}$
6. (b) U is an enlargement. centre $(0, 0)$, scale factor 3
   (e) V is a reflection in $y = -x$
7. $(0, 2); 90°; P'(-3, 6), Q'(-3, 10), R'(-5, 6)$
8. (e) 3   (f) $1:3:9$

Exercise 25a

2. (a) $\begin{pmatrix} 4 \\ 5 \end{pmatrix}$ (b) $\begin{pmatrix} 1 \\ 7 \end{pmatrix}$ (c) $\begin{pmatrix} 6 \\ 0 \end{pmatrix}$ (d) $\begin{pmatrix} 3 \\ -6 \end{pmatrix}$

   (e) $\begin{pmatrix} 0 \\ -6 \end{pmatrix}$ (f) $\begin{pmatrix} 2 \\ 7 \end{pmatrix}$

3.

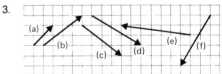

4. (a) $2.83, 45°$ (b) $5, 37°$
   (c) $5, 323°$ (d) $5.83, 329°$
   (e) $7.07, 172°$ (f) $5.83, 239°$
5. (a) $13, 67.4°$ (b) $13, 112.6°$
   (c) $13, 247.4°$ (d) $13, 292.6°$
   (e) $13, 22.6°$ (f) $13, 202.6°$
6. (a) $\begin{pmatrix} -3 \\ -2 \end{pmatrix}$ (b) 3.61 (c) 3.61
7. (a) $6.4, 128.7°$ (b) $12.8, 128.7°$
   (c) $16.01, 128.7°$; the vectors are parallel
8. **c** $\parallel$ **e**

Exercise 25b

3. $12.8; 19.2; 3.2; 16.0$

4. $\begin{pmatrix} 4 \\ 3 \end{pmatrix}$

5. $\begin{pmatrix} -2 \\ 5 \end{pmatrix}$

6. $\begin{pmatrix} 2 \\ 8 \end{pmatrix}$

7. $\begin{pmatrix} 4 \\ 9 \end{pmatrix}$

8. $\begin{pmatrix} -4 \\ 5 \end{pmatrix}$

9. $\begin{pmatrix} 5 \\ 1 \end{pmatrix}$

10. $\begin{pmatrix} 2\frac{1}{2} \\ \frac{1}{2} \end{pmatrix}$

11. $\begin{pmatrix} -9 \\ -3 \end{pmatrix}$

12. $\begin{pmatrix} -7 \\ -18 \end{pmatrix}$

13. $\begin{pmatrix} 4 \\ \frac{1}{2} \end{pmatrix}$

14. $\begin{pmatrix} 21 \\ -2 \end{pmatrix}$

15. $\begin{pmatrix} -9 \\ 10 \end{pmatrix}$

16. 1
17. 3
18. -2 or 3
19. 2
20. $m = 0, n = 2$
21. $p = 1\frac{1}{2}, q = \frac{1}{4}$
22. $r = 0, s = 2$
23. $c = -2$
24. $x = 5$

Exercise 25c

1. (a) $-a$ (b) $b-a$ (c) $a-b$
   (d) $2a+b$

2. (a) b (b) a (c) $a+b$
   (d) $b-a$ (e) $-b$ (f) $-a$
   (g) $-a-b$ (h) $a-b$

3. (a) $b-a$ (b) $d-b$ (c) $c-b$
   (d) $d-a$ (e) $a-d$ (f) $b-d$
   (g) $c-d$ (h) $-d$

4. (a) $b-a$ (b) $b-a$ (c) $-a$
   (d) $\frac{1}{2}b$ (e) $-\frac{1}{2}b$ (f) $\frac{1}{2}b-a$
   (g) $a-\frac{1}{2}b$

5. (a) c (b) $a+c$ (c) $c-a$
   (d) $-a$ (e) $-c$ (f) $a-c$
   (g) $2(a-c)$ (h) $2a-c$ (i) $a-2c$
   (j) $a+c$

6. (a) $q-p$ (b) $\frac{3}{4}(q-p)$
   (c) $\frac{3}{4}q+\frac{1}{4}p$

7. (a) $2a$ (b) $2a+b$ (c) $b-a$
   (d) $a+b; \overrightarrow{OP} = \frac{1}{3}(2a+b); 1:2$

8. (a) b (b) $b-2a$ (c) $\frac{2}{3}(b-2a)$
   (d) $\frac{2}{3}(a+b)$ (e) $2b-2a$ (f) $b-a$
   (g) $a+b$
   $2:1; \overrightarrow{OL} = a; \overrightarrow{BL} = a-2b; \overrightarrow{BA} = 2a-2b$
   $\overrightarrow{BG} = \frac{2}{3}(a-2b) = \frac{2}{3}BL$

9. $\overrightarrow{AB} = b-a; \overrightarrow{MN} = 3(b-a);$
   $\overrightarrow{AX} = \frac{1}{4}(3b-a); \overrightarrow{BX} = \frac{1}{4}(3a-b);$
   $\overrightarrow{BM} = 3a-b$

10. (a) $2v$ (b) $2v+z$ (c) $z-v$
    (d) $\frac{1}{3}(z-v)$
    (e) $v+\frac{1}{3}(z-v) = \frac{1}{3}(2v+z) = \frac{1}{3}\overrightarrow{OW}$

12. (a) $\overrightarrow{PQ} = a+2b; \overrightarrow{PR} = 6a+12b$
    (c) PR and XZ are parallel; their ratio is $1:6$

Exercise 25d

1. $346°$
2. $102°$
3. (a) $039°$ (b) 6 min   (c) 400 m
4. (a) $034°$ (b) 2 min   (c) 66.7 m
5. $37°; 3$ km/h; 10 min
6. $48°; 2$ min 41 s
7. (a) 130 km/h; $337°$
   (b) $025°$; 109 km/h
8. (a) $030°$; 22.4 knots
   (b) $066°$
9. (a) $028°$; 24.7 knots   (b) $057°$
10. $120°$; 91.5 min; $330°$; 161 min

Miscellaneous Exercise 25

1. (a) 5 (b) 5 (c) 7.1; no
   (d) 3.5 (e) 5 (f) 13.0

2. (a) (i) $\begin{pmatrix} 16 \\ -12 \end{pmatrix}$ (ii) $\begin{pmatrix} -5 \\ 5\frac{1}{2} \end{pmatrix}$ (iii) $h = 7, k = 2$
   (b) $\overrightarrow{PQ} = q-p; \overrightarrow{OM} = \frac{1}{2}(p+q)$

3. (a) (i) $-\mathbf{p}$ (ii) $\mathbf{p}+\mathbf{q}$ (iii) $\mathbf{p}-\mathbf{q}$
$\mathbf{OU}=\frac{1}{2}(\mathbf{p}-\mathbf{q}); \mathbf{OV}=\frac{1}{4}(\mathbf{p}+\mathbf{q})$
(b) $\mathbf{OS}=\mathbf{u}-\mathbf{v}=\frac{1}{4}\mathbf{p}-\frac{3}{4}\mathbf{q}$
(c) $\mathbf{p}=\mathbf{u}+2\mathbf{v}; \mathbf{q}=2\mathbf{v}-\mathbf{u}; \mathbf{OA}=2\mathbf{u}+\mathbf{v}$

V . . . A
. . .
O U

4. (a) (i) $\mathbf{b}-\mathbf{a}$ (ii) $\frac{3}{4}(\mathbf{b}-\mathbf{a})$ (iii) $\frac{1}{4}(3\mathbf{b}+\mathbf{a})$
(iv) $2(\mathbf{b}-\mathbf{a})$
(b) (i) $40°$ (ii) $2\frac{1}{2}$
5. (a) $\mathbf{OB}=\mathbf{a}+\mathbf{c}; \mathbf{OP}=\frac{3}{4}(\mathbf{a}+\mathbf{c});$
$\mathbf{AP}=\frac{3}{4}\mathbf{c}-\frac{1}{4}\mathbf{a}$
(b) $\mathbf{OQ}=(1-\frac{1}{4}x)\mathbf{a}+\frac{3}{4}x\mathbf{c}$
(c) $\mathbf{OQ}=\mathbf{c}+y\mathbf{a}$
(d) $x=1\frac{1}{3}; y=\frac{2}{3}$
(e) $\frac{2}{1}$
6. (a) (i) $\mathbf{b}-\mathbf{a}$ (ii) $\frac{1}{4}(\mathbf{b}-\mathbf{a})$ (iii) $\frac{3}{4}\mathbf{a}+\frac{1}{4}\mathbf{b}$

(b) (i) $\begin{pmatrix}3\\4\end{pmatrix}$ (ii) $\sqrt{5}$ (iii) $(2,-1)$

$5l+m=8; 3l+m=2; l=3, m=-7$
7. $\overrightarrow{SA}=\frac{2}{3}\mathbf{p}; \overrightarrow{AP}=\frac{1}{3}\mathbf{q}; \overrightarrow{SP}=\frac{1}{3}(2\mathbf{p}+\mathbf{q});$
$\overrightarrow{PQ}=\frac{1}{3}(2\mathbf{q}-\mathbf{p}); \overrightarrow{QS}=-\frac{1}{3}\mathbf{p}-\mathbf{q};$
$\overrightarrow{PR}=\frac{1}{3}\mathbf{q}-\mathbf{p}$ 2.98 at $333°$
8. (a) $\mathbf{a}$ (b) $\mathbf{a}-\mathbf{b}$
(c) $2\mathbf{a}-\mathbf{b}; -\mathbf{b}+k\mathbf{a}; 3\mathbf{a}-\mathbf{b}$
9. (a) $166°$ (b) 48 km/h
(c) 165.5 km
10. (a) N $24°$W; 4.6 m/s
(b) N : N $24°$W; 4.6 m/s
E : due east; 7 m/s
S : S $24°$W; 4.6 m/s
W : due west ; 3 m/s
6 min 4 s

10. 0.2
11. 0.05
12. $\frac{99}{100}$

Exercise 26b

1. (a) $\frac{1}{2}$ (b) $\frac{2}{13}$
2. (a) $\frac{1}{3}$ (b) $\frac{1}{2}$
3. (a) $\frac{7}{12}$ (b) $\frac{7}{12}$ (c) $\frac{5}{6}$
4. $\frac{2}{5}$
5. $\frac{4}{25}$
6. (a) $\frac{1}{5}$ (b) $\frac{29}{100}$
7. $\frac{1}{2}$
8. $\frac{7}{12}$
9. $\frac{12}{35}; \frac{23}{35}$
10. $\frac{17}{24}$

Exercise 26c

1. (a) $\frac{1}{36}$ (b) $\frac{1}{18}$
2. (a) $\frac{4}{663}$ (b) $\frac{8}{663}$
3. (a) $\frac{1}{8}$ (b) $\frac{3}{8}$
4. $\frac{8}{729}$
5. (a) $\frac{3}{64}$ (b) $\frac{9}{64}$
6. (a) $\frac{1}{18}$ (b) $\frac{1}{12}$ (c) $\frac{1}{9}$ (d) $\frac{5}{18}$
7. (a) $\frac{1}{216}$ (b) $\frac{1}{216}$ (c) $\frac{5}{216}$ (d) $\frac{3}{216}$
(e) $\frac{15}{216}$
8. (a) $\frac{2}{9}$ (b) $\frac{1}{6}$ (c) $\frac{1}{3}$
9. (a) $\frac{1}{4}$ (b) $\frac{3}{20}$ (c) $\frac{3}{10}$
10. (a) $\frac{20}{539}$ (b) $\frac{120}{539}$

Exercise 26d

1. (a) $\frac{1}{36}$ (b) $\frac{5}{18}$ (c) $\frac{25}{36}$ (d) $\frac{11}{36}$
2. (a) $\frac{1}{4}$ (b) $\frac{1}{2}$ (c) $\frac{3}{4}$
3. (a) $\frac{1}{8}$ (b) $\frac{7}{8}$
4. $\frac{7}{16}$
5. $0.328; 0.672$
6. $\frac{64}{729}; \frac{665}{729}$
7. 0.65
8. $\frac{1}{2}; \frac{5}{9}; \frac{7}{9}$
9. $\frac{55}{62};$ (a) $\frac{55}{62}$ (b) $\frac{367}{620}$
10. (a) $\frac{47}{85}$ (b) $\frac{15}{17}$ (c) $\frac{997}{1700}$

Exercise 26a

1. (a) $\frac{1}{6}$ (b) $\frac{1}{6}$ (c) $\frac{1}{2}$
2. $\frac{1}{5}$
3. (a) $\frac{1}{52}$ (b) $\frac{1}{13}$ (c) $\frac{1}{4}$
4. $\frac{1}{491}$
5. yes; $p(3$ heads$)$ must be less than 1
6. 1
7. 0
8. $\frac{17}{20}$
9. 0.9

Exercise 26e

1.

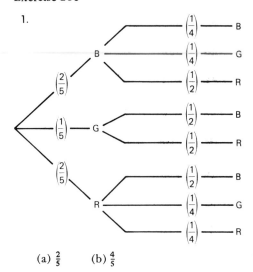

(a) $\frac{2}{5}$ (b) $\frac{4}{5}$

2.

1st draw 2nd draw 3rd draw

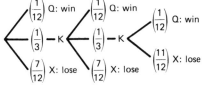

$\frac{13}{108}$

3.

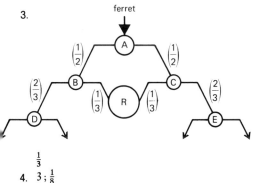

$\frac{1}{3}$

4. $3;\frac{1}{8}$

5. (a) $\frac{4}{15}$ (b) $\frac{4}{5}$

Miscellaneous Exercise 26

1. (a) $\frac{1}{36}$ (b) $\frac{11}{36}$ (c) $\frac{1}{9}$ (d) $\frac{1}{1296}$
   (e) $\frac{7}{432}$

2. (a) $\frac{5}{36}$ (b) $\frac{1}{12}$ (c) $\frac{1}{6}$

3. (a) (i) $\frac{4}{5}$ (ii) $\frac{1}{60}$ (iii) $\frac{2}{5}$ (iv) $\frac{3}{5}$
   (b)

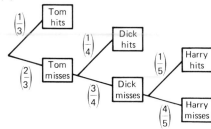

(i) $\frac{1}{6}$ (ii) $\frac{1}{2}$ (iii) $\frac{1}{10}$ (iv) $\frac{3}{5}$

4. (a) $\frac{2}{5}$ (b) $\frac{1}{7}$ (c) $\frac{6}{7}$
   (d) $\frac{216}{455}$; $\frac{117}{125}$

5. $\frac{2}{3}$ (a) $\frac{4}{9}$ (b) $\frac{5}{9}$ (c) $\frac{1}{40}$
   (d) $\frac{11}{40}$; 203

6. (a) $\frac{3}{8}$ (b) $\frac{1}{4}$ (c) $\frac{5}{8}$ (d) $\frac{3}{64}$
   (e) $3;\frac{1}{64}$

7. (a) 18 (b) 44 (c) $\frac{4}{25}$

8. (a) (i) $\dfrac{x}{x+30}$ (ii) 35 (b) $\frac{1}{8}$

Exercise 27a

1. (i) 4 (ii) 2 and 4 (iii) 4
2. (i) 5 (ii) 3 (iii) 4
3. (i) 8 (ii) 9 (iii) 9
4. (i) 2 (ii) no mode (iii) 1
5. (i) 53.2 (ii) no mode (iii) 53.1
6. (i) 105 (ii) 104 (iii) $104\frac{1}{2}$
7. $57\frac{1}{2}\%$
8. The workers are using the mode; the boss is using the mean
9. 12
10. 7.6
11. 3, 3, 5, 7
12. 6
13. 3
14. 135 ; 96 ; 7.7
15. 10.2
16. 54
17. $19\frac{2}{3}$
18. 11
19. (i) 195 (ii) 19
20. 0
21. 17 years and 7 months

Exercise 27b

1. (a) 3.5 (b) 3 (c) 3
2. (a) 5 (b) 5 (c) 5
3. (a) $1\frac{1}{3}$ (b) 0 (c) 1

4. (a) 1   (b) 2   (c) 1.98
5. (a) 6   (b) 7   (c) 7.6

6.

Score	0	1	2	3	4	5
f	14	13	13	9	3	2

mode = 0

7. (a) 3   (b) 4   (c) 3.7   (d) 3.6
8. 2.2; $m = 1.9$ Mid-point 3

9.

x	f	fx
3	11	33
8	12	96
13	15	195
18	9	162
23	3	69
	50	555

mean = 11.1

10. (a) 10; 12; 11

(b)

Marks	f
1–4	2
5–8	8
9–12	13
13–16	6
17–20	2

mean = 10.24

11. 10.7
12. 16.2
13. 12.1
14. 10.2

Exercise 28a

1. (a) 1   (b) 2   (c) 30; 53; 1.77
3. 45%; 61.2°
4. 27 min
5. £3640 m
7. (a) (i) 20% (ii) 28% (iii) 32%

Exercise 28b

1. (i) (a) 10, 20, 5   (b) 10, 20, 10
   (c) 2; mode = 1.9
   (ii) (a) 1, 3, 4, 1.6   (b) 5, 15, 10, 12
   (c) 10–12.5; mode = 10.75
2. (a) 17.5–20   (b) 18.5
3. (a) 14–15   (b) 14.4
4. (a) 115–117.5   (b) 116
5. (a) 10–12   (b) 10.25
6. (a) 10–14   (b) 11
7. (a) 5   (b) 4.95
8. (a) 10–19   (b) 14.5
9. (b) 4.37   (c) 4.5

Exercise 28c

1. (c) (i) 176 (ii) $174\frac{1}{2}$ (iii) 179 (iv) 175
   (d) $4\frac{1}{2}$
2. (c) (i) 24 (ii) 18 (iii) 28 (iv) 21
   (d) 10
3. (c) (i) $10\frac{1}{2}$ (ii) $8\frac{1}{2}$ (iii) 12 (iv) $9\frac{1}{2}$
   (d) $3\frac{1}{2}$
4. (b) 49   (c) 45   (d) 74
5. (a) 25   (b) 5, 44
6. (a) 23 200
   (b) (i) 770 (ii) 56 (iii) $\frac{7}{50}$

INDEX